MVP

ROBERT W. COHEN

A CONTROVERSIAL LOOK AT BASEBALL'S GREATEST PLAYERS: WHO WON THE AWARD, AND WHO SHOULD HAVE

MVP

ROBERT W. COHEN

**A CONTROVERSIAL LOOK AT BASEBALL'S GREATEST PLAYERS:
WHO WON THE AWARD, AND WHO SHOULD HAVE**

CARDOZA PUBLISHING

Cardoza Publishing has a library of more than 200 up-to-date and easy-to-read books on gaming and sports information. With more than 10,000,000 books in print, these titles represent the best-selling and most popular gaming books anywhere.

First Edition

Copyright © 2010 by Robert W. Cohen
- All Rights Reserved -

Library of Congress Catalog No: 2010933138
ISBN 10:   1-58042-266-7
ISBN 13: 978-1-58042-266-6

Visit the Cardoza Publsihing website or write us for a full list of our more than 200 titles.

CARDOZA PUBLISHING

P.O. Box 98115, Las Vegas, NV 89193
Phone (800)577-WINS
email: cardozabooks@aol.com
www.cardozabooks.com

TABLE OF CONTENTS

Acknowledgments

I wish to express my appreciation to Bill Deane, whose Awards and Honors section in *Total Baseball* proved to be an invaluable source of information to me during my research. Mr. Dean's material provided a great deal of the historical information presented on the Most Valuable Player Award, as well as the voting results through the 1992 season.

Dedication

In loving memory of my mom, who passed away shortly before this book was completed...Mom, I know I didn't tell you how much you meant to me nearly as often as I should have, but you were always my own personal MVP—the Most Valuable Person in my life.

AN HISTORICAL OVERVIEW

The award that is presented annually to the most valuable baseball player in each of the two major leagues is perhaps the most prestigious and coveted award in all of professional sports. While a similar honor is bestowed upon the player who is perceived to be most indispensable to his team in each of the other major team sports of football, basketball, and hockey, not one of those seems to generate quite as much interest among fans or the media. Only the Heisman Trophy, presented to the outstanding college football player of the year, attracts as much media attention and creates as much controversy. As a result, with the exception of being selected to the Baseball Hall of Fame after the conclusion of one's career, being named Most Valuable Player is considered to be the greatest individual honor a player can achieve during his playing days. However, the award did not always carry with it the significance it has had for the better part of the past century. In fact, it was not even presented at the end of each season at one time, and it initially was instituted primarily as a means of promoting the sport.

Prior to the start of the 1910 season, baseball fan Hugh Chalmers, who was President and General Manager of the Chalmers Motor Company, announced that he would present one of his company's automobiles to the major league player who compiled the highest batting average. The rules stated that, depending on his position, a player must accumulate a certain number of at-bats to qualify for the award. Infielders and outfielders were to have tallied a minimum of 350 at-bats; catchers, a minimum of 250 at-bats; and pitchers, at least 100 at-bats. The concept created a tremendous amount of interest among both fans and players, but it left a sour taste in everyone's mouth by season's end.

As the 1910 campaign evolved, it became apparent that only Detroit's Ty Cobb and Cleveland's Napoleon Lajoie, both American Leaguers, had a serious chance of compiling the highest batting average and, thereby, winning the automobile. The two men could not have been perceived more differently by both fans and players alike. Lajoie was well-liked and respected by all, while Cobb, with his contentious and hostile disposition, was the most hated man in baseball. Many observers believed that the latter placed more importance on winning the prize than on helping his team to win, while Lajoie was viewed as being a consummate team player. Controversy continued to grow during the season, with allegations being made of favoritism by official scorers in various cities. The popular Lajoie seemed to be almost everyone's favorite, with the only possible exceptions being those people associated with the Tigers. This last fact became most evident on the final day of the campaign when the St. Louis Browns devised a plot they hoped would enable Lajoie to come away with the prize.

Cobb entered the season's final day with a batting average of .383, while Lajoie's mark stood at .376. Thinking he had the batting crown locked up, Cobb chose to sit out his final game, leaving Lajoie the almost impossible task of raising his batting average eight points in one day. However, the Cleveland second baseman was able to collect eight hits in eight times at-bat in a doubleheader against St. Louis because Browns' manager Jack O'Connor instructed his third baseman to play Lajoie unusually deep. The Cleveland star subsequently bunted safely seven times to finish a fraction of a point ahead of Cobb in the batting race. Charges of a conspiracy followed, raising questions as to the legitimacy of Lajoie's batting title.

O'Connor ended up losing his job due to his role in the alleged fix, and American League President Ban Johnson subsequently announced that a "discrepancy" had been found in the official records, and that Cobb had actually won the batting crown after all. Hugh Chalmers, in an attempt to placate all the parties involved, presented automobiles to both Cobb and Lajoie. However, the incident made Chalmers rethink his approach to the award and come up with a new proposal for the 1911 season that essentially served as the precursor for what eventually became the Most Valuable Player Award.

Prior to the start of that campaign, Chalmers announced that a car would be awarded to one player in each league who "should prove himself as the most important and useful player to his club and to the league at large in point of deportment and value of services rendered." The decision for this honor was to be made by a committee of baseball writers, comprised of one writer from each club city in each league. Each writer was to select eight players, with his first choice receiving eight points in the scoring, and his last choice receiving one point.

This *Chalmers Award* was presented annually from 1911 to 1914. However, the public's attention was gradually drawn away from its pursuit by major league baseball's battles with the new Federal League and the escalation of World War I in Europe. As a result, the award quietly faded away, with no such honor being bestowed upon any professional baseball player again until 1922, when the American League decided to present an award that had its roots in the Chalmers Award. The rules devised by the newly formed American League Trophy Committee specified that "the purpose of the American League Trophy is to honor the baseball player who is of greatest all-round service to his club and credit to the sport during each season; to recognize and reward uncommon skill and ability when exercised by a player for the best interests of his team, and to perpetuate his memory." The rules also instructed voters to seek out the "winning ball player", suggesting to them that "combined offensive and defensive ability is not always indicated by any system of records."

As had been the case with the Chalmers Award, the selection committee was to be comprised of eight baseball writers, one from each American League city, with each voter required to select exactly one player from each team, for a total of eight selections. Player-managers and previous winners were to be excluded from consideration, and points were to be distributed in exactly the same fashion as they had been with the Chalmers Award, with eight points going to the voter's first choice, all the way down to one for his eighth choice.

The National League followed suit in 1924, when it announced that it would also present an award at the end of each season to the player deemed to be most valuable to his team by a panel of experts. While the senior circuit also stipulated that one writer from each of its member cities was to serve on the selection committee, it made several modifications to the selection process earlier instituted by the American League. Firstly, each writer was to vote for ten players, with a first-place vote equating to 10 points in the scoring system, on down to one point for a tenth-place vote. In addition, each voter was free to select a player-manager, he could select more than one player from each team, and he was permitted to consider previous winners of the award.

These last two points were particularly significant since the American League's system met with much criticism during the 1920s for its inflexibility, which prevented its voters from truly considering the most worthy candidates. For example, the writers were permitted to select only one player from each team. Therefore, when the St. Louis Browns' George Sisler was named the league's Most Valuable Player in 1922 he was named on all eight ballots, thereby disqualifying any of his teammates from possible consideration. However, another St. Louis player, outfielder Ken Williams, led the A.L. in home runs (39), runs batted in (155), and total bases (367) that year, and also became the first player in major league history to hit 30 home runs and steal 30 bases in the same season. If not the league's most valuable player that year, he was certainly a close second to Sisler. Yet, Williams did not receive a single vote since Sisler was named on all eight ballots.

The provision that did not permit voters to enter the names of previous winners on their ballots was even more ludicrous because it often excluded from consideration some of the league's top performers. While the purpose of this ruling was to create more of an opportunity for the award to be shared by players throughout the league, it ended up creating what amounted to a hollow honor. Thus, since Babe Ruth won the award in 1923, he was not eligible to be considered again in either 1924 or 1926—both seasons in which he was clearly the league's dominant player. He was also ineligible in 1927, when he hit 60 home runs, and again the following season, when he and teammate Lou Gehrig were clearly the two most deserving players in the league. In fact, Gehrig was not eligible for the award in that 1928 season either, since he was named league MVP the previous year. As a result, Philadelphia Athletics catcher Mickey Cochrane was named the recipient, in spite of the fact that the Yankees won the pennant and both Ruth and Gehrig had much better seasons than him.

These flaws in the system, along with management's concerns that the winners might attempt to use the awards as a bargaining tool when it came time to discuss salary at season's end, led to the eventual demise of the American League Award. In a special league meeting held early during the 1929 campaign, the A.L. Award was officially voted out. The National League soon elected to do away with the award as well, but it agreed to present the honor one final time at the conclusion of the 1929 season. Thus, it seemed that the Most Valuable Player Award had seen its final days.

However, in October of 1929, the Baseball Writers Association of America (BBWAA) decided to select its own "unofficial" winner of the A.L MVP Award, naming Cleveland Indians first baseman Lew Fonseca as its choice. Two months later, *The Sporting News* announced the results of another "unofficial" poll, in which the eight A.L. writers who had previously voted on the league Award were asked to select a winner. They chose Philadelphia A's outfielder Al Simmons, who *The Sporting News* proclaimed to be its "unofficial" winner.

Such "unofficial" polls were taken at the end of the 1930 season as well, naming multiple winners in both leagues. However, the BBWAA, in an attempt to unify the selection process, decided prior to the start of the 1931 campaign to appoint two committees (one in each league) to elect most valuable players. The former restrictions placed on the American League voters were lifted, and they were now permitted to vote for player-managers, multiple players from the same team, and former winners of the award. Thus, in essence, the first *true* Most Valuable Player Awards (at least in the American League) were presented in 1931.

Two additional changes to the voting process were implemented by the BBWAA in 1938. For the first time, three writers in each major league city were polled, rather than just one. That number remained in effect until 1961, when it was changed to two writers per city. Also, in 1938, it was decided to award 14 points for each first-place vote, rather than 10. A second-place vote would continue to equate to nine points, all the way down to one point for a tenth-place vote. That system has remained in effect to this day.

The Sporting News, though, continued to make its own selections until 1938, when it agreed to unify the award by naming as its winners the players chosen by the BBWAA. This solidarity lasted only a few years, however, with the publication returning to its earlier practice of naming its own MVP winners in 1944, something it has done ever since. Yet, for some reason, the public has never really given much credibility to the selections made by *The Sporting News*, and the players selected by the BBWAA have always been widely accepted as the "true" winners.

INTERPRETATION OF AWARD

"BEST PLAYER" OR "MOST VALUABLE"

One of the things that has always made selecting the Most Valuable Player of each league so difficult is that the term *Most Valuable* is open to different interpretations. What makes someone the *most valuable* player in his league, or even on his own team for that matter? Is it the player who accumulates the most impressive numbers during the regular season? If this approach is taken, the award should be presented to the league's *best*, or, at the very least, *most dominant* player. Is it the player who best combines statistical compilation, defensive prowess, and leadership skills? If so, it would seem that only those outstanding performers who played on winning teams should be seriously considered. Or should the award be presented to the best all-around player in terms of offense and defense (or pitching), regardless of the quality of the team for which he played?

It was mentioned earlier that the American League Trophy Committee specified in 1922 that "the purpose of the American League Trophy is to honor the baseball player who is of greatest all-round service to his club and credit to the sport during each season; to recognize and reward uncommon skill and ability when exercised by a player for the best interests of his team, and to perpetuate his memory." None of those provisions state that the player must have played for a winning team. Thus, one could certainly surmise that the purpose of the trophy is to reward the league's *best* player at season's end. However, there is also that phrase at the end saying, "...for the best interests of his team..." This would seem to suggest that the player's efforts should have a positive effect on the performance of his team, and in some way impact its place in the standings. Furthermore, the voters were instructed to seek out the "winning ball player" and were reminded that "combined offensive and defensive ability is not always indicated by any system of records."

These last two provisions are particularly noteworthy since they would clearly seem to indicate that statistics should not be used as the sole measuring stick of a player's value to his team. They are also an indication that the player's team should have benefited greatly from his outstanding performance during the season, and that he should have, at least to some degree, improved their place in the standings.

Through the years, the voters seem to have given this a great deal of consideration when casting their MVP ballots, since roughly two-thirds of their choices have been players whose teams either won the pennant, or their own division. In several of these instances, the statistics of the players selected were not nearly as impressive as those compiled by other players in the league. Following are just a few examples of these occurrences:

> **1931**—The St. Louis Cardinals won the N.L. pennant by 13 games over the New York Giants. Cardinals second baseman Frankie Frisch (4 home runs, 82 runs batted in, 96 runs scored, .311 batting average) was selected league MVP over the Giants Bill Terry (9 home runs, 112 runs batted in, 121 runs scored, .349 batting average) and Mel Ott (29 home runs, 115 runs batted in, 104 runs scored, .292 batting average), among others.

> **1942**—The Yankees finished first, nine games ahead of the second-place Red Sox. New York second baseman Joe Gordon (18 home runs, 103 runs batted in, 88 runs scored, .322 Average) was named league MVP in spite of the fact that Boston's Ted Williams led the A.L. with 36 home runs, 137 runs batted in, 141 runs scored, and a .356 batting average, thereby capturing the league's Triple Crown.

> **1947**—The Yankees won the A.L. pennant by 12 games over the second-place Tigers. The Red Sox finished third, 14 games back. New York's Joe DiMaggio (20 home runs, 97 runs batted in, 97 runs scored, .315 batting average)

was named league MVP. Boston's Ted Williams finished second in the voting despite winning another Triple Crown by hitting 32 home runs, driving in 114 runs, batting .343, and scoring 125 runs.

1960—The Pittsburgh Pirates won the N.L. pennant by 7 games over the Milwaukee Braves. Pirates shortstop Dick Groat was named league MVP. While he did lead the league with a .325 batting average, Groat hit only two home runs, knocked in just 50 runs, and scored only 85 others. Meanwhile, the Braves Eddie Mathews hit 39 home runs, drove in 124 runs, scored 108 others, and batted .277, while Mathews' teammate, Hank Aaron hit 40 home runs, knocked in 126 runs, scored 102 others, and batted .292.

These are just some of the instances in which the voters placed more importance on the final league standings than on individual statistics when evaluating the qualifications of possible MVP candidates. In several ballots, though, the voters were swayed more by a player's outstanding individual performance, since his team was unable to finish first in the standings. In virtually all of these cases, however, the player's dominant performance was at least able to keep his team in contention for much of the season. Following are some examples of players who won the award under these circumstances:

1932, 1933, 1938—Jimmie Foxx was named A.L. MVP in each of these years even though his team never finished any higher than second in any of them. In 1932, his A's finished 13 games behind the first-place Yankees, but Foxx's league- leading 58 home runs, 169 runs batted in, 151 runs scored, and .364 batting average earned him MVP honors. The following season, Foxx was named MVP again despite the fact his A's finished in third-place, 19 1/2 games behind the first- place Washington Senators. That year, Foxx's 48 home runs, 163 runs batted in, and .356 batting average all led the American League. In 1938, as a member of the Red Sox, Foxx won his third MVP Award even though Boston finished second, 9½ games behind the first-place Yankees. Foxx hit 50 home runs and led the league with 175 runs batted in and a .349 batting average.

1948—The Braves won the N.L. pennant by 6½ games over the second-place Cardinals, but Stan Musial was named league MVP for hitting 39 home runs and leading the league with 131 runs batted in, a .376 batting average, and 135 runs scored.

1949—The Red Sox finished one game behind the pennant-winning Yankees, but Ted Williams was voted league MVP for leading the league with 43 home runs, 159 runs batted in, and 150 runs scored, while finishing a close second in the batting race with an average of .343.

1953—The Yankees finished 8½ games ahead of the second-place Indians, but Cleveland slugger Al Rosen was named A.L. MVP for leading the league with 43 home runs, 145 runs batted in, and 115 runs scored, while batting .336.

1969—The Braves finished three games ahead of the Giants in the N.L. West, but San Francisco's Willie McCovey was voted N.L. MVP. He led the league with 45 home runs and 126 runs batted in, and compiled a .320 batting average.

1972—Oakland finished 5½ games ahead of Chicago in the A.L. West, but White Sox first baseman Dick Allen was named league MVP for leading the league with 37 home runs and 113 runs batted in, and finishing third in batting with an average of .308.

1977—The Dodgers finished 10 games ahead of second-place Cincinnati in the N.L. West, but Reds slugger George Foster, who led the league with 52 home runs, 149 runs batted in, and 124 runs scored, while batting .320, was named MVP.

These are all examples of players who, while unable to lead their teams to a pennant or division title, at least helped their teams to respectable finishes. However, in certain elections, the voters seemed to pay virtually no attention to the final standings and seemed to focus more on the outstanding candidates' individual statistics. In 1952, Chicago Cubs slugger Hank Sauer was named N.L. MVP even though the Cubs finished in fifth place, 19½ games behind the first-place Dodgers. Cubs shortstop Ernie Banks was voted N.L. MVP in both 1958 and 1959 despite Chicago's sixth-place finishes both seasons. Orioles shortstop Cal Ripken Jr. was selected A.L. MVP for the second time in 1991, in spite of Baltimore's sixth-place finish in the A.L. East. And, of course, Andre Dawson was voted N.L. MVP in 1987, and Alex Rodriguez was selected A.L. MVP in 2003 in spite of their respective teams' last-place finishes.

Thus, there seems to be no consistent pattern to the mind-set of the voters. While playing for a winning team certainly seems to enhance a top candidate's chances, it does not necessarily guarantee him election. Sometimes, overwhelming individual statistics can have just as much influence on the outcome of the vote.

That being said, as we proceed to analyze all the MVP selections that have been made through the years and suggest possible alternative choices, what should our approach be, and what should our interpretation of the term *Most Valuable* be? How much importance should be placed on the team concept, and how much emphasis should be given to individual statistics? The feeling here is that a leading candidate has a decided advantage if his team finished in first-place, or somewhere near the top of the standings. The only instance in which a player whose team finished well out of contention should be given serious consideration would be if his statistics are so overwhelmingly superior to those of the other top candidates that they are difficult to ignore. However, it would be difficult to find any scenario under which a player on a last-place team could be seriously considered for MVP honors. Used within this context, the term *Most Valuable* implies that the player should have had a positive effect on his team, and on its place in the standings. Even if there is not a more talented player in the league, how valuable could a player have been to his team if it finished in last place? We will have to look at the individual cases of Dawson and Rodriguez later to determine if there were any other viable candidates, but, at this juncture, it would be difficult to justify the selection of either man.

POSITION PLAYERS VS. PITCHERS

Another point of contention in the MVP balloting has always been the extent to which pitchers should be given consideration. There are those who feel that, since a pitcher generally works only once every fourth or fifth day, it is impossible for him to be as valuable to his team as an every day position player. Some voters have even gone on record as saying that they would never cast their ballot for a pitcher since they have their own award (the Cy Young Award, instituted in 1956). Others feel that pitchers deserve as much consideration for the award as anyone else. However, the roles of pitchers have changed dramatically through the years, and this must be taken into consideration when analyzing the winners of past elections.

During the first part of the 20th century in the Deadball Era, starting pitchers had a far more prevalent role in the fortunes of their teams. Runs were often at a premium, and games were usually low-scoring chess matches that featured slap-hitting, bunting, and base stealing. Pitchers were more dominant than they would become in later years, and they were expected to finish the majority of their starts. They also pitched far more frequently, with top starters appearing in perhaps as many as 45 or 50 games a year. A team's top pitcher was considered to be the backbone of his team, and, often, its most important player.

With the rules changes and livelier ball that were implemented during the 1920s, runs were scored much more frequently, and pitchers became far less dominant. In addition, teams started going to four-man rotations, with top pitchers rarely making more than 40 starts a year. This practice existed more than 50 years, until five-man rotations became more the norm during the 1970s. Since then, the role of relief pitchers has increased dramatically, thereby further lessening the impact of starting pitchers. The end result has been a gradual diminishing of the role of starting pitchers and a lessening of their credibility as viable MVP candidates.

However, one thing that has not changed is the impact that outstanding pitchers have on the game, and the importance that every team places on having them. Through the years, this has been recognized on numerous occasions by the BBWAA when it came time for the writers to cast their MVP ballots. While there have been a few exceptions, the general approach the voters seem to have taken, though, is that a pitcher must have had a truly dominant season—even more dominant than the top position player—and that his team must have finished in first place for him to be named the winner. Some examples follow:

1931—Lou Gehrig had a tremendous year for the second-place Yankees, hitting 46 home runs, driving in an American League record 184 runs, and batting .341. However, Lefty Grove had an even more dominant year for the first-place Athletics. He finished 31-4, with a league-leading 2.06 earned run average and 175 strikeouts, and was named A.L. MVP at the end of the season.

1933—Chuck Klein won the National League's Triple Crown, hitting 28 home runs, knocking in 120 runs, and batting .368 for the seventh-place Phillies. However, he finished second in the MVP voting to New York lefthander Carl Hubbell, who finished 23-12 with a league-leading 1.66 earned run average for the first-place Giants.

1934—The Giants finished second, just two games behind the first-place Cardinals. New York outfielder Mel Ott led the N.L. with 35 home runs and 135 runs batted in, while batting .326 and scoring 119 runs. However, St. Louis righthander Dizzy Dean was named league MVP for finishing 30-7 with a 2.66 earned run average and league-leading 195 strikeouts.

1963—Hank Aaron led the National League with 44 home runs, 130 runs batted in, and 121 runs scored. However, his Braves finished sixth, 15 games behind the first-place Dodgers, who were led by Sandy Koufax. The lefthander won the pitcher's version of the Triple Crown by compiling a record of 25-5, with a 1.88 earned run average and 306 strikeouts. Koufax was named league MVP at season's end.

1968—Willie McCovey led the National League with 36 home runs and 105 runs batted in, and his Giants finished second, nine games behind the first-place Cardinals. St.

Louis righthander Bob Gibson was named league MVP for finishing 22-9, with a league-leading 1.12 earned run average, 268 strikeouts, and 13 shutouts.

However, the voters have proven to be somewhat inconsistent in their approach to pitchers as well. In some years, a pitcher on a pennant-winning team displayed a level of dominance that equalled or exceeded that of the finest position player in the league and yet still failed to win the award.

In 1965, the Dodgers won the National League pennant by two games over the second-place Giants. Sandy Koufax led the league with 26 wins (against only 8 losses), a 2.04 earned run average, and 382 strikeouts, but finished a close second to San Francisco's Willie Mays in the MVP voting. Mays led the league with 52 home runs, knocked in 112 runs, scored 118 others, and batted .317 for the Giants.

The following season, the Dodgers repeated as N.L. champs, edging out the Giants by 1½ games and the third-place Pirates by three games. Koufax had another brilliant season, leading N.L. pitchers in virtually every statistical category. He finished 27-9, with a 1.73 earned run average, 317 strikeouts, 323 innings pitched, 27 complete games, and 5 shutouts. Yet, Pirates rightfielder Roberto Clemente was named league MVP at season's end for his outstanding year. Clemente hit 29 home runs, drove in 119 runs, batted .317, and scored 105 runs.

In 1978, the Yankees defeated the Red Sox in a one-game playoff to capture the A.L. East title. New York's Ron Guidry kept his team in the pennant race for much of the year with his incredible season. He finished 25-3, with a 1.74 earned run average, 248 strikeouts, and nine shutouts. Yet, Boston's Jim Rice was named league MVP for his brilliant year. Rice finished with 46 home runs, 139 runs batted in, a .315 batting average, and 121 runs scored.

Thus, there seems to be no exact formula for determining when a pitcher's outstanding performance during the regular season is deemed sufficient by the baseball writers to earn him MVP honors. For the most part, it seems that the writers have leaned in the direction of the every day position players. However, there have been instances in which a pitcher's dominant performance has been able to overcome any predisposition some of the members of the BBWAA may already have had.

INTERPRETATION OF AWARD

As we analyze the outcomes of previous MVP elections, the approach that will be taken throughout this book is that a pitcher should only be given serious consideration if he had a truly dominant season; that is, one in which he was clearly the league's best pitcher, having led his circuit in numerous statistical categories. He also should have displayed a level of dominance at least equal to that shown by the league's most dominant position player, and/or played for a team that finished higher in the standings.

Now that the guidelines that will be used going forward have been set, it is time to begin our analysis of all the MVP winners since the beginning of the 20th century.

HYPOTHETICAL AWARDS FOR THE PRE-MVP YEARS

It was noted earlier that, prior to the Chalmers Award in 1911, no official league MVP Awards were presented annually. Therefore, the first ten years of the twentieth century, as well as other miscellaneous years in which no award was presented, are completely unaccounted for. These "missing" years will be addressed in the ensuing chapters, as we select the *hypothetical* winners in each league for each of those seasons. These are the players who, based on my interpretation of all available statistical data, appear to have been most valuable to their respective teams in each of those seasons. These selections will be based not only on outstanding individual statistical compilation, but also on team placement in the final standings, as well as any reputation the player may have had as being either an outstanding defensive player or team leader. The analysis begins with the years 1900-1910.

HYPOTHETICAL MVP WINNERS

	AMERICAN LEAGUE	NATIONAL LEAGUE
1900	***	Honus Wagner
1901	Napoleon Lajoie	Honus Wagner
1902	Cy Young	Honus Wagner
1903	Cy Young	Christy Mathewson
1904	Jack Chesbro	Joe McGinnity
1905	Rube Waddell	Christy Mathewson
1906	Napoleon Lajoie	Mordecai Brown
1907	Ty Cobb	Honus Wagner
1908	Ed Walsh	Christy Mathewson
1909	Ty Cobb	Honus Wagner
1910	Jack Coombs	Sherry Magee

*** Note: The American League's inaugural season was 1901.

1900

NATIONAL LEAGUE

There were three outstanding performers who merited serious consideration for National League MVP honors. The first was righthander *Iron Man* Joe McGinnity, who pitched for pennant-winning Brooklyn. McGinnity led all pitchers with 28 wins, while losing only 8 games and leading the league with 343 innings pitched and a .778 winning percentage. His earned run average was a solid 2.94, but it was not good enough to place him in the top five in the league rankings. Therefore, his level of dominance is somewhat debatable.

Philadelphia outfielder Elmer Flick finished second in the league in home runs (11), batting average (.367), slugging percentage (.545), and total bases (297), and led the N.L. with 110 runs batted in. His team finished third, though, 8 games behind first-place Brooklyn. Therefore, there is some doubt as to whether or not he was more valuable to Philadelphia than McGinnity was to Brooklyn.

However, there was someone who was more valuable to his team than McGinnity and Flick were to their respective squads. Pittsburgh's Honus Wagner placed among the league leaders in every major offensive category, except home runs, and his Pirates finished second, just 4½ games behind Brooklyn in the standings. Wagner led the league with a .381 batting average, and he also topped the circuit in triples (22), doubles (45), slugging percentage (.573), and total bases (302). He finished third in runs batted in (100) and hits (201), and fifth in runs scored (107). Wagner was clearly the best all-around player in the league, and he was most deserving of being named its Most Valuable Player.

1901

AMERICAN LEAGUE

In the American League's inaugural season, Cy Young had a tremendous year for the second-place Boston Red Sox. He finished 33-10, and he also led the league with a 1.62 earned run average and 158 strikeouts, completing 38 of his 41 starts in the process.

As good as Young was, Philadelphia second baseman Napoleon Lajoie was even more dominant. Lajoie led his team to a respectable fourth-place finish, nine games out of first, by leading the league in almost every major offensive category. In addition to winning the Triple Crown by topping the junior circuit in home runs (14), runs batted in (125), and batting average (.426), Lajoie finished first in runs scored (145) and hits (232). His .643 slugging percent was *120 points* higher than the mark posted by the league runner-up, and his .426 batting average remains the highest since the start of the last century.

NATIONAL LEAGUE

Honus Wagner was once again the National League's dominant player. His Pittsburgh Pirates won the pennant, finishing 7½ games ahead of second-place Philadelphia, and Wagner was Pittsburgh's acknowledged leader and the finest all-around player in the game. He led the league with 126 runs batted in and 49 stolen bases, and he also finished in the top five in batting average (.353), hits (194), doubles (37), and on-base percentage (.416).

1902

AMERICAN LEAGUE

The Philadelphia A's won the American League pennant and their third baseman, Lave Cross, was their best player. Cross placed among the league leaders in runs batted in (108), batting average (.342), hits (191), and doubles (39). Yet Cross failed to lead the league in any statistical category.

On the other hand, Cy Young led his Boston Red Sox to a relatively close third-place finish, just 6½ games behind the A's, and he finished first among A.L. hurlers in several categories. Young won more games than any other pitcher, finishing with a record of 32-11, and he also threw more innings (384) and completed more games (41) than anyone else. He also finished fourth in earned run average (2.15) and second in strikeouts (160). Overall, Young had more of an impact on his team and on the pennant race than anyone else in the league. He would have to be considered the league's Most Valuable Player.

NATIONAL LEAGUE

The Pittsburgh Pirates ran away with the National League pennant in 1902, finishing 27½ games ahead of their closest competition. The Pirates were so dominant that they featured the league's top three MVP candidates. Pitcher Jack Chesbro finished 28-6, to lead the league in victories. He also compiled an outstanding 2.17 earned run average while completing 31 of his 33 starts. Outfielder Ginger Beaumont led the league with a .357 batting average and 193 hits. However, he finished well behind teammate Honus Wagner in most other offensive categories. Wagner batted .330 and led the league with 91 runs batted in, 105 runs scored, 30 doubles, 42 stolen bases, and a .463 slugging percentage. The Pittsburgh shortstop was the National League's top performer for the third straight year, and also the circuit's most valuable player.

1903

AMERICAN LEAGUE

Napoleon Lajoie, now playing for Cleveland, had another outstanding year, leading the American League with a .344 batting average and finishing in the top five in several other offensive categories. However, his team finished a distant third, 15 games behind first-place Boston.

Red Sox outfielders Patsy Dougherty and Buck Freeman both had solid seasons for the A.L. champions. Dougherty batted .331 and led the league with 107 runs scored and 195 hits. Freeman led the league with 13 home runs and 104 runs batted in. However, the former knocked in only 59 runs, while the latter batted only .287 and scored just 74 runs. In addition, both players finished well behind Lajoie in most offensive categories. Neither man could be seriously considered for league MVP honors.

Boston righthander Cy Young was a far more viable candidate. Having another brilliant year, Young was clearly the driving force behind his team's first-place finish. He led the league in wins for the third consecutive season, finishing 28-9 with a 2.08 earned run average, and he also finished first in innings pitched (341), complete games (34), and shutouts (7).

NATIONAL LEAGUE

The Pittsburgh Pirates won the National League pennant for the third straight year, this time finishing 6½ games ahead of the second-place New York Giants. Honus Wagner had another outstanding year, leading the league with a .355 batting average and 19 triples, finishing second with 101 runs batted in, and placing in the top five in several other offensive categories. However, he had a great deal of help from his Pittsburgh teammates.

Ginger Beaumont had an excellent season, leading the league with 137 runs scored and 209 hits. Fellow outfielder Fred Clarke finished second to Wagner in batting, with a mark of .351, and he led the league with a .532 slugging percentage. There were others who contributed greatly to Pittsburgh's success over the course of the season. But Wagner, Beaumont, and Clarke, in particular, helped establish the Pirates as the class of the National League.

Meanwhile, John McGraw's Giants were not nearly as talented. They certainly had a solid team, but it was their two outstanding pitchers, Joe McGinnity and Christy Mathewson, who kept them in the pennant race for most of the season. McGinnity led the league with 31 wins, 434 innings pitched, 44 complete games, and 55 appearances, and he pitched to a 2.43 earned run average. He was the most durable pitcher in the game and a tremendous asset to his team. The only thing that prevented him from being selected over Mathewson as hypothetical MVP was his 20 losses.

Mathewson wasn't quite as durable as his teammate, throwing "only" 366 innings and completing "just" 37 games. However, he was slightly more effective than McGinnity. Mathewson finished the season with a record of 30-13 and an earned run average of 2.26, and he led the league with 267 strikeouts. In fact, he finished either first or second in the league in every pitching category. Thus, even though Mathewson pitched for a second-place team that finished 6½ games behind Honus Wagner's Pittsburgh Pirates, the hurler was a more integral part of his team's success. Therefore, he deserved to be named the league's Most Valuable Player in 1903.

1904

AMERICAN LEAGUE

Pitchers were the dominant forces in both leagues in 1904. While Napoleon Lajoie had a superb season for fourth-place Cleveland in the American League, finishing first in batting average (.376), runs batted in (102), hits (208), doubles (49), on-base percentage (.413), and slugging percentage (.552), the New York Highlanders' Jack Chesbro was clearly the league's Most Valuable Player. The righthander, who signed with New York the previous year after jumping from the rival National League's Pittsburgh Pirates, led the Highlanders to an extremely close second-place finish, just 1½ games behind pennant-winning Boston. In finishing 41-12, Chesbro set a 20th century record for most wins in a season. He also compiled an earned run average of 1.82, with 239 strikeouts and a league-leading 454 innings pitched and 48 complete games.

NATIONAL LEAGUE

The New York Giants ended Pittsburgh's three-year reign as league champions by finishing 13 games ahead of the second-place Chicago Cubs. Christy Mathewson and Joe McGinnity won a total of 68 games between them, enabling the Giants to run away with the N.L. flag. Mathewson finished 33-12, with a 2.03 earned run average, 367 innings pitched, and 33 complete games in 48 appearances.

As brilliant as Mathewson was, McGinnity was even better. The latter finished with a record of 35-8, and he led the league in virtually every statistical category. In addition to winning the most games, McGinnity topped the circuit with a 1.61 earned run average, 408 innings pitched, nine shutouts, five saves, and 51 appearances, completing 38 of his starts.

1905

AMERICAN LEAGUE

Pitchers dominated the scene once more in 1905. Lefthanders Eddie Plank and Rube Waddell were the driving forces behind the Philadelphia Athletics' first-place finish in the American League. The

A's edged out the Chicago White Sox by two games, largely on the strength of the 51 wins compiled by their two aces. Plank finished 24-12, with a 2.26 earned run average, 210 strikeouts, and a league-leading 35 complete games. However, he was overshadowed by his teammate, who won the pitcher's Triple Crown by finishing 27-10, with a 1.48 earned run average and 287 strikeouts. Waddell also completed 27 of his 34 starts, appearing in a total of 46 games and throwing seven shutouts.

NATIONAL LEAGUE

Cincinnati outfielder Cy Seymour was clearly the circuit's top offensive player in 1905. He led the league in batting average (.377), runs batted in (121), hits (219), doubles (40), triples (21), slugging percentage (.559), and total bases (325), and he placed second in home runs, with eight. However, his Reds finished a distant fifth in the standings, 26 games behind the first-place Giants, ruining any chance he may have had of being named league MVP.

New York won its second consecutive pennant by finishing nine games ahead of the second-place Pirates, and, once again, it was pitching that carried the Giants to the championship. Christy Mathewson had his finest season to date, winning the pitcher's Triple Crown by finishing 31-9, with a 1.28 earned run average and 206 strikeouts. He also led the league with eight shutouts, and he finished third with 338 innings pitched. Mathewson was clearly his team's best player in 1905, and he was the most dominant player in the league.

1906

AMERICAN LEAGUE

Napoleon Lajoie breaks the four-year reign that pitchers had on the American League MVP Award by becoming the first position player since himself, in 1901, to come away with the honor. Lajoie led Cleveland to a third-place finish, just five games behind the pennant-winning White Sox and two games behind second-place New York. Despite finishing first, Chicago really did not have an outstanding MVP candidate in 1906. New York's Al Orth led the league with 27 wins, 338 innings pitched, and 36 complete games, and he also finished with a fine 2.34 earned run average. However, he also lost 17 games, preventing him from being seriously considered for the award.

Meanwhile, Lajoie led the league in hits (214) and doubles (48), and he finished second in batting average (.355), runs batted in (91), on-base percentage (.392), and slugging percentage (.465).

NATIONAL LEAGUE

The Chicago Cubs began a three-year reign as National League champions in 1906, dominating the league with an incredible record of 116-36, and finishing 20 games ahead of the second-place Giants. The Cubs featured outstanding defense and a solid lineup that included future Hall of Fame infielders Joe Tinker, Johnny Evers, and Frank Chance, but the thing that truly separated them from the rest of the league was their exceptional pitching. Chicago had four starters that finished among the league leaders in earned run average, with the best of them being Mordecai Brown. The righthander was absolutely magnificent all season, compiling a 26-6 record and a league-leading nine shutouts, while completing 27 of his 32 starts and establishing a 20th century record by pitching to a 1.04 earned run average.

1907

AMERICAN LEAGUE

Ty Cobb follows Napoleon Lajoie as only the second position player to earn American League MVP honors. Cobb's Detroit Tigers finished 1½ games ahead of the Philadelphia Athletics to capture their first league championship. Detroit pitcher "Wild Bill" Donovan was a major contributor to his team's success, going 25-4, with a 2.19 earned run average and 271 innings pitched, and completing 27 of his 28 starts. However, he didn't lead league pitchers in any statistical category. Meanwhile, Cobb won the first of his 10 batting championships by hitting .350. He also led the league in runs batted in (119), hits (212), stolen bases (49), slugging percentage (.468), and total bases (283).

NATIONAL LEAGUE

The Chicago Cubs dominated the National League once more in 1907, finishing with a regular-season record of 107-45, 17 games ahead of the second-place Pittsburgh Pirates.

As was the case the previous year, the pitching staff was the backbone of the team. Mordecai Brown finished 20-6 with a 1.39 earned run average, Jack Pfiester went 14-9 with a league-leading 1.15 earned run average, Carl Lundgren compiled a record of 18-7 and an earned run average of 1.17, and Orval Overall finished 23-7 with a 1.68 earned run average. The Cubs were so much better than the rest of the league, and their pitchers were all so outstanding, that it would seem that none of them were indispensable to the team. Had one of the members of their staff gone down with an injury, in all likelihood, Chicago still would have won the pennant, albeit by a smaller margin. Therefore, it would be difficult to pinpoint one member as the team's most valuable player.

As a result, even though his Pirates finished a distant second to the Cubs, Honus Wagner would have to be considered the league's MVP. He placed in the top five in every major statistical category, and he led the league in batting (.350), doubles (38), on-base percentage (.407), slugging percentage (.513), and total bases (264).

1908

AMERICAN LEAGUE

The Tigers repeated as American League champions in 1908, edging out Cleveland by just ½ game and Chicago by 1½ games. Detroit star Ty Cobb won his second consecutive batting title, finishing with a mark of .324, and he also led the league in runs batted in, hits, doubles, triples, slugging percentage, and total bases. However, the American League's dominant player was White Sox spitball artist Ed Walsh. The right-hander kept his team in the pennant race almost single-handedly, leading league pitchers in almost every statistical category. He finished with a record of 40-15 and an earned run average of 1.42 (third in the league), while topping the circuit in strikeouts (269), innings pitched (464), complete games (42), shutouts (11), and saves (6).

NATIONAL LEAGUE

The choice for National League MVP was a far more difficult one. Unlike the previous two seasons, the Cubs struggled to win the N.L. flag in 1908, finishing just one game ahead of both the Giants and the Pirates. Pittsburgh had an excellent candidate in Honus Wagner, and New York had one of their own in Christy Mathewson.

Wagner led the league in nine different offensive categories, including batting average (.354), runs batted in (109), and stolen bases (53). With a career-high 10 home runs, he also came within two long balls of winning the Triple Crown. Under normal circumstances, Wagner would have been the easy choice to come away with his fifth Most Valuable Player trophy.

However, the decision was made much more difficult by the fabulous year Christy Mathewson had for New York. The Giant hurler led National League pitchers in every major statistical category. In perhaps his greatest season, Mathewson finished 37-11, with a 1.43 earned run average, 259 strikeouts, 390 innings pitched, 34 complete games, 11 shutouts, and five saves. He appeared in 56 of his team's games, and he rivaled the American League's Ed Walsh for preeminence among major league pitchers that year.

Both Wagner and Mathewson were extremely dominant in 1908, and both were deserving of being named Most Valuable Player. A valid case could be made for splitting the vote and giving each of them a share of the trophy. However, the thing that finally tipped the scales ever so slightly in Mathewson's favor was his slightly greater level of dominance. While both men dominated their respective statistical categories, Wagner actually put up comparable numbers in at least two or three other seasons. Certainly, his MVP seasons of 1900 and 1902 were just as good, and his 1903 campaign was quite comparable as well. On the other hand, not only was Mathewson's year the best of his career, but it may well have been the finest any pitcher turned in the entire decade. He gets the nod over Wagner in a photo-finish.

1909

AMERICAN LEAGUE

The Detroit Tigers won their third consecutive American League championship in 1909, finishing 3½ games ahead of the second-place Philadelphia Athletics, and there is little doubt as to who was primarily responsible. Ty Cobb captured the A.L. Triple Crown by leading the league in home runs (9), runs batted in (107), and batting average (.377). He also finished first in runs scored (116), base hits (216), stolen bases (76), on-base percentage (.431), slugging percentage (.517), and total bases (296). It was in 1909 that Cobb replaced Honus Wagner as the game's greatest all-around player.

NATIONAL LEAGUE

Nevertheless, the Pirates shortstop still had a lot left in him, and he remained the National League's finest position player. Wagner's Pirates ended Chicago's three-year reign as league champions by finishing 6½ games ahead of the Cubs. Chicago's Mordecai Brown had a fabulous season, leading the league with 27 victories, against only 9 losses, pitching to a 1.31 earned run average, and leading N.L. pitchers with 342 innings pitched and 32 complete games. He was certainly deserving of MVP consideration.

So, too, was the Giants' Christy Mathewson, who had another brilliant year. He finished 25-6, led the league with a 1.14 earned run average, threw 275 innings and eight shutouts, and completed 26 games. However, New York finished a distant third, 18½ games behind the first-place Pirates, thus squelching the argument that might have been made on his behalf.

It would seem that the argument backing Brown would be a more valid one, especially when it is considered that his Cubs remained in the pennant race for virtually the entire season. However, the pennant-winning Pirates had an outstanding candidate of their own. Honus Wagner led the league with 100 runs batted in and a batting average of .339, and he also finished first in four other offensive categories. While he was starting to approach the twilight of his career, Wagner was still clearly the league's top player and the unquestioned leader of his team. For leading Pittsburgh to the pennant, he is the choice for league MVP.

1910

AMERICAN LEAGUE

As we saw earlier, both Ty Cobb and Napoleon Lajoie received automobiles from Hugh Chalmers for their outstanding 1910 seasons. Cobb finished a close second to Lajoie in the batting race with a mark of .383, and he led the American League with 106 runs scored, a .456 on-base percentage, and a .551 slugging percentage. He also finished second in runs batted in, hits, doubles, stolen bases, and total bases. In addition to leading the league with a .384 batting average, Lajoie finished first in the league rankings in hits (227), doubles (51), and total bases (304). However, both Detroit and Cleveland finished well back in the standings, making it difficult to select either Cobb or Lajoie as the league's Most Valuable Player.

The Philadelphia Athletics ran away with the American League flag in 1910, finishing 14½ games ahead of second-place New York. Philadelphia second baseman Eddie Collins led the league with 81 stolen bases, and he also finished in the top five in batting average, runs batted in, and hits. He, therefore, deserved consideration for league MVP honors. However, the A's most dominant player was righthanded pitcher Jack Coombs, who had the greatest season of his career. Coombs finished 31-9, to lead the league in victories, and he also finished second in earned run average with a superb mark of 1.30. Coombs threw a league-leading 13 shutouts, and he finished third in innings pitched (353) and strikeouts (224), while appearing in 45 games and completing 35 of his 38 starts.

NATIONAL LEAGUE

After a brief one-year hiatus, Chicago returned to the top of the National League standings in 1910, finishing 13 games ahead of the second-place Giants. Once again, the most outstanding player on each of those teams was their great pitcher—Mordecai Brown for the Cubs, and Christy Mathewson for the Giants.

Let's take a look at the numbers posted by the two righthanders:

PITCHER	WINS	LOSSES	ERA	IP	CG	SHUTOUTS
MORDECAI BROWN	25	14	1. 86	295	27*	6*
CHRISTY MATHEWSON	27*	9	1. 89	318	27*	2

This graphic would seem to indicate that there was little separating the two hurlers in 1910. In fact, their statistics were so similar that it is hard to determine which pitcher was actually better. Mathewson finished with a better won-lost record. But the two men posted virtually identical earned run averages, completed the same number of games, and threw practically the same number of innings. Brown, though, did have more shutouts. It could be argued that Mathewson was slightly more effective than Brown since he compiled a better won-lost record on a weaker team. Yet, it is difficult to ignore the fact that Brown's Cubs won the pennant, finishing 13 games ahead of Mathewson's Giants in the process. It would, therefore, be hard to select Mathewson as the league's Most Valuable Player. Similarly, it would be difficult to award the honor to Brown, since it is highly debatable as to whether or not he was even the league's best pitcher.

There was, however, one player who demonstrated that he was clearly the circuit's most outstanding performer during the regular season. Although his Philadelphia Phillies finished in fourth place, 25½ games behind the first-place Cubs, outfielder Sherry Magee finished in the top five in every major offensive category, except home runs. He led the N.L. in batting average (.331), runs batted in (123), runs scored (110), on-base percentage (.445), slugging percentage (.507), and total bases (263), and he finished fourth in stolen bases, with 49. Magee was so dominant that his 123 runs batted in exceeded his nearest rival's mark by a total of 35. Although the Phillies finished well behind the pennant winners, Magee led them to a respectable fourth-place finish. He, is, therefore, the choice for league MVP.

---

* Note: Throughout this book, when listing players' statistics, any numbers in bold print indicate that the player led his league in that category.

THE FIRST PRESENTATIONS

4

The Chalmers Award was presented annually from 1911 to 1914 to the player in each league who "should prove himself as the most important and useful player to his club and to the league at large in point of deportment and value of services rendered." Even though the award bore a different name, it conceptualized for the first time the true meaning of the Most Valuable Player Award. The winner in each league was determined by a committee of baseball writers, just as the MVP winners would be selected in future years. This represented a change in philosophy to the strictly statistical method devised by Hugh Chalmers prior to the start of the 1910 season. For the first time, the selection of the winners was made on a somewhat subjective basis, leaving the choices of the baseball writers open to a great deal of second-guessing and critical analysis.

Such an analysis will be performed here, with the validity of each selection closely examined. The "actual" award winners for each year will be listed, and a list of "suggested" winners will be provided as well. In some instances, the choices will differ. Arguments supporting the alternative winners proposed herein will be presented so that the reader may formulate his or her own opinion.

	ACTUAL MVP WINNERS		**SUGGESTED WINNERS**	
	A.L.	**N.L.**	**A.L.**	**N.L.**
1911	Ty Cobb	Frank Schulte	Ty Cobb	Frank Schulte
1912	Tris Speaker	Larry Doyle	Walter Johnson	Heinie Zimmerman
1913	Walter Johnson	Jake Daubert	Walter Johnson	Gavvy Cravath
1914	Eddie Collins	Johnny Evers	Eddie Collins	Bill James

1911

AMERICAN LEAGUE

The Philadelphia A's repeated as American League champions, finishing 13½ games in front of second-place Detroit. The Athletics were led by third baseman Frank "Home Run" Baker, second baseman Eddie Collins, and 1910 MVP selection Jack Coombs. Baker batted .334, scored 96 runs, led the league with 11 home runs, and finished third with 115 runs batted in. Collins batted .365, knocked in 73 runs, scored 92 others, played brilliantly in the field, and provided leadership in the infield. Although Coombs' earned run average jumped more than two runs a game to 3.53, he once again led the league in victories, finishing with a record of 28-12.

However, Coombs was not the best pitcher in the league in 1911, and none of the aforementioned Philadelphia players were even among the leading candidates for MVP honors. Chicago's Ed Walsh was the league's top hurler, compiling a 27-18 record, a 2.22 earned run average, and a league-leading 255 strikeouts, 368 innings pitched, and 56 appearances for the fourth-place White Sox. He finished second in the Chalmers Award voting.

In his first full major league season, Cleveland outfielder Shoeless Joe Jackson compiled the highest single-season batting average ever by a first-year player, finishing second in the batting race with a mark of .408. He also finished second in runs scored (126) and hits (233). However, Cleveland finished a distant third to the A's, 22 games back. Thus, Jackson could do no better than fourth in the balloting.

The man who overshadowed Jackson, and every other player in the league for that matter, was Ty Cobb. While his Tigers finished second, 13½ games behind the A's, Cobb led A.L. batters in nine different offensive categories. He batted .420, drove in 127 runs, scored 147 others, compiled 248 hits, collected 47 doubles and 24 triples, stole 83 bases, and finished with a .621 slugging percentage and 367 total bases. He also finished just one percentage point behind Jackson in on-base percentage (.467) and just three home runs behind Baker, with 8. There is certainly no second-guessing the writers on this selection— Cobb was clearly the league's dominant player all year.

NATIONAL LEAGUE

The Giants returned to the top of the National League standings for the first time in six years in 1911, finishing 7½ games ahead of second-place Chicago. Although he received a great deal of help from second baseman Larry Doyle, who hit 13 home runs, knocked in 77 runs, batted .310, scored 102 runs, and finished tied for third in the Chalmers Award voting, Christy Mathewson was once again New York's most outstanding performer. He finished with a record of 26-13, and a league-leading 1.99 earned run average, 307 innings pitched, and 29 complete games. Yet, Mathewson, who finished second in the voting, was not the best pitcher in the National League that year. Philadelphia rookie Grover Cleveland Alexander compiled a record of 28-13 to lead the league in victories. He also pitched to a 2.57 earned run average and led league hurlers in innings pitched (367), complete games (31), and shutouts (7). However, the Phillies finished fourth in the standings, 19½ games behind New York, ruining any chance Alexander had of winning the award. He finished tied for third in the voting.

The Chicago Cubs, though, fared much better than Philadelphia, finishing in second place, just 7½ games behind the Giants. They were led by outfielder Frank Schulte, who led the N.L. with a most impressive total of 21 home runs. He also finished first with 107 runs batted in, 308 total bases, and a .534 slugging percentage, while batting .300 and placing among the league leaders with 105 runs scored, 173 hits, and 21 triples. With the Cubs no longer the dominant team they were for much of the first decade of the century, it was Schulte's play that kept them in the pennant race for much of the season. For his efforts, he was most deserving of the Chalmers Award that was presented to him at the end of the year.

1912

AMERICAN LEAGUE

The Boston Red Sox dominated the American League in 1912, finishing 14 games ahead of the second-place Washington Senators and 15 games ahead of third-place Philadelphia. Red Sox outfielder Tris Speaker was rewarded for his brilliant play by being voted the

Chalmers Award winner in the A.L. at season's end. Speaker led the league with 10 home runs, 53 doubles, and a .464 on-base percentage. He also knocked in 90 runs, batted .383, scored 136 runs, collected 222 hits and 329 total bases, stole 52 bases, and was acknowledged to be the finest defensive outfielder in the game. Speaker was clearly the best all-around position player in baseball in 1912, and he was not a bad choice by the baseball writers.

However, two men stood above all others that year as the dominant figures in the game. Speaker's teammate with the Red Sox, Smokey Joe Wood, and Washington's Walter Johnson completely dominated American League hitters all year. Let's take a look at their numbers, along with those of Chicago's Ed Walsh, who finished runner-up in the voting for the second consecutive year:

PITCHER	W	L	ERA	IP	G	GS	CG	SO	BB	SHO
Smokey Joe Wood	**34**	5	1.91	344	43	38	**35**	258	82	**10**
Walter Johnson	33	12	**1.39**	368	50	37	34	**303**	76	7
Ed Walsh	27	17	2.15	**393**	**62**	41	32	254	94	6

Between them, the three men finished first in the league in virtually every statistical category. While Walsh led the league in appearances and innings pitched, his overall numbers were not as impressive as those compiled by either Wood or Johnson. In addition, Walsh's team finished well out of contention. Therefore, his second-place finish in the voting seems somewhat curious. Meanwhile, Wood and Johnson were the dominant forces in the game in 1912. Both men ran off 16-game winning streaks at one point during the season. Wood won 34 games and finished with a phenomenal .872 winning percentage. Johnson's .733 winning percentage wasn't as good, but he didn't have nearly the supporting cast in Washington that Wood had in Boston, and his 1.39 earned run average was considerably better than Wood's mark of 1.91. Boston's regular season record was a superb 105-47, meaning that the team posted a mark of 71-42 in games that Wood was not involved in the final decision. On the other hand, Washington's record was 91-61, meaning that the Senators compiled a record of just 58-49 without Johnson.

Therefore, as great as Smokey Joe was that year, Johnson was slightly better, and he was a far more integral part of the success his team experienced. The writers recognized that fact by giving Johnson enough votes for a third-place finish, while Wood had to settle for fifth. However, the feeling here is that it just wasn't enough.

As great a year as Speaker had, both Wood and Johnson probably should have finished ahead of him in the voting. Both men were more dominant, and, even though Boston won the pennant, Johnson should have won the award.

NATIONAL LEAGUE

The Giants won the National League pennant for the second straight year in 1912, beating out the second-place Pirates by 10 games and the third-place Cubs by 11½ games. Giants second baseman Larry Doyle had another solid season, hitting 10 home runs, driving in 90 runs, scoring 98 others, batting .330, and collecting 184 hits. At season's end, the baseball writers voted him the Chalmers Award winner, giving him 48 points to Honus Wagner's 43. Wagner, then 38 years old, managed to lead Pittsburgh to a second-place finish by leading the league with 102 runs batted in, hitting .324, scoring 91 runs, and tallying 181 hits. His numbers were actually quite comparable to those compiled by Doyle, so it is certainly understandable why the latter received more votes from the writers.

However, it is difficult to explain the lack of support received by Cubs third baseman Heinie Zimmerman, who finished a distant sixth in the voting with only 16 points. Zimmerman scored 95 runs, placed third in the league with 99 runs batted in, and topped the circuit with 14 home runs, a .372 batting average, 207 hits, and a .571 slugging percentage. His Cubs finished a very respectable third, just 1½ games behind Wagner's Pirates, and Zimmerman finished well ahead of the Pittsburgh great in most offensive categories. Zimmerman hit twice as many home runs as Wagner, batted almost 50 points higher, scored more runs, collected more hits, and finished with a slugging percentage that was 75 points higher. Perhaps Wagner's reputation influenced the voters, but Zimmerman was clearly more of an offensive force in 1912.

Zimmerman's numbers were also superior to those of Doyle, even though it could be argued on the latter's behalf that his team won the pennant and finished 11½ games ahead of Zimmerman's. However, it is debatable as to whether or not Doyle was even the most valuable player on his own team. Giants lefthander Rube Marquard finished

26-11, to lead the league in wins, and he also compiled a 2.57 earned run average, 175 strikeouts, 294 innings pitched, and 22 complete games. Marquard probably had as much to do with New York's success as Doyle.

The feeling here is that the award should have gone to Zimmerman.

1913

AMERICAN LEAGUE

Connie Mack's Philadelphia Athletics recaptured the American League pennant in 1913 after a disappointing third-place finish the previous year. Mack's A's finished 6½ games ahead of second-place Washington and 9½ in front of third-place Cleveland. The Athletics had two viable Chalmers Award candidates in second baseman Eddie Collins and third baseman Frank Baker. Collins hit only three home runs and drove in just 73 runs, but he batted .345, scored a league-leading 125 runs, collected 184 hits, and stole 55 bases. He finished third in the voting. Baker led the league with 12 home runs and 117 runs batted in, finished second to Collins with 116 runs scored, batted .337, and collected 190 hits. He finished fifth in the balloting.

The driving force behind Cleveland's third-place finish was outfielder Shoeless Joe Jackson. Although he hit only seven home runs and knocked in just 71 runs, Jackson led the league with 226 hits and 26 triples, placed second with a .373 batting average, and finished third with 109 runs scored. The writers placed him second in the balloting.

The man who received the greatest number of votes was Walter Johnson of the second-place Senators. Although it is hard to believe, Johnson actually improved upon his previous year's performance in 1913. He led A.L. pitchers in every major statistical category, compiling a brilliant 36-7 record and 1.14 earned run average, with 243 strikeouts, 346 innings pitched, 29 complete games, and 11 shutouts. Johnson's season would have to rank among the greatest ever by a pitcher.

There may have been some doubt as to who was most deserving of league MVP honors in 1912, but there certainly wasn't in 1913.

NATIONAL LEAGUE

The writers' selection of Brooklyn first baseman Jake Daubert as the 1913 National League Chalmers Award winner was the first truly poor choice they made. While it was clearly a reflection of the thinking of the times, Daubert's selection remains almost inexplicable. Let's take a closer look.

The Giants won their third consecutive pennant in 1913, finishing 12½ games in front of the second-place Phillies. The Dodgers finished sixth, 34½ games behind the Giants. New York's Christy Mathewson had an outstanding year, finishing with a record of 25-11, a league-leading 2.06 earned run average, 306 innings pitched, and 25 complete games. He was clearly his team's most valuable player. However, he only led the league in one statistical category, and he finished among the leaders in just three others. While he was still an outstanding pitcher, Mathewson was no longer the dominant hurler he was earlier in his career—certainly not dominant enough to be named league MVP.

The National League's most dominant player in 1913 was Philadelphia outfielder Gavvy Cravath, who finished second in the Chalmers Award voting. Cravath led the league with 19 home runs, 128 runs batted in, 179 hits, and a .568 slugging percentage, finished second with a .341 batting average, and scored 78 runs. Yet, the writers chose to vote for Daubert instead, even though his statistics were not nearly as impressive as Cravath's, and in spite of the fact that Brooklyn finished four places and 22 games behind Cravath's Phillies in the standings. While Daubert led the league with a .350 batting average, his other numbers were quite ordinary. The first baseman scored 76 runs, collected 178 hits, hit only two home runs, and knocked in just 52 runs (not even half as many as Cravath). The writers obviously placed a great deal of importance on the fact that Daubert won the batting title, which was considered to be the most important individual accomplishment at that time. However, his overall numbers paled by comparison to those of Cravath, his team was not nearly as successful, and Daubert never should have been selected league MVP. That honor should have gone to Gavvy Cravath.

1914

AMERICAN LEAGUE

The Philadelphia Athletics repeated as American League champions in 1914, finishing 8½ games ahead of second-place Boston. Leading candidates for the Chalmers Award included Walter Johnson and Detroit outfielder Sam Crawford. Johnson had another outstanding year for Washington, finishing 28-18, to lead the league in victories, compiling a superb 1.72 earned run average, and leading A.L. pitchers with 225 strikeouts, 371 innings pitched, 33 complete games, and nine shutouts. However, Johnson's Senators finished a distant third, 19 games behind the first-place A's, thereby negating his chances of being selected league MVP once more. Crawford hit just eight home runs, but he led the league with 104 runs batted in and 26 triples, while batting .314, scoring 74 runs, and collecting 183 hits. Crawford's Tigers finished fourth, though, 19½ games out of first.

Second-place Boston's leading candidate was Tris Speaker, who finished second in the batting race with a mark of .338, led the league with 193 hits, 46 doubles, 287 total bases, and a .503 slugging percentage, and also finished among the leaders in runs batted in, runs scored, triples, stolen bases, and on-base percentage. Speaker was the league's best all-around player in 1914.

However, Eddie Collins of the pennant-winning Athletics wasn't far behind Speaker, and his team's first-place finish made the Philadelphia second baseman the man most deserving of league MVP honors. Collins topped the circuit with 122 runs scored, a .344 batting average, and a .452 on-base percentage. He also finished second with 58 stolen bases, and he placed among the leaders in runs batted in, hits, doubles, total bases, and slugging percentage.

It was very close, but the Athletics' first-place finish was just enough to validate the writers' selection of Collins over Speaker as the Chalmers Award winner.

NATIONAL LEAGUE

However, it is far more difficult to agree with the National League writers' 1914 selection of Boston Braves second baseman Johnny Evers as the senior circuit's Chalmers Award winner. The surprising Braves upset the favored Giants, finishing 10½ games ahead of second-place New York in the final standings. As a result, when the writers' votes were tabulated at season's end, the names of three Boston players were at the top of the list. Evers, who came over to the Braves at the start of the season after spending the previous 12 years with the Cubs, finished first. Shortstop Rabbit Maranville finished a close second, and pitcher Bill James came in third.

The final tally seemed a bit surprising since no other player had previously won the award with such feeble numbers. Evers hit one home run, knocked in 40 runs, batted .279, scored 81 runs, and collected 137 hits, including three triples and 20 doubles. Many people felt that his doubleplay partner, Maranville, should have won the award instead, even though the latter's numbers weren't much better. While the shortstop knocked in almost twice as many runs as Evers (78 to 40), he hit just four home runs, batted only .246, scored just 74 runs, and collected only 144 hits, including six triples and 23 doubles. Neither player finished in the top five in the league in any offensive category, prompting one to think that they both must have been very strong defensively and possessed many intangible qualities that made an impression on the voters.

The feeling here, though, is that righthander Bill James was far more deserving of the honor. Although he spent parts of just four seasons in the big leagues, finishing with a career won-lost record of only 37-21, James was superb in 1914. He finished 26-7, with a 1.90 earned run average, 332 innings pitched, and 30 complete games. While neither of his teammates finished anywhere near the league leaders in any offensive category, James finished in the top five in virtually every pitching department. He was second in both wins and earned run average, third in innings pitched and complete games, and fifth in strikeouts. James' one shining moment in the majors should have been enough to earn him the N.L. Chalmers Award.

MORE HYPOTHETICAL WINNERS

With interest in the Chalmers Award waning, the award quietly disappeared at the end of the 1914 season. Thus, there were no official presentations made in either league from 1915 to 1921. Therefore, those years will now be addressed, and the hypothetical most valuable players in both leagues will be selected.

HYPOTHETICAL MVP WINNERS

	AMERICAN LEAGUE	NATIONAL LEAGUE
1915	Ty Cobb	Grover Cleveland Alexander
1916	Shoeless Joe Jackson	Grover Cleveland Alexander
1917	Ed Cicotte	Grover Cleveland Alexander
1918	Babe Ruth	Hippo Vaughn
1919	Ed Cicotte	Edd Roush
1920	Babe Ruth	Rogers Hornsby
1921	Babe Ruth	Rogers Hornsby

1915

AMERICAN LEAGUE

After capturing the previous two American League pennants, Connie Mack decided to purge the Philadelphia Athletics roster of much of its high-priced talent at the conclusion of the 1914 season. As a result, the team that contended for the A.L. pennant throughout most of the league's early years spent much of the ensuing decade floundering near the bottom of the American League rankings.

The Boston Red Sox were the first team to take advantage of Philadephia's weakened state as they won their first league championship since 1912, finishing just 2½ games ahead of second-place Detroit. Despite winning the pennant, Boston really did not have an outstanding MVP candidate in 1915, thereby leaving the race wide open. Walter Johnson had another great year for the Senators, finishing 27-13, to lead A.L. pitchers in wins, compiling a 1.55 earned run average and 336 innings pitched, and leading the league with 203 strikeouts, seven shutouts, and 35 complete games. However, Washington finished fourth, 17 games out of first place, eliminating Johnson from serious MVP consideration.

The second-place Tigers had a more viable candidate for that honor; someone whose qualifications were even more impressive than Johnson's. Ty Cobb led the league with a .369 batting average, 144 runs scored, 208 hits, a .486 on-base percentage, and 96 stolen bases, while finishing third with 99 runs batted in. His 96 steals stood as the single-season major league record for 47 years, until finally surpassed in 1962 by the Dodgers Maury Wills.

Cobb was clearly the American League's best player in 1915, and his team's close second-place finish made him the only logical selection for league MVP honors.

NATIONAL LEAGUE

The Philadelphia Phillies captured their first National League pennant since the turn of the century in 1915, finishing seven games ahead of the second-place Boston Braves. On offense, Philadelphia was once again led by slugging outfielder Gavvy Cravath, who led the league with 24 home runs, 115 runs batted in, 89 runs scored, and a .393 on-base percentage. He also batted .285 and finished with a .510 slugging percentage. Cravath was the league's top hitter that year, but he was not its best player.

Cravath's teammate with the Phillies, pitcher Grover Cleveland Alexander, began a three-year reign as the best pitcher in baseball. Alexander led N.L. pitchers in every major statistical category, finishing 31-10, with a 1.22 earned run average, 241 strikeouts, 12 shutouts, 376 innings pitched, and 36 complete games. The Philadelphia righthander clearly replaced Christy Mathewson as the league's top pitcher that year.

Alexander was also the driving force behind Philadelphia's first-place finish, and he was unquestionably the league's Most Valuable Player in 1915.

1916

AMERICAN LEAGUE

The Red Sox repeated as American League champions in 1916, finishing two games ahead of second-place Chicago and four games in front of third-place Detroit.

After trading away star centerfielder Tris Speaker to Cleveland during the off-season, Boston's best player subsequently became a young lefthanded pitcher named Babe Ruth. In just his second full season as a starter, Ruth was the league's best pitcher. He finished 23-12, with a league-leading 1.75 earned run average and nine shutouts. Ruth also struck out 170 batters, threw 323 innings, and completed 23 games. He was clearly Boston's most valuable player during the season, but, having led A.L. pitchers in just two statistical categories, he wasn't quite dominant enough to be considered league MVP.

The two leading candidates for that honor were former Boston star, Tris Speaker, and Shoeless Joe Jackson, who was traded from Cleveland to Chicago the previous year.

In his first season with his new team, Speaker posted numbers that were slightly superior to those of Jackson. The Cleveland centerfielder led the league with a .386 batting average, 211 hits, a .470 on-base percentage, and a .502 slugging percentage, finished fourth with 79 runs batted in, placed second with 274 total bases, and collected 41 doubles. Although Jackson's numbers weren't quite as good, they were actually quite comparable. He finished third in batting (.341), second in hits (202), fourth in on-base percentage (.393), and second in slugging percentage (.495). Jackson finished with one less RBI (78) and double (40) than Speaker, but he led the league with 21 triples and 293 total bases. Of even greater significance is the fact that Speaker's Indians finished sixth, 14 games behind first-place Boston, while Jackson's White Sox finished just two games back, in second place.

While Speaker may have been a slightly better player in 1916, Jackson was more valuable to his team.

NATIONAL LEAGUE

Grover Cleveland Alexander continued his dominance of National League hitters in 1916, leading his Philadelphia Phillies to a second-place finish, just 2½ games behind the pennant-winning Brooklyn Dodgers. Brooklyn outfielder Zack Wheat had a solid season for the N.L. champs, finishing fourth in the league with nine home runs, fifth in runs batted in (73) and batting average (.312), third in hits (177), and second in doubles (32), while scoring 76 runs, collecting 13 triples, and leading the league with 262 total bases and a .461 slugging percentage. However, his performance could hardly be described as dominant.

Meanwhile, Alexander led league pitchers in every major statistical category for the second consecutive year. He finished 33-12, with a 1.55 earned run average, 167 strikeouts, 388 innings pitched, 38 complete games, and a major league record 16 shutouts. Alexander was once again the National League's best player, and his team's close second-place finish was clearly enough to validate his selection as the league's Most Valuable Player.

1917

AMERICAN LEAGUE

The Chicago White Sox replaced Boston at the top of the American League standings in 1917, finishing nine games ahead of the second-place Red Sox. With both Shoeless Joe Jackson and former Athletics star Eddie Collins members of their everyday lineup, the White Sox became the league's most formidable team. However, neither Jackson nor Collins was Chicago's best player in 1917. The team's most dominant performer was righthanded pitcher Ed Cicotte, who eventually became one of the infamous "Black Sox" involved in throwing the 1919 World Series to the Cincinnati Reds. Cicotte led A.L. pitchers in victories, earned run average, and innings pitched, finishing 28-12, with a 1.53 earned run average and 346 innings pitched. He also finished second in strikeouts (150), third in complete games (29), and fourth in shutouts (7).

In spite of Cicotte's outstanding year for Chicago, Detroit's Ty Cobb was actually the league's top player. Cobb led the A.L. with a .383 batting average, 225 hits, 44 doubles, 24 triples, 55 stolen bases, 335 total bases, a .444 on-base percentage, and a .570 slugging percentage, and he also finished second with 102 runs batted in and

107 runs scored. Had the Tigers finished a little closer in the standings, Cobb would have been the choice as league MVP. However, Detroit finished a distant fourth, 21½ games behind first-place Chicago. The Tiger great is denied his fifth MVP selection, and the honor goes to Cicotte instead.

NATIONAL LEAGUE

The National League pennant moved up north in the city of New York, from Brooklyn to Manhattan, in 1917, as the Giants replaced the Dodgers as league champions. New York outfielder, George Burns (no, not the comedian who was married to Gracie Allen), was extremely instrumental in his team's first-place finish. Burns led the N.L. with 103 runs scored, placed second with 180 hits, and finished fifth with a .302 batting average. He also finished in the top five in total bases, stolen bases, on-base percentage, and slugging percentage. However, Burns' total of only 45 runs batted in clearly indicates that he was not a dominant player.

Once again, Grover Cleveland Alexander was the league's most outstanding performer. He led the Phillies to a very respectable second-place finish, 10 games behind the Giants. Alexander won at least 30 games for the third consecutive year, finishing 30-13, to lead the league in victories. He also topped the circuit in strikeouts (200), innings pitched (387), complete games (34), and shutouts (8), and he finished second in earned run average, with a mark of 1.83.

Alexander's selection as league MVP makes him the first pitcher to earn the honor three consecutive seasons.

1918

AMERICAN LEAGUE

The Red Sox won their third pennant in four years in 1918—a season that became historic in that it marked the last time in the twentieth century that Boston captured the world championship. The Sox finished just 2½ games ahead of second-place Cleveland and four games in front of third-place Washington.

Detroit's Ty Cobb was once again the top offensive performer in the American League. He led the league with a .382 batting average, a .440 on-base percentage, a .515 slugging percentage, and 14 triples. However, injuries caused Cobb to miss several games, enabling him to drive in just 64 runs, score only 83 others, and collect just 161 hits. In addition, his Tigers finished next-to-last in the league, a full 20 games out of first place. Therefore, it would be difficult to give him serious consideration for league MVP honors.

Walter Johnson had an excellent season for third-place Washington, and he was clearly the league's best pitcher. He finished 23-13 to lead A.L. pitchers in victories, and he also compiled a league-leading 1.27 earned run average, 162 strikeouts, and eight shutouts, while placing second in innings pitched (325) and third in complete games (29). He would have to be considered a leading candidate.

So, too, would Boston's Babe Ruth. Splitting his time between pitching and playing the outfield, Ruth had a tremendous impact on the pennant-race, and on his team's eventual first-place finish. Although the numbers Ruth compiled over the course of the season would seem to indicate that he failed to dominate the league either as a hitter or as a pitcher, Ruth's level of proficiency in both aspects of the game was exceptional. As a pitcher, he appeared in 20 games, 19 of them starts. He finished with a won-lost record of 13-7 and an earned run average of 2.22, threw 166 innings, and completed 18 of his 19 starts. In just 95 games and 317 at-bats as an outfielder, Ruth tied for the league lead with 11 home runs, finished third with 66 runs batted in, and batted .300.

While Johnson's pitching unquestionably enabled the Senators to remain in the pennant race for much of the season, it would seem that it was the combined efforts of Ruth, as both a pitcher and as a hitter, that allowed the Red Sox to capture the league championship. As a result, Ruth is the choice for league MVP.

NATIONAL LEAGUE

After failing to win the National League pennant in each of the previous seven seasons, the Chicago Cubs returned to the top of the league standings in 1918, finishing 10 games ahead of the second-place Giants. In a year in which offensive numbers were down somewhat throughout all of baseball, few N.L. hitters truly distinguished themselves. Neither the first-place Cubs nor the second-place Giants had any player in their respective lineups that could legitimately be called a leading candidate for MVP honors.

However, Chicago did feature a pitcher whose performance was worthy of such accolades. With Grover Cleveland Alexander spending time in the military during World War I, Cubs lefthander Hippo Vaughn replaced the Phillie great as the league's dominant pitcher. He led league hurlers in virtually every statistical category, finishing 22-10, with a 1.74 earned run average, 148 strikeouts, 290 innings pitched, and eight shutouts, and he finished second with 27 complete games.

1919

AMERICAN LEAGUE

The Chicago White Sox replaced Boston at the top of the American League standings in 1919, winning their second pennant in three seasons. Although they ended up throwing the World Series to Cincinnati, the Sox were baseball's strongest team in 1919. They finished 3½ games ahead of second-place Cleveland. Despite a tremendous year from Babe Ruth, who became a full-time outfielder prior to the start of the season, the defending champion Boston Red Sox could do no better than sixth, finishing 20½ games behind first-place Chicago. Nevertheless, Ruth deserved some consideration for MVP honors, having established a new major league record by hitting 29 home runs, and also leading the league with 114 runs batted in, 103 runs scored, a .456 on-base percentage, and a .657 slugging percentage, white batting .322.

White Sox outfielder Shoeless Joe Jackson also merited consideration. Generally considered to be one of the game's greatest hitters and finest all-around players, Jackson finished third in the league with 96 runs batted in, fourth in batting average (.351), third in on-base percentage (.422), and fifth in slugging percentage (.506).

However, for the second time in three years, Chicago's most dominant player was not a member of its everyday lineup. Once again, righthander Ed Cicotte was the driving force behind the team's first-place finish. He finished 29-7, to lead the league in wins, placed second with a 1.82 earned run average, threw five shutouts, and led the league with 306 innings pitched and 30 complete games. With the regular season shortened to just 140 games in 1919 due to the war, the White Sox finished the year with a record of 88-52. In winning 29 games, Cicotte won almost one-third of his team's games, thereby justifying his selection as league MVP.

NATIONAL LEAGUE

Although they were not as strong as the White Sox, the Cincinnati Reds actually had an easier time capturing the National League flag in 1919. The Reds finished nine games ahead of the second-place Giants. With offensive numbers still generally down in both leagues, there really was no outstanding offensive performer in the National League. No player was able to establish himself as the league's dominant hitter, and no pitcher even had the type of year that was worthy of MVP consideration.

Almost by default, the Award would have to go to Cincinnati outfielder Edd Roush, who led the league with a .321 batting average while finishing in the top five in several other categories as well.

1920

AMERICAN LEAGUE

Having seen the kind of excitement that Babe Ruth was able to generate amongst fans with his 29 home runs the previous year, baseball began implementing certain changes in 1920 that it hoped would bring more offense to the game, thereby increasing fan interest even more. The size of the strike zone was decreased, the spitball was outlawed, new balls were put into play more frequently, and the ball was wound a bit more tightly, allowing hitters to drive it farther, thereby increasing power numbers and run-production. The changes had their desired effect as offensive numbers improved dramatically in both leagues.

American League fans also had a close pennant race to hold their interest for much of the year. The Cleveland Indians won the pennant, finishing just two games ahead of the second-place White Sox and just three games ahead of the Yankees, who acquired Babe Ruth from Boston during the off-season.

Cleveland featured two legitimate MVP candidates. The first was pitcher Jim Bagby, who finished 31-12 and also led league pitchers with 339 innings pitched and 30 complete games, while finishing fifth with a 2.89 earned run average. Cleveland's other contender for league MVP honors was outfielder Tris Speaker, who had one of his best seasons for the Indians. Although Speaker hit only eight home runs, he knocked in 107 runs, placed second in the league with a .388 batting average, finished tied for second with 137 runs scored, finished fifth with 214 hits, led the league with 50 doubles, collected 11 triples, and finished in the top five in on-base percentage, slugging percentage, and total bases.

Second-place Chicago also had an outstanding candidate in Shoeless Joe Jackson. In what turned out to be his final big league season, Jackson had a tremendous year. Although he hit just 12 home runs, Jackson drove in 121 runs, scored 105 others, batted .382, collected 218 hits, and led the league with 20 triples.

First baseman George Sisler of the St. Louis Browns had an even better year, though. He led the league with a .407 batting average, 257 hits, and 399 total bases. Sisler also finished second in home runs (19), runs batted in (122), runs scored (137), doubles (49), triples (18), stolen bases (42), and slugging percentage (.632), and he finished third in on-base percentage (.449). However, Sisler's Browns finished fourth, 21 1/2 games behind the Indians.

As great as Sisler was, he was surpassed by Babe Ruth. In his first season in New York, Ruth established a new major league record by hitting an astounding 54 home runs. He also led the league with 137 runs batted in, 158 runs scored, a .530 on-base percentage, and an amazing .847 slugging percentage. Ruth finished second behind Sisler in total bases, with 388, and he compiled the fourth highest batting average in the league, with a mark of .376.

Leading his team to a close third-place finish, and making an instant contender out of a team that had consistently finished in the second division, Ruth was unquestionably the league's Most Valuable Player in 1920.

NATIONAL LEAGUE

The National League pennant race was not nearly as interesting, with the Brooklyn Dodgers finishing seven games ahead of the second-place Giants. Brooklyn pitcher Burleigh Grimes was the only legitimate MVP candidate that the team featured. He compiled a 23-11 record, with a 2.22 earned run average, 131 strikeouts, 303 innings pitched, and 25 complete games. Grimes managed just a third-place finish in each of those categories, though, and he was not close to being the best pitcher in the league in 1920.

That honor fell to Grover Cleveland Alexander, who, following time spent in the military during the war and his subsequent battles with alcoholism and epilectic seizures, was dealt to the Chicago Cubs. With Chicago, Alexander proved he was still the best pitcher in the game, leading league hurlers in practically every statistical category. He finished 27-14, with a 1.91 earned run average, 173 strikeouts, 363 innings pitched, and 33 complete games. However, his Cubs finished tied for fifth with the Cardinals, 18 games out of first.

While Alexander was the league's dominant pitcher, the Cardinals Rogers Hornsby established himself as the circuit's best hitter. He led the league with a .370 batting average, 94 runs batted in, 218 hits, 44 doubles, a .431 on-base percentage, and a .559 slugging percentage, while finishing second with 20 triples and fourth with 96 runs scored.

It really is a difficult choice between the two men for MVP. Who was more worthy—Alexander or Hornsby? Both men played for teams that finished tied for fifth, well out of first-place. In spite of their teams' mediocre performances, both men dominated the league in their respective statistical categories. Yet, one man did not play every day, while the other did.

With everything else being virtually equal, we'll opt for the everyday player and select Hornsby for league MVP.

1921

AMERICAN LEAGUE

The New York Yankees captured their first American League pennant in 1921, finishing 4½ games ahead of second-place Cleveland. New York and Cleveland had easily the most potent offenses in the game that year, scoring significantly more runs than any other team. New York led the majors in scoring with a total of 948 runs, while the

Indians finished second, with 925. The National League champion New York Giants finished a distant third, with 840 runs scored.

However, neither the Yankees nor the Indians were one-dimensional, since they both had solid pitching as well, finishing first and second in the American League in runs allowed. Cleveland featured future Hall of Fame pitcher, Stan Coveleski, who won 23 games and completed 28 of his 40 starts. New York's Carl Mays tied for the league lead in victories, with 27, finished third in earned run average with a mark of 3.05, threw 30 complete games, and led the league with 336 innings pitched, 49 appearances, and seven saves.

Still, it was their powerful offenses that truly separated these two teams from the rest of the pack in the American League in 1921. Yet, other teams had their fair share of hitting stars as well.

Detroit outfielder Harry Heilmann led the league with a .394 batting average and 237 hits, while finishing second with 139 runs batted in. Teammate Ty Cobb finished second in the league with a .389 batting average, and fellow Tiger outfielder Bobby Veach knocked in 128 runs.

Although his Browns finished third, 17½ games out of first, George Sisler had another tremendous year for St. Louis, compiling a .371 batting average, 125 runs scored, and a league-leading 35 stolen bases. Teammate Ken Williams hit 24 home runs, knocked in 117 runs, scored 115 others, and batted .347, while fellow Brownie Jack Tobin batted .352, led the league with 18 triples, scored 132 runs, and collected 236 hits..

On the pennant contenders, Cleveland's Tris Speaker batted .362 and led the league with 52 doubles, while teammate Larry Gardner drove in 120 runs and scored 101 others.

Outfielder Bob Meusel hit 24 home runs, knocked in 135 runs, scored another 104, and batted .318 for New York. However, Meusel was merely a member of Babe Ruth's supporting cast. Having perhaps the greatest single season in baseball history, Ruth was once again the league's dominant player and unquestionably its MVP. He established new major league records with 59 home runs, 171 runs batted in, 177 runs scored, 457 total bases, a .512 on-base percentage, and an .846 slugging percentage, while finishing third in the league with a .378 batting average, and placing second with 44 doubles. Ruth was so dominant that his .846 slugging percentage was *240* points higher than that of runner-up Harry Heilmann.

NATIONAL LEAGUE

The New York Giants won the National League pennant in 1921, finishing four games ahead of the second-place Pirates and seven games ahead of the third-place Cardinals. While hitting was not as dominant in the senior circuit as it was in the A.L. in 1921, two players stood out above all others. Frankie Frisch had an outstanding season for the pennant-winning Giants, while fellow second baseman Rogers Hornsby had a tremendous year for third-place St. Louis. In fact, Hornsby came within just two home runs of capturing the league's triple crown.

Let's look at the statistics of both players:

PLAYER	AB	HITS	RUNS	2B	3B	HR	RBI	AVG	OBP	SLG PCT	SB
Rogers Hornsby	592	235	131	44	18	21	126	.397	.458	.639	13
Frankie Frisch	618	211	121	31	17	8	100	.341	.384	.485	49

Hornsby clearly dominated the various National League hitting categories, finishing first in everything except home runs and stolen bases. Frisch led in stolen bases and finished second to Hornsby in runs scored and hits. He also played for the pennant-winning team, which is a point in his favor. However, the Cardinals finished just seven games back, in third place, and Hornsby was unquestionably the league's most outstanding player. He must also be considered its Most Valuable Player.

A MIXED BAG

6

The 1922 and 1923 seasons represented a mixed bag of sorts as far as the MVP Award was concerned in that the American League announced a winner at the end of each season, while the National League did not. However, as we saw earlier, the rules devised by the American League Trophy Committee had several flaws in it, including the exclusion from consideration of any previous winners and the limitation placed on voters to select just one player from each team. The exclusion of previous winners did not impact either the 1922 or the 1923 election, but the ability of voters to select only one player from each team certainly did. With St. Louis Brown George Sisler being named on all eight ballots in the 1922 election, teammate Ken Williams was automatically excluded from consideration even though he led the A.L. in both home runs and runs batted in.

Such an injustice will not take place here as we attempt to discern who the league's Most Valuable Player actually was in each of those years. A hypothetical award winner will also be selected for the National League.

	ACTUAL MVP WINNERS AMERICAN LEAGUE	HYPOTHETICAL MVP WINNERS NATIONAL LEAGUE
1922	George Sisler	Rogers Hornsby
1923	Babe Ruth	Frankie Frisch

1922

AMERICAN LEAGUE

The Yankees repeated as American League champions in 1922 despite the fact that Babe Ruth missed more than a month of the season due to a suspension. The St. Louis Browns finished a close second, just one game behind New York. With Ruth missing a considerable amount of playing time, the Yankee offense was much less potent than it was the previous year. While New York's 758 runs scored represented the fourth highest total in the American League in 1922, the team scored almost 200 fewer runs than it did the previous year when it led the majors with a total of 948 runs scored. As a result, the Yankees had to depend far more on their pitching, which was able to compile the second lowest team earned run average in the league (3.39), just one point higher than the Browns' mark of 3.38.

The most effective pitcher on the New York pitching staff was righthander Joe Bush, who compiled a 26-7 record, for a league-leading .788 winning percentage. He also finished with a 3.31 earned run average and 20 complete games. Teammate Bob Shawkey was also a primary contributor to the team's success. He finished 20-12, with a 2.91 earned run average and 22 complete games. However, neither pitcher was dominant enough to merit serious consideration for league MVP honors.

Tris Speaker had another outstanding season for Cleveland, finishing third in batting with an average of .378 and leading the league with 48 doubles and a .474 on-base percentage. However, the Indians finished fourth, 16 games behind the Yankees.

Detroit's Ty Cobb finished second in the league with 211 hits and a .401 batting average, and he also placed among the league leaders in doubles, triples, total bases, and on-base percentage. But the Tigers finished third, 15 games off the pace.

Despite appearing in only 110 games and accumulating just 406 official at-bats, Babe Ruth managed to finish third in the league with 35 home runs. He also knocked in 99 runs, scored 94 others, batted .315, and led the league with a .672 slugging percentage. However, Ruth was not the American League's top slugger in 1922. St. Louis Browns outfielder Ken Williams was. Williams led the league with 39 home runs, 155 runs batted in, and 367 total bases, and he also finished among the league leaders in runs scored, stolen bases, and slugging percentage. He may well have been the best all-around player in the league that year. If not, he was certainly a close second to teammate

George Sisler, who finished among the league leaders in every offensive category, except home runs.

Let's take a look at the numbers of both men:

PLAYER	AB	HITS	RUNS	2B	3B	HR	RBI	AVG	OBP	SLG PCT	SB
George Sisler	586	246	134	42	18	8	105	.420	.467	.594	51
Ken Williams	585	194	128	34	11	39	155	.332	.413	.627	37

Between them, Sisler and Williams led the league in almost every major statistical category. They also played on a team that finished second, just one game behind the first-place Yankees. Therefore, they were clearly the two players most deserving of the league MVP Award that year. But, which one was **more** deserving? Williams had better power numbers, hitting far more home runs and finishing with a higher slugging percentage. However, Sisler more than compensated for that by hitting almost 90 points higher, compiling a higher on-base percentage, stealing more bases, and finishing with more doubles and triples. He also scored a few more runs, but Williams was the greater run-producer of the two, having knocked in 50 more runs. When one takes into consideration, though, that Williams batted right behind Sisler in the St. Louis lineup and, therefore, benefited greatly from having the latter constantly on base when he came to the plate, the RBI discrepancy becomes much less significant.

As a result, it would seem that Sisler was slightly more valuable than Williams to the team, and that the baseball writers were correct in naming him league MVP.

NATIONAL LEAGUE

The Giants also repeated as champions, finishing seven games ahead of the second-place Reds. The Cardinals and Pirates finished tied for third, eight games behind New York. The Giants were led by first baseman George Kelly, who finished among the league leaders in home runs and runs batted in, outfielder Emil Meusel, who finished second in the league with 132 runs batted in, and shortstop Dave Bancroft, who finished among the league leaders in runs scored and base hits.

Second-place Cincinnati's outstanding performer was pitcher Eppa Rixey, who led the league with 25 wins and 313 innings pitched. Pittsburgh was paced by centerfielder Max Carey, who led the league with 51 stolen bases, finished second with 140 runs scored, and collected 207 hits. Outfielder Carson Bigbee was also a primary contributor to Pittsburgh's success. He batted .350, knocked in 99 runs, scored 113 others, and finished second in the league with 215 hits.

However, the accomplishments of every other player paled in comparison to those of Rogers Hornsby. The Cardinals second baseman kept his team in the pennant race for most of the season almost singlehandedly, leading the league in every major statistical category. Hornsby became the first National League player to win the coveted triple crown by finishing first in home runs (42), runs batted in (152), and batting average (.401). He also led the league in runs scored (141), base hits (250), doubles (46), on-base percentage (.459), slugging percentage (.722), and total bases (450).

There is little doubt that Hornsby was the Most Valuable Player in the National League in 1922.

1923

AMERICAN LEAGUE

The Yankees won their third conseutive American League pennant in 1923, beating out the second-place Tigers by 16 games and the third-place Indians by 16½ games. Each of those three teams had a legitimate MVP candidate—Harry Heilmann, for Detroit; Tris Speaker, for Cleveland; and Babe Ruth, for New York.

Heilmann won his second batting title, finishing with a mark of .403. He also finished in the top five in home runs (18), runs batted in (115), runs scored (121), hits (211), doubles (44), on-base percentage (.481), slugging percentage (.632), and total bases (331).

At the age of 35, Speaker had his most productive major league season for the Indians, establishing career highs in home runs (17) and runs batted in (130), scoring 133 runs, batting .380, and leading the league in doubles for the fourth straight year, with 59. He also finished in the top five in hits, on-base percentage, and slugging percentage.

However, following his suspension-marred 1922 season, Babe Ruth returned to the New York lineup with a vengeance, leading the American League with 41 home runs, 131 runs batted in, 151 runs scored, 399 total bases, a .545 on-base percentage, and a .764 slugging percentage. Ruth also set a new major league record by walking 170 times, while finishing second in the A.L. to Heilmann with a .393 batting average. In addition, he finished in the top five in the circuit in base hits and runs scored.

There can be no questioning of the baseball writers' selection of Ruth as league MVP in 1923.

NATIONAL LEAGUE

New York made it a clean sweep as the Giants also repeated as National League champs in 1923, finishing 4½ games in front of second-place Cincinnati. The Cardinals finished fifth, 16 games behind the first-place Giants, and Rogers Hornsby, while winning his fourth consecutive batting title, did not have nearly as much impact on the pennant race as he had the previous two years. Appearing in only 107 games and accumulating just 424 at-bats due to injury, Hornsby led the league with a .384 batting average, but hit only 17 home runs, drove in just 83 runs, and scored only 89 others. Therefore, his string of three successive hypothetical league MVP Awards must come to an end.

The second-place Reds had an outstanding MVP candidate in pitcher Dolf Luque. The righthander finished 27-8, to lead the league in victories, and he also finished first among N.L. pitchers in earned run average (1.93) and shutouts (6). Luque also placed second in the league with 322 innings pitched and 28 complete games.

The pennant-winning Giants had several key contributors to their success. George Kelly once again finished among the league leaders in run batted in, with 103, while outfielder Ross Youngs led the N.L. with 121 runs scored. However, the best player on the Giants, and the Most Valuable Player in the league, was Frankie Frisch. The New York second baseman finished among the league leaders in several different categories. He led the circuit with 223 hits and 311 total bases, and he also finished in the top five in runs batted in (111), batting average (.348), and runs scored (116). Frisch may not have dominated the offensive statistical categories as much as Luque dominated the pitching statistics, but he played every day, his team finished first, and he was the league's best all-around player. Therefore, he was most deserving of the league MVP Award for 1923.

THE SUPERFICIAL WINNERS

7

In 1924, the National League decided to follow the American League's lead and once again present an award to its Most Valuable Player at season's end. However, the senior circuit did not make the same mistakes the A.L. made two years earlier when it elected to exclude previous winners of the award from consideration and limit representation for each team to just one player. Therefore, the National League selections made between the years 1924 and 1928 were far more reflective of the players' performances during each of those seasons than were the A.L. choices, which were extremely flawed in some instances. As a result, this chapter has been entitled *The Superficial Winners* because several American League MVP honorees during this period were exactly that.

	ACTUAL MVP WINNERS		SUGGESTED WINNERS	
	A.L.	**N.L.**	**A.L.**	**N.L.**
1924	Walter Johnson	Dazzy Vance	Babe Ruth	Dazzy Vance
1925	Roger Peckinpaugh	Rogers Hornsby	Al Simmons	Rogers Hornsby
1926	George Burns	Bob O'Farrell	Babe Ruth	Jim Bottomley
1927	Lou Gehrig	Paul Waner	Lou Gehrig	Paul Waner
1928	Mickey Cochrane	Jim Bottomley	Lou Gehrig/ Babe Ruth	Jim Bottomley

1924

AMERICAN LEAGUE

The Washington Senators captured their first American League pennant in 1924, ending New York's three-year reign as league champions by finishing two games ahead of the Yankees in the standings. The season was a tremendous one for Washington's Walter

Johnson for a number of reasons. Firstly, the campaign ended 17 years of frustration for the great pitcher, since it marked the first time his team made it to the World Series. In addition, the 36-year-old hurler made something of a comeback, surpassing 20 victories for the first time in five years. Thought to be well past his prime, Johnson led all A.L. pitchers with 23 victories, against only 7 defeats, and he also finished first with a 2.72 earned run average, 158 strikeouts, and six shutouts. He was rewarded by the baseball writers at season's end by being named league MVP.

There were other major contributors to Washington's success in 1924. Young outfielder Goose Goslin led the league with 129 runs batted in, and also finished among the leaders in batting average (.344), base hits (199), triples (17), and slugging percentage (.516). Fellow outfielder Sam Rice batted .334, scored 106 runs, stole 24 bases, and led the league with 216 hits. However, with teammate Johnson being named on the ballots of all eight writers, neither Goslin nor Rice received as much as a single point in the voting.

The third-place Detroit Tigers, who finished six games behind the Senators, also had a legitimate MVP candidate in Harry Heilmann. The Tiger outfielder finished among the league leaders in batting average (.346), runs batted in (114), runs scored (107), on-base percentage (.428), slugging percentage (.533), doubles (45), and triples (16).

However, the man who was most deserving of MVP honors, in spite of Walter Johnson's great comeback season, was someone who was not even eligible for the award. Having been named league MVP the prior year, Babe Ruth was not among those players who could even be considered for the award in 1924. Yet, having led the Yankees to a close second-place finish, Ruth was not only the American League's top performer, but also its most valuable player. The New York outfielder finished second to Goslin with 121 runs batted in, and led the league with 46 home runs, a .378 batting average, 143 runs scored, a .513 on-base percentage, and a .739 slugging percentage, which was *206* points higher than that of runners-up Heilmann and Ken Williams.

NATIONAL LEAGUE

The Giants won their fourth consecutive National League pennant in 1924, finishing just 1½ games ahead of second-place Brooklyn. The primary contributors to the Giants' success were first baseman George Kelly and the previous year's hypothetical MVP selection, Frankie Frisch. Kelly hit 21 home runs, batted .324, and led the league with 136 runs batted in. Frisch batted .328, collected 198 hits, and led the N.L. with 121 runs scored.

Rogers Hornsby had a fabulous year for the Cardinals, compiling the highest batting average of his career with a league-leading mark of .424. He also topped the circuit in six other categories, including runs scored (121), base hits (227), doubles (43), total bases (373), on-base percentage (.507), and slugging percentage (.696). However, St. Louis finished a distant sixth, 28½ games off the pace.

First baseman Jack Fournier and outfielder Zack Wheat both had outstanding seasons for second-place Brooklyn. Fournier led the N.L. with 27 home runs, finished second with 116 runs batted in, and batted .334. Wheat finished second to Hornsby with 212 hits and a batting average of .375, and also drove in 97 runs.

However, Brooklyn's best player in 1924 was pitcher Dazzy Vance, who was also the league's Most Valuable Player. Vance dominated the statistical categories for pitchers and clearly earned the MVP Award voted him by the baseball writers. The righthander finished 28-6, with a 2.16 earned run average, 262 strikeouts, 308 innings pitched, and 30 complete games in leading the Dodgers to a 92-62 record that left them just 1½ games behind the first-place Giants.

1925

AMERICAN LEAGUE

The Senators repeated as American League champions in 1925, finishing 8½ games ahead of second-place Philadelphia. Amazingly, Roger Peckinpaugh was selected league MVP by the writers even though he posted relatively modest numbers and failed to finish among the league leaders in any statistical category. Appearing in just 126 of his team's 151 games and compiling a total of just 422 official at-bats, the Washington shortstop hit a solid .294 but knocked in only 64 runs, scored just 67 others, and collected only 124 hits. Furthermore, Peckinpaugh was not even close to being his own team's best player. Goose Goslin hit 18 home runs for the Senators, while finishing fourth in the league with 113 runs batted in and 116 runs scored, compiling a .334 batting average and 201 hits, and leading the league with 20 triples. Sam Rice hit .350 and finished among the league leaders with 111 runs scored, 227 hits, and 26 stolen bases. In addition, pitcher Stan Coveleski, a member of Washington's pitching staff in 1925, finished 20-5, with a league-leading 2.84 earned run average.

However, the best player in the American League in 1925, and the man who should have been voted the circuit's MVP, was Philadephia outfielder Al Simmons. In just his second full year in the majors Simmons led the A's to an extremely respectable second-place finish—the first time since 1914 that they finished out of the second division. Simmons placed among the league leaders with 24 home runs, 129 runs batted in, 122 runs scored, 43 doubles, and a .387 batting average, and led the A.L. with 253 base hits and a .599 slugging percentage.

It is mystfying that Simmons received a total of just 41 points in the voting, while Peckinpaugh received 45 points from the writers.

NATIONAL LEAGUE

The New York Giants' four-year reign as National League champions was ended in 1925 by the Pittsburgh Pirates, who finished 8½ games ahead of the second-place Giants in the final standings. The Pirates had many outstanding performers who made major contributions to their success. Shortstop Glenn Wright finished among the league leaders with 121 runs batted in, and also hit 18 home runs, batted .308, and scored 97 runs. Third baseman Pie Traynor hit only six home runs, but drove in 106 runs, batted .320, and scored 114 runs.

Pittsburgh's best player in 1925 was future Hall of Fame outfielder Kiki Cuyler, who hit 18 home runs, knocked in 102 runs, batted .357, collected 220 hits, and led the National League with 144 runs scored and 26 triples. Cuyler was unquestionably the Pirates' most valuable player, and he probably would have been named league MVP in almost any other year. However, he was only able to finish second in the voting because Rogers Hornsby had another amazing season for the Cardinals. Hornsby won his second triple crown by leading the league with 39 home runs, 143 runs batted in, and a .403 batting average. He also finished second in runs scored (133), collected 203 hits, and led the league with a .489 on-base percentage and a .756 slugging percentage.

The only thing working against Hornsby was that his Cardinals finished fourth in the standings, 18 games behind first-place Pittsburgh, with a record of only 77-76. However, St. Louis finished second in the league in runs scored, and Hornsby was clearly the focal point of the team's offense. Furthermore, there is no telling where the Cardinals would have finished in the standings had it not been for his great year. Kiki Cuyler had an excellent season for the Pirates, and he would not have been a particularly bad selection by the writers. But his numbers were dwarfed by Hornsby's, whose selection as league MVP was the correct one.

1926

AMERICAN LEAGUE

After a two-year absence, the Yankees returned to the World Series in 1926, capturing the American League pennant by finishing three games ahead of the second-place Indians. Several players contributed greatly to New York's first-place finish. Pitcher Herb Pennock finished second in the league with 23 wins, and he also placed among the leaders with 19 complete games and 266 innings pitched. Rookie second baseman Tony Lazzeri finished third in the league with 18 home runs and finished tied for second with 114 runs batted in. In just his second full season, Lou Gehrig led the league with 20 triples and finished among the leaders with 112 runs batted in, 135 runs scored, 47 doubles, and 105 bases on balls.

However, New York's best player, and the man most responsible for the team's first-place finish, was Babe Ruth. He led the league in seven different offensive categories and was clearly the A.L.'s dominant player in 1926. Yet, since he was named league MVP in 1923, Ruth was not eligible to be selected again by the writers. Therefore, Cleveland first baseman George Burns, who played a huge role in the Indians' second-place finish, was voted league MVP instead. Although Burns was probably the best selection the writers could have made under the circumstances, Ruth was clearly more deserving of the honor.

A look at the numbers of both players indicates that last fact:

PLAYER	AB	HITS	RUNS	2B	3B	HR	RBI	AVG	OBP	SLG PCT	SB
George Burns	603	216	97	64	3	4	114	.358	.394	.494	13
Babe Ruth	495	184	139	30	5	47	146	.372	.516	.737	11

In over 100 fewer official at-bats, Ruth finished well ahead of Burns in every department, except base hits, doubles, and stolen bases. Ruth led the league with 144 walks, thereby explaining his relatively low number of official plate appearances. His 47 home runs, which more than doubled the total of 19 compiled by league runner-up Al Simmons, exceeded Burns' total by 43. Ruth also scored many more runs than Burns, finished with a much higher on-base percentage, and compiled a slugging percentage that was almost 250 points higher.

It is unfortunate that The Babe was not eligible for consideration because he was unquestionably the Most Valuable Player in the American League in 1926.

NATIONAL LEAGUE

Just as the American League writers' selection of Washington Senators shortstop Roger Peckinpaugh was completely inexplicable the previous year, the N.L. writers' choice of Cardinals catcher Bob O'Farrell in 1926 was equally puzzling. While St. Louis did capture the National League pennant, finishing just two games ahead of second-place Cincinnati and 4½ in front of third-place Pittsburgh, O'Farrell's numbers were hardly overwhelming. He finished with just seven home runs, 68 runs batted in, 63 runs scored, and 144 hits, while batting .293.

The selection of O'Farrell perhaps reflected the thinking of the times, when a tremendous amount of emphasis was placed on intangible qualities such as field leadership and a catcher's handling of his team's pitching staff. In fact, as we continue to move through the first half of the twentieth century, this thought process will become increasingly evident. However, in spite of the *intangible* qualities O'Farrell may have provided to his team, he was clearly not the most deserving player in the league that year.

Kiki Cuyler had another fine season for the third-place Pirates, finishing among the league leaders with 92 runs batted in, 197 hits, and a .321 average, and leading the N.L. with 113 runs scored. However, even more deserving was O'Farrell's teammate with the Cardinals, Jim

Bottomley. The St. Louis first baseman finished second in the league with 19 home runs, led the circuit with 120 runs batted in, batted .299, scored 98 runs, collected 180 hits, and led the N.L. with 40 doubles. Yet, for some reason, the writers curiously chose not to give Bottomley as much as a single point on their ballots. Six other Cardinals received at least minimal support, but the player who should have been named league MVP was completely ignored.

1927

AMERICAN LEAGUE

Perhaps more than any other team, in any other year, the Yankees dominated the American League and all of baseball in 1927. They breezed through the regular season, compiling a won-lost record of 110-44 and finishing 19 games ahead of the second-place Philadelphia Athletics. New York's 975 runs scored surpassed the league's second-highest scoring team by a total of *130* runs. The Yankees also allowed just 599 runs, far fewer than any other team. New York's run-differential was an astounding *376*, meaning that the team scored almost 2½ more runs per-game than it allowed. The Yankees followed up their magnificent regular season by sweeping the Pittsburgh Pirates in the World Series in four games, outscoring the National League champions by a combined score of 23-10.

Such a level of dominance has rarely been approached in any sport. Needless to say, New York also dominated most of the individual pitching and hitting statistical categories. Pitcher Waite Hoyt finished tied for the league lead with 22 victories, and he also finished second in earned run average (2.63), third in complete games (23), and fifth in innings pitched (256). Herb Pennock placed in the top five with 19 wins, Urban Shocker won 18 games and finished third in the league with a 2.84 earned run average, and, in his only season of note, Wilcy Moore won 19 games and led the league with 13 saves and a 2.28 earned run average.

Yet, it was the Yankee offense that struck fear into the hearts of their opponents. Tony Lazzeri finished third in the league with 18 home runs, drove in 102 runs, and batted .309. Outfielder Bob Meusel hit .337, drove in 103 runs, and finished among the league leaders with 47 doubles and 24 stolen bases. Centerfielder Earle Combs led the league with 231 hits and 23 triples, and also finished in the top five with 137 runs scored, 331 total bases, and a .356 batting average. But it was the combination of Babe Ruth and Lou Gehrig that truly made the Yankees baseball's dominant team. The two men finished first and second in six different statistical categories, and one or the other led the league in eight out of the 12 major offensive departments. Ruth topped the circuit in home runs, runs scored, bases on balls, on-base percentage, and slugging percentage, while Gehrig finished first in runs batted in, doubles, and total bases. It follows that the two Yankee sluggers were unquestionably the most qualified candidates for league MVP.

Let's take a look at the numbers of both players:

PLAYER	AB	HITS	RUNS	2B	3B	HR	RBI	AVG	OBP	SLG PCT
Lou Gehrig	584	218	149	**52**	18	47	**175**	.373	.474	.765
Babe Ruth	540	192	**158**	29	8	**60**	164	.356	**.487**	.772

The statistics of the two men were actually quite comparable, with the only decided advantages going to Gehrig in doubles and triples. Ruth ended up breaking his own single-season home run record that he established six years earlier in 1921, but Gehrig actually kept pace with him for most of the season. It was really just Ruth's fabulous month of September, well after the pennant race was over, that allowed him to pull away from Gehrig in that department. Other than Ruth's historic home run total, when the overall numbers are closely examined, it becomes apparent that Gehrig actually had a slightly better year. He drove in more runs, hit for a higher average, and collected far more doubles and triples.

With Ruth once again ineligible to be named league MVP, the honor was appropriately awarded to Gehrig, who finished well ahead of everyone else in the voting. However, when it is considered that the thinking of the writers has often been swayed through the years by the setting of historical records, it would have been extremely interesting to see which man they would have selected had Ruth been eligible as well.

NATIONAL LEAGUE

The National League was far more competitive than the A.L. in 1927, with the Pirates edging out the Cardinals by just 1½ games, and beating out the third-place Giants by only two games. Each team had an outstanding candidate for Most Valuable Player.

Prior to the start of the season, the Giants and Cardinals exchanged star second basemen, with Frankie Frisch going from New York to St. Louis, and Rogers Hornsby leaving the Cardinals and going to the Giants. Both men had exceptional years for their new teams. Hornsby hit 26 home runs, drove in 125 runs, and finished second in the league with a .361 batting average and 133 runs scored. He finished third in the MVP voting. Frisch hit only 10 home runs and drove in just 78 runs, but he batted .337, scored 112 runs, collected 208 hits, led the league with 48 stolen bases, and led league second basemen in both putouts and assists. He finished second in the balloting.

The man who finished first was Pirates outfielder Paul Waner. Although he received a great amount of support in the Pittsburgh lineup from Pie Traynor, who batted .342 and knocked in 106 runs, and brother Lloyd, who batted .355 and led the N.L. with 237 hits and 133 runs scored, Waner was the Pirates' most outstanding performer in 1927, and the best all-around player in the league. Although he hit only nine home runs, Waner led the league with 131 runs batted in, a .380 batting average, 237 hits, 18 triples, and 342 total bases. He also scored 114 runs, compiled a .437 on-base percentage and a .549 slugging percentage, and collected 42 doubles. It would be difficult to find fault with Waner's selection by the baseball writers.

1928

AMERICAN LEAGUE

The fast-improving Philadelphia Athletics closed the gap considerably on the powerful Yankees in 1928, finishing just 2½ games behind pennant-winning New York. The Yankees won 101 games and were the class of baseball for the second straight year, but it became apparent that they would have to deal with the hard-charging A's in the coming years.

Philadelphia featured four future Hall of Famers in young first baseman Jimmie Foxx, outfielder Al Simmons, catcher Mickey Cochrane, and pitcher Lefty Grove. In just his first full season, Foxx hit 13 home runs, drove in 79 runs, scored 85 others, and batted .327. Simmons, the hypothetical MVP winner for 1925, hit 15 homers, knocked in 107 runs, and batted .351. Grove tied for the league lead with 24 victories, against only 8 defeats, led the league with 183 strikeouts, and also finished among the league leaders with a 2.58 earned run average, 261 innings pitched, and 24 complete games. All three men had fine seasons, but only Grove had the type of year that merited serious consideration for MVP honors. However, all three players put up numbers superior to those of teammate Mickey Cochrane, who was the rather dubious selection of the writers for league MVP.

Cochrane hit only 10 home runs, knocked in just 57 runs, batted .293, scored 92 runs, and collected just 137 hits. With such modest numbers, it would seem that the voters must have been extremely impressed with Cochrane's leadership skills, and with his fiery, competitive nature—for which he was well-known. However, those qualities should not have been enough to earn him MVP honors. There were several other men, aside from some of his own teammates, who were far more deserving.

Future Hall of Fame outfielder Heinie Manush had a tremendous year for the St. Louis Browns. Manush led the league with 241 hits and 47 doubles, and he also finished among the league leaders in batting average (.378), runs batted in (108), triples (20), slugging percentage (.575), and total bases (367). However, the Browns finished a distant third, 19 games behind first-place New York. As a result, Manush finished a very close second to Cochrane in the voting. Yet, the feeling here is that, since St. Louis finished seventh in the standings the prior year, with only 59 victories, their 82 wins and third-place finish in 1928 should have been enough to propel Manush past Cochrane in the voting.

Still, we are forgetting about the first-place Yankees. Pitcher George Pipgras tied Grove for the league lead with 24 victories and led A.L. pitchers with 300 innings pitched. Waite Hoyt finished with a superb 23-7 record, threw 273 innings, completed 19 of his 31 starts, and led the league with eight saves. Outfielder Bob Meusel finished third in the league with 113 runs batted in and 45 doubles. Earle Combs batted .310, led the league with 21 triples, and also finished among the league leaders with 118 runs scored, 194 hits, and 290 total bases.

Once again, though, it was the combination of Lou Gehrig and Babe Ruth that formed the backbone of the team. Although the rules governing the American League elections made both Gehrig and Ruth ineligible for MVP consideration, the two sluggers were clearly the league's most deserving players for the second consecutive year. Let's take a look at their numbers for the season:

PLAYER	AB	HITS	RUNS	2B	3B	HR	RBI	AVG	OBP	SLG PCT
Lou Gehrig	562	210	139	47	13	27	142	.374	.467	.648
Babe Ruth	536	173	163	29	8	54	142	.323	.461	.709

The statistics of both men were down slightly from the previous year, but they were still outstanding, and they were easily the most impressive in the league. The two men tied for the A.L. lead in runs batted in, and they were also very close in on-base percentage. However, Ruth hit twice as many home runs as Gehrig, scored 24 more runs, and compiled a slugging percentage that was some 60 points higher. On the other hand, Gehrig's batting average was 50 points higher than Ruth's and he once again finished with far more doubles and triples. It would seem that the statistics favored Ruth, ever so slightly, but it really was too close to call. We'll split our vote and give both Ruth and Gehrig a share of the MVP Award.

NATIONAL LEAGUE

In a three-team race, the Cardinals captured the National League pennant in 1928, finishing just two games ahead of the second-place Giants and three in front of the third-place Cubs. Each team had viable MVP candidates, as did a few other teams that finished further down in the standings.

Pitcher Dazzy Vance had a tremendous year for Brooklyn, finishing 22-10, with a league-leading 2.09 earned run average and 200 strikeouts. He also finished among the league leaders with 280 innings pitched, 24 complete games, and four shutouts. However, Vance's chances were hurt by the fact that the Dodgers finished sixth, 17½ games out of first.

Burleigh Grimes, Pie Traynor, and Paul Waner all had outstanding seasons for the fourth-place Pirates, who finished nine games off the pace. Grimes tied for the league lead with 25 wins, against 14 losses, pitched to a solid 2.99 earned run average, and led N.L. pitchers with 330 innings pitched, 28 complete games, and 48 appearances. Traynor batted .337 and finished second in the league with 124 runs batted in. Waner led the league with 142 runs scored and 50 doubles, and he also finished among the league leaders with a .370 batting average, 223 hits, 19 triples, and 329 total bases.

Among the pennant contenders, Chicago's Hack Wilson tied for the league lead with 31 home runs and finished third in the circuit with 120 runs batted in. New York righthander Larry Benton tied Grimes for the league lead with 28 complete games and 25 victories, against only 9 defeats, and he also finished among the league leaders with 310 innings pitched and a 2.73 earned run average. Giants third baseman Fred Lindstrom led the league with 231 hits, and he also finished among the leaders with a .358 batting average, 107 runs batted in, and 39 doubles.

The pennant-winning Cardinals, though, had an outstanding MVP candidate of their own in Jim Bottomley. The St. Louis first baseman tied for the league lead with 31 home runs, and he finished first with 136 runs batted in, 20 triples, and 362 total bases. He also batted .325 and placed among the league leaders with 123 runs scored, 42 doubles, and a .628 slugging percentage. In hitting 31 home runs and collecting 20 triples and 42 doubles, Bottomley became one of just a handful of players in baseball history to top the 20-mark in each category in the same season. He was the National League's best all-around player in 1928 and the major reason why St. Louis was able to capture the pennant.

Bottomley's selection by the baseball writers, who inexplicably snubbed him in the MVP voting just two years earlier, was one that should not be questioned.

THE FINAL SET OF HYPOTHETICAL WINNERS

8

There were no official selections made for the American League in 1929, or for either league in 1930. Therefore, the final set of hypothetical MVP winners will be presented, and the actual National League winner for the 1929 season will be discussed in this chapter.

	HYPOTHETICAL MVP WINNERS		ACTUAL WINNERS
	A.L.	**N.L.**	**N.L.**
1929	Al Simmons		Rogers Hornsby
1930	Al Simmons	Hack Wilson	

1929

AMERICAN LEAGUE

The Philadelphia Athletics replaced the Yankees as the American League's dominant team in 1929, running away with the league title by finishing a full 18 games in front of the defending champions. The combination of the A's rapid development into a powerhouse team and the gradual aging of New York's pitching staff ended the Yankees' three-year reign as league champions and marked the beginning of Philadelphia's mini-dynasty. While the A's did not have quite the offensive firepower that the Yankees displayed the prior three seasons, they actually had superior pitching to New York. Philadelphia finished second in the league in runs scored in 1929, with a total of 901. The Detroit Tigers led the A.L. with 926 runs scored, and the Yankees finished a close third, with 899. But, while Detroit allowed a league-high 928 runs and New York permitted the opposition 775 runs, the A's allowed their opponents a total of just 615 runs, by far the fewest in the American League (St. Louis was second, with 713). Therefore, even though Philadelphia's offense was quite formidable, it was actually their pitching that separated them from the rest of the pack.

The A's staff was headed by Lefty Grove and George Earnshaw. Grove finished 20-6, for a league-leading .769 winning percentage, led the league with a 2.81 earned run average and 170 strikeouts, threw 275 innings, and completed 19 of his 37 starts. In his first full major league season, the 29-year-old Earnshaw led the league with 24 wins, against only 8 losses, finished fourth in the league with a 3.29 earned run average, placed second to Grove with 149 strikeouts, and threw 254 innings. However, as good as Grove and Earnshaw were, neither hurler was dominant enough to be seriously considered for MVP honors.

Several position players throughout the league had outstanding seasons. Detroit second baseman Charlie Gehringer led the A.L. in four different offensive categories, including runs scored (131), base hits (215), triples (19), and stolen bases (27), and he placed among the leaders in two others. Teammate Dale Alexander finished near the top of the league rankings with 25 home runs, 137 runs batted in, 215 hits, and 363 totals bases, while batting .343 and scoring 110 runs. However, the Tigers finished 36 games behind Philadelphia, in sixth place.

Babe Ruth and Lou Gehrig had extremely productive years for New York, enabling the Yankees to finish second, in spite of their mediocre pitching. Ruth led the league with 46 home runs and a .697 slugging percentage, while also finishing among the league leaders in runs batted in (154), runs scored (121), on-base percentage (.430), and total bases (348). Gehrig finished second to Ruth with 35 home runs, and he also placed in the top five in runs batted in (126), runs scored (127), on-base percentage (.431), slugging percentage (.584), and bases on balls (122). But, with the Yankees finishing a distant second, it would be difficult to select either man over one of the first-place A's outstanding performers.

Mickey Cochrane actually had a much better year than he did in 1928, when the writers foolishly voted him league MVP. Cochrane batted .331, knocked in 95 runs, and scored 113 others. Establishing himself as a major offensive force for the first time, Jimmie Foxx finished among the league leaders in several categories, including home runs (33), runs batted in (118), batting average (.354), runs scored (123), slugging percentage (.625), and bases on balls (103). He also led the league with a .463 on-base percentage.

The A's best player, though, was Al Simmons, who led the league with 157 runs batted in and 373 total bases, finished second with a .365 batting average and .642 slugging percentage, and also placed third with 34 home runs and 212 hits. After missing more than a month of both the 1927 and 1928 seasons, Simmons' daily presence in the middle of the A's batting order in 1929 was as big a factor as any in their overwhelming regular season performance. He was clearly the league's Most Valuable Player. *The Sporting News* recognized that by naming him its "unofficial" winner at the end of the season.

Something that was not nearly as clear was why another "unofficial" poll taken of the Baseball Writers Association of America named Cleveland first baseman Lou Fonseca the league's Most Valuable Player. Although Fonseca had an outstanding year for the Indians, leading the league with a .369 batting average, his overall numbers were not even close to those of Simmons. He hit just six home runs, drove in only 103 runs, scored just 97 others, and finished in the top five in a total of just three offensive categories (batting average, hits, and doubles). Although Fonseca's team finished a very respectable third in the standings, they won just 81 games, 23 fewer than the 104 victories compiled by Simmons' A's.

Perhaps the BBWAA members felt that Simmons had a much better supporting cast in Philadelphia, which he did, but there is no question that he was a much better player than Fonseca that year, and that he was the only logical selection for league MVP.

NATIONAL LEAGUE

The National League began experimenting with a livelier ball in 1929, and the results were immediate and significant. Only two players hit more than 30 home runs in the senior circuit the previous year. In 1929, that number jumped to five, with four men hitting as many as 39 long balls. In 1928, no player in the league drove in as many as 140 runs, and only one scored as many as 130. In 1929, the number in both categories jumped to four. Throughout the league as a whole, 5,769 runs were scored in 1928. In 1929, the number rose to 6,609.

Needless to say, there were several players who put up outstanding offensive numbers that year.

While the Chicago Cubs won the pennant, finishing 10½ games in front of the second-place Pirates, three of the top players in the league came from other teams. Philadelphia's Lefty O'Doul and Chuck Klein both had tremendous seasons. O'Doul led the league with a .398 batting average, 254 hits, and a .465 on-base percentage, and he also finished among the league leaders with 32 home runs, 122 runs batted in, 152 runs scored, and 397 total bases. Klein led the league with 43 home runs, and he also finished among the leaders with 145 runs batted in, 126 runs scored, a .356 batting average, 219 hits, 45 doubles, 405 total bases, and a .657 slugging percentage. The Phillies, though, finished fifth, 27½ games out of first, thereby diminishing their chances of being selected league MVP.

The New York Giants finished third, 13½ games behind the first-place Cubs. Their most outstanding performer was Mel Ott, who batted .328 in his breakout season, led the league with 113 bases on balls, finished second to Klein with 42 homers, and also finished among the leaders with 151 runs batted in, 138 runs scored, a .449 on-base percentage, and a .635 slugging percentage. Teammate Bill Terry also had a superb year, batting .372, driving in 117 runs, scoring 103 others, and collecting 226 hits.

The top two candidates for league MVP, though, came from the pennant-winning Cubs. Outfielder Hack Wilson hit 39 home runs, led the league with 159 runs batted in, scored 135 others, and batted .345. As impressive as his numbers were, it was his teammate, Rogers Hornsby, who was most deserving of the honor. Playing for his fourth team overall, and his third in the last three seasons, Hornsby was once again the best hitter on his team. He hit 39 home runs, drove in 149 runs, batted .380, led the league with 156 runs scored, 409 total bases, and a .679 slugging percentage, and also finished among the league leaders with 229 hits, 47 doubles, and a .459 on-base percentage.

In what turned out to be his last healthy and productive season, Hornsby was the very best player in the game.

1930

AMERICAN LEAGUE

Offense continued to dominate both leagues in 1930, with the most prolific hitting attack belonging to the New York Yankees, who established a new major league record by scoring a total of 1,062 runs. However, they also allowed the opposition 898 runs, the second highest total in the American League. As a result, New York could do no better than third, finishing 16 games behind the first-place Athletics, and eight games back of the second-place Washington Senators. Washington's improved pitching, which allowed the fewest runs in the league (689) and posted the lowest team earned run average (3.96), helped them to improve their record by 23 games over the previous year and jump three places in the standings. Another major contributor to the Senators' improvement was shortstop Joe Cronin, who was elected "unofficial" league MVP at season's end by *The Sporting News*. However, there were several other players worthy of consideration, who were perhaps even more deserving of the honor.

In spite of the decided edge the hitters seemed to have gained over pitchers in recent seasons, the league still had its fair share of outstanding hurlers. Cleveland's Wes Ferrell finished second in the league with 25 wins, 296 innings pitched, 25 complete games, and a 3.31 earned run average. The Indians finished fourth, though, 21 games back, and Ferrell was not even the league's best pitcher. That honor fell to Philadelphia's Lefty Grove, who merited serious consideration for MVP honors with his exceptional performance. Grove won the pitcher's triple crown, finishing with a 28-5 record, a 2.54 earned run average, and 209 strikeouts. He was so outstanding that his 2.54 earned run average was *79* points lower than league runner-up Ferrell. Grove also finished among the league leaders with 291 innings pitched, 22 complete games, and 50 appearances, which included a league-leading nine saves. However, there were several position players whose MVP credentials would be hard to overlook in favor of someone who played only every fourth day.

The most dominant everyday performers were New York's Babe Ruth and Lou Gehrig, and Grove's teammates in Philadelphia, Al Simmons and Jimmie Foxx. Let's take a look at the numbers posted by each of these four men, along with those of Joe Cronin, who was selected by *The Sporting News* as league MVP:

PLAYER	AB	HITS	RUNS	2B	3B	HR	RBI	AVG	OBP	SLG PCT
Joe Cronin	587	203	127	41	9	13	126	.346	.422	.513
Lou Gehrig	581	220	143	42	17	41	**174**	.379	.473	.721
Babe Ruth	518	186	150	28	9	**49**	153	.359	**.493**	**.732**
Jimmie Foxx	562	188	127	33	13	37	156	.335	.429	.637
Al Simmons	554	211	**152**	41	16	36	165	**.381**	.423	.708

Of the five men, Ruth, Gehrig, and Simmons had the best overall numbers, but the Yankees finished 16 games behind the A's in the standings. Therefore, it would be difficult to argue on behalf of either Ruth or Gehrig. Furthermore, in spite of the vastly superior numbers posted by the two New York stars, a valid case could be made for selecting Cronin over them as well, since the Senators finished well ahead of the Yankees in the standings.

The same cannot be said, though, about Foxx and Simmons, whose A's finished eight games in front of Cronin's Senators. Both A's stars put up better numbers than Cronin, and Simmons was particularly outstanding. He led the league in batting average and runs scored, finished second to Gehrig in runs batted in, and also finished in the top five in home runs, triples, hits, total bases, and slugging percentage. He hit almost three times as many home runs as Cronin, knocked in almost 40 more runs, scored 25 more times, and compiled a slugging percentage that was almost *200* points higher.

It follows then that, for the second consecutive year, and for the third time overall, Simmons is the hypothetical selection for league MVP.

NATIONAL LEAGUE

Hitting dominated the National League as well in 1930, with the pennant-winning Cardinals scoring a league-high 1,004 runs. The second-place Cubs, who finished just two games behind St. Louis, and the third-place Giants, who finished five games back, were quite close to the Cardinals in the run-scoring derby. Chicago scored 998 runs, and New York finished third in the league with 959 runs. Ironically, the team that compiled the fourth highest run total was the last-place Phillies, who scored 944 runs. Philadelphia still had 1929 batting champion Lefty O'Doul, who followed up his league-leading performance with a .383 mark in 1930. The Phillies also had perhaps the finest all-around player in the league in Chuck Klein, who hit .386, led the circuit with 158 runs scored, 59 doubles, and 445 total bases, and finished second with 40 home runs, 170 runs batted in, and 250 hits. However, Philadelphia's last-place finish spoiled any chance he may have had of being named league MVP.

Both Frankie Frisch and outfielder Chick Hafey had outstanding seasons for the pennant-winning Cardinals. Frisch hit only 10 home runs, but he knocked in 114 runs, scored 121 others, and batted .346. Hafey hit 26 homers, drove in 107 runs, scored another 108, and batted .336. None of those numbers, though, even came close to placing either player in the top five in the league.

Fred Lindstrom had a fine season for the third-place Giants, compiling a .379 batting average and tallying 231 hits. But those figures placed him no higher than fourth in either category.

Catcher Gabby Hartnett put up big numbers for second-place Chicago, hitting 37 home runs, driving in 122 runs, and batting .339. However, he wasn't close to being the Cubs' best player in 1930. Outfielder Hack Wilson had a monster year for Chicago, establishing a then single-season National League record by hitting 56 home runs, driving in a major league record 190 runs, and batting .356. The only man who posed a serious threat to Wilson for league MVP honors was Giants first baseman Bill Terry, who became the last N.L. player to hit .400 when he led the league with a .401 batting average and 254 base hits.

Let's look at the numbers of Wilson and Terry to determine who was more deserving:

PLAYER	AB	HITS	RUNS	2B	3B	HR	RBI	AVG	OBP	SLG PCT
Bill Terry	633	254	139	39	15	23	129	.401	.452	.619
Hack Wilson	585	208	146	35	6	56	190	.356	.454	.723

Terry finished with far more hits and batted 45 points higher than Wilson, but the latter was far more productive, finished with a much higher slugging percentage, and, because of his greater penchant for drawing walks, actually finished with a slightly higher on-base percentage. Perhaps the greatest argument that could be made on Terry's behalf is that he had a much better reputation than Wilson for being a team leader. However, the latter's incredibly productive year and distinct statistical advantage far outweigh any edge Terry may have had in other areas.

Wilson is, therefore, the choice for the 1930 National League MVP.

MVP CONTROVERSIES

Due largely to the subjective nature of the MVP balloting, the selections made by the BBWAA have resulted in a great deal of controversy in some years. With the true meaning of *Most Valuable* open to different interpretations, rarely has one player stood out so far among his peers that his election has resulted in total accord among both voters and fans.

In numerous instances, the primary source of controversy has been a difference of opinion between the writers and the majority of fans. On most of those occasions, the BBWAA selected a player whose statistics did not measure up to those of some of the other leading candidates. A prime example would be the American League election of 1934, when Mickey Cochrane of the pennant-winning Tigers was named league MVP despite posting numbers that were far less impressive than the figures compiled by several other players in the league, including Lou Gehrig, who won the Triple Crown. Even two of Cochrane's own teammates, Charlie Gehringer and Hank Greenberg, put up numbers that would lead one to think they were far more deserving of the honor. Another example would be the National League election of 1944, when the writers selected Cardinals shortstop Marty Marion over teammate Stan Musial, despite the latter's overwhelmingly superior numbers.

In other years, phenomenal seasons turned in by multiple players proved to be the source of much discord. In 1941, New York's Joe DiMaggio hit in 56 consecutive games and led the Yankees to the pennant. Meanwhile, Boston's Ted Williams batted .406, to outhit the Yankee Clipper by almost 50 points. The Red Sox slugger also led the Red Sox to a very respectable second-place finish. Yet Boston finished 17 games behind first-place New York, and many people still feel that DiMaggio's hitting streak was a greater accomplishment than Williams' .406 batting average. Needless to say, the writers were split when it came time to select a winner that year.

OBJECTIVITY, INTERPRETATIONS, AND INCONSISTENCIES

Another source of controversy has been the lack of objectivity demonstrated by the voters from time to time. Ted Williams, who was not particularly popular with the press during his playing days, was discriminated against more than once during the voting process. One such instance occurred in 1947, when Williams finished one point behind DiMaggio in the balloting because a Boston writer who didn't get along with the Red Sox slugger left him completely off his ballot.

There are also various interpretations of how pitchers should be treated during the elections. Some writers feel they should be given the same opportunity to win the award as everyday position players, while others feel that someone who takes the field just once every fourth or fifth day could not possibly be as valuable to his team as someone who mans his position every day. These varying viewpoints have resulted in voting inconsistencies through the years, with position players winning close elections in some years and pitchers coming out on top in others. Examples would be the National League election of 1965, the American League election of 1978, and the A.L. election of 1986.

In the first instance, Willie Mays of the Giants edged out the Dodgers Sandy Koufax even though Los Angeles won the N.L. pennant primarily because of Koufax. Thirteen years later, in1978, the Yankees defeated the Red Sox in a one-game playoff to capture the American League pennant, and Ron Guidry was absolutely brilliant for New York all year. Yet Boston's Jim Rice walked off with the MVP trophy for the great year he had for the Sox. Then, in 1986, the writers opted for Roger Clemens of the pennant-winning Red Sox over New York's Don Mattingly, even though the latter's superb season enabled the Yankees to finish a close second to Boston in the American League East.

Such apparent inconsistency in the thought process of the voters has prompted a considerable amount of debate through the years. We will now take a closer look at the aforementioned MVP elections, along with some of the other more controversial ones that have been conducted through the years.

It was mentioned earlier that there have been instances in which the writers seem to have looked beyond sheer numbers when casting their MVP ballots. This has been especially true with shortstops and catchers, who man the two most important and demanding defensive positions on the diamond. Shortstops are often considered to be the leaders in the infield, while catchers are valued for their ability to call a good game, handle a pitching staff, and be on-field generals and team leaders. Since having good players at these positions has always been viewed as being vital to the success of any team, the writers have often shown a preference for these men in the voting. Catchers have fared particularly well, often winning the award despite posting numbers that were far inferior to those of other position players.

We have already seen that Cardinals catcher Bob O'Farrell was named National League MVP in 1926, despite hitting just seven home runs, driving in only 68 runs, and scoring just 63 others. Two years later, in 1928, the Philadelphia Athletics Mickey Cochrane was selected American League MVP in spite of his team's second-place finish and his rather unimpressive stat-line (10 home runs, 57 runs batted in, .293 batting average, 92 runs scored). In both instances, the writers must have felt these men possessed many intangible qualities that were not reflected in the boxscores. Cochrane, in particular, in spite of his well-known dark side, was considered to be a gritty and determined player, and a true team leader. In fact, after he was traded from the A's to the Tigers following the 1933 season, he became player-manager for Detroit.

Cochrane's reputation must have made a very strong impression on the writers because there is no other plausible explanation for his winning the American League MVP in 1934.

1934: THE END OF ELIGIBILITY RESTRICTIONS

When the Most Valuable Player Award was reinstituted in both leagues prior to the start of the 1931 campaign, the American League wisely decided to remove the eligibility restrictions it previously placed on candidates. No longer were player-managers prohibited from winning the award; multiple players from the same team could be selected; and prior winners were no longer excluded. As a result, unlike 1928, when Cochrane was selected league MVP primarily because neither Babe Ruth nor Lou Gehrig of the pennant-winning Yankees was eligible, all players were considered eligible for the award in 1934.

Voters were free to include former winners Cochrane and Gehrig on their ballots, along with two of Cochrane's Detroit teammates, Charlie Gehringer and Hank Greenberg.

The Tigers won the American League pennant in 1934, finishing seven games ahead of the second-place Yankees. Player-manager Cochrane had a good year for Detroit, batting .320 and compiling a .428 on-base percentage. He was also considered to be the Tigers' veteran presence and, needless to say, their on-field leader. However, with only two home runs, 76 runs batted in, and 74 runs scored, his numbers were dwarfed by those of teammates Gehringer and Greenberg. The former finished the season with 11 home runs, 127 runs batted in, a .356 batting average, and a league-leading 134 runs scored and 214 hits. Gehringer was also an outstanding defensive second baseman, generally considered to be among the finest all-around players in the game. Greenberg, while somewhat limited in his mobility as a first baseman, was a prolific slugger who had his breakout season. He hit 26 home runs, drove in 139 runs, scored 118 others, and batted .339. While Cochrane may have been the Tigers' on-field leader, it would be difficult to imagine him being any more valuable to the team in 1934 than either Gehringer or Greenberg. Yet, when all the votes were counted, Cochrane came away with his second MVP trophy, finishing with a total of 67 points, to runner-up Gehringer's 65 points. Greenberg could do no better than sixth, finishing with a total of just 29 points.

And what of New York's Lou Gehrig? The first baseman was clearly the league's best player, winning the Triple Crown with 49 home runs, 165 runs batted in, and a .363 batting average. With Babe Ruth finally succumbing to Father Time, Gehrig became the backbone of the Yankees in 1934, carrying their offense most of the year and leading the team to a very respectable second-place finish. Yet he finished fifth in the voting, with a total of just 54 points.

1941: JOE DIMAGGIO AND TED WILLIAMS

Two men were the focal points of the baseball world in 1941. The first was New York Yankees centerfielder Joe DiMaggio, who compiled a record 56-game hitting streak from May 15th to July 16th . The other was Boston Red Sox leftfielder Ted Williams, who captivated everyone with his chase of the magical .400-mark during the latter stages of the season. The tremendous accomplishments of both players left the writers with an extremely difficult choice at season's end, in trying to determine which man was truly the American League's Most Valuable Player.

Through mid-May, New York was barely a .500 team, sitting in fourth-place and striving to find some kind of consistency. Then, during a 13-1 loss to the Chicago White Sox at Yankee Stadium on May 15th, Joe DiMaggio connected for a single against Chicago pitcher Edgar Smith that turned out to be just the first in a long string of hits. DiMaggio hit safely in each of the next 55 games as well, batting an astonishing .408 with 15 home runs and 55 runs batted in in 223 at-bats during the streak, which turned into a national obsession. Baseball followers everywhere checked boxscores on a daily basis to see if DiMaggio was able to continue "the streak", which finally ended in Cleveland on July 17th.

The Yankees followed DiMaggio's lead and played exceptional ball during his hitting streak. The team compiled a .750 winning percentage over that stretch, building up a huge lead in the American League that no team was able to challenge the remainder of the year. New York finished the season with a record of 101-53, 17 games in front of the second-place Boston Red Sox. DiMaggio's hitting streak clearly sparked the Yankees, leading them to their outstanding record. But there was someone else in Boston doing incredible things as well.

Ted Williams, in just his third major league season, was already beginning to draw comparisons to the greatest hitters of all-time. While he watched DiMaggio with admiration during the Yankee Clipper's amazing hitting streak, Williams was having a phenomenal season in his own right. He was batting close to .400—something that had not been done in the majors since 1930, when Bill Terry hit .401 for the Giants—and he was ahead of DiMaggio in numerous statistical categories. With the latter's hitting streak over by mid-July, the nation began focusing on Williams' pursuit of .400. Before the season's final day, Boston Manager Joe Cronin asked Williams if he wanted to sit out a doubleheader against the Philadelphia Athletics so that his batting average, which was just a fraction under .400, could be rounded up to the magical number and he could finish the year with a

.400 average. Williams declined the offer and ended up going 6-for-8 in the doubleheader, thereby raising his average to .406 and creating the legend of *The Splendid Splinter*.

Needless to say, this presented the voters with quite a dilemma at season's end as to who to vote for in the MVP balloting. Should it be DiMaggio, who captivated the nation for two months with his remarkable hitting streak and led his team to the American League flag? Or should it be Williams, who hit an astounding .406 and actually finished the year with slightly better numbers than DiMaggio? The writers opted for DiMaggio, who received a total of 291 points in the voting, to the 254 that Williams received.

1942 TED WILLIAMS AND ANOTHER CONTROVERSY

Just one year later, in 1942, Williams was involved in another controversial MVP election. His Red Sox finished second during the regular season to the pennant-winning Yankees, who beat out Boston by nine games. The Yankees were led by their outstanding second baseman, Joe Gordon, who rivaled Boston's Bobby Doerr as the game's finest player at that position at the time. Gordon hit 18 home runs, knocked in 103 runs, batted .322, and scored 88 runs that year. He also played a solid second base, and he was thought to have more range and more athleticism than perhaps any other middle infielder in the league.

However, Williams posted significantly better numbers than Gordon over the course of the season. The Boston leftfielder won the American League Triple Crown by leading the league with 36 home runs, 137 runs batted in, and a .356 batting average. He also finished first with 141 runs scored, a .499 on-base percentage, and a .648 slugging percentage. Williams hit twice as many home runs as Gordon, knocked in 34 more runs, hit 34 points higher, scored 53 more runs, and finished with an on-base percentage that was 90 points higher and a slugging average that was 157 points higher. He also led the Red Sox to a very respectable second-place finish and a very solid 93-59 record. Yet, when all the votes were tabulated, it was Gordon who was named league MVP, finishing with a total of 270 points, to Williams' 249 points.

1944 NATIONAL LEAGUE MVP CONTROVERSY

In the war year of 1944, with many of the game's finest players in the service, the National League writers seemed to pay little attention to statistics when evaluating possible MVP candidates. The Cardinals ran away with the pennant that year, finishing 14½ games ahead of the second-place Pirates. St. Louis shortstop Marty Marion, who was generally acknowledged to be the finest defensive shortstop of the era, played brilliantly in the field all year and put up decent offensive numbers, hitting six home runs, driving in 63 runs, and batting .267. At season's end, the writers elected him league MVP by awarding him a total of 190 points in the balloting.

However, a teammate of Marion's compiled numbers that were far more impressive than those of the St. Louis shortstop. Stan Musial, who won the award the previous year, hit only 12 home runs (which was still twice as many as Marion's total), but he knocked in 94 runs, scored 112 others, batted .347, and led the league with 51 doubles. Musial's 112 runs scored were 62 more than the 50 Marion tallied, his .347 batting average was 80 points higher than the shortstop's mark, his league-leading .440 on-base percentage was 116 points higher than Marion's, and his league-leading .549 slugging average was almost 200 points higher. Yet Musial finished fourth in the voting, 54 points behind Marion.

The man who finished second in the balloting, just one point behind the Cardinals shortstop, was Chicago Cubs outfielder Bill Nicholson, who led the league with 33 home runs, 122 runs batted in, and 116 runs scored, while batting .287. While a valid case could be made for not selecting Nicholson MVP since the Cubs finished a distant fourth in the standings, 30 games behind St. Louis, it would certainly seem that he had more of a claim to the honor than Marion. And what of Musial, who played for the same team as the man who was selected, and put up far better numbers?

1947 AMERICAN LEAGUE MVP CONTROVERSY

Ted Williams came out second-best in the American League MVP voting a third time in 1947, losing this time by the very slimmest of margins. The Yankees won the pennant that year, finishing 12 games in front of the second-place Detroit Tigers. Boston finished third, 14 games back.

After spending three years in the military during World War II, both Joe DiMaggio and Ted Williams returned to the game in 1946. The three-year layoff didn't seem to have too much of an effect on Williams, who led the Red Sox to the pennant that year by hitting 38 home runs, collecting 123 runs batted in, and batting .342. On the other hand, DiMaggio's performace was impacted significantly. In his first season back, he hit 25 home runs, knocked in just 95 runs, and batted below .300 for the first time in his career, hitting just .290. He clearly was not the same player he was prior to entering the service.

DiMaggio had another sub-par year in 1947, finishing with just 20 home runs and 97 runs batted in, and hitting .315. While most players would have been happy with those numbers, they represented a major drop-off for the *Yankee Clipper*. Yet, with New York easily winning the pennant, DiMaggio was selected the league's Most Valuable Player by the writers, who gave him a total of 202 points in the voting—just one more than they gave Williams.

However, while DiMaggio struggled to regain his earlier form, Williams was his usual dominant self. He won the second Triple Crown of his career, leading the league with 32 home runs, 114 runs batted in, and a .343 batting average. He also finished first with 125 runs scored, a .499 on-base percentage, and a .634 slugging average. In so doing, not only did Williams finish well ahead of DiMaggio in home runs, runs batted in, and batting average, but he also scored 28 more runs and surpassed *Joltin' Joe* by 108 points in on-base percentage and 112 points in slugging percentage. Unfortunately for Williams, he was on bad terms with one of the Boston sportswriters, who elected not to include him anywhere on his ballot, thereby depriving him of the points he would have needed to out-poll DiMaggio for the award.

1960: ONE OF THE MOST CONTROVERSIAL MVP ELECTIONS

The election for the National League's Most Valuable Player in 1960 was one of the more controversial ones of the second half of the twentieth century. The Pittsburgh Pirates won the pennant that year, finishing seven games ahead of the second-place Milwaukee Braves. Pirates shortstop Dick Groat, generally considered to be the leader of the team, led the N.L. in batting with a mark of .325. He was rewarded by the BBWAA by being selected league MVP at season's end. However, it is extremely debatable as to whether or not Groat was truly deserving of the honor, or if he was even the most valuable player on his own team.

While it is true that Groat led the league in batting, he hit just two home runs, drove in only 50 runs, and scored just 85 others. He was a solid defensive player, but he was slow afoot and he had very limited range. Therefore, it would seem that Groat's selection as league MVP was based more on the Pirates winning the pennant than on anything else. However, there were other Pittsburgh players who were more deserving than Groat.

Third baseman Don Hoak finished a distant second to Groat in the voting, totaling 162 points to Groat's 276. Yet Hoak finished well ahead of the MVP winner in home runs (16 to 2), runs batted in (79 to 50), and runs scored (97 to 85), and he also batted a solid .285. Yet, since Groat played the more demanding position of the two, and since Hoak's numbers were hardly overwhelming, a valid case could be made for selecting the shortstop over the third baseman.

Far more disturbing was Roberto Clemente's eighth-place finish in the balloting. The Pirates outfielder, like Hoak, hit 16 home runs, but he knocked in 15 more runs (94), hit 32 points higher (.314), and scored almost as many runs (89). Clemente's numbers were actually superior to those of both Hoak and Groat, and he was also a much better fielder and baserunner than either of his teammates. Yet the writers chose to give him a total of just 62 points in the balloting—100 fewer than Hoak, and 214 fewer than Groat. Clemente had clearly established himself as the Pirates' best player by 1960, but it seemed that both the press and the broadcasting media had a difficult time accepting that fact.

While dark-skinned players always had a difficult time being accepted into the world of white baseball in the early days, things were particularly hard on Clemente. As the first great Latin player, he not only had to deal with the prejudices that were bound to come his way because of the color of his skin, but he also had to learn a new culture and a new language. Those early days were especially difficult for him because the newspaper columnists and broadcasters of the day did not appear ready to fully accept his Latin heritage. The manner in which the writers quoted Clemente in the newspapers revealed their disdain for him, since they openly mocked the outfielder's speech. For example, if he said: "I hit the ball", his quote appeared in the paper the next day as: "I heet thee ball." And broadcasters attempted to Americanize his name by referring to him as either "Bob" or "Bobby" Clemente, instead of "Roberto", which was the name he preferred.

Therefore, it should come as no surprise that Clemente did not receive the proper amount of respect in the MVP balloting either. In later years, Roberto commented that he did not have a particularly strong objection to not winning the award that year. The thing that bothered him far more was his eighth-place finish. He felt he deserved to finish higher in the voting, which he most certainly did.

So, too, did two players from the second-place Braves, who finished just seven games behind the Pirates. Eddie Mathews hit 39 home runs, knocked in 124 runs, scored 108 others, batted .277, and led the league with 111 walks. He finished tenth in the voting, with a total of just 52 points. Teammate Hank Aaron hit 40 home runs, led the league with 126 runs batted in, hit .292, and scored 102 runs. He finished just behind Mathews in the balloting, in eleventh place, with only 49 points.

It is difficult to imagine what the writers were thinking in 1960.

1979 MVP ELECTION: THE ONLY TIE IN HISTORY

The 1979 election for National League MVP marked the only time in the history of the MVP voting that two players ended up finishing tied for first in total points, each earning a share of the award as a result. Both the Pittsburgh Pirates Willie Stargell and the St. Louis Cardinals Keith Hernandez received 216 points from the BBWAA, finishing well ahead of third-place finisher Dave Winfield.

Pittsburgh finished first in the N.L. East that year, just two games ahead of the second-place Montreal Expos. That Pirates bunch was a close-knit family group that adopted Sister Sledge's *We Are Family* as their theme song. The patriarch of that family was veteran slugger Willie Stargell, who was admired and respected by everyone on the team. Well into the twilight of his Hall of Fame career, Stargell was moved in from the outfield a few seasons earlier to be the team's first baseman. However, at 39 years of age, he was no longer able to play every day. Appearing in 126 games that year, and totaling 424 official at-bats, Stargell hit 32 home runs, knocked in 82 runs, and batted .281. Decent numbers, to be sure, but hardly MVP-caliber. The writers, though, were keenly aware of the influence Stargell had on his teammates and the manner in which he held the team together. They undoubtedly placed a great deal of importance on the intangible qualities he brought to his team when they cast their ballots. However, they may also have been influenced somewhat by the outcomes of two prior elections.

Eight years earlier, in 1971, Stargell's Pirates finished first in the National League East, seven games ahead of the second-place Cardinals. The Pittsburgh slugger had a tremendous year, leading the league with 48 home runs, knocking in 125 runs, and batting .295. However, he was beaten out for MVP honors by the Cardinals Joe Torre, who had an absolutely phenomenal season, leading the league with 137 runs batted in, a batting average of .363, and 230 hits.

In 1973, Pittsburgh finished a close third in the N.L. East and Stargell had another great year, leading the league with 44 home runs and 119 runs batted in, and batting .299. Stargell, though, finished a close second in the MVP voting to Cincinnati's Pete Rose, who led the league with a .338 batting average.

Truth be told, Stargell actually deserved to win the award more in either of those years than he did in 1979 because the third-place Cardinals, who finished 12 games behind Pittsburgh in the N.L. East, had an outstanding candidate of their own in co-winner Keith Hernandez. The first baseman hit only 11 home runs, but he drove in 105 runs and led the league with a .344 batting average, 116 runs scored, and 48 doubles. Yet, when the votes were counted, Stargell received the same number of points as Hernandez. Perhaps it was the writers' knowledge of Stargell's past frustrations with the MVP balloting, in addition to his tremendous contribution to Pittsburgh's team chemistry, that prompted many of them to vote for him. It is quite possible that his being named co-winner of the award in 1979 was essentially the writers' way of presenting Stargell with a "lifetime achievement" award of sorts.

FOUR INCONSISTENT YEARS

Another source of controversy has been the inconsistency that the voters have shown in various elections. This has been most obvious in the way they have voted in different years in which both a pitcher on a pennant-winning team and an everyday player on a contender have had superb seasons. Prime examples would be the National League elections of 1965 and 1966, and the American League elections of 1978 and 1986.

1965 AND 1966

The Los Angeles Dodgers won the National League pennant in 1965, finishing just two games ahead of the second-place San Francisco Giants. While several other players contributed greatly to the success that Los Angeles experienced that year, most notably shortstop Maury Wills and pitcher Don Drysdale, the Dodgers' most outstanding performer was clearly Sandy Koufax. The lefthander won the pitcher's Triple Crown by dominating all league pitching categories. He finished 26-8, with a 2.04 earned run average and 382 strikeouts. There is little doubt that the Dodgers would not even have come close to winning the pennant without him.

Yet, Willie Mays also had an exceptional season for the second-place Giants. He led the league with 52 home runs, drove in 112 runs, scored 118 others, and batted .317. Mays helped San Francisco to remain in the pennant race to the very end with his outstanding performance, and he was rewarded for his efforts at season's end by being named National League MVP, out-pointing Koufax in the balloting, 224 to 177. This, despite the fact that Koufax's Dodgers won the pennant and Koufax led N.L. pitchers in five major categories, while Mays led league batsmen in just one.

The very next year, the Dodgers repeated as N.L. champs, once again edging out the Giants in a very close pennant race, this time by just 1½ games. The Pirates finished third, just three games back. In what turned out to be his final season, Koufax had another phenomenal year, winning his second straight Triple Crown. He finished the season with a record of 27-9, an earned run average of 1.73, and 317 strikeouts. He also led the league in innings pitched, complete games, and shutouts.

Willie Mays had another outstanding season for the Giants, hitting 37 home runs and driving in 103 runs. However, he was not the league's top outfielder that year. Pittsburgh's Roberto Clemente had the most productive season of his career, hitting 29 home runs, driving in 119 runs, scoring 105 others, and batting .317. He was rewarded by being named league MVP, narrowly out-pointing Koufax in the voting, 218 to 208. Yet, Koufax's Dodgers finished ahead of Clemente's Pirates, and the Dodger lefthander led the league in six statistical categories while Clemente failed to lead the league in any.

1978 AND 1986

The Yankees and Red Sox went right down to the wire in the American League East in 1978, both finishing the regular season with 99 wins. As a result, the two teams were forced to play a one-game playoff, with the winner becoming division champions. New York prevailed and then went on to win the pennant and World Series. None of that would have been possible, though, had it not been for their slight-of-build lefthander, Ron Guidry, who had an absolutely amazing year. *Louisiana Lightning*, as he was known, kept the Yankees within striking distance for much of the year as Boston streaked while New York struggled. When the Red Sox finally began to show signs of vulnerability in late July, the Yankees seized the opportunity to gradually make up a 14½ game deficit over the season's final two months. However, they wouldn't even have been that close if Guidry had not been able to virtually guarantee them a victory every fifth day. The lefty led the league with 25 victories, against only 3 defeats, and he also topped the circuit with a 1.74 earned run average and nine shutouts.

Boston outfielder Jim Rice, though, also had a fabulous year. He led the league with 46 home runs and 139 runs batted in, batted .315, and scored 121 runs. Rice also finished first in hits, triples, slugging average, and total bases. At season's end, he was selected league MVP, out-pointing Guidry, 352 to 291.

It seemed that the BBWAA clearly set a precedent in these three elections. In each instance, it opted for an outstanding everyday player on a pennant-contending team over a superb pitcher who played for the pennant-winner. However, that trend was reversed in 1986 when

Boston's Roger Clemens was selected A.L. MVP over New York's Don Mattingly.

The Red Sox captured the American League East title that year, finishing 5½ games in front of the second-place Yankees. Boston's Roger Clemens had a great year, finishing 24-4, to lead the league in wins. He also led the league with a 2.48 earned run average, and he finished among the leaders with 238 strikeouts and 254 innings pitched.

Mattingly, though, kept New York in the pennant race for virtually the entire year with his finest all-around season. He hit 31 home runs, drove in 113 runs, batted .352, scored 117 runs, and led the league with 238 hits, 53 doubles, and a .573 slugging percentage. Yet, the writers selected Clemens over Mattingly in the MVP voting, by a margin of 339 to 258.

The BBWAA's selection of Clemens over Mattingly in 1986 is a bit confusing since, even though the former's team finished first in the standings, his numbers were not as good as those posted by Koufax in either 1965 or 1966, or by Guidry in 1978. Clemens also did not dominate the various pitching categories to the same degree that both Koufax and Guidry dominated them in each of their outstanding seasons. Meanwhile, Mattingly's year could be put up against those of Mays, Clemente, and Rice in their MVP seasons. Although he hit far fewer home runs and finished with a slugging percentage that was some 70 points lower than that of Mays, Mattingly compiled virtually the same number of runs batted in and runs scored, hit 35 points higher, and collected far more hits and doubles than Willie. Rice's numbers in his MVP season of 1978 were slightly better than Mattingly's, but the latter actually posted numbers that were slightly superior to those that Clemente put up in 1966. Thus, there does not appear to be a definite pattern in the thinking of the members of the BBWAA, and the result is invariably controversy.

THE AWARDS RETURN

10

Both major leagues decided to resume the practice of presenting a Most Valuable Player Award at the end of each season prior to the start of the 1931 campaign—a practice that has remained intact ever since. However, unlike past elections, the voters in the American League did not have any restrictions placed upon them. They could include the names of more than one player from each team on their ballots, they were free to vote for player-managers, and they could select players who had previously won the award.

As a result, the subsequent elections held in both leagues theoretically should have been far more accurate than those conducted prior to 1931 since the voters began operating under essentially the same rules that govern the current elections.

	ACTUAL MVP WINNERS		**SUGGESTED WINNERS**	
	A.L.	**N.L.**	**A.L.**	**N.L.**
1931	Lefty Grove	Frankie Frisch	Lefty Grove	Bill Terry
1932	Jimmie Foxx	Chuck Klein	Jimmie Foxx	Chuck Klein
1933	Jimmie Foxx	Carl Hubbell	Jimmie Foxx	Carl Hubbell
1934	Mickey Cochrane	Dizzy Dean	Lou Gehrig	Dizzy Dean

1931

AMERICAN LEAGUE

The Philadelphia Athletics continued their dominance of the American League in 1931, capturing their third consecutive pennant and finishing 13½ games in front of the second-place Yankees. The Athletics' top offensive player was once again Al Simmons, who won his second consecutive batting title with a mark of .390. He also hit 22 home runs, drove in 128 runs, and scored 105 others. However, it would be difficult to make a case for Simmons being the Most

Valuable Player in the league since two members of the second-place Yankees posted numbers that were far superior to his in most offensive categories. Both Babe Ruth and Lou Gehrig had years that were among the best of their respective careers, with Gehrig driving in an American League record 184 runs.

Let's take a look at their statistics alongside those of Simmons:

PLAYER	AB	HITS	RUNS	2B	3B	HR	RBI	AVG	OBP	SLG PCT
Lou Gehrig	619	211	163	31	15	46	184	.341	.446	.662
Babe Ruth	534	199	149	31	3	46	163	.373	.495	.700
Al Simmons	513	200	105	37	13	22	128	.390	.444	.641

Ruth and Gehrig tied for the league lead in home runs, hitting twice as many homers as Simmons in the process. Both men also finished well ahead of the Philadelphia outfielder in runs batted in and runs scored, with Gehrig leading the league in both departments. Gehrig also topped the circuit in base hits. Simmons won the batting title, but the superior ability of Ruth and Gehrig to draw bases on balls enabled both men to compile higher on-base percentages than the Philadelphia outfielder. In fact, Ruth led the league in both on-base and slugging percentage. Neither Ruth nor Gehrig held a distinct statistical advantage over the other, but a slight edge could be given to Gehrig due to his greater run production. Therefore, it would seem that an evaluation of the MVP credentials of the three men would result in a final placement of Gehrig first, Ruth second, and Simmons third.

However, we are forgetting about someone who was even more valuable to the A's that year than Simmons. After winning 28 games the prior year and capturing the pitcher's Triple Crown, Lefty Grove improved upon his performance in 1931, winning his second consecutive Triple Crown and finishing with a superb 31-4 record. Grove led the league with a 2.06 earned run average, 175 strikeouts, 27 complete games, and four shutouts, and he finished second with 288 innings pitched. Grove's 2.06 earned run average was 61 points lower than that of league runner-up Lefty Gomez, and it was two runs per-game better than the league average. As great an offensive year as Gehrig had for New York, Grove had an even more dominant season for Philadelphia. While Gehrig established a new American League record for runs batted in and led the league in three other categories, his overall numbers were only slightly better than Ruth's. However, Grove's performance far exceeded that of any other pitcher in the league. Furthermore, his team won the pennant.

Therefore, it would be difficult to find fault with the writers' selection of Grove as league MVP, over Gehrig, who finished second in the voting.

NATIONAL LEAGUE

The St. Louis Cardinals repeated as National League champions in 1931, finishing 13 games ahead of the second-place Giants. St. Louis second baseman Frankie Frisch was selected by the writers as the league's Most Valuable Player even though he didn't have one of his best seasons. Frisch hit only four home runs, drove in just 82 runs, batted .311, and scored 96 runs. While he led the league with 28 stolen bases, Frisch was not among the league leaders in any other statistical category. The writers must have been very impressed with Frisch's fiery temperament and leadership skills because he wasn't even the best player on his own team that year. Cardinals outfielder Chick Hafey put up much better numbers than the second baseman, hitting 16 home runs, knocking in 95 runs, scoring 94 others, and batting .349. Yet Hafey could do no better than fifth in the voting.

The man who finished runner-up to Frisch in the balloting was the Philadelphia Phillies Chuck Klein, who was probably the best all-around player in the league. Klein led the N.L. with 31 homers, 121 runs batted in, and 121 runs scored, and he also batted .337. However, the Phillies finished a distant sixth, 35 games behind the first-place Cardinals, greatly diminishing Klein's credentials as a legitimate MVP candidate. Let's take a look at his numbers, though, along with those of Frisch, Hafey, and two members of the second-place Giants— Mel Ott and Bill Terry:

PLAYER	AB	HITS	RUNS	2B	3B	HR	RBI	AVG	OBP	SLG PCT
Frankie Frisch	518	161	96	24	4	4	82	.311	.368	.396
Chick Hafey	450	157	94	35	8	16	95	**.349**	**.404**	.569
Mel Ott	497	145	104	23	8	29	115	.292	.392	.545
Bill Terry	611	213	**121**	43	**20**	9	112	.349	.397	.529
Chuck Klein	594	200	**121**	34	10	**31**	**121**	.337	.398	**.584**

Based strictly on statistics, it is extremely difficult to make a valid argument on Frisch's behalf. Teammate Hafey's numbers were far superior in virtually every category, and the outfielder led the league in two departments. The primary thing working against Hafey was that he appeared in only 122 of his team's games, accumulating a total of just 450 official at-bats in the process. Mel Ott also compiled fewer than 500 at-bats, and his batting average was much lower than that of any of the other players. However, Ott finished among the league leaders in home runs, runs batted in, and slugging percentage, he scored 104 runs, and his ability to draw bases on balls enabled him to place among the league leaders in on-base percentage.

The feeling here, though, is that the man most worthy of being selected league MVP was Bill Terry. Although he hit only nine home runs, Terry finished near the top of the league rankings in both runs batted in and on-base percentage. The first baseman also tied for the league lead in runs scored, he topped the circuit in triples, and he finished just a fraction of a point behind league-leader Hafey in batting average. Terry played in virtually all of New York's games, and his team finished second in the standings. Philadelphia's Klein had a slightly better year, but the outfielder's team finished sixth, four places and 22 games behind Terry's Giants in the standings.

It is somewhat mystifying that Terry finished third in the balloting, behind both Frisch and Klein.

1932

AMERICAN LEAGUE

New York ended Philadelphia's three-year reign as American League champions in 1932, finishing 13 games ahead of the second-place Athletics. With a much improved pitching staff that featured future Hall of Famers Lefty Gomez and Red Ruffing, the Yankees compiled an outstanding 107-47 record and led the league with a team earned run average of 3.98. In just his second full year, Gomez won 24 games and tasted defeat only seven times. Ruffing, acquired from Boston two years earlier, compiled a record of 18-7, led the league with 190 strikeouts, and finished second in earned run average (3.09) and third in complete games (22).

New York's offense remained extremely potent. With young stars Bill Dickey and Ben Chapman, and veteran infielder Joe Sewell joining a lineup that already included Babe Ruth, Lou Gehrig, and Earle Combs, the Yankees led the majors with 1,002 runs scored. Catcher Dickey drove in 84 runs and batted .310. Chapman, who replaced the retired Bob Meusel in left-field one year earlier, knocked in 107 runs, scored 101 others, stole a league-leading 38 bases, and batted .299. Third baseman Sewell, acquired from Cleveland the previous year, scored 95 runs and set a major league record by striking out just three times in 503 at-bats. Combs batted .321 and finished third in the league with 143 runs scored.

As usual, the Yankees attack was led by Ruth and Gehrig. The Babe led the league with a .489 on-base percentage, and he finished second with 41 home runs and a .661 slugging percentage. He also finished fourth with 137 runs batted in and a .341 batting average. Gehrig was even better, finishing among the league leaders with 34 home runs, 151 runs batted in, 138 runs scored, a .349 batting average, 208 hits, 370 total bases, a .451 on-base percentage, and a .621 slugging percentage. He was clearly New York's most valuable player in 1932. However, there were several other outstanding candidates who performed for other teams.

Cleveland outfielder Earl Averill finished among the league leaders in home runs (32), runs batted in (124), batting average (.314), runs scored (116), and hits (198). Heinie Manush, a member of the Washington Senators that year, finished in the top five in batting average (.342), runs scored (121), hits (214), and total bases (325). The MVP credentials of both Averill and Manush were greatly diminished, though, by the fact that the Indians finished fourth, 19 games behind the Yankees, while the Senators finished third, 14 games out of first place.

Al Simmons had another tremendous year for the second-place A's. Although his batting average of .322 represented a 68-point drop from his league-leading 1931 average of .390, Simmons finished among the league leaders with 35 home runs, 151 runs batted in, 144 runs scored, and 367 total bases, and he led the league with 216 hits. His numbers were actually quite similar to the figures posted by Gehrig in numerous offensive categories. But, with the Athletics finishing 13 games behind the Yankees, it would be difficult to make a valid argument for naming Simmons league MVP over Gehrig.

However, there was one man whose statistics far exceeded those of any other player in the league. Simmons' teammate in Philadelphia, Jimmie Foxx, had one of the most dominant seasons ever. Foxx led the league with 58 home runs, 169 runs batted in, and 151 runs scored, batted .364, collected 213 hits, and posted a .469 on-base percentage and a league-leading .749 slugging percentage. His 438 total bases were 68 more than the 370 bases runner-up Gehrig compiled for the Yankees.

In 1932, Foxx replaced Al Simmons as his own team's best player, and Babe Ruth and Lou Gehrig as the game's most dominant hitter. Foxx's extraordinary season, coupled with the A's second-place finish, more than justified his selection by the writers as the league's Most Valuable Player.

NATIONAL LEAGUE

The Chicago Cubs replaced St. Louis as National League champions in 1932, finishing four games ahead of the second-place Pittsburgh Pirates. Finishing fourth in the league in both team batting average (.278) and runs scored (720), it was actually Chicago's pitching that enabled the team to capture the N.L. flag. The Cubs' team earned run average of 3.44 was the lowest in the majors, and they had the best pitcher in the league that year. Righthander Lon Warneke finished 22-6 to top the circuit in victories. He also led in earned run average (2.37) and winning percentage (.786), and he finished second in complete games (25) and third in innings pitched (277). Although Warneke was clearly the league's best pitcher, he wasn't quite dominant enough to be considered its Most Valuable Player. Let's take a look at some of the league's top hitters that year.

Second-place Pittsburgh's top candidate was Paul Waner, who led the league with 62 doubles and also finished among the leaders with a .341 batting average and 215 hits. The third-place Dodgers Lefty O'Doul was even better. He led the league with a .368 batting average, and he also finished in the top five in runs scored (120), base hits (219), on-base percentage (.423), and slugging percentage (.555). Neither player, though, was really dominant enough to overtake Warneke as the league's top candidate, considering Chicago's first-place finish.

However, fourth-place Philadelphia had someone who was more dominant than either Waner or O'Doul. Chuck Klein was clearly the

National League's best player in 1932. He tied Mel Ott for the league lead with 38 home runs, and he topped the circuit with 152 runs scored, 226 hits, 20 stolen bases, 420 total bases, and a .646 slugging percentage. Klein also finished second with 137 runs batted in and 50 doubles, and he placed third with a .348 batting average. His 420 total bases were almost 50 more than the total compiled by league runner-up Bill Terry.

Although the Phillies finished fourth, they were only 12 games behind first-place Chicago in the final standings, thereby justifying Klein's selection as league MVP. Warneke appropriately finished second in the balloting.

1933

AMERICAN LEAGUE

The Washington Senators claimed the American League pennant in 1933, finishing seven games ahead of the second-place Yankees. Washington was a well-balanced team, finishing second in the league with a team earned run average of 3.82, third with 850 runs scored, and leading the A.L. with a team batting average of .287. The Senators' top pitcher was Alvin Crowder, who led the league with 24 victories (against 15 defeats), and also finished second with 299 innings pitched. Washington's offense was led by Heinie Manush and Joe Cronin. Manush led the league with 221 hits and 17 triples, and he also finished in the top five in batting average (.336) and runs scored (115). Cronin placed among the league leaders with 118 runs batted in, hit .309, led the league with 45 doubles, and led A.L. shortstops in fielding.

Lou Gehrig had a better year than either man, though, for second-place New York. He led the league with 138 runs scored, finished second with 139 runs batted in, 359 total bases, and a .605 slugging percentage, and also placed among the leaders with 32 home runs, a .334 batting average, and 198 hits. Still, Gehrig was not the league's best player.

For the second consecutive year, Philadelphia's Jimmie Foxx dominated the American League statistical categories, winning the Triple Crown with 48 home runs, 163 runs batted in, and a .356

batting average. He also finished second to Gehrig with 125 runs scored, and he topped the circuit with 403 total bases. His league-leading .703 slugging percentage was almost 100 points higher than runner-up Gehrig's mark of .605. The only thing working against Foxx was that his A's finished 19½ games behind the first-place Senators. Yet, they managed to finish third, even though team owner and manager Connie Mack already began disassembling the Athletics' mini-dynasty that ruled the American League from 1929 to 1931. Gone were Al Simmons, third baseman Jimmy Dykes, and centerfielder Mule Haas—all dealt to the White Sox at the end of the 1932 season. Although Lefty Grove and Mickey Cochrane were still members of the A's in 1933, they were both shown the door as well at the end of the season. With the A's clearly in a state of flux, Foxx had all he could do to keep the team in contention.

Only his tremendous year enabled them to finish as high as they did in the standings. Foxx, therefore, was clearly the league's Most Valuable Player in 1933.

NATIONAL LEAGUE

There were several teams in contention for the National League pennant in 1933. Although the Giants were finally able to capture the title, Pittsburgh, Chicago, Boston, and St. Louis all remained within striking distance for much of the season. The Pirates finished second, five games back; the Cubs were third, six back; the Braves fourth, nine back; and the Cardinals finished fifth, 9½ games off the pace.

Pittsburgh was led by Paul Waner, who batted over .300 for the eighth straight year and finished among the league leaders with 101 runs scored, 191 hits, 38 doubles, and 16 triples. St. Louis had two stand-out performers in Joe Medwick and Pepper Martin. Medwick finished in the top five in home runs, runs batted in, runs scored, doubles, and total bases. Martin led the league with 122 runs scored and 26 stolen bases, and he also finished among the leaders in batting average, hits, triples, and on-base percentage. Boston outfielder Wally Berger finished second in the league in home runs, runs batted in, total bases, and slugging percentage.

The man who finished ahead of Berger in all four categories was the best player in the league for the third consecutive year. Philadelphia's Chuck Klein won the National League Triple Crown by hitting 28 home runs, driving in 120 runs, and batting .368. He also finished first in hits, doubles, total bases, on-base percentage, and slugging percentage. However, it would be difficult to make a valid case for Klein being the league's Most Valuable Player since his Phillies finished next-to-last, 31 games behind the first-place Giants, who had a legitimate candidate of their own..

After experimenting with a livelier ball in 1930, the National League reverted back to a more conventional ball the following year. The result was a marked decrease in the total number of runs that were scored throughout the league—7,025 in 1930, and 5,537 in 1931. By 1933, the run total dropped to just 4,908—the lowest figure since 1920. For the first time in years, National League pitchers thrived, with the league earned run average gradually dropping from a 20th century high of 4.97 in 1930, to just 3.34 in 1933. New York's staff compiled the lowest team earned run average in the league with a mark of just 2.71. The Giants' best pitcher, and the best hurler in baseball that year, was Carl Hubbell. The lefthander finished 23-12, to lead the league in wins. He also finished first in earned run average (1.66), innings pitched (308), and shutouts (10), and he placed among the leaders in strikeouts and complete games as well. Hubbell was unquestionably the most dominant player in the league.

That last fact, combined with the Giants' first-place finish, clearly earned Hubbell the MVP trophy the writers awarded him at season's end.

1934

AMERICAN LEAGUE

It was mentioned earlier that the selection of Detroit's Mickey Cochrane as the American League's Most Valuable Player in 1934 was a rather dubious one. Let us now examine more closely the circumstances surrounding his election that year.

The Detroit Tigers captured their first American League pennant in 25 years in 1934, finishing seven games in front of the second-place Yankees. Detroit boasted a solid pitching staff that compiled the second lowest team earned run average (4.06) in the league. The Tigers' two best pitchers were righthanders Tommy Bridges and "Schoolboy"

Rowe. Bridges won 22 games and finished among the league leaders with 151 strikeouts, 23 complete games, and 275 innings pitched. Rowe compiled a 24-8 record and also finished among the leaders in strikeouts, complete games, and innings pitched.

It was the Detroit offense, though, that truly separated the team from the rest of the American League in 1934. Although they finished fourth in the league with just 74 home runs, the Tigers' team batting average of .300 was easily the highest in the A.L., and their 958 runs scored were 116 more than the 842 tallied by the runner-up Yankees. Detroit's attack was led by slugging first baseman Hank Greenberg, superb second baseman Charlie Gehringer, and catcher Mickey Cochrane, who was also the team's manager. Greenberg led the Tigers with 26 home runs, led the league with 63 doubles, and also finished among the league leaders with 139 runs batted in, 118 runs scored, and a .339 batting average. Gehringer led the American League with 134 runs scored and 214 hits, and he also finished among the leaders with 127 runs batted in, a .356 batting average, and 50 doubles. Cochrane's numbers were not nearly as impressive, but he did hit .320, compile a .428 on-base percentage, and provide on-field leadership for the pennant-winners.

None of these men, though, were even among the top two offensive players in the league. Philadelphia's Jimmie Foxx finished second in the A.L. with 44 home runs and a .653 slugging percentage. He also placed among the leaders with a .334 batting average, 130 runs batted in, 120 runs scored, and a .449 on-base percentage. However, with former teammates Al Simmons, Mickey Cochrane, and Lefty Grove all playing for other teams in 1934, Foxx had very little support and the A's could do no better than fifth, finishing 31 games behind the first-place Tigers. Therefore, it would be difficult to give him serious consideration for MVP honors. Furthermore, Foxx wasn't even the league's most dominant player, since New York's Lou Gehrig had one of his greatest seasons.

Let's look at Gehrig's numbers, along with those of Greenberg, Gehringer, and Cochrane:

PLAYER	AB	HITS	RUNS	2B	3B	HR	RBI	AVG	OBP	SLG PCT
Mickey Cochrane	437	140	74	32	1	2	76	.320	.428	.412
Hank Greenberg	593	201	118	63	7	26	139	.339	.404	.600

Charlie Gehringer	601	**214**	**134**	50	7	11	127	.356	.450	.517
Lou Gehrig	579	210	128	40	6	**49**	**165**	**.363**	**.465**	**.706**

Two things become quite clear from this graphic. The first is that Cochrane's selection as the league's Most Valuable Player was a poor one. If the writers felt a need to present the award to a Detroit player, the honor should have gone to either Gehringer, who finished second in the voting, or to Greenberg, who finished sixth. Both men had much better seasons than Cochrane, who, even as his team's manager, had much less of an impact on the pennant race.

The second thing that becomes rather obvious is that Lou Gehrig was unquestionably the best player in the American League in 1934. He won the Triple Crown, and his league-leading .706 slugging percentage was almost 200 points higher than Gehringer's, and almost 300 points higher than Cochrane's. With teammate Babe Ruth no longer a major offensive force (he hit only 22 home runs and drove in just 84 runs), Gehrig received far less support in the New York lineup than he did in previous seasons, and he became the Yankees' primary offensive threat.

Although Lefty Gomez, who finished ahead of Gehrig in the voting, had an outstanding season for New York, winning the pitcher's Triple Crown with 26 victories, a 2.33 earned run average, and 158 strikeouts, Gehrig was clearly the team's best player. He was also the most dominant player in the league. New York's second-place finish should have been enough to earn him MVP honors.

NATIONAL LEAGUE

The St. Louis Cardinals, who finished fifth in the National League the prior year, overtook the New York Giants in 1934, finishing just two games ahead of the defending champions in the standings. The St. Louis offense was the best in the league, finishing first in both team batting average (.288) and runs scored (799). A major contributor was outfielder Joe Medwick, who hit 18 home runs, drove in 106 runs, scored 110 others, batted .319, and led the league with 18 triples. The Cardinals' best hitter, though, was first baseman "Ripper" Collins, who finished among the league leaders in several offensive categories.

Let's take a look at his numbers, along with those of Mel Ott, who led the second-place Giants' attack that year:

PLAYER	AB	HITS	RUNS	2B	3B	HR	RBI	AVG	OBP	SLG PCT
Ripper Collins	600	200	116	40	12	35	128	.333	.393	.615
Mel Ott	582	190	119	29	10	35	135	.326	.415	.591

The statistics of the two players were actually quite comparable, and, with their teams finishing first and second in the standings, both men could be considered viable MVP candidates. Yet, for some reason, Ott finished fifth in the voting and Collins finished sixth, behind other players whose numbers were not nearly as impressive.

One player who finished ahead of them in the voting, though, deserved a higher ranking. Cardinals pitcher Dizzy Dean easily out-polled the rest of the field following his superb season. Dean was the league's dominant player, compiling a 30-7 record for the pennant-winning Cards and leading the league with 195 strikeouts and seven shutouts. He also finished second with a 2.66 earned run average and 24 complete games, and third with 311 innings pitched.

In a close pennant race, Dean was the difference between the Cardinals finishing first, or losing out to the Giants.

SLUGGERS DOMINATE

11

From 1935 to 1942, sluggers dominated the MVP voting, except for an occasional triumph by a pitcher who performed at an exceptionally high level. This trend was particularly noticeable in the American League, where a top slugger won the award in six of the eight years during this period. A.L. honorees included Hank Greenberg, Lou Gehrig, Jimmie Foxx, and Joe DiMaggio, relegating many other fine players to honorable-mention status. Yet, several other outstanding candidates surfaced each year, presenting serious challenges to these prolific hitters for league MVP honors.

Let's look at the top performers in each league over this eight-year stretch.

	ACTUAL MVP WINNERS		SUGGESTED WINNERS	
	A.L.	**N.L.**	**A.L.**	**N.L.**
1935	Hank Greenberg	Gabby Hartnett	Hank Greenberg	Dizzy Dean
1936	Lou Gehrig	Carl Hubbell	Lou Gehrig	Carl Hubbell
1937	Charlie Gehringer	Joe Medwick	Joe DiMaggio	Joe Medwick
1938	Jimmie Foxx	Ernie Lombardi	Jimmie Foxx	Mel Ott
1939	Joe DiMaggio	Bucky Walters	Joe DiMaggio	Bucky Walters
1940	Hank Greenberg	Frank McCormick	Hank Greenberg	Bucky Walters
1941	Joe DiMaggio	Dolph Camilli	Joe DiMaggio	Dolph Camilli
1942	Joe Gordon	Mort Cooper	Ted Williams	Mort Cooper

1935

AMERICAN LEAGUE

The Tigers repeated as American League champions in 1935, beating out the Yankees by only three games in a close pennant race. Once again, Detroit's lineup was the best in the league, finishing first in batting average (.290) and runs scored (919), and placing second in home runs (106). The Tigers also had solid pitching, finishing second in the league with a team earned run average of 3.82. Tommy Bridges and "Schoolboy" Rowe were again the staff aces, combining for 40 wins and finishing among the league leaders in both complete games and innings pitched. However, they were not the best pitchers in the league.

Wes Ferrell and Lefty Grove both had outstanding seasons for fourth-place Boston. Grove won 20 games and led the league with a 2.70 earned run average. Ferrell led the league with 25 wins, and he also finished first with 31 complete games and 322 innings pitched.

Cleveland also had an outstanding pitcher in Mel Harder, who won 22 games and finished among the league leaders with a 3.29 earned run average and 287 innings pitched. Harder was not the only Indians player, though, who performed at an extremely high level. First baseman Hal Trosky finished near the top of the league rankings in both home runs, with 26, and runs batted in, with 113. Outfielder Joe Vosmik finished second in the league with a .348 batting average and led the A.L. with 47 doubles, 20 triples, and 216 hits. Harder, Trosky, and Vosmik led Cleveland to a very respectable third-place finish, 12 games behind the pennant-winning Tigers. However, none of the three Indians was worthy of serious consideration for league MVP honors.

Neither was Athletics slugger Jimmie Foxx, who had another excellent year for Philadelphia. He tied for the league lead with 36 home runs, led the A.L. with a .636 slugging percentage, and finished among the leaders with 115 runs batted in, 118 runs scored, a .346 batting average, a .461 on-base percentage, and 340 total bases. However, the A's finished last, 34 games off the pace, ruining any chance Foxx might have had of winning his third Most Valuable Player Award.

Lou Gehrig finished among the league leaders with 30 home runs, 119 runs batted in, a .329 batting average, and a .583 slugging percentage. He also led the league with 125 runs scored, 132 bases on balls, and a .466 on-base percentage. Having played a major role in the Yankees' second-place finish, Gehrig certainly deserved consideration for MVP honors.

So, too, did Detroit's Charlie Gehringer, who hit 19 home runs for the first-place Tigers and finished among the league leaders with a .330 batting average, 108 runs batted in, 123 runs scored, and 201 hits. The Tigers' best player, though, and unquestionably the league's Most Valuable Player, was Hank Greenberg. The big first baseman tied for the league lead with 36 home runs, finished first with 170 runs batted in and 389 total bases, and placed among the leaders with a .328 batting average, 121 runs scored, 203 hits, 46 doubles, 16 triples, and a .628 slugging percentage. His 170 runs batted in topped runner-up Gehrig's total of 119 by a margin of 51, clearly illustrating the fact that Greenberg was the league's top run-producer.

As a result, the Tiger first baseman was able to easily outpoll everyone else in the balloting for league MVP.

NATIONAL LEAGUE

The decision for National League MVP was much less obvious. The Cubs won the pennant, beating out the second-place Cardinals by four games, the third-place Giants by 8½, and the fourth-place Pirates by 13½. Each of those teams had at least one legitimate MVP candidate.

For Pittsburgh, there was shortstop Arky Vaughan, who led the league with a .385 batting average, a .491 on-base percentage, and a .607 slugging percentage. St. Louis had Joe Medwick, who finished second in the league with 126 runs batted in, 132 runs scored, 224 hits, and a .353 batting average. New York had Mel Ott, who finished among the leaders with 31 home runs, 114 runs batted in, and 113 runs scored. Chicago had two players who were deserving of consideration—catcher Gabby Hartnett and second baseman Billy Herman. Hartnett batted .344 and drove in 91 runs in just 413 at-bats, and Herman batted .341 and led the league with 227 hits and 57 doubles.

Let's take a look at the statistics of all five men:

PLAYER	AB	HITS	RUNS	2B	3B	HR	RBI	AVG	OBP	SLG PCT
Billy Herman	666	227	113	57	6	7	83	.341	.383	.476
Arky Vaughan	499	192	108	34	10	19	99	.385	.491	.607
Mel Ott	593	191	113	33	6	31	114	.322	.407	.555
Gabby Hartnett	413	142	67	32	6	13	91	.344	.404	.545
Joe Medwick	634	224	132	46	13	23	126	.353	.386	.576

From this graphic, it would seem that Vaughan and Medwick were the two best players in the league that year, while Hartnett was the least effective. Yet, it was Hartnett who was selected as the league's Most Valuable Player. While it is true that the Chicago catcher had a good year and that the Cubs won the pennant, Hartnett appeared in only 116 of his team's games and accumulated just 413 official at-bats. Meanwhile, teammate Herman played in all of Chicago's 154 games and came to bat more than 250 more times. The second baseman also had a fine year, finishing with better overall numbers than Hartnett. Therefore, if a Chicago player was to be named league MVP, it probably should have been Herman. Nevertheless, the feeling here is that Medwick was more valuable to his team than any of the other four men. St. Louis finished a close second in the standings, and he put up the best numbers.

However, one of Medwick's Cardinals teammates also had an outstanding year. Dizzy Dean followed up his 30-win 1934 campaign with another 28 victories in 1935. He finished 28-12 and also led the league with 190 strikeouts, 325 innings pitched, and 29 complete games. His 3.04 earned run average was among the lowest in the league, and he appeared in 50 of his team's games, 36 of them starts.

Dean was the league's best pitcher for the second consecutive season, and he should have been selected its Most Valuable Player again.

1936

AMERICAN LEAGUE

After a three-year hiatus, the Yankees returned to the top of the American League standings in 1936, finishing 19½ games ahead of second-place Detroit. New York's offense was the most potent in baseball, scoring a total of 1,065 runs, just two short of the major-league record 1,067 the team scored five years earlier, in 1931. Two players, in particular, were largely responsible for New York's increased run-production. The first was Bill Dickey, who was an outstanding hitter from the day he first put on the pinstripes. However, the catcher greatly increased his offensive production in 1936, batting a career-high .362, while hitting 22 home runs and knocking in 107 runs in just 423 at-bats.

New York's lineup also featured Joe DiMaggio for the first time. The brilliant rookie centerfielder hit 29 home runs, drove in 125 runs, batted .323, scored 132 runs, collected 206 hits, and led the league with 15 triples. The Yankees, who badly needed someone to support Lou Gehrig in their lineup after they released Babe Ruth prior to the start of the 1935 campaign, found their man in DiMaggio. In addition to providing a perfect righthanded complement to the lefthanded swinging Gehrig, DiMaggio replaced the aging Earle Combs in centerfield, playing the position better than almost anyone else had up to that point.

New York was not the only team, though, that had a powerful offense in 1936. Detroit and Cleveland finished tied for second in the league with 921 runs scored, and both teams sported stars of their own. The Tigers' attack was led by Charlie Gehringer, who had another superb year for the Bengals. He batted .354, knocked in 116 runs, scored 144 others, and collected 227 hits and 60 doubles. The Indians featured Hal Trosky and Earl Averill, both of whom had perhaps their finest seasons. Trosky led the league with 162 runs batted in, finished second with 42 home runs, batted .343, and scored 124 runs. Averill hit 28 home runs, drove in 126 runs, finished second in the league with a .378 batting average, scored 136 runs, and led the A.L. with 232 hits. Had Cleveland not finished fifth, 22½ games off the pace, both Trosky and Averill would have been serious contenders for league MVP honors. As it is, Averill finished third in the voting.

The man who finished second was Chicago shortstop Luke Appling, who had the finest season of his career. Appling led the league with a .388 batting average, finished second with a .474 on-base percentage, knocked in 128 runs, scored 111 others, and collected 204 hits. His .388 average remains a major league record for shortstops. Appling was the primary reason the White Sox finished third in the standings, thereby justifying his second-place finish in the balloting.

Yet, Chicago finished a full 20 games behind the pennant-winning Yankees, who featured the best player in baseball that year. Lou Gehrig had one of his greatest seasons, leading the league with 49 home runs, and finishing second with 152 runs batted in and third with a .354

batting average. He also led the A.L. with 167 runs scored, a .478 on-base percentage, and a .696 slugging percentage.

Even though the exceptional play of the brilliant rookie DiMaggio drew a great deal of attention from both the fans and the media, Gehrig remained the Yankees' dominant player and the driving force behind their first-place finish. As such, he was most deserving of his selection as the league's Most Valuable Player.

NATIONAL LEAGUE

The Giants made it an all-New York World Series in 1936, capturing the National League pennant by finishing five games in front of both the Cardinals and Cubs. All three teams had viable MVP candidates, most of whom also received a great deal of consideration the previous year.

The Giants' Mel Ott was again a prime candidate. He led the league with 33 home runs and also finished among the leaders with 135 runs batted in, a .328 batting average, and 120 runs scored. The Cardinals' Joe Medwick was also once more a leading candidate. He hit 18 home runs, led the league with 138 runs batted in, finished second with a .351 batting average, scored 115 runs, and led the N.L. with 223 hits and 64 doubles. Billy Herman had another solid season for Chicago, batting .334, driving in 93 runs, scoring 101 runs, and collecting 211 hits. Still, Herman may not have been the Cubs' best player. Teammate Frank Demaree batted .350, knocked in 96 runs, scored 93 others, and tallied 212 hits.

In spite of the outstanding offensive performances turned in by these four men, the league's most exceptional player in 1936 was Giants pitcher Carl Hubbell. The lefthander compiled a 26-6 record for the pennant-winners, thereby leading the league in victories. He also topped the circuit in earned run average (2.31), and he finished third with 304 innings pitched and second with 25 complete games. Ott and Medwick may have been the league's best hitters, but Hubbell was the most dominant player in the N.L. that year, and the player most responsible for the Giants winning the pennant. He clearly deserved the MVP honor that was bestowed upon him at season's end.

1937

AMERICAN LEAGUE

Combining excellent pitching and tremendous hitting, the Yankees repeated as American League champions in 1937, finishing the season with a record of 102-52, 13 games ahead of the second-place Tigers. New York's pitching staff was headed by Lefty Gomez, who won the pitcher's Triple Crown by going 21-11, with a 2.33 earned run average and 194 strikeouts. He also finished second in the league with 25 complete games and 278 innings pitched.

It was really New York's offense, though, that led them to their second straight pennant. Third baseman Red Rolfe joined the list of Yankee All-Stars, finishing second in the league with 143 runs scored. Bill Dickey had an even more productive year than he had in 1936, establishing career highs with 29 home runs and 133 runs batted in, and batting .332. Yet, it was the combination of Gehrig and DiMaggio that truly made the New York offense the most prolific in the game. Let's take a look at their numbers, along with those of Hank Greenberg and Charlie Gehringer of the second-place Tigers—the only other viable MVP candidates that year:

PLAYER	AB	HITS	RUNS	2B	3B	HR	RBI	AVG	OBP	SLG PCT
Hank Greenberg	594	200	137	49	14	40	**183**	.337	.436	.668
Charlie Gehringer	564	209	133	40	1	14	96	**.371**	.458	.520
Lou Gehrig	569	200	138	37	9	37	159	.351	**.473**	.643
Joe Dimaggio	621	215	**151**	35	15	**46**	167	.346	.412	**.673**

Gehringer won the only batting title of his career with a mark of .371, but, with 96 runs batted in, he actually had other, more productive years. He hit far fewer home runs and triples than any of the other three players, and his slugging percentage was more than 100 points lower. Yet, Gehringer was the writers' choice as league MVP. It would seem that his Detroit teammate, Greenberg, who came within one RBI of tying Lou Gehrig's A.L. record of 184, would have been a far better choice. Gehrig, whose numbers also compared favorably to Gehringer's, and whose team finished 13 games ahead in the standings, also would have been a better selection.

But the player who was most deserving of the honor was Joe DiMaggio. He led the league in home runs, runs scored, and slugging percentage, and he finished with only 16 fewer runs batted in than Greenberg. DiMaggio also played a tremendous centerfield—a more demanding position than those played by any of the other men under consideration. DiMaggio was the best player on the pennant-winning team, and the best player in the league. That should have been enough to allow him to finish first in the MVP voting, instead of placing second in the balloting to Gehringer.

NATIONAL LEAGUE

The Giants made it a New York sweep for the second year in a row by capturing the National League pennant in 1937, finishing just three games ahead of the second-place Cubs. Carl Hubbell and Mel Ott were again the Giants' leading candidates for MVP honors. Hubbell finished 22-8, with a 3.20 earned run average and a league-leading 159 strikeouts. Ott finished tied for the league lead with 31 homers, drove in 95 runs, batted .294, and scored 99 runs.

The second-place Cubs also had a pair of legitimate MVP candidates. Second baseman Billy Herman batted .335 and scored 106 runs. Outfielder Frank Demaree had his second consecutive outstanding season, hitting 17 home runs, finishing second in the league with 115 runs batted in, hitting .324, and scoring 104 runs.

Johnny Mize of the fourth-place Cardinals also had an excellent year, hitting 25 home runs, driving in 113 runs, and finishing second in the league with a .364 batting average. Mize's teammate, Joe Medwick, though, was clearly the National League's most dominant player in 1937. The outfielder won the Triple Crown by hitting 31 home runs, knocking in 154 runs, and batting .374. He also led the league with 111 runs scored, 237 hits, 56 doubles, a .641 slugging percentage, and 406 total bases.

The fact that St. Louis finished fourth, 15 games out of first, certainly worked against Medwick. But, in the end, the fabulous numbers he posted could not be overlooked. He was most deserving of league MVP honors.

1938

AMERICAN LEAGUE

The Yankees won their third consecutive American League pennant in 1938, finishing 9½ games ahead of Boston in the standings. Red Rolfe and Bill Dickey were again primary contributors to the New York offense. Rolfe hit .311 and finished among the league leaders with 132 runs scored. Dickey hit 27 home runs, drove in 115 runs, and batted .313. Surprisingly, he finished second in the MVP voting, ahead of teammate Joe DiMaggio, whose numbers were far more impressive. DiMaggio hit 32 homers, knocked in 140 runs, batted .324, and scored 129 runs. Yet, the centerfielder finished sixth in the balloting.

The Yankees were not the only team that featured players worthy of MVP consideration. Charlie Gehringer hit 20 home runs for fourth-place Detroit, drove in 107 runs, batted .306, and scored 133 runs. Outfielder Jeff Heath had an outstanding year for third-place Cleveland. He hit 21 home runs, knocked in 112 runs, finished second in the league with a .343 batting average, scored 104 runs, and led the A.L. with 18 triples. Yet, neither Gehringer nor Heath was truly deserving of serious consideration for MVP honors. Only two men in the league were that year, and, surprisingly, neither played for the pennant-winning Yankees.

Detroit's Hank Greenberg had a superb season, leading the league with 58 home runs and 144 runs scored, finishing second with 146 runs batted in, and batting .315. Even though the Tigers finished fourth, 16 games out of first, Greenberg's tremendous year made him a leading candidate for league MVP. However, there was one player who had an even better year—Boston's Jimmie Foxx. He finished second to Greenberg with 50 homers and 139 runs scored, and he led the league with 175 runs batted in, a .349 batting average, a .462 on-base percentage, a .704 slugging percentage, and 398 total bases. Foxx's fabulous season enabled the Red Sox to finish second in the league, two places and 6 1/2 games ahead of Greenberg's Tigers in the standings. He clearly earned the MVP trophy that the writers awarded him at the end of the year.

NATIONAL LEAGUE

The Cubs finished on top in a four-team pennant race in the National League in 1938, beating out the Pirates by two games, the Giants by five, and the Reds by six. Chicago's offense was led by third baseman and leadoff hitter, Stan Hack, who batted .320, scored 109 runs, and collected 195 hits. However, Hack was not the Cubs' most outstanding performer that year. Righthander Bill Lee finished 22-9, to lead N.L. hurlers in victories. He also compiled a league-leading 2.66 earned run average and nine shutouts, and he threw 291 innings and 19 complete games. Those numbers were certainly quite impressive, but were they good enough to earn him MVP honors? The writers didn't think so, since Lee finished second in the balloting.

Outfielder Johnny Rizzo was second-place Pittsburgh's top player in 1938. Rizzo hit 23 home runs, knocked in 111 runs, batted .301, and scored 97 runs. Nice numbers, but hardly MVP caliber.

The third-place Giants and fourth-place Reds each had an outstanding candidate of their own. New York's Mel Ott led the league in three different offensive categories, while Cincinnati's Ernie Lombardi won the National League batting title with a mark of .342. Let's take a look at the numbers posted by both men:

PLAYER	AB	HITS	RUNS	2B	3B	HR	RBI	AVG	OBP	SLG PCT
Ernie Lombardi	489	167	60	30	1	19	95	**.342**	.391	.524
Mel Ott	527	164	**116**	23	6	**36**	116	.311	**.442**	.583

Ott's numbers were clearly far more impressive than Lombardi's. He hit almost twice as many home runs, drove in 20 more runs, scored almost twice as many runs, and compiled a much higher slugging percentage. While Lombardi hit for a higher average, Ott finished with a much higher on-base percentage. Yet, for some reason, the writers selected Lombardi as the league's Most Valuable Player, while Ott finished fourth in the voting. It is difficult to imagine what they were thinking since, not only was Ott the better player, but his team finished a game ahead of Lombardi's in the standings. Lombardi clearly did not deserve to be selected over either Ott or Chicago's Bill Lee. The award should have gone to one of those two men, with the nod here going to Ott.

1939

AMERICAN LEAGUE

The Yankees won an unprecedented fourth consecutive American League pennant in 1939, finishing 17 games ahead of the second-place Red Sox. Once again, New York combined solid pitching with a potent offense to distance themselves from the rest of the league. The pitching staff was led by Red Ruffing, who compiled a 21-7 record and a 2.94 earned run average. The offense featured Red Rolfe, who had his finest season, Bill Dickey, and young second baseman Joe Gordon. Rolfe hit .329 and led the league with 139 runs scored, 213 hits, and 46 doubles. Dickey clubbed 24 home runs, drove in 105 runs, batted .302, and scored 98 runs. Gordon added another powerful bat to the Yankee lineup, hitting 28 homers and driving in 111 runs. None of these players, though, finished any higher than fifth in the MVP voting.

One player who did was righthander Bob Feller. Pitching for third-place Cleveland, Feller finished 24-9, to lead the league in victories. He also compiled a 2.85 earned run average and led A.L. pitchers with 246 strikeouts, 296 innings pitched, and 24 complete games. Feller was clearly the league's best pitcher, but he wasn't its Most Valuable Player.

The Red Sox had two players who certainly were in contention for that coveted honor. Both Jimmie Foxx and Ted Williams had excellent years for Boston, helping their team to a second-place finish. Foxx led the league with 35 home runs, knocked in 105 runs, batted .360, scored 130 runs, and finished first in the league with a .464 on-base percentage and a .694 slugging percentage. Rookie Williams hit 31 homers, led the league with 145 runs batted in, hit .327, and scored 131 runs. Had the Red Sox finished closer to the Yankees in the standings, a valid case could have been made for picking either man for league MVP. However, with a 17-game margin separating the two teams, it would be difficult to justify the selection of either Foxx or Williams over Joe DiMaggio, who had an exceptional year for New York. Although he missed almost a month of the season, DiMaggio hit 30 home runs, drove in 126 runs, scored 108 others, and led the league with a .381 batting average. He also finished third in the league with a .448 on-base percentage, and he placed second with a .671 slugging percentage.

DiMaggio was clearly the driving force behind the Yankees' early pennant-clinching, and he was most deserving of his selection as the league's Most Valuable Player.

NATIONAL LEAGUE

The National League pennant race was much closer in 1939, with the Cincinnati Reds beating out the second-place Cardinals by 4½ games. Although several players contributed to the success of both teams, the top players for both Cincinnati and St. Louis were their respective first basemen. The Reds' Frank McCormick hit 18 home runs, led the league with 128 runs batted in and 209 hits, batted .332, and scored 99 runs. The Cards' Johnny Mize led the N.L. with 28 home runs and a .349 batting average, knocked in 108 runs, and scored 104 others. Both men were leading candidates for league MVP, with the aforementioned numbers favoring McCormick ever so slightly due to Cincinnati's first-place finish. However, when one considers that Mize's .444 on-base percentage was 70 points higher than McCormick's mark of .374, and that his league-leading .626 slugging percentage exceeded the Reds' first baseman's by 131 points, the case for Mize becomes a better one. In addition, Mize's team finished a very close second to Cincinnati. Therefore, it really is difficult to choose between the two men.

However, there was another player on the Reds who was more dominant than either McCormick or Mize. Righthander Bucky Walters led National League pitchers in virtually every statistical category. He finished 27-11, with a 2.29 earned run average, 137 strikeouts, 319 innings pitched, and 31 complete games.

Walters was clearly the league's best pitcher in 1939, and its most dominant player as well. The writers recognized that fact by voting him the league's MVP, in an easy win over runner-up Mize.

1940

AMERICAN LEAGUE

New York's domination of the American League ended in 1940 as three teams battled right down to the wire. The Yankees and Indians both remained in contention until the season's final days, but it was the Detroit Tigers that prevailed in the end. Detroit finished just one game ahead of Cleveland, and just two ahead of New York. Each team had an outstanding MVP candidate, with Hank Greenberg leading the way for the Tigers, Bob Feller being the Indians' best player, and Joe DiMaggio having another exceptional year for the Yankees. However, they were not the only players that deserved consideration.

Both Ted Williams and Jimmie Foxx had excellent years for the fourth-place Red Sox, who finished eight games off the pace. Williams hit 23 home runs, drove in 113 runs, batted .344, and led the league with 134 runs scored and a .442 on-base percentage. Foxx hammered 36 homers, knocked in 119 runs, hit .297, and scored 106 runs.

Slugger Rudy York provided ample support for Greenberg in the Detroit lineup. The big first baseman hit 33 home runs, drove in 134 runs, batted .316, and scored 105 runs. But DiMaggio, Feller, and Greenberg were clearly the top three candidates for league MVP honors. DiMaggio hit 31 home runs, drove in 133 runs, and led the league in batting for the second straight year with a .352 average. Feller dominated the American League statistical categories for pitchers, almost as much as he dominated league hitters. He finished 27-11, with a 2.61 earned run average, 261 strikeouts, 320 innings pitched, 31 complete games, and four shutouts. He placed second in the MVP voting.

The man who finished ahead of Feller was Greenberg. Prior to the start of the season, Greenberg agreed to move to left-field to make room at first base for Rudy York. In earning MVP honors at season's end, he became the first player to win the award at two different positions. Greenberg was named league MVP for topping the circuit with 41 home runs, 150 runs batted in, 50 doubles, 384 total bases, and a .670 slugging percentage. He also finished among the leaders with a .340 batting average and 129 runs scored.

NATIONAL LEAGUE

Cincinnati repeated as National League champions in 1940, this time having a much easier time, finishing 12 games ahead of the second-place Dodgers. As was the case the previous year, the Reds' Frank McCormick and Bucky Walters, and the Cardinals' Johnny Mize were the top three candidates for league MVP honors.

Mize led the league with 43 home runs and 137 runs batted in, finished second with a .314 batting average, and scored 111 runs. McCormick hit 19 home runs, drove in 127 runs, batted .309, scored 93 runs, and led the league with 191 hits. Mize had better numbers than the Cincinnati first baseman but,.since St. Louis finished a full 16 games behind the pennant-winning Reds, it is more difficult to make a legitimate case for him being league MVP than it was the prior year. Yet, Mize was clearly a better player than McCormick, finishing with better numbers in virtually every statistical category. The disparity was particularly noticeable in home runs (43 to 19) and slugging percentage (.636 to .482). Still, McCormick was the top hitter on the first-place Reds, and he was their best everyday player. The writers acknowledged the first baseman's importance to his team by selecting him as the league's Most Valuable Player, over runner-up Mize.

There was someone else, though, who was perhaps equally important to Cincinnati's success. Bucky Walters was the league's best pitcher for the second consecutive season. He finished 22-10, to lead the N.L. in wins, and he also topped the circuit with a 2.48 earned run average, 305 innings pitched, and 29 complete games. While his numbers were down slightly from the previous season, Walters was unquestionably the top pitcher in the league. In finishing first in four different pitching categories, he was far more dominant than teammate McCormick, who only led the league in one offensive category.

As a result, the feeling here is that Walters should have been named the league's MVP for the second straight year, instead of finishing third in the voting, behind both McCormick and Mize.

1941

AMERICAN LEAGUE

The Yankees recaptured the American League flag in 1941, finishing the season with a record of 101-53, 17 games ahead of the second-place Red Sox. We saw earlier that Joe DiMaggio, with his 56-game hitting streak, and Ted Williams, with his .406 batting average, were clearly the focal points of the baseball world that year. However, several other players also had outstanding seasons.

Washington Senators shortstop Cecil Travis finished second to Williams with a .359 batting average, he led the league with 218 hits, and he also knocked in 101 runs and scored 106 others.

Jeff Heath and Bob Feller both had tremendous years for the fifth-place Indians. Heath hit 24 home runs, drove in 123 runs, batted .340, and led the league with 20 triples. In also collecting 32 doubles, he became one of a select few in the history of baseball to finish with at least 20 home runs, 20 triples, and 20 doubles in the same season. Feller led the league in wins for the third straight year with a record of 25-13, while also compiling a 3.15 earned run average and leading league hurlers with 260 strikeouts and 343 innings pitched.

In most other years, both Heath and Feller would have been legitimate MVP candidates. However, they were mere afterthoughts in 1941 due to DiMaggio and Williams. With the Red Sox-Yankees rivalry beginning to intensify, the two men waged their own personal battle for hitting supremacy, clearly establishing themselves as the two greatest players in the game.

Let's look at their numbers for the season:

PLAYER	AB	HITS	RUNS	2B	3B	HR	RBI	AVG	OBP	SLG PCT
Joe DiMaggio	541	193	122	43	11	30	**125**	.357	.440	.643
Ted Williams	456	185	**135**	33	3	**37**	120	**.406**	**.551**	**.735**

While it was DiMaggio who captivated the nation for two months with his incredible hitting streak, Williams actually put up better numbers. DiMaggio led the league in runs batted in, finished with more doubles and triples, and was relatively close to Williams in home runs and runs scored, but the Red Sox slugger out-hit him by almost 50 points, and he compiled an on-base percentage that was more than

100 points higher and a slugging percentage that was 90 points better. Yet, DiMaggio's numbers were nothing to scoff at, he was a more complete player than Williams, and his team finished 17 games ahead of second-place Boston. It is certainly true that *The Yankee Clipper* received a great deal of support from his teammates that year. Tommy Henrich hit 31 home runs and scored 106 runs, and Charlie Keller hammered 33 homers, knocked in 122 runs, batted .298, and scored 102 runs.

But DiMaggio was clearly the team's best player, and it was his hitting streak that provided the impetus for New York's successful season. When the streak began, the Yankees were in fourth place, but, by the time it ended, they were in first, well ahead of the rest of the American League. Even though Williams' incredible year undoubtedly presented quite a dilemma to many of the writers when it came time for them to cast their ballots, there can be no questioning of their selection of DiMaggio over Williams as the league's Most Valuable Player.

NATIONAL LEAGUE

The pennant race in the National League was a much closer one in 1941, with the Dodgers capturing their first league championship in 21 years by finishing just 2½ games ahead of the second-place Cardinals. With many new faces on their roster, Brooklyn quickly went from a perennial also-ran to league champions. Two of those new faces were veteran first baseman Dolph Camilli, who was acquired from the Phillies a few seasons earlier, and young outfielder Pete Reiser, who was in just his first full major league season. Camilli and Reiser were unquestionably the Dodgers' two best players and the leading candidates for league MVP honors. Johnny Mize of the second-place Cardinals also deserved some consideration, but, with 16 home runs, 100 runs batted in, a .317 batting average, and only 67 runs scored, his credentials were not nearly as impressive as those of either Reiser or Camilli.

Let's look at their statistics for the year:

PLAYER	AB	HITS	RUNS	2B	3B	HR	RBI	AVG	OBP	SLG PCT
Pete Reiser	536	184	117	39	17	14	76	.343	.406	.558
Dolph Camilli	529	151	92	29	6	34	120	.285	.407	.556

Reiser led the league in four different categories, as opposed to two for Camilli, and, despite the latter's big edge in home runs, the centerfielder actually finished with a slightly higher slugging percentage. However, Camilli drove in far more runs and, even though Reiser batted almost 60 points higher, the first baseman finished with a slightly higher on-base percentage. Based strictly on the numbers, it would appear that a valid case could be made on either player's behalf. Reiser would certainly not have been a bad choice. However, we'll opt instead for Camilli since he was the greater run-producer, and also because he brought veteran leadership to the Dodgers. The writers must have felt the same way since they selected Camilli over Reiser by a fairly wide margin—300 points to 183.

1942

AMERICAN LEAGUE

New York and Boston finished first and second in the American League standings for the second straight year in 1942, with the Yankees coming out on top once more, this time by nine games. With 102 victories, the Yankees actually won one more game than they did the previous season. However, the Red Sox improved their record by nine games, thereby closing the gap on their rivals considerably.

Several players contributed to the Red Sox improvement. Dom DiMaggio (Joe's younger brother) played a brilliant centerfield, batted .286, and scored 110 runs. Second baseman Bobby Doerr knocked in 102 runs and batted .290. Shortstop Johnny Pesky led the league with 205 hits and finished second with a .331 batting average. And, of course, there was Ted Williams, who won the Triple Crown by leading the league with 36 home runs, 137 runs batted in, and a .356 batting average. He also led the A.L. with 141 runs scored, a .499 on-base percentage, and a .648 slugging percentage. In spite of his great year, though, Williams could do no better than second in the MVP voting.

The man who finished ahead of Williams in the balloting was Yankees second baseman Joe Gordon. Let's take a look at his numbers, alongside those of *The Splendid Splinter*:

PLAYER	AB	HITS	RUNS	2B	3B	HR	RBI	AVG	OBP	SLG PCT
Joe Gordon	538	173	88	29	4	18	103	.322	.409	.491
Ted Williams	522	186	141	34	5	36	137	.356	.499	.648

While, as a second baseman, one would not expect Gordon's numbers to be on a par with the figures posted by Williams, the latter's statistics were far superior to Gordon's in almost every offensive category. Williams hit twice as many home runs, drove in 34 more runs, batted 34 points higher, scored 53 more runs, and compiled an on-base percentage that was 90 points higher and a slugging percentage that was *157* points higher. It is true that the Red Sox lineup provided Williams with an ample amount of support. However, Gordon also received a great deal of help from his Yankees teammates. Charlie Keller hit 26 home runs, drove in 108 runs, batted .292, and scored 106 runs. Joe DiMaggio hit "only" 21 home runs and batted "just" .305, but he knocked in 114 runs and scored 123 others.

Therefore, the determining factor ended up being which player had the better year, and which one had a greater impact on his team. Gordon had a fine year, the Yankees won the pennant, and their second baseman certainly had a lot to do with that. However, Boston won 93 games and moved eight games closer to New York in the standings. Furthermore, Williams' numbers far exceeded those of Gordon, he won the Triple Crown, and he was clearly the best player in the league. That should have been enough to earn Williams MVP honors for the first time in his career.

NATIONAL LEAGUE

Brooklyn and St. Louis both had tremendous years in 1942. The Dodgers finished the regular season with a record of 104-50. Unfortunately for Brooklyn, the Cardinals won 106 games and lost only 48, to finish two games ahead of their rivals in the standings. The third-place Giants also had a pretty good year, compiling a record of 86-68. However, that left them 20 games off the pace, well out of pennant-contention. As a result, neither Johnny Mize nor Mel Ott, both of whom had fine years for New York, merited serious consideration for league MVP honors. Mize finished second in the league with 26 home runs, led the N.L. with 110 runs batted in, hit .305, and led the league with a .521 slugging percentage. Ott led the league with 30 homers and 118 runs scored, and he also knocked in 93 runs and batted .295. The only serious contenders for the award, though, played for Brooklyn and St. Louis.

The Dodgers were led for the second straight year by Pete Reiser and Dolph Camilli. Although neither player was as productive as he was in 1941, both men were among the league's top performers. Reiser batted .310, scored 89 runs, and led the N.L. with 20 stolen bases. Camilli finished among the league leaders with 26 homers and 109 runs batted in, but batted only .252.

The pennant-winning Cardinals had an even better MVP candidate. Outfielder Enos Slaughter hit only 13 home runs, but he finished third in the league with 98 runs batted in and second with 100 runs scored, while leading the N.L. with a .318 batting average, 17 triples, and 188 hits. The writers selected him first among all position players, placing him second in the MVP voting. The man who finished first was Slaughter's Cardinals teammate, pitcher Mort Cooper. The righthander had a tremendous year, finishing the season with a 22-7 record, and leading the league with a superb 1.78 earned run average and 10 shutouts. Cooper also finished second with 152 strikeouts and 278 innings pitched, and third with 22 complete games.

He may not have played every day as his teammate Slaughter did, but Cooper was clearly the league's best player in 1942, and he was most deserving of the trophy he received.

12

THE 1943-1945 SEASONS—
THE WAR YEARS

Like the rest of the world, baseball was impacted tremendously by World War II. Many of the nation's finest players were either drafted, or chose to enlist in the armed forces, causing the level of play in the major leagues to invariably suffer. Detroit's Hank Greenberg was among the very first to enlist, joining the military early during the 1941 campaign. Cleveland's Bob Feller was another early entrant, enlisting one year later. Greenberg was gone from the game almost five years, while Feller didn't return for three-and-a-half years. Others, such as Boston's Ted Williams and New York's Joe DiMaggio, weren't gone quite as long, serving in the military from 1943 to 1945. But every team was affected, with some players returning after just one or two years, while others never made it back.

Needless to say, with many of the game's top players gone, both leagues experienced a period of transition, with the traditional baseball hierarchy being torn asunder. Perennial also-rans such as the Washington Senators and St. Louis Browns suddenly became contenders. In fact, the Browns won their only pennant in St. Louis in 1944 (they eventually moved to Baltimore and became the Orioles). Lesser-known players also became legitimate MVP candidates, with the names of Williams, DiMaggio, Feller, Greenberg, and Mize being replaced with those of Nicholson, Holmes, Chandler, and Cavaretta.

Let us now take a look at some of the players who excelled during these "War Years."

	ACTUAL MVP WINNERS		SUGGESTED WINNERS	
	A.L.	**N.L.**	**A.L.**	**N.L.**
1943	Spud Chandler	Stan Musial	Spud Chandler	Stan Musial
1944	Hal Newhouser	Marty Marion	Hal Newhouser	Stan Musial
1945	Hal Newhouser	Phil Cavaretta	Hal Newhouser	Phil Cavaretta

1943

AMERICAN LEAGUE

Even with Joe DiMaggio in the military, the Yankees managed to repeat as American League champions in 1943. The Tigers and Red Sox, who were forced to play without their great stars Hank Greenberg and Ted Williams, didn't fare nearly as well. Detroit fell to fifth in the standings, 20 games behind New York, while Boston finished out of the first division for the first time since 1937, coming in 29 games off the pace, in seventh place. Detroit's and Boston's annual first-division slots were taken by the Senators, who finished second, 13½ games back, and the Indians, who finished third, 15½ back. The White Sox, who featured league batting champion Luke Appling (.328), finished fourth, 16 games out. Washington was led by outfielder George Case, considered by many to be the fastest player in the game. Case led the league with 102 runs scored and 61 stolen bases, and he also finished among the leaders with a .294 batting average and 180 hits. Cleveland was led by Jeff Heath, who placed among the league leaders in home runs and slugging percentage, Lou Boudreau, who batted .286 and led league shortstops in fielding, and pitchers Al Smith and Jim Bagby Jr., both of whom won 17 games.

The fifth-place Tigers featured three of the league's top players. Righthander "Dizzy" Trout tied for the A.L. lead with 20 victories and 5 shutouts, and he also finished in the top five in earned run average (2.48), innings pitched (246), and complete games (18). Outfielder Dick Wakefield led the American League with 200 hits and 38 doubles, and he also finished among the leaders with a .316 batting average and 91 runs scored. Slugger Rudy York led the league with 34 home runs and 118 runs batted in, scored 90 runs, and also led the A.L. in total bases and slugging percentage. He was among the top MVP candidates in 1943, but his chances were hurt by his .271 batting average and Detroit's distant, fifth-place finish.

With run production down considerably in the American League, the Yankees were able to finish atop the league rankings with only 669 runs scored. Their attack was led by outfielder Charlie Keller and first baseman Nick Etten. Keller finished second in the league with 31 home runs and 97 runs scored, drove in 86 runs, and led the A.L.

with 106 walks. Etten finished second in the league with 107 runs batted in.

It was really the Yankees' pitching that enabled them to capture their third straight league championship. New York's team earned run average of 2.93 was the lowest in the league, and their staff included the two individual leaders in that category. Ernie "Tiny" Bonham, who won 21 games the previous year, compiled a 15-8 record and the second lowest earned run average in the league (2.27). The league leader in that department was Bonham's teammate, Spurgeon "Spud" Chandler. The righthander, who generally posted extremely high winning-percentages, had the greatest season of his career. He tied for the league lead with 20 wins (against only 4 losses) and five shutouts, and he led the A.L. with a 1.64 earned run average and 20 complete games. Chandler also finished fourth with 253 innings pitched. He was clearly his team's top performer in 1943, and he was the league's Most Valuable Player.

NATIONAL LEAGUE

The St. Louis Cardinals ran away with the National League pennant in 1943, finishing 18 games in front of second-place Cincinnati. Mort Cooper, the previous year's MVP winner, had another outstanding season for the Cards, tying for the league lead with 21 victories (against just 8 defeats), and also finishing among the leaders with a 2.30 earned run average, 274 innings pitched, and 24 complete games. He finished fifth in the MVP voting, three places behind his brother and batterymate, Walker. The younger Cooper batted .318 and drove in 81 runs for St. Louis, to finish runner-up in the balloting, just ahead of Chicago's Bill Nicholson. The Cubs outfielder was the most productive hitter in the league, finishing first in both home runs (29) and runs batted in (128), and also placing among the leaders with a .309 batting average, 95 runs scored, 188 hits, and a .531 slugging percentage. Had Chicago not finished fifth, 30½ games off the pace, Nicholson may well have been named league MVP, instead of finishing third in the voting.

However, with St. Louis dominating the National League with 105 wins, Stan Musial was the only logical selection for the honor. In just his second full season, Musial was the Cardinals' best player, and the league's most complete hitter. Although he hit only 13 home runs and knocked in just 81 runs, Musial won his first batting title with a mark of .357. He also finished second in the league with 108 runs scored, and he led the N.L. with 220 hits, 20 triples, 48 doubles, a .425 on-base percentage, and a .562 slugging percentage.

1944

AMERICAN LEAGUE

The St. Louis Browns won their only American League pennant in 1944, finishing just one game ahead of the Detroit Tigers and six games in front of the third-place Yankees in the standings. The Browns' top player was shortstop Vern Stephens, who finished second in the league with 20 home runs, led the A.L. with 109 runs batted in, batted .293, and scored 91 runs. He finished third in the MVP voting.

Rudy York had another productive year for the second-place Tigers, finishing among the league leaders with 18 home runs and 98 runs batted in. There were other outstanding offensive performers in the league as well, though. Nick Etten led the A.L. with 22 home runs for third-place New York. He also knocked in 91 runs and batted .293. Teammate George "Snuffy" Stirnweiss filled in admirably for the enlisted Joe Gordon at second base, batting .319 and leading the league with 125 runs scored, 205 hits, 16 triples, and 55 stolen bases.

Cleveland's Lou Boudreau led the league with a .327 batting average, and Boston teammates Bobby Doerr and Bob Johnson finished second and third with averages of .325 and .324, respectively. Doerr also scored 95 runs and led the A.L. with a .528 slugging percentage, while Johnson hit 17 homers, drove in 106 runs, scored another 106, and led the league with a .431 on-base percentage. Had Boston finished higher than fourth, 12 games out of first, Johnson likely would have been a leading candidate for MVP.

However, with the Tigers finishing just one game behind the pennant-winning Browns, the top two candidates for that honor both came from Detroit. Pitchers "Dizzy" Trout and Hal Newhouser dominated the league statistical categories for pitchers, finishing first and second in virtually every department. Newhouser led the league with 29 wins and 187 strikeouts, with Trout finishing second in both categories. Meanwhile, Trout led in earned run average, complete games, shutouts, and innings pitched. Newhouser finished right behind him in each department.

Let's look at the numbers compiled by both pitchers:

PITCHER	W	L	ERA	IP	G	GS	CG	SO	BB	SHO
Dizzy Trout	27	14	2.12	352	49	40	33	144	83	7
Hal Newhouser	29	9	2.22	312	47	34	25	187	102	6

The statistics posted by righthander Trout and lefthander Newhouser were quite comparable. Trout was a bit more of a workhorse, throwing 40 more innings and completing eight more games. He also threw one more shutout and finished with a slightly lower earned run average, but the discrepancy in both areas was negligible. On the other hand, Newhouser struck out more batters and won two more games, finishing with a much higher winning percentage—.763 to .659. It's really very close, and the writers thought so as well, selecting Newhouser by the slimmest of margins—236 points to 232. We'll go along with them, taking into account the lefthander's two extra wins and higher winning percentage.

NATIONAL LEAGUE

The Cardinals repeated as National League champions for the third consecutive year in 1944, finishing 14½ games ahead of second-place Pittsburgh and 16 games in front of the third-place Reds. Once again, Stan Musial of the Cards and Bill Nicholson of the Cubs were the top two players in the league. Musial led the N.L. in hits, doubles, on-base percentage, and slugging percentage, while Nicholson finished first in home runs, runs batted in, and runs scored. Yet, neither man was selected by the writers as the league's Most Valuable Player. That honor instead went to Musial's St. Louis teammate, shortstop Marty Marion, who edged out Nicholson by one point in the voting, 190 to 189.

Let's look at the numbers posted by all three players, along with those of Dodger outfielder Dixie Walker, who finished third in the balloting, just ahead of Musial:

PLAYER	AB	HITS	RUNS	2B	3B	HR	RBI	AVG	OBP	SLG PCT
Dixie Walker	535	191	77	37	8	13	91	.357	.434	.529
Stan Musial	568	197	112	51	14	12	94	.347	.440	.549
Marty Marion	506	135	50	26	2	6	63	.267	.324	.362
Bill Nicholson	582	167	116	35	8	33	122	.287	.391	.545

Based strictly on statistics, it is difficult to make a case for Marion's selection. While it is true that he was an excellent defensive player at one of the most demanding positions on the diamond, his numbers do not even approach those of the other three men. Teammate Musial hit twice as many home runs, drove in 31 more runs, batted 80 points higher, scored more than twice as many runs, and had an on-base percentage that was more than 100 points higher and a slugging percentage that was almost 200 points better. He clearly deserved the award more than Marion.

Almost as confusing was Dixie Walker's third-place finish in the voting, just ahead of Musial. While the two men had comparable numbers in most categories, Musial scored 35 more runs and finished with far more doubles and triples. Of even greater significance is the fact that Walker's Dodgers finished seventh, *42* games behind Musial's Cardinals. Even if one wished to make a case for Walker being as good a player as Musial that year (which he wasn't), it would be impossible to argue that he was more valuable to his team than Musial. It is difficult to comprehend what the National League writers were thinking in 1944. Nicholson was the only player whose numbers rivaled those compiled by Musial, but his Cubs finished fourth, 30 games back.

Stan The Man was the only logical selection for league MVP.

1945

AMERICAN LEAGUE

Detroit edged out Washington for the American League pennant in 1945, finishing just 1½ games ahead of the team from the nation's capital. The defending-champion Browns finished third, six games back, while New York finished fourth, 6½ out. The Senators had the best pitching staff in the A.L., leading the league in team earned run average with a mark of 2.92, while the Yankees topped the circuit with 676 runs scored.

Washington's staff featured two of the top hurlers in the league in Dutch Leonard and Roger Wolff. Leonard compiled a 17-7 record and finished among the league leaders with a 2.13 earned run average. Wolff, who in seven major league seasons finished over .500 only once, had a career year. He finished 20-10, with a 2.12 earned run average, 21 complete games, and 250 innings pitched.

New York's offense was again led by Nick Etten and George Stirnweiss. Etten hit 18 home runs, led the league with 111 runs batted in, and batted .285. Stirnweiss was perhaps the best all-around player in the league. He won the batting title with a mark of .309, and he also led the A.L. with 195 hits, 107 runs scored, 22 triples, and 33 stolen bases. He was certainly a leading candidate for MVP honors, as was the third-place Browns' Vern Stephens. The St. Louis shortstop led the league with 24 home runs, and he also finished among the leaders with 89 runs batted in, 90 runs scored, and a .289 batting average.

However, there was someone else who stood above all others that year as the league's top performer. Detroit's Hal Newhouser dominated the statistical categories for pitchers and was clearly the American League's best player. He won the pitcher's Triple Crown by compiling a record of 25-9, with a 1.81 earned run average and 212 strikeouts. He also led league hurlers with 313 innings pitched, 29 complete games, and eight shutouts. It is true that the Tigers received a huge lift when Hank Greenberg returned to the team at mid-season after a 4½ year stint in the military. In only 270 at-bats over 78 games, the slugger hit 13 home runs, drove in 60 runs, scored another 47, and batted .311.

Detroit never would have been in a position to capture the American League flag had it not been for Newhouser's great year. The Tiger lefthander was unquestionably the league's Most Valuable Player.

NATIONAL LEAGUE

The Cubs broke the Cardinals' string of three successive National League pennants in 1945, finishing three games ahead of St. Louis and capturing their first league championship since 1938. The Cubs led the N.L. with a team batting average of .277, but they finished just fourth in runs scored and they hit only 57 home runs, placing them in a fifth-place tie in the league rankings in that category. However, Chicago's pitching was easily the best in the National League. Their league-leading team earned run average of 2.98 was considerably lower than that of the runner-up Cardinals (3.24), and it was almost a run per-game less than that of any other team. In fact, three of the five lowest earned run averages in the league belonged to Cubs pitchers. Lefthander Ray Prim led the league with a mark of 2.40, and he also won 13 games. Righthander Claude Passeau finished second to Prim with a 2.46 earned run average, won 17 games, and led the league with five shutouts. Chicago righthander Hank Wyse was the league's best pitcher, compiling a record of 22-10, an earned run average of 2.68, 278 innings pitched, and 23 complete games.

The Cubs were not without offensive standouts as well. Third baseman Stan Hack finished among the league leaders with a .323 batting average, 110 runs scored, and 193 hits. Outfielder Andy Pafko knocked in 110 runs and batted .298. First baseman Phil Cavaretta— the man selected by the writers as the league's Most Valuable Player— led the N.L. with a .355 batting average and a .449 on-base percentage.

However, the two best offenses in the league belonged to the third-place Dodgers and the second-place Cardinals. Brooklyn led the league with 795 runs scored and featured defending batting champion Dixie Walker, who batted .300, scored 102 runs, and led the N.L. with 124 runs batted in. St. Louis finished second in the league in runs scored and, playing without Stan Musial, who was serving in the military in 1945, were led by third baseman Whitey Kurowski, who finished among the league leaders in home runs, runs batted in, and batting average.

Let's take a look at Kurowski's numbers, along with those of Cavaretta and outfielder Tommy Holmes, who played for the Boston Braves:

PLAYER	AB	HITS	RUNS	2B	3B	HR	RBI	AVG	OBP	SLG PCT
Whitey Kurowski	511	165	84	27	3	21	102	.323	.383	.511
Phil Cavaretta	498	177	94	34	10	6	97	**.355**	**.449**	.500
Tommy Holmes	636	**224**	125	**47**	6	**28**	117	.352	.420	**.577**

Holmes was clearly the best player in the National League in 1945. He led the league in four different offensive categories and finished among the leaders in four others. His numbers were far superior to those of both Cavaretta and Kurowski. However, Holmes' Braves finished sixth, 30 games behind the pennant-winning Cubs. With a record of 67-85, Boston was out of contention for virtually the entire year. Therefore, as good as Holmes was, it would be difficult to consider him the league's Most Valuable Player. The writers agreed, placing him second in the voting.

On the other hand, Kurowski's Cardinals finished just three games behind Cavaretta's Cubs. The St. Louis third baseman posted numbers that were quite comparable to those of Cavaretta, and he hit many more home runs and drove in five more runs as well. However, the Chicago first baseman finished with better numbers in virtually every other category, and his team finished first. Therefore, it would be difficult to find fault with Cavaretta's selection as league MVP.

THE STARS RETURN

13

With World War II over, most of the game's finest players returned to the national pastime in 1946. The level of play improved dramatically with players such as Ted Williams, Joe DiMaggio, Bob Feller, and Johnny Mize returning to their former teams after lengthy absences. One year later, in 1947, Jackie Robinson broke the color barrier, creating a brand new source of competition, and improving the level of play even more.

	ACTUAL MVP WINNERS		SUGGESTED WINNERS	
	A.L.	**N.L.**	**A.L.**	**N.L.**
1946	Ted Williams	Stan Musial	Ted Williams	Stan Musial
1947	Joe DiMaggio	Bob Elliott	Ted Williams	Johnny Mize
1948	Lou Boudreau	Stan Musial	Lou Boudreau	Stan Musial
1949	Ted Williams	Jackie Robinson	Ted Willaims	Jackie Robinson
1950	Phil Rizzuto	Jim Konstanty	Phil Rizzuto/ Yogi Berra	Jim Konstanty

1946

AMERICAN LEAGUE

The Boston Red Sox replaced Detroit at the top of the American League standings in 1946, compiling an outstanding 104-50 record and finishing 12 games in front of the defending A.L. champions. Boston combined solid pitching with the best offense in baseball to separate themselves from the rest of the league. Their staff's earned run average of 3.38 was the fourth lowest in the circuit, and its leader was Dave "Boo" Ferriss, who posted a superb 25-6 record and finished among the league leaders with 274 innings pitched and 26 complete games. Ferriss was not the best pitcher in the league, though.

Cleveland's Bob Feller tied for the A.L. lead with 26 victories (against 15 losses), compiled an excellent 2.18 earned run average, and led the league with 348 strikeouts, 371 innings pitched, 36 complete games, and 10 shutouts. However, the Indians finished sixth, 36 games behind the Red Sox. Therefore, it would be difficult to make a strong case for Feller being the league's Most Valuable Player.

A valid argument could be made on behalf of Detroit's Hal Newhouser, though. The Tiger lefthander posted numbers that were almost as impressive as Feller's, and his team finished second in the standings. In fact, Newhouser actually had a better won-lost record than the Cleveland fireballer, finishing 26-9, while also leading the league with a 1.94 earned run average. In addition, he finished right behind Feller in strikeouts (275), innings pitched (292), complete games (29), and shutouts (6). Newhouser finished runner-up in the MVP balloting.

The American League also had its fair share of outstanding offensive performers. Washington's Mickey Vernon led the league with a .353 batting average and 51 doubles, and he finished second with 207 hits. Detroit's Hank Greenberg led the A.L. with 44 home runs and 127 runs batted in, and he finished second with a .604 slugging percentage.

The pennant-winning Red Sox featured the league's top offense. Their .271 team batting average was the highest in the A.L., they scored a league-leading 792 runs (almost 100 more than any other team in the circuit), and they posted the third-highest home-run total (109). Rudy York, acquired from Detroit during the off-season, finished third in the league with 119 runs batted in. Dom DiMaggio placed among the leaders with a .316 batting average. Bobby Doerr hit 18 home runs, knocked in 116 runs, and scored another 95. Johnny Pesky batted .335, scored 115 runs, and led the league with 208 hits. And, of course, there was Ted Williams, who picked up right where he had left off some three years earlier before he joined the war effort. Williams finished second to Greenberg with 38 home runs and 123 runs batted in, he placed second to Vernon with a .342 batting average, and he led the league with 142 runs scored, 156 walks, 343 total bases, a .497 on-base percentage, and a .667 slugging percentage. He was clearly the focal point of the Boston attack and the league's Most Valuable Player.

NATIONAL LEAGUE

After a close, second-place finish the previous year, St. Louis returned to the top of the National League standings in 1946, capturing their fourth pennant in five seasons. Their only competition was provided by the Dodgers, who finished just two games back. The Cardinals' team batting average of .265 was the best in the league, as was their total of 712 runs scored and team earned run average of 3.01.

The St. Louis staff was headed by lefthander Howie Pollet, who finished 21-10 to lead the league in victories. He also led N.L. hurlers with a 2.10 earned run average and 266 innings pitched, and he finished second with 22 complete games. Pollet ended up finishing fourth in the MVP voting, behind the top three offensive players in the league.

Dixie Walker had another outstanding year for second-place Brooklyn, finishing among the league leaders in batting average, runs batted in, and hits. Enos Slaughter had his finest season for the pennant-winning Cardinals, leading the league in runs batted in, and also finishing among the leaders in batting, runs scored, hits, total bases, and slugging percentage. Let's look at the numbers of both Walker and Slaughter, along with those of Stan Musial, the man selected by the baseball writers as the league's MVP:

PLAYER	AB	HITS	RUNS	2B	3B	HR	RBI	AVG	OBP	SLG PCT
Dixie Walker	576	184	80	29	9	9	116	.319	.391	.448
Enos Slaughter	609	183	100	30	8	18	130	.300	.374	.465
Stan Musial	624	228	124	50	20	16	103	.365	.434	.587

Walker knocked in more runs than Musial, but the latter finished well ahead of the Dodger outfielder in every other offensive category. Slaughter played for the same team as Musial, hit two more home runs, and drove in almost 30 more runs. However, Musial finished well ahead of his teammate in every other category. His batting average was 65 points higher than Slaughter's, and both his on-base and slugging percentages were much higher. Musial also scored many more runs and finished with far more doubles, triples, and hits. He led the league in six different offensive categories and played for the pennant-winning team.

It would be hard to find fault with Musial's selection as league MVP.

1947

AMERICAN LEAGUE

New York captured the Ameican League pennant in 1947, finishing 12 games ahead of second-place Detroit and 14 in front of defending A.L. champion Boston. The Yankees did not have any one player that dominated the individual statistical categories, but they were an extremely well-balanced team that led the league in home runs (115), runs scored (794), batting average (.271), and earned run average (3.39). Their pitching staff was led by righthanded starter Allie Reynolds and lefty reliever Joe Page. Reynolds, acquired in an off-season deal with Cleveland for Joe Gordon, finished 19-8, with a 3.20 earned run average and 17 complete games. Page was the league's top relief pitcher, compiling a 14-8 record and a 2.48 earned run average, and leading the A.L. with 17 saves.

The New York offense was led by Tommy Henrich and Joe DiMaggio. Henrich finished second in the league in both runs batted in (98) and runs scored (109), batted .287, and led the league with 13 triples. DiMaggio finished among the league leaders with 20 home runs, 97 runs batted in, 97 runs scored, a .315 batting average, and a .522 slugging percentage. Both men were among the top offensive players in the league.

So, too, were Cleveland's Joe Gordon and Lou Boudreau. Gordon hit 29 home runs, drove in 93 runs, and scored 89 others for the fourth-place Indians, while Boudreau batted .307 and led the league with 45 doubles. Second-place Detroit was led by third baseman George Kell, who batted .320 and knocked in 93 runs.

However, the best player in the American League in 1947 was unquestionably Ted Williams. The Boston outfielder won the second Triple Crown of his career, topping the circuit in seven different offensive categories.

Let's look at his numbers, alongside those of DiMaggio, who was selected as the league's MVP:

PLAYER	AB	HITS	RUNS	2B	3B	HR	RBI	AVG	OBP	SLG PCT
Joe Dimaggio	533	168	97	31	10	20	97	.315	.391	.522
Ted Williams	528	181	125	40	9	32	114	.343	.499	.634

Williams' statistics were much better than DiMaggio's. He finished well ahead of the *Yankee Clipper* in virtually every offensive category, and he was clearly the better player. In what was actually a sub-par year for him, DiMaggio failed to lead the league in any department. Yet, because Williams was at odds with some of the writers, he didn't receive as much support as he should have in the voting. In fact, one Boston writer left him completely off his ballot, thereby denying him the points he would have needed to win the award. Instead, DiMaggio outpolled the more deserving Williams by the slimmest of margins, 202 points to 201.

NATIONAL LEAGUE

The Dodgers claimed their third National League pennant in 1947, finishing five games ahead of the second-place Cardinals and eight games in front of the third-place Braves. Brooklyn was led by outstanding rookie Jackie Robinson and young right-handed pitcher, Ralph Branca. Even though he hit just 12 home runs and knocked in only 48 runs, Robinson had a major impact on his new team. In addition to batting .297, scoring 125 runs, and leading the league with 29 stolen bases, Robinson's speed and aggressiveness brought a new dimension to the Dodgers' attack, and his competitive nature had a positive effect on his teammates. The writers recognized the former Negro League star's contributions to his team by placing him fifth in the MVP voting. Branca didn't finish as high in the balloting, but his statistics were very impressive. He finished 21-12, with a 2.67 earned run average, 280 innings pitched, and 15 complete games.

Even more effective than Branca were Cincinnati's Ewell Blackwell and Boston's Warren Spahn. Blackwell finished 22-8, to lead the league in wins. He also compiled an outstanding 2.47 earned run average and topped the circuit with 193 strikeouts and 23 complete games. Spahn finished 21-10, threw 22 complete games, and led the league with a 2.33 earned run average, 289 innings pitched, and seven shutouts. Still, neither Blackwell nor Spahn was among the top two MVP candidates.

The feeling here is that the two men who deserved the greatest amount of consideration for league MVP were Johnny Mize and Bob Elliott. Mize, playing for the fourth-place Giants, led the N.L. with 51 home runs, 138 runs batted in, and 137 runs scored. Elliott, who was selected by the writers as the league's Most Valuable Player, drove in 113 runs and batted .317 for the third-place Braves.

Let's look at their numbers, along with those of Pirates slugger Ralph Kiner:

PLAYER	AB	HITS	RUNS	2B	3B	HR	RBI	AVG	OBP	SLG PCT
Johnny Mize	586	177	137	26	2	51	138	.302	.384	.614
Bob Elliott	555	176	93	35	5	22	113	.317	.410	.517
Ralph Kiner	565	177	118	23	4	51	127	.313	.417	.639

Kiner was the league's best player. In spite of the fact that he had a weak supporting cast in Pittsburgh, his numbers were actually quite comparable to those compiled by Mize. He hit the same number of home runs, and he finished close to Mize in most other categories. However, it would be difficult to give Kiner serious consideration for MVP honors since the Pirates finished tied for last in the league, 32 games behind pennant-winning Brooklyn.

As a result, we are left with Mize and Elliott. The latter hit for a slightly higher batting average, finished with more doubles and triples, and compiled a slightly higher on-base percentage. However, Mize hit more than twice as many home runs, knocked in 25 more runs, scored 44 more, and finished with a much higher slugging percentage. It would seem that the statistical edge would have to go to Mize. Yet, the writers selected Elliott and placed Mize third in the voting. Perhaps they were influenced by Boston's higher finish in the standings. But the Braves finished third, eight games out, while the Giants were fourth, 13 games back.

The feeling here is that one place and five games in the standings should not have been enough to deter the writers from selecting Mize over Elliott. Johnny Mize should have been the National League's Most Valuable Player in 1947.

1948

AMERICAN LEAGUE

The Cleveland Indians defeated the Boston Red Sox in a one-game playoff in 1948 to capture their first American League pennant since 1920. Both Cleveland and Boston, as well as third-place New York, who finished just 2½ games off the pace, were talented teams that featured several outstanding players who deserved MVP consideration. The Indians' pitching staff included two 20-game winners, and another hurler who won 19. Righthander Bob Lemon finished 20-14 with a 2.82 earned run average, and he led the league with 293 innings pitched, 20 complete games, and 10 shutouts. Lefthander Gene Bearden compiled an outstanding 20-7 record and a league-leading 2.43 earned run average, while throwing 229 innings, 15 complete games, and six shutouts. Bob Feller won 19 games, threw 280 innings and 18 complete games, and led the A.L. with 164 strikeouts.

The Cleveland offense was just as imposing. Shortstop and team manager Lou Boudreau had the finest season of his career, hitting .355 with 18 home runs, 106 runs batted in, and 116 runs scored. Second baseman Joe Gordon hit 32 home runs and knocked in 124 runs. Third baseman Ken Keltner finished among the league leaders with 31 home runs and 119 runs batted in, and batted .297. Outfielder Dale Mitchell finished third in the league with a .336 batting average, and he placed second in the circuit with 204 hits.

Boston also had a powerful offense, with Ted Williams and Vern Stephens supplying much of the firepower. Williams hit 25 home runs, knocked in 127 runs, scored another 124, and led the league with a .369 batting average. Stephens added 29 homers, 137 runs batted in, and 114 runs scored.

New York's attack was led by Joe DiMaggio and Tommy Henrich. DiMaggio led the league with 39 homers and 155 runs batted in, and he also batted .320. Henrich chipped in with 25 homers, 100 runs batted in, a .308 batting average, and a league-leading 138 runs scored and 14 triples.

With so many outstanding candidates, it is difficult to select just one for league MVP. However, the field can probably be pared down to just five. Let's look at their numbers in order to deduce who was most deserving:

PLAYER	AB	HITS	RUNS	2B	3B	HR	RBI	AVG	OBP	SLG PCT
Ken Keltner	558	166	91	24	4	31	119	.297	.395	.522
Joe Gordon	550	154	96	21	4	32	124	.280	.371	.507
Lou Boudreau	560	199	116	34	6	18	106	.355	.453	.534
Ted Williams	509	188	124	**44**	3	25	127	**.369**	**.497**	**.615**
Joe Dimaggio	594	190	110	26	11	**39**	**155**	.320	.396	.598

Keltner and Gordon can be ruled out because, in spite of their exceptional years, neither man was as valuable to the Indians as Boudreau. They both drove in more runs than their teammate, but neither Keltner nor Gordon scored as many times as Boudreau, and the shortstop finished with a much higher batting average and on-base percentage than either of his infield mates. Boudreau's MVP credentials were further enhanced by the fact that he served the Indians as player/manager.

Therefore, we are left with Williams, DiMaggio, and Boudreau. Williams and DiMaggio put up slightly better numbers than Boudreau, and the latter certainly had a great deal of help from his teammates. Yet, the shortstop played the most demanding defensive position of the three men, and he also served as his team's manager. Furthermore, Boudreau proved to be the star of the one-game playoff held between Cleveland and Boston, hitting two home runs during the contest to help deliver the pennant to the Indians.

All things considered, it would be difficult to find fault with the writers' selection of Boudreau over DiMaggio, who finished second in the voting, and Williams, who finished third.

NATIONAL LEAGUE

While Indians fans had to wait 28 years for their team to make it into the World Series, Braves fans had to wait even longer. Having won their last pennant in 1914, it took Boston 34 years to capture their next National League flag. The Braves did so in 1948 by finishing 6½ games ahead of the second-place Cardinals and 7½ in front of the third-place Dodgers.

The Braves were led by their fine pitcher Johnny Sain, who finished 24-15 to top the circuit in wins. He also led N.L. pitchers with 314 innings pitched and 28 complete games, while compiling the third lowest earned run average in the league (2.60). He certainly deserved serious consideration for MVP honors.

Meanwhile, Boston's offense was led by outfielders Tommy Holmes and Bob Elliott. Holmes finished among the league leaders with a .325 batting average, and Elliott hit 23 home runs, drove in 100 runs, batted .283, scored 99 runs, and led the N.L. with 131 walks. Neither man was even among the top three or four offensive players in the league, though.

Johnny Mize had an outstanding year for the fifth-place Giants, who finished 13½ games behind the Braves in the standings. Mize tied for the league lead with 40 home runs, finished second with 125 runs batted in, batted .289, and scored 110 runs. Ralph Kiner had an equally impressive campaign for the fourth-place Pirates, who finished just 8½ games off the pace. Kiner tied Mize for the league lead with 40 homers, drove in 123 runs, and scored another 104. Jackie Robinson was the best player for the third-place Dodgers. He hit 12 home runs, knocked in 85 runs, batted .296, and scored 108 runs. The second-place Cardinals featured Enos Slaughter, who batted .321 and finished with 90 runs batted in and 91 runs scored.

However, the league's top player was Stan Musial. Having his finest all-around season, Musial led the N.L. in nine different offensive categories, and he came within one home run of capturing the Triple Crown. He hit 39 homers and led the league with 131 runs batted in, a .376 batting average, 135 runs scored, 230 hits, 46 doubles, 18 triples, a .450 on-base percentage, a .702 slugging percentage, and 429 total bases.

Although the Cardinals were unable to beat out the Braves for the pennant, their second-place finish was the direct result of Musial's fabulous year. He was clearly the National League's Most Valuable Player.

1949

AMERICAN LEAGUE

The Boston Red Sox came ever so close again in 1949 to capturing the American League pennant, this time being eliminated by the Yankees on the very last day of the regular season. Boston finished just one game behind New York, who finished eight games ahead of third-place Cleveland and 10 games in front of fourth-place Detroit.

The Tigers were led by third baseman George Kell, who led the league with a .343 batting average, and outfielder Vic Wertz, who hit 20 homers, knocked in 133 runs, and batted .304. Cleveland's best players were Dale Mitchell, who batted .317 and led the A.L. with 203 hits and 23 triples, and Bob Lemon, who finished 22-10, with a 2.99 earned run average, 279 innings pitched, and 22 complete games. Yet, none of these players merited serious consideration for MVP honors since both the Red Sox and Yankees had several leading candidates of their own.

Boston second baseman Bobby Doerr hit 18 home runs, knocked in 109 runs, and batted .309. Johnny Pesky batted .306 and scored 111 runs. Dom DiMaggio hit .307 and finished among the league leaders with 126 runs scored and 186 hits. Vern Stephens finished second in the league with 39 home runs, tied for the league lead with 159 runs batted in, batted .290, and scored 113 runs. Righthander Ellis Kinder compiled a 23-6 record, a 3.36 earned run average, 252 innings pitched, 19 complete games, and a league-leading six shutouts. Mel Parnell was even better. The Boston lefthander finished 25-7, with a 2.77 earned run average and a league-leading 295 innings pitched and 27 complete games.

Yogi Berra hit 20 home runs and knocked in 91 runs for New York, while Phil Rizzuto batted .275 and scored 110 runs. Tommy Henrich followed up his outstanding 1948 season with another good year, hitting 24 homers, driving in 85 runs, batting .287, and scoring 90 runs. Vic Raschi won 21 games, threw 274 innings, and completed 21 of his starts. Reliever Joe Page was the team's most valuable player. He appeared in 60 games, finished with a record of 13-8 and an earned run average of 2.59, and saved a league-leading 27 games. New York also received a huge lift midway through the season when Joe DiMaggio returned to the lineup after missing the first three months with a leg injury. In just 76 games and 272 at-bats, he hit 14 home runs, knocked in 67 runs, scored another 58, and compiled a .346 batting average.

Nevertheless, even with all the outstanding performers in the league, one man stood above all others. Ted Williams came within a fraction of a point of winning an unprecedented third Triple Crown by batting .343 and leading the league with 43 home runs and 159 runs batted in. He also led the A.L. with 150 runs scored, 39 doubles, a .490 on-base percentage, and a .650 slugging percentage.

More than anyone, Williams was responsible for keeping the Red Sox in the pennant race until the very last day of the season. Therefore, he was most deserving of the MVP Award he was presented with at the end of the year.

NATIONAL LEAGUE

The National League pennant race was equally competitive in 1949, with Brooklyn edging out St. Louis by just one game. Both the Dodgers and Cardinals had several players who made major contributions to the success of their respective teams. For St. Louis, Howie Pollet finished 20-9, with a 2.77 earned run average and a league-leading five shutouts. Enos Slaughter finished third in the league with a .336 batting average, drove in 96 runs, scored another 92, and led the N.L. with 13 triples. For Brooklyn, rifle-armed outfielder Carl Furillo hit 18 home runs, knocked in 106 runs, and batted .322. Gil Hodges hit 23 homers, drove in 115 runs, and batted .285. In his first big year, Duke Snider hit 23 home runs, knocked in 92 runs, batted .292, and scored 100 runs. But none of those players were among the leading candidates for league MVP honors.

One player who certainly would have been had his team fared a little better in the standings was Pittsburgh's Ralph Kiner. The Pirates slugger led the N.L. with 54 home runs and 127 runs batted in, batted .310, and scored 116 runs. However, Pittsburgh finished sixth, 26 games behind Brooklyn, greatly reducing Kiner's legitimacy as a possible candidate. As a result, the top two contenders came from the league's two best teams. The Dodgers' Jackie Robinson led the league with a .342 batting average, while the Cardinals' Stan Musial finished first in four different offensive categories.

A look at their numbers reveals just how evenly matched the two players were that year:

PLAYER	AB	HITS	RUNS	2B	3B	HR	RBI	AVG	OBP	SLG PCT
Jackie Robinson	593	203	122	38	12	16	124	**.342**	.432	.528
Stan Musial	612	**207**	128	**41**	**13**	36	123	.338	**.438**	.624

Musial led the league in hits, doubles, triples, and on-base percentage, but Robinson was right behind him in every category. The two players were also extremely close in batting average, runs batted in, and runs scored. The only appreciable differences were in home runs, where Musial hit more than twice as many as Robinson, and in slugging percentage, where he finished almost 100 points higher than his rival. However, the Dodger second baseman led the league with 37 stolen bases, and he drove opposing teams crazy with his daring baserunning, thereby making the players around him better. In addition, Robinson was a fierce competitor who inspired his teammates and brought the Negro Leagues' aggressive style of play to the major leagues. The fact that Robinson possessed a number of intangible qualities that simply did not show up in the boxscores certainly enhanced his MVP candidacy. His claim to that honor was further legitimized by Brooklyn's first-place finish. It's an extremely close call, but we'll go along with the writers' selection of Robinson over Musial as the league's Most Valuable Player.

1950

AMERICAN LEAGUE

The Yankees won another close pennant race in 1950, this time finishing just three games ahead of the second-place Tigers, four in front of the Red Sox, and six ahead of the Indians. Cleveland was actually in the process of assembling a team that proved to be New York's primary nemesis over the next several seasons. Featuring a solid pitching staff and a potent lineup, the Indians had already formed much of the nucleus of the team that ended up dominating the American League in 1954. Their top starter was Bob Lemon, who finished 23-11 in 1950 and led the league with 170 strikeouts, 288 innings pitched, and 22 complete games. Centerfielder Larry Doby and young third baseman Al Rosen comprised the middle of the Cleveland lineup. Doby, the American League's first black player, hit 25 home runs, knocked in 102 runs, batted .326, and scored 110 runs. Rosen, in just his second season, led the league with 37 home runs, drove in 116 runs, batted .287, and scored 100 runs.

Second-place Detroit was again led by George Kell and Vic Wertz. The Tiger third baseman finished second in the league with a .340 batting average, knocked in 101 runs, scored 114 others, and led the A.L. with 218 hits and 56 doubles. Wertz hammered 27 home runs, drove in 123 runs, and batted .308.

Boston's lineup was probably the strongest in the league. Rookie first baseman Walt Dropo joined a team that already featured table-setters Dom DiMaggio and Billy Goodman, and sluggers Ted Williams and Vern Stephens. Dropo hit 34 home runs, tied for the league lead with 144 runs batted in, batted .322, and scored 101 runs. Although Williams appeared in only 89 games and accumulated just 334 official at-bats, he managed to slug 28 home runs, drive in 97 runs, score 82 others, and bat .317. Stephens was perhaps the team's most valuable player, hitting 30 home runs and tying teammate Dropo for the league lead with 144 runs batted in. Let's look at the shortstop's numbers, along with those of Phil Rizzuto, Yogi Berra, and Joe DiMaggio—the leading MVP candidates from the pennant-winning Yankees:

PLAYER	AB	HITS	RUNS	2B	3B	HR	RBI	AVG	OBP	SLG PCT
Vern Stephens	628	185	125	34	6	30	144	.295	.361	.511
Phil Rizzuto	617	200	125	36	7	7	66	.324	.418	.439
Yogi Berra	597	192	116	30	6	28	124	.322	.383	.533
Joe DiMaggio	525	158	114	33	10	32	122	.301	.394	.585

Stephens' statistics were as impressive as anyone's on the list, but he finished 25th in the voting for some reason, with a total of only six points. His poor showing perhaps reflected the opinion that many members of the media had of the Red Sox at that time. Boston was considered to have as formidable a lineup as any team in baseball. However, the Red Sox were also thought to be lacking somewhat in the basic fundamentals of the game, and they were generally viewed as being weak defensively. Many of their players were thought to be too concerned with their own numbers to be willing to make the sacrifices necessary to help their team. Players such as Stephens and Ted Williams were thought to be too selfish to do the "little things", such as bunting or hitting behind a base- runner. Whether or not this line of thinking was accurate is certainly very much open to debate, especially since hitters such as Williams and Stephens, or New York's Joe DiMaggio, for that matter, were rarely asked to sacrifice a time at-bat. Nevertheless, that was apparently the thinking of the writers because Stephens received virtually no support, while his New York counterpart, Phil Rizzuto, who epitomized this "selfless" approach to the game, finished first in the balloting.

But, was Rizzuto truly deserving? The *Scooter* certainly had his finest season, establishing career highs in virtually every offensive category. He finished among the league leaders in base hits, runs scored, batting average, and doubles, and he played brilliantly in the field as well. Rizzuto's power numbers and RBI total were not on a par with those of either Berra or DiMaggio, but they weren't expected to be since he was a leadoff hitter. Rizzuto was most definitely the Yankees' offensive catalyst that year, and he provided a spark to the team both in the field and on the basepaths. DiMaggio's overall numbers were better than Rizzuto's, but the centerfielder was nearing the end of his career and he clearly did not contribute to the team in as many ways as he once did.

On the other hand, Yogi Berra was in the early stages of his illustrious career, and he contributed to the Yankees' success in many ways. Firstly, Berra had perhaps the finest all-around season of his career. Although the Yankee catcher eventually went on to win three Most Valuable Player Awards, his numbers were not as good in any of those years as they were in 1950. With 28 home runs, 124 runs batted in, 116 runs scored, and a .322 batting average, Berra had a tremendous year. In addition, he played a position that was even more demanding than the one manned by Rizzuto, and one that was perhaps even more important to the success of the team. It was New York's outstanding pitching that enabled them to finish atop the American League standings several times during the first half of Berra's career. As the team's catcher, it was Berra's responsibility to call a good game and get the most out of his pitching staff. He needed to gain the trust of veteran starters such as Vic Raschi, Allie Reynolds, and Ed Lopat, and he also had to help build the confidence of young Whitey Ford.

Perhaps Berra did not receive enough credit from the writers for the superb job he did in 1950 since it was so early in his career. As a result, he finished just third in the MVP voting. It is also quite possible that Rizzuto received a little more credit than he deserved for the Yankees' successful season, since the writers may have thought that their acknowledgement of the "little things" he did to help the team win demonstrated their knowledge of the game. The fact is, both Rizzuto and Berra had tremendous years and they were equally responsible for New York's successful pennant-run.

Since it is so difficult to judge their respective contributions quantitatively, the feeling here is that the efforts of both players should have been acknowledged by naming them co-winners of the American League MVP Award for the 1950 season.

NATIONAL LEAGUE

Philadelphia's *Whiz Kids* captured the Phillie franchise's first National League pennant in 35 years in 1950, finally prevailing in an extremely close pennant-race. The Phillies' combination of solid pitching, timely hitting, and youthful exuberance helped them to overcome the heavily-favored Dodgers on the next-to-last-day of the regular season, as they edged out Brooklyn by just two games. Youngsters such as outfielders Richie Ashburn and Del Ennis, and pitcher Robin Roberts all performed at an extremely high level. They also added some much-needed enthusiasm to a team that had been stagnant for almost two decades. Meanwhile, catcher Andy Seminick provided veteran leadership. Seminick did a fine job of handling Philadelphia's young pitching staff, while also contributing offensively with 24 home runs and a .288 batting average. Ashburn batted .303, scored 84 runs, led the league with 14 triples, and established himself as one of the finest defensive centerfielders in the game. Ennis hit 31 home runs, batted .311, and knocked in a league-leading 126 runs. They were joined in the Philadelphia lineup by first baseman Dick Sisler, who drove in 83 runs and batted .296. Robin Roberts led the pitching staff with a record of 20-11, an earned run average of 3.02, 304 innings pitched, 21 complete games, and five shutouts.

However, the Phillies player who was recognized by the writers as having had the greatest impact on the team's success was righthanded relief pitcher Jim Konstanty, who was selected as the league's Most Valuable Player. Konstanty appeared in 74, or nearly one-half of his team's games, compiling a 16-7 record and a 2.66 earned run average, and saving a league-leading 22 games. He also threw 152 innings—an inordinately high number for a relief pitcher, even in those days.

Yet, the Phillies were not the only team with legitimate MVP candidates. Jackie Robinson, Gil Hodges, and Duke Snider all had outstanding seasons for the second-place Dodgers. Robinson batted .328, drove in 81 runs, and scored another 99. Hodges hit 32 home runs, knocked in 113 runs, batted .283, and scored 98 runs. Snider had his finest season to-date, hammering 31 homers, driving in 107 runs, scoring 109 others, batting .321, and leading the league with 199 hits. He had to be considered a leading candidate for MVP honors.

So, too, did Stan Musial. Although his Cardinals finished fifth in the league, 12½ games out of first, Musial rivaled Pittsburgh's Ralph Kiner as the finest all-around offensive player in the N.L. He hit 28 homers, drove in 109 runs, scored another 105, and led the league with a .346 batting average and a .596 slugging percentage. Kiner led the league with 47 home runs, and he also finished among the leaders with 118 runs batted in and 112 runs scored. However, the Pirates finished last, 33½ games back, eliminating Kiner from serious MVP consideration.

Therefore, let's look at the numbers posted by Musial, Snider, and Del Ennis, who were the top three candidates for league MVP, along with Konstanty:

PLAYER	AB	HITS	RUNS	2B	3B	HR	RBI	AVG	OBP	SLG PCT
Del Ennis	595	185	92	34	8	31	**126**	.311	.372	.551
Duke Snider	620	**199**	109	31	10	31	107	.321	.379	.553
Stan Musial	555	192	105	41	7	28	109	**.346**	.437	**.596**

Musial finished with the highest batting average, on-base percentage, and slugging percentage, but his numbers were quite comparable to those compiled by Snider and Ennis in every other category. As a result, his team's fifth-place finish prevents Musial from being viewed as the league's Most Valuable Player. The statistics of Snider and Ennis were actually quite similar, with the only major advantages being held by the former in runs scored (109 to 92) and the latter in runs batted in (126 to 107). A valid case could be made for either man, but we'll opt for Ennis since his team won the pennant.

That leaves us with two Phillies—Ennis and Konstanty. While both men had outstanding seasons, neither player was truly dominant. They each led the league in only one major statistical category. Ennis led the N.L. in runs batted in, while Konstanty led the league in saves. In such a situation, preference would ordinarily be given to the everyday player.

However, Konstanty appeared in almost half of his team's games, and he had a hand in 38 of their victories. Therefore, it would be difficult to find fault with his selection as the league's Most Valuable Player.

THE CHANGING FACE OF BASEBALL

The major leagues underwent dramatic changes during the 1950s, seriously disrupting the status quo that had previously remained in effect for so many years. In 1954, the St. Louis Browns moved to Baltimore, where they subsequently became the *Orioles*. Just one year later, a 54-year association ended when the Athletics relocated from Philadelphia to Kansas City. Then, the unthinkable happened at the end of the 1957 season when the Giants and Dodgers both left New York and headed for the West Coast. The Giants settled in the city of San Francisco, while Brooklyn's beloved Dodgers left their disillusioned fans for the bright lights of Los Angeles.

The exodus of these teams from their original cities essentially marked the beginning of the end of the age of innocence in baseball. Patrons of the game subsequently arrived at the inevitable conclusion that the sport was merely nothing more than a business. Fans realized that team owners were more concerned with turning a profit than they were with returning to them the same allegiance they showed their teams.

This period in baseball history also forced most people to reevaluate themselves and their outlook on life, since it was during the decade of the 1950s that the national pastime became increasingly integrated. While Jackie Robinson broke the color barrier in 1947, it was another 10 years before every team in the majors included at least one black player on its roster. The National League was quicker to accept integration than was its American League counterpart. As a result, the senior circuit became the stronger of the two leagues during this period, featuring many of the game's most dynamic and exciting players.

In fact, while Elston Howard, in 1963, eventually became the first black player to win the American League's Most Valuable Player Award, a black player won the National League trophy in eight out of the nine years between 1951 and 1959.

	ACTUAL MVP WINNERS		**SUGGESTED WINNERS**	
	A.L.	**N.L.**	**A.L.**	**N.L.**
1951	Yogi Berra	Roy Campanella	Yogi Berra	Roy Campanella
1952	Bobby Shantz	Hank Sauer	Bobby Shantz	Robin Roberts
1953	Al Rosen	Roy Campanella	Al Rosen	Roy Campanella
1954	Yogi Berra	Willie Mays	Yogi Berra	Willie Mays
1955	Yogi Berra	Roy Campanella	Mickey Mantle	Duke Snider
1956	Mickey Mantle	Don Newcombe	Mickey Mantle	Don Newcombe
1957	Mickey Mantle	Hank Aaron	Mickey Mantle	Hank Aaron
1958	Jackie Jensen	Ernie Banks	Mickey Mantle	Ernie Banks
1959	Nellie Fox	Ernie Banks	Nellie Fox	Hank Aaron

1951

AMERICAN LEAGUE

The Yankees won their third straight American League pennant in 1951, finishing five games ahead of the second-place Indians. However, in capturing his third consecutive league championship, Manager Casey Stengel used a slightly different formula than the one Miller Huggins used in managing New York's *Murderers' Row* squads of the late 1920s, or the one Joe McCarthy employed in capturing four straight world championships between 1936 and 1939. While those teams had solid pitching as well, it was really their powerful offenses that allowed them to dominate the rest of the baseball world. Huggins had Ruth, Gehrig, Lazzeri, Combs and Meusel at his disposal, while McCarthy could always turn to Gehrig, DiMaggio, Dickey and Gordon.

Meanwhile, Stengel had an aging DiMaggio, a budding star in Yogi Berra, a young and extremely talented—but also extremely raw—player in Mickey Mantle, and a group of role players. Phil Rizzuto was the most talented player in that group, which also included the likes of Hank Bauer, Gene Woodling, Billy Martin, and Gil McDougald. Lacking the firepower of some of the Yankee powerhouse teams of the past, Stengel's approach was to build his team around pitching and defense, while also employing a system of platooning, which enabled him to maximize the strengths of the players he had at his disposal. Therefore, while the Yankee teams of this era had stars such as Mantle and Berra on offense, it was really their strong defense and excellent pitching that enabled them to win so many championships.

That fact was most evident in 1951, when New York featured three of the top starting pitchers in the American League. Vic Raschi finished 21-10 with a 3.27 earned run average, and he led the league with 164 strikeouts. Allie Reynolds compiled a record of 17-8, a 3.05 earned run average, 16 complete games, and a league-leading seven shutouts. New York's most effective pitcher was lefthander Ed Lopat, who finished the year with a 21-9 record, a 2.91 earned run average, and 20 complete games.

The team's outstanding trio of starters, solid bullpen, and exceptional defense, combined with Stengel's clever manipulation of several of his players, enabled the Yankees to finish ahead of the Indians, who rivaled New York in talent. On the mound, Cleveland had Bob Feller, who finished 22-8 to lead the league in victories. The Cleveland lineup featured Al Rosen, who hit 24 home runs and knocked in 102 runs, Larry Doby, who hit 20 homers and batted .295, and big first baseman Luke Easter, who clubbed 27 home runs and drove in 103 runs. Yet, none of these men were among the leading candidates for league MVP in 1951.

Someone who was a contender for the award was Chicago outfielder Minnie Minoso, who placed among the league leaders with a .326 batting average and 112 runs scored, while topping the circuit with 14 triples. However, Minoso's MVP aspirations were hurt considerably by Chicago's fourth-place finish, 17 games behind the pennant-winning Yankees.

Ted Williams posted the best offensive numbers of any player in the league. The Boston slugger hit 30 home runs, knocked in 126 runs, scored 109 others, and batted .318. But the Red Sox finished a distant third in the pennant race, 11 games off the pace, preventing Williams from even placing in the top 10 in the MVP voting.

Yankee catcher Yogi Berra was the selection of the writers. Berra put up solid but unspectacular numbers over the course of the season, hitting 27 home runs, driving in 88 runs, scoring 92 others, and batting .294. But the catcher's contributions to the success of the team could not be measured by statistics alone. Berra and Phil Rizzuto were the only players whose names appeared on the Yankee lineup virtually every day. With Mickey Mantle struggling in his first season in pinstripes, and with Joe DiMaggio just a shell of his former self (he hit only 12 home runs, knocked in just 71 runs, and batted only .263 in 415 at-bats in his final big league season), Berra held the Yankees together. He was the team's best player, and he was the one to whom everyone looked in clutch situations.

Berra did a masterful job of handling New York's pitching staff and, in many ways, he established himself as the leader of the team. Therefore, while his statistics may not have been the most impressive in the league, Berra was the Most Valuable Player in the A.L. in 1951.

NATIONAL LEAGUE

One of baseball's all-time great pennant races took place in the National League in 1951, with the Giants and Dodgers battling it out right to the very end. Trailing Brooklyn by 13½ games in early August, the Giants went on to win 37 of their final 43 games to tie the Dodgers on the next-to-last day of the regular season. With both teams winning their final contest, the stage was set for a three-game playoff between the bitter rivals. The Giants won the first game, but the Dodgers came back to take the second contest, creating the dramatic setting for the decisive third game in New York's Polo Grounds. With Brooklyn leading 4-1 heading into the bottom of the ninth, the Giants mounted a rally, scoring one run and putting two men on base with only one man out. Ralph Branca came in to relieve Dodger starter Don Newcombe with the tying run on second base and Bobby Thomson stepping to the plate for the Giants. As they say, the rest is history. Thomson hit Branca's second pitch into the left field stands, winning the pennant for the Giants and sending the Polo Grounds into a frenzy.

With the Giants and Dodgers dominating the baseball headlines for most of the season's final month, it should come as no surprise that virtually all of the leading candidates for National League MVP honors were members of those two teams. Playoff hero Bobby Thomson had an outstanding year for the Giants, leading the team with 32 home runs, knocking in 101 runs, and batting .293. Giants righthanders

Sal Maglie and Larry Jansen tied for the league lead with 23 victories apiece. Maglie finished 23-6, with a 2.93 earned run average, 298 innings pitched, and 22 complete games. Jansen compiled a record of 23-11, with a 3.04 earned run average, 278 innings pitched, and 18 complete games.

Gil Hodges hit 40 home runs for the Dodgers, drove in 103 runs, and scored 118 others. Teammate Jackie Robinson homered 19 times, knocked in 88 runs, batted .338, and scored 106 runs. Don Newcombe finished 20-9, with a 3.28 earned run average and a league-leading 164 strikeouts, while Preacher Roe, with a record of 22-3, led the league with an .880 winning percentage, while also pitching to a 3.04 earned run average.

The top two candidates from the Dodgers and Giants, though, were Brooklyn catcher Roy Campanella and New York leftfielder Monte Irvin. Let's take a look at the numbers of both players:

PLAYER	AB	HITS	RUNS	2B	3B	HR	RBI	AVG	OBP	SLG PCT
Monte Irvin	558	174	94	19	11	24	121	.312	.415	.514
Roy Campanella	505	164	90	33	1	33	108	.325	.393	.590

It's an extremely close call, based strictly on the numbers. Irvin led the league in runs batted in, scored a few more runs than Campanella, collected far more triples, and finished with a slightly higher on-base percentage. But the Dodger catcher had the edge in home runs, doubles, batting average, and slugging percentage. Stan Musial of the Cardinals actually put up better numbers than either man. He hit 32 homers, drove in 108 runs, and led the league with 124 runs scored and a .355 batting average. But St. Louis finished third, 15½ games out of first, making Irvin and Campanella the top two contenders for league MVP honors in spite of Musial's second-place finish in the balloting.

In addition to their outstanding seasons, both players contributed to their respective teams in ways that did not show up in the boxscores. Campanella was a superb handler of pitchers, and he did an excellent job of calling a game. He was also a fine defensive receiver. Irvin was a very good all-around player, but one of his greatest contributions to the Giants that year came off the field. The lack of success experienced by Willie Mays early in the season caused the rookie centerfielder to struggle tremendously with his self- confidence. Mays turned to Irvin and Manager Leo Durocher for emotional support. Durocher treated Mays as if he were his own son, and Irvin, a longtime veteran of the Negro Leagues before he signed with the Giants, kept a watchful eye on the youngster. Considerably older than the 20-year-old rookie, and much wiser in the ways of the world, Irvin looked after Mays. He roomed with him on the road, took him under his wing, and helped to restore the rookie's shattered confidence. As a result, Mays became a primary contributor to the Giants' incredible comeback during the latter stages of the season.

Therefore, even though Irvin finished a distant third in the MVP voting, a strong case could be made for him being the league's Most Valuable Player. Nevertheless, it would be difficult to dispute the decision of the writers. Campanella played the more demanding defensive position of the two men, and he had an outstanding year.

1952

AMERICAN LEAGUE

The Yankees tied their own American League record by capturing their fourth consecutive pennant in 1952, finishing just two games ahead of the hard-charging Indians. New York's offense was led by Yogi Berra and Mickey Mantle, who took over for the retired Joe DiMaggio in centerfield. Mantle hit 23 home runs, knocked in 87 runs, scored another 94, and batted .311. Berra followed up his 1951 MVP season by hitting 30 home runs, driving in 98 runs, batting .273, and scoring 97 runs. Mantle and Berra finished third and fourth, respectively, in the league MVP voting, well ahead of Cleveland's top two offensive performers, Al Rosen and Larry Doby.

Rosen hit 28 homers, led the league with 105 runs batted in, batted .302, and scored 101 runs. Doby led the A.L. with 32 home runs and 104 runs scored, drove in another 104 runs, and batted .276. The numbers compiled by Rosen and Doby were actually slightly better than the figures posted by Mantle and Berra. Furthermore, Cleveland finished just two games behind New York in the standings. Therefore, it is somewhat mystifying that Rosen finished tenth in the MVP balloting, while Doby could do no better than twelfth.

In fact, three other members of the Indians received more support than both Rosen and Doby. Pitchers Bob Lemon, Mike Garcia, and Early Wynn all had outstanding seasons for Cleveland, earning them a great deal of consideration in the MVP voting. Lemon finished 22-11, with a 2.50 earned run average, 28 complete games, and a league-leading 309 innings pitched. Garcia compiled an identical 22-11 record, with a 2.37 earned run average, 292 innings pitched, 19 complete games, and a league-leading six shutouts. Wynn finished 23-12, with a 2.90 earned run average, 285 innings pitched, and 19 complete games. With such impressive numbers, it is difficult to believe that none of the three Tribe hurlers were even among the two best pitchers in the league. But the American League's top two pitchers were New York righthander Allie Reynolds and Philadelphia lefthander Bobby Shantz, who were also the two leading candidates for league MVP honors.

Let's look at the numbers posted by both men:

PITCHER	W	L	ERA	IP	G	GS	CG	SO	BB	SHO
Allie Reynolds	20	8	**2.06**	244	194	29	24	**160**	97	**6**
Bobby Shantz	**24**	7	2.48	279	230	33	27	152	63	5

The statistics of the two pitchers were actually quite comparable. Shantz finished with a better won-lost record, threw more innings, completed more games, and finished with a better strikeout-to-walk ratio. However, Reynolds led the league in earned run average, threw one more shutout, and allowed slightly fewer hits per innings pitched. The most telling number, though, was the percentage of their respective teams' victories that each hurler was able to win. Reynolds, who pitched for a much better team, won 20 games, or 21 percent of the Yankees' 95 victories. Shantz was not as fortunate, since he pitched for the fourth-place Athletics, who won only 79 games. His 24 victories represented 30 percent of his team's wins. In addition, Philadelphia's Shibe Park, where the A's played their home games, was much less of a pitcher's park than Yankee Stadium.

It follows that the earned run average advantage held by Reynolds was basically insignificant, and that Shantz was clearly the more effective pitcher of the two. He was also more valuable to his team. True, Philadelphia finished fourth, 16 games behind New York in the standings. But the A's wouldn't even have finished that high had it not been for Shantz. That being the case, it would be difficult to find fault with his selection as the American League's Most Valuable Player for the 1952 season.

NATIONAL LEAGUE

The Dodgers were able to rebound from their heartbreaking playoff defeat the prior year to capture the National League pennant in 1952. The arch-rival Giants finished second, 4½ games back in the standings. Brooklyn was led by Jackie Robinson, Duke Snider, and Gil Hodges. Robinson hit 19 home runs, drove in 75 runs, and finished third in the league with a .308 batting average and 104 runs scored. Snider hit 21 homers, knocked in 92 runs, and batted .303. Hodges led the team with 32 homers and 102 runs batted in. The Giants' top players were pitcher Sal Maglie and 1951 playoff hero Bobby Thomson. Maglie compiled an 18-8 record and a 2.92 earned run average, while Thomson hit 24 home runs and drove in 108 runs. None of these five men, though, even finished among the top five in the league MVP voting.

The man selected by the writers as the National League's Most Valuable Player was Chicago Cubs outfielder Hank Sauer, who tied Ralph Kiner for the league lead with 37 home runs and led the league with 121 runs batted in. In spite of his impressive power numbers, it is somewhat difficult to defend Sauer's selection since he not only batted just .270 and scored only 89 runs, but his Cubs finished fifth in the league, 19½ games behind Brooklyn. Making his selection even more dubious is the fact that Robin Roberts had a truly magnificent year for the fourth-place Philadelphia Phillies.

Roberts was clearly the National League's best pitcher in 1952. He compiled a brilliant 28-7 record and 2.59 earned run average, and he led the league with 330 innings pitched and 30 complete games. His 28 victories were *10* more than any other pitcher in the league posted, and he led a staff that compiled the lowest team earned run average in the league. In fact, Philadelphia's team mark of 3.07 was almost a-half-a-run per game less than the 3.53 earned run average compiled by league runner-up Brooklyn. With 28 victories, Roberts was responsible for almost one-third of his team's 87 wins. It is true that the Phillies finished just fourth in the National League standings, but they were only 9½ games out of first, 10 games ahead of Sauer's fifth-place Cubs. In addition, Roberts was easily the league's top pitcher, while it is debatable if Sauer was even the top offensive player in the N.L.

Robin Roberts was unquestionably the most dominant player in the league in 1952, and there is little doubt he should have been selected its Most Valuable Player.

1953

AMERICAN LEAGUE

The Yankees established a new major league record by winning their fifth consecutive pennant and world championship in 1953, eclipsing their own mark set from 1936 to 1939. Once again, New York combined solid pitching with timely hitting and strong defense to distance themselves from the rest of the American League. The pitching staff was led by crafty lefthander Ed Lopat, who finished the season with a 16-4 record and a league-leading 2.42 earned run average. Mickey Mantle and Yogi Berra were again the primary threats on offense. In just 127 games and 461 official at-bats, Mantle collected 21 homers and 92 runs batted in, batted .295, and scored 105 runs. Berra led the team with 27 home runs and 108 runs batted in, batted .296, and scored 80 runs. There were several other outstanding offensive performers in the league, though, whose numbers were superior to those compiled by the two New York sluggers.

Outfielder Gus Zernial hit 42 home runs, drove in 108 runs, and batted .284 for the Athletics. However, Philadelphia finished seventh, 41½ games behind New York, ruining any chance he may have had of being considered for league MVP honors. First baseman Mickey Vernon had perhaps the finest season of his career for Washington. He knocked in 115 runs, scored another 101, collected 205 hits, and led the league with a .337 batting average and 43 doubles. But the Senators finished fifth, 23½ games off the pace. Chicago's Minnie Minoso batted .313, both drove in and scored 104 runs, and led the league with 25 stolen bases. The White Sox finished third, 11½ games back, thereby making Minoso a leading candidate. Another contender for the award was Larry Doby, who had another solid season for

Cleveland. Doby hit 29 home runs, knocked in 102 runs, and scored 92 others for the Indians, who finished second, 8½ games behind the Yankees.

However, Doby's teammate, Al Rosen, was unquestionably the American League's Most Valuable Player in 1953. The third baseman dominated the league's offensive statistical categories, coming within one percentage point of winning the Triple Crown. Rosen led the circuit with 43 home runs, 145 runs batted in, and 115 runs scored, and he finished just one point behind Mickey Vernon in the batting race, with an average of .336. Cleveland may have failed to win the pennant, but they finished a very respectable second, and there is no doubt that Rosen was the league's best player.

NATIONAL LEAGUE

The Dodgers won their second straight pennant, and their fourth in seven seasons in 1953, finishing 13 games ahead of the second-place Boston Braves. Brooklyn had the most balanced team in the National League, and the most talented team in baseball. On the mound, there was Carl Erskine, who led the team with 20 wins. The lineup was a veritable collection of All-Stars. Rookie second baseman Jim Gilliam joined Gil Hodges, Pee Wee Reese, and Jackie Robinson to form the best infield in the league. Gilliam batted .278, scored 125 runs, stole 21 bases, and led the N.L. with 17 triples. Hodges hammered 31 home runs, drove in 122 runs, batted .302, and scored 101 runs. The versatile Robinson, who split time between third base and left field to make room at second for Gilliam, knocked in 95 runs, scored another 109, and batted .329.

The Dodger outfield included Carl Furillo in right and Duke Snider in center. Furillo, who probably had a stronger throwing arm than any other outfielder in the game, was the National League's batting champion, hitting a career high .344. He also hit 21 homers and knocked in 92 runs. Snider was Brooklyn's best all-around player. The centerfielder hit 42 home runs, knocked in 126 runs, batted .336, and led the league with 132 runs scored. He and catcher Roy Campanella were both among the leading candidates for league MVP honors.

Let's look at their numbers, along with those of Braves third baseman Eddie Mathews, another top candidate:

PLAYER	AB	HITS	RUNS	2B	3B	HR	RBI	AVG	OBP	SLG PCT
Duke Snider	590	198	**132**	38	4	42	126	.336	.419	.627
Roy Campanella	519	162	103	26	3	41	**142**	.312	.395	.611
Eddie Mathews	579	175	110	31	8	**47**	135	.302	.406	.627

Aside from these three sluggers, there were others that deserved consideration as well. Warren Spahn compiled a 23-7 record for the Braves, led the league with a 2.10 earned run average, and threw 265 innings and 24 complete games. Pitching for the fourth-place Phillies, Robin Roberts tied Spahn for the league lead with 23 victories, compiled a 2.75 earned run average, and led N.L. hurlers with 198 strikeouts, 346 innings pitched, and 33 complete games.

But Snider, Campanella, and Mathews were clearly the three players that deserved the most serious consideration for the coveted prize. Mathews' numbers actually compared quite favorably to those of both Snider and Campanella. He hit the most home runs and triples, and he tied Snider for the highest slugging percentage. He drove in more runs than Snider and scored more times than Campanella. Although he finished with the lowest batting average, Mathews drew the most bases on balls. Therefore, his on-base percentage was better than Campanella's, and only slightly lower than Snider's. Overall, it would seem that Mathews had as good a year as either Snider or Campanella. In addition, when one considers the superior supporting cast that both Dodger players had, it becomes quite evident that Eddie Mathews was the National League's best player in 1953. However, the Braves finished 13 games behind Brooklyn in the standings.

Had they finished a little closer, a stronger case could have been made for selecting Mathews as league MVP. But, with both Snider and Campanella posting numbers that were quite comparable to his, it would be difficult to suggest that Mathews deserved the award more than either Dodger player.

That leaves us with the two Brooklyn sluggers. Campanella led the league in runs batted in, but Snider finished ahead of him in every other offensive category. While the two men were extremely close in most statistical categories, Snider scored almost 30 more runs and out-hit Campanella by 24 points. Statistically, the edge would have to go to Snider. But Campanella played the more demanding position of the two, and, as a catcher, he had a greater overall impact on the game.

He was a tremendous handler of pitchers, and he was more of a team leader than Snider.

Campanella would have to be rated ever so slightly above Snider as the league's Most Valuable Player.

1954

AMERICAN LEAGUE

After three consecutive second-place finishes, the Indians finally overcame the Yankees in 1954, putting together one of the greatest seasons in American League history. Although they were swept by the Giants in four straight games in the World Series, Cleveland's 111 regular-season victories (against only 43 losses) enabled them to finish eight games ahead of New York, in spite of the Yankees' tremendous 103-51 record.

Several players made major contributions to Cleveland's incredible season. The team's pitching staff, which featured three 20-game winners, was headed by Early Wynn and Bob Lemon. Wynn finished 23-11, with a 2.73 earned run average, 20 complete games, and a league- leading 270 innings pitched. Lemon, with a record of 23-7, tied his teammate for the league lead in victories. He also compiled a 2.72 earned run average, threw 258 innings, and led the league with 21 complete games. Cleveland's lineup was almost as impressive. Second baseman Bobby Avila finished second in the league with a .341 batting average and scored 112 runs. Larry Doby led the A.L. with 32 home runs and 126 runs batted in, and he also scored 94 runs. Al Rosen hit 24 homers, knocked in 102 runs, and batted .300.

Yet, Cleveland's lineup was not the most formidable one in the league that year. Although they led the A.L. with 156 home runs, the Indians placed second in runs scored, with 746, and they finished fourth in the league with a team batting average of .262. The most potent offense in the league belonged to the Yankees, who led the A.L. with 805 runs scored and a .268 team batting average, and finished second with 133 home runs. New York's attack was led by Yogi Berra and Mickey Mantle.

Let's look at their numbers, along with those of Doby and Rosen, the Indians' top two offensive threats:

PLAYER	AB	HITS	RUNS	2B	3B	HR	RBI	AVG	OBP	SLG PCT
Larry Doby	577	157	94	18	4	32	126	.272	.368	.484
Al Rosen	466	140	76	20	2	24	102	.300	.412	.506
Yogi Berra	584	179	88	28	6	22	125	.307	.371	.488
Mickey Mantle	543	163	129	17	12	27	102	.300	.411	.525

Rosen played in fewer games than any of the other three players. As a result, his run- production was down quite a bit from the previous season, and he posted lower numbers than the other three men. Mantle knocked in fewer runs than either Berra or Doby, but he scored many more times, collected far more triples, hit a comparable number of home runs, and finished with much higher on-base and slugging percentages. A valid case could certainly be made for selecting him over either Berra or Doby as league MVP. Yet, surprisingly, Berra and Doby finished first and second in the voting, while Mantle finished a distant 15th. Therefore, it is safe to conclude that the writers did not feel Mantle was nearly as valuable to his team as either Berra or Doby, whose numbers were actually quite comparable. The two players drove in almost the same number of runs and finished with almost identical on-base and slugging percentages. Doby hit 10 more home runs and scored a few more runs, but Berra hit for a higher average and finished with more doubles and triples.

It's very close, but we'll go along with the writers' selection of Berra for a couple of reasons. Firstly, he was a catcher, and, as has previously been noted, that is the most demanding position on the field. Even more important is the fact that, even though the Indians had a solid offense, their pitching was actually their greatest strength. While they were outscored by New York by almost 60 runs during the season, the Indians allowed the opposition almost half-a-run per-game less. Their team earned run average of 2.78 was easily the lowest in the league, and it was far superior to the Yankees' team mark of 3.26. Thus, it is fair to say that it was Cleveland's pitching staff that enabled them to finish eight games ahead of New York in the standings. That being the case, it also follows that Yogi Berra, the best hitter in the most potent lineup in the league, was more valuable to his team than Larry Doby, the top hitter in the Cleveland lineup, was to his.

Considering that New York's 103 victories were certainly nothing to scoff at, it would be hard to disagree with the writers' selection of Berra as the league's MVP.

1951-1959

NATIONAL LEAGUE

The Giants replaced the Dodgers at the top of the National League standings in 1954, finishing five games ahead of their crosstown rivals. Both teams featured several outstanding performers. For Brooklyn, Gil Hodges hit 42 home runs, knocked in 130 runs, batted .304, and scored 106 runs. Jim Gilliam batted .282 and scored 107 runs. Carl Furillo hit 19 home runs, drove in 96 runs, and batted .294. Giants outfielder Don Mueller finished second in the league with a .342 batting average, scored 90 runs, and led the N.L. with 212 hits. Lefthander Johnny Antonelli compiled a 21-7 record and led all league pitchers with a 2.30 earned run average and six shutouts. Yet, none of these men were among the leading candidates for league MVP honors.

Someone who was a top contender was the Cardinals' Stan Musial. He finished among the league leaders with 35 home runs, 126 runs batted in, and a .330 batting average, and he led the N.L. with 120 runs scored and 41 doubles. But, with St. Louis finishing sixth, 25 games off the pace, it would be difficult to suggest that he deserved to be named league MVP.

Powerful Cincinnati first baseman Ted Kluszewski was the most imposing hitter in the league. He led the N.L. with 49 home runs and 141 runs batted in, scored 104 runs, and batted .326. However, with the Reds finishing fifth, 23 games out of first, he, too, would be a hard sell.

We have yet to mention the best players on the top two teams, though. New York's Willie Mays and Brooklyn's Duke Snider led their respective teams to first and second place finishes, and were the most complete players in the league in 1954.

A look at their numbers reveals just how outstanding their seasons were, and, also, just how comparable they were:

PLAYER	AB	HITS	RUNS	2B	3B	HR	RBI	AVG	OBP	SLG PCT
Duke Snider	584	199	120	39	10	40	130	.341	.427	.647
Willie Mays	565	195	119	33	**13**	41	110	**.345**	.415	**.667**

Snider and Mays were extremely close in most statistical categories, with the only decided advantage going to the Dodger centerfielder in runs batted in. However, Snider also played in a better hitter's park, in tiny Ebbets Field. While Mays' home park of the Polo Grounds was exceptionally short down the lines, it was cavernous in centerfield and in the power alleys. Furthermore, Mays was a better outfielder and baserunner than Snider, and the Giants won the pennant. He was most deserving of his selection as the National League's Most Valuable Player.

1955

AMERICAN LEAGUE

After a one-year absence from the World Series, New York returned to the top of the American League standings in 1955, beating out Cleveland by three games. The Indians' pitching staff remained the best in the league, with Bob Lemon and Early Wynn again leading the way. Lemon finished 18-10, to tie for the league lead in victories, while Wynn compiled a record of 17-11 and a 2.82 earned run average. However, with both Al Rosen and Larry Doby suffering through sub-par seasons, Cleveland's offense was not nearly as potent as it was the previous few years. Outfielder Al Smith did what he could to pick up the slack, hitting 22 home runs, driving in 77 runs, batting .306, and scoring a league-leading 123 runs. But, in spite of his third-place finish in the MVP balloting, Smith was not even close to being the top offensive player in the league, and the Indians lineup was not nearly the most prolific.

Fourth-place Boston featured one of the top offenses in the league in 1955, with Jackie Jensen and Ted Williams providing much of the firepower. Jensen hit 26 home runs, led the league with 116 runs batted in, and scored 95 runs. In only 98 games and 320 at-bats, Williams finished with 28 home runs, 83 runs batted in, 77 runs scored, and a .356 batting average. Had he been available for more of the season, the Red Sox undoubtedly would have finished higher than they did in the standings. But, with the Sox finishing 12 games back, and with several other viable candidates, it would be difficult to make a case for either Williams or Jensen being the league's Most Valuable Player.

Both Nellie Fox and Billy Pierce had outstanding seasons for the third-place White Sox, who finished just five games out of first. Fox batted .311, scored 100 runs, and collected 198 hits. Pierce finished 15-10 and led the league with a 1.97 earned run average. Whitey Ford had an excellent year for New York. He tied for the league lead with 18 victories (against only 7 defeats), compiled a 2.63 earned run average, and led the A.L. with 18 complete games.

However, none of these men were among the leading candidates for MVP honors. Two of the three men who were played for the pennant-winning Yankees, while the other came from the fifth-place Tigers. Mickey Mantle and Yogi Berra led the New York attack, while Al Kaline had a superb year for Detroit.

Let's take a look at the numbers posted by all three players:

PLAYER	AB	HITS	RUNS	2B	3B	HR	RBI	AVG	OBP	SLG PCT
Yogi Berra	541	147	84	20	3	27	108	.272	.352	.470
Mickey Mantle	517	158	121	25	11	37	99	.306	.433	.611
Al Kaline	588	200	121	24	8	27	102	.340	.425	.546

Mantle and Kaline were extremely close in run-production, with the two men scoring the exact same number of runs and Kaline driving in three more runs. Mantle hit 10 more home runs, but Kaline out-hit him by 34 points. However, Mantle led the league with 113 walks, giving him a slightly higher on-base percentage than Kaline. Mantle also finished with a much higher slugging percentage. Overall, it would seem that Mantle had a slightly better year. In addition, the Tigers finished 17 games behind the Yankees in the standings. Yet, Kaline was *The Sporting News'* selection as the American League's Player of the Year, and he finished a close second to Berra in the MVP voting. Meanwhile, Mantle finished fifth in the balloting.

The comparison of Berra to Mantle isn't nearly as close. Mantle finished well ahead of Berra in every offensive category, except for runs batted in. He probably would have knocked in more runs as well had pitchers been more willing to pitch to him with men on base. But, as was noted earlier, Mantle led the league in walks. He scored almost 40 more runs than Berra, his on-base percentage was some 80 points higher, and his slugging percentage was 140 points better. Mantle was clearly New York's best player, and he was far more deserving than Berra of the league's Most Valuable Player Award. However, at that particular point in time, it appears that Berra may have been given slightly more credit than he deserved for New York's success, while Mantle wasn't being given enough. The centerfielder's fifth-place finish in the balloting was a travesty.

NATIONAL LEAGUE

The National League election for the 1955 season was equally perplexing. Brooklyn captured the pennant, finishing 13½ games ahead of the second-place Braves. The Dodgers' best pitcher was Don Newcombe, who compiled a record of 20-5, with a 3.20 earned run average and 17 complete games. Brooklyn's offense was led by Roy Campanella, who hit 32 home runs and drove in 107 runs, and Duke Snider, who hit 42 homers and led the league with 136 runs batted in and 126 runs scored. There were also several other outstanding performers in the league that year.

Robin Roberts won 23 games for Philadelphia and led N.L. hurlers with 305 innings pitched and 26 complete games. Ted Kluszewski had another huge year for Cincinnati. The big first baseman hit 47 homers, drove in 113 runs, batted .314, scored 116 runs, and led the N.L. with 192 hits. Shortstop Ernie Banks hit 44 home runs, knocked in 117 runs, batted .295, and scored 98 runs for Chicago. However, the Phillies finished fourth, the Reds fifth, and the Cubs sixth, all well out of contention, hurting the chances of all three men of being named league MVP.

Hank Aaron and Eddie Mathews both had excellent years for the second-place Braves. In just his second season, Aaron hit 27 home runs, drove in 106 runs, batted .314, and scored 105 runs. Mathews hit 41 homers, knocked in 101 runs, scored another 108, batted .289, and led the N.L. with 109 walks. Considering his team's second-place finish, Mathews was certainly worthy of serious consideration for MVP honors. Yet, he surprisingly received virtually no support, finishing 18th in the balloting with a total of just six points. Meanwhile, Banks, whose numbers were only slightly better, and whose team finished four places and 12½ games behind Mathews' Braves in the standings, finished third in the voting, with 195 points. Go figure.

Equally puzzling was the writers' selection of Campanella as league MVP. Let's look at his numbers, alongside those of teammate Snider and the Giants' Willie Mays, the other top two candidates:

PLAYER	AB	HITS	RUNS	2B	3B	HR	RBI	AVG	OBP	SLG PCT
Willie Mays	580	185	123	18	13	51	127	.319	.404	.659
Roy Campanella	446	142	81	20	1	32	107	.318	.402	.583
Duke Snider	538	166	126	34	6	42	136	.309	.421	.628

The numbers posted by Mays and Snider were fairly comparable, and, with the Giants finishing third, 18½ games behind the Dodgers, you could make a valid case for choosing Snider, and perhaps even Campanella, over Mays, who finished fourth in the voting. However, it is difficult to explain the writers' selection of Campanella over Snider. Duke finished with better numbers in every offensive category, except batting average. He hit more homers, finished with far more doubles and triples, compiled higher on-base and slugging percentages, knocked in almost 30 more runs, and scored 45 more. In addition, Campanella played in only 123 games, thereby missing more than 30 of his team's games. Yet, he received more votes than Snider, who finished a close second in the balloting.

Snider had to settle for being selected by *The Sporting News* as the league's Player of the Year. But he also should have been named its Most Valuable Player by the BBWAA.

1956

AMERICAN LEAGUE

Cleveland came out second-best to New York for the fifth time in six years in 1956, finishing nine games behind the Yankees, who captured their seventh pennant in eight seasons. Yogi Berra had another outstanding year for the league champions, hitting 30 homers, driving in 105 runs, scoring another 93, and batting .298. Whitey Ford anchored the pitching staff by compiling a 19-6 record and a league-leading 2.47 earned run average, and completing 18 games. Meanwhile, Vic Wertz was the Indians' top player, hitting 32 home runs and knocking in 106 runs.

Among the other leading candidates for league MVP honors was Detroit's Al Kaline, who followed up his superb 1955 campaign with another exceptional season. The Tiger outfielder hit 27 home runs, finished second in the league with 128 runs batted in, batted .314, and knocked in 96 runs.

However, there is little doubt that Mickey Mantle was the American League's Most Valuable Player in 1956. Mantle led not only the A.L., but both major leagues in five different offensive categories in winning the Triple Crown. He finished first with 52 home runs,

130 runs batted in, a .353 batting average, 132 runs scored, and a .705 slugging percentage. Mantle also finished second in the league with a .467 on-base percentage and 112 walks, and fourth in hits, with 188. For his efforts, in addition to being selected the American League's Most Valuable Player, Mantle was named the winner of the Hickock Belt as the Professional Athlete of the Year.

NATIONAL LEAGUE

The pennant race, and the balloting for league MVP, were both much closer in the National League in 1956. Milwaukee closed the gap considerably on Brooklyn, finishing just one game behind the Dodgers in the standings. Cincinnati finished a very close third, just two games off the pace.

In fact, the Reds had the most powerful lineup in baseball that year. Featuring five players who hit at least 28 home runs, Cincinnati established a new National League record by hitting 221 round-trippers. Rookie Frank Robinson led the assault with 38 homers, 83 runs batted in, a .290 batting average, and a league-leading 122 runs scored. He was joined by Ted Kluszewski, who clubbed 35 homers, drove in 102 runs, batted .302, and scored 91 runs. Outfielders Wally Post and Gus Bell added 36 and 29 four-baggers, respectively, and catcher Ed Bailey chipped in with 28.

The second-place Braves also had an impressive lineup that included sluggers Hank Aaron, Eddie Mathews, and Joe Adcock. Aaron hit 26 homers, drove in 92 runs, led the league with a .328 batting average and 200 hits, and scored 106 runs. He finished third in the MVP voting. Mathews clubbed 37 homers, knocked in 95 runs, and scored another 103. Adcock led the team with 38 home runs and 103 runs batted in, and batted .291.

Both the Braves and Reds fell just short, though, as the Dodgers won what turned out to be their last pennant in the borough of Brooklyn. Duke Snider led the offense with a league-leading 43 homers, and also knocked in 101 runs, scored 112 others, and batted .292. However, the Dodgers' dominant player, and the league's Most Valuable Player in 1956, was Don Newcombe. The big righthander finished 27-7, with a 3.06 earned run average, 268 innings pitched, 18 complete games, and five shutouts. Although he led N.L. hurlers in only one major statistical category, his 27 victories were 7 more than any other pitcher in the league compiled, and he finished in the top five in every other category.

In a year that was devoid of any dominating offensive performers in the National League, Newcombe was the league's best player and the logical selection for MVP.

1957

AMERICAN LEAGUE

New York repeated as American League champions in 1957, finishing eight games in front of second-place Chicago. The Yankees were the most well-balanced team in the league, finishing first in batting average (.268), runs scored (723), and earned run average (3.00). In fact, three of the top five earned run averages in the league belonged to members of the New York pitching staff. Former league MVP Bobby Shantz, who was acquired from the Athletics during the off-season, led A.L. hurlers with a 2.45 earned run average, and also compiled a record of 11-5. Tom Sturdivant's record was an impressive 16-6, and he finished second to teammate Shantz with an earned run average of 2.54. Bob Turley compiled a record of 13-6 and finished with the fourth lowest earned run average in the league, with a mark of 2.71. All three men were major contributors to the Yankees' success.

Several players also contributed to Chicago's second-place finish. Lefthander Billy Pierce finished with a record of 20-12, an earned run average of 3.26, and a league-leading 16 complete games. Second baseman Nellie Fox batted .317, scored 110 runs, and led the A.L with 196 hits. Outfielder Minnie Minoso knocked in 103 runs, scored another 96, and batted .310.

However, none of these men merited serious consideration for league MVP honors. Neither did Washington outfielder Roy Sievers, despite his outstanding offensive performance. Sievers led the league with 42 home runs and 114 runs batted in, batted .301, and scored 99 runs. But the Senators finished last, 43 games behind first-place New York, preventing Sievers from being a leading contender for the cherished award.

The Red Sox, though, finished much closer to the Yankees in the standings, and Ted Williams had another exceptional season for Boston. Although limited to 420 official at-bats, the 38 year-old Williams remained a great hitter, smashing 38 home runs, driving in 87 runs, scoring another 96, and leading the league with a .388 batting average. If Boston had not finished 16 games behind New York, Williams' great year might have been able to earn him another MVP Award to put in his trophy case. But Mickey Mantle had an equally impressive season for the pennant-winning Yankees. Mantle followed up his Triple Crown performance one year earlier by hitting 34 home runs, driving in 94 runs, batting .365, and leading the league with 121 runs scored and 146 walks. Mantle accumulated a total of just 474 official at-bats because, as his 146 bases on balls indicate, opposing pitchers just did not want to pitch to him with men on base.

Although the statistics for Williams and Mantle were fairly comparable in 1957, the latter was clearly the more complete player of the two at that particular point in their respective careers. He was much faster than Williams, a better baserunner, and a better outfielder. Mantle's Yankees also won the pennant, further validating his selection as A.L. MVP.

NATIONAL LEAGUE

In 1957, the Braves won their first pennant since leaving Boston for Milwaukee, finishing eight games ahead of the second-place Cardinals. Milwaukee combined solid hitting with the league's deepest pitching staff to capture their first league championship since 1948. That staff was headed by Warren Spahn, who finished 21-11, to lead the league in victories. He also compiled a 2.69 earned run average, threw 271 innings, and led N.L. pitchers with 18 complete games. For his efforts, Spahn was named the winner of the Cy Young Award, presented at that time to the major leagues' most outstanding pitcher. Spahn was joined by Bob Buhl, who finished 18-7 with a 2.74 earned run average, and Lew Burdette, who compiled a record of 17-9 and defeated the Yankees three times in the World Series to bring the world championship to the city of Milwaukee.

On offense, Eddie Mathews hit 32 homers, knocked in 94 runs, batted .292, and scored 109 runs. He and Spahn both deserved consideration for league MVP honors. So, too, did Willie Mays, Ernie Banks, and Stan Musial, all of whom had excellent years for their respective teams.

Mays hit 35 home runs, drove in 97 runs, scored another 112, batted .333, and led the league with 38 stolen bases. However, the Giants finished sixth, 26 games behind the Braves. Banks finished second in the league with 43 homers, knocked in 102 runs, batted .285, and scored 113 runs. But, with the Cubs finishing last, 33 games off the pace, it would be difficult to make a strong case for him.

However, Stan Musial's Cardinals finished second to Milwaukee, and Musial was the primary reason why. He hit 29 homers, drove in 102 runs, and led the league with a .351 batting average. Musial was surrounded by other talented players earlier in his career, and St. Louis was a perennial contender. However, by 1957, players such as Enos Slaughter, Marty Marion, Red Schoendist, and Mort and Walker Cooper were no longer with the Cardinals, and Musial had to shoulder much of the burden alone. Therefore, the Cardinals' second-place finish made him a very strong candidate. The writers felt so, too, placing him a very close second in the voting, with a total of 230 points.

The man who finished just ahead of Musial, with 239 points, was Milwaukee's Hank Aaron. He led the league with 44 home runs, 132 runs batted in, and 118 runs scored, finished fourth in batting with a mark of .322, collected the second most hits (198), and led the N.L. with 369 total bases. It is true that Aaron had a better supporting cast in Milwaukee than Musial had in St. Louis, but he was his team's best player and the primary reason why the Braves were able to capture the pennant.

While Musial out-hit him by almost 30 points, Aaron finished well ahead of the Cardinal great in almost every other offensive category. He was clearly the league's best player in 1957, and the balloting for league MVP should not have been as close as it was.

1958

AMERICAN LEAGUE

The Yankees captured their fourth consecutive American League championship, and their ninth in ten seasons in 1958, finishing ten games ahead of the second-place White Sox. Once again, New York had the most balanced team in the league. They finished first with 164 home runs, 759 runs scored, a .268 batting average, and a 3.22 earned run average. Yogi Berra, with 22 home runs and 90 runs batted in, was a major contributor on offense, while the pitching staff was headed by Whitey Ford and Bob Turley. Ford finished 14-7, with a league-leading 2.01 earned run average and seven shutouts. Turley led A.L. pitchers with 21 victories (against only 7 defeats), compiled a 2.97 earned run average, and led the league with 19 complete games. He was named the major leagues' Cy Young Award winner at the end of the year, and he also finished second in the MVP balloting.

The top players for second-place Chicago were Nellie Fox and Billy Pierce. Fox batted .300 and led the league with 187 hits. Pierce finished 17-11 with a 2.68 earned run average, and tied Turley for the league lead with 19 complete games.

The leading candidates for league MVP, though, were Boston's Jackie Jensen, Cleveland's Rocky Colavito, and New York's Mickey Mantle.

Let's look at their numbers:

PLAYER	AB	HITS	RUNS	2B	3B	HR	RBI	AVG	OBP	SLG PCT
Mickey Mantle	519	158	**127**	21	1	**42**	97	.304	.445	.592
Jackie Jensen	548	157	83	31	0	35	**122**	.286	.398	.535
Rocky Colavito	489	148	80	26	3	41	113	.303	.407	**.620**

There was no appreciable difference in the number of home runs, triples, or doubles compiled by the three players. Jensen led the league in runs batted in, and both he and Colavito finished well ahead of Mantle in that category. However, that was largely because opposing pitchers refused to give Mantle the chance to beat them, as can be evidenced by his league-leading 129 walks. In addition, Mickey compensated for the disparity in runs batted in by finishing with far more runs scored than either Jensen or Colavito. The three men were relatively close in batting average, but Mantle was well ahead in on-base percentage, while Colavito finished with the highest slugging percentage.

Based strictly on statistics, it would seem that Mantle had a slightly better year than either Jensen or Colavito. When you factor into the equation New York's first-place finish, it becomes rather apparent that he should have been named the league's Most Valuable Player. Yet, Jensen, whose Red Sox finished third, 13 games behind New York, was selected league MVP. Colavito, whose Indians finished fourth, 14½ games out of first, finished third in the balloting, while Mantle came in fifth.

Perhaps the writers were hesitant to award Mantle a third consecutive MVP trophy, but he was the most deserving player in the league.

NATIONAL LEAGUE

The Braves repeated as National League champions in 1958, finishing eight games ahead of the second-place Pirates. Once again, Milwaukee's pitching staff was headed by Warren Spahn, who finished 22-11, with a 3.07 earned run average, and a league-leading 290 innings pitched and 23 complete games. Lew Burdette, 1957's World Series hero, finished 20-10, with a 2.91 earned run average, 275 innings pitched, and 19 complete games. On offense, Eddie Mathews hit 31 home runs and knocked in 97 runs, while outfielder Wes Covington, in just 294 at-bats, hit 24 homers, drove in 74 runs, and batted .330.

Bob Friend was Pittsburgh's best pitcher, compiling a record of 22-14, with 274 innings pitched and 16 complete games. Outfielder Bob Skinner batted .321 and drove in 83 runs, while fellow outfielder Frank Thomas was Pittsburgh's most productive hitter. He led the team with 35 home runs and 109 runs batted in, and batted .281. Thomas finished fourth in the MVP voting, just behind the three leading candidates—Ernie Banks, Willie Mays, and Hank Aaron.

Let's take a look at their numbers:

PLAYER	AB	HITS	RUNS	2B	3B	HR	RBI	AVG	OBP	SLG PCT
Willie Mays	600	208	121	33	11	29	96	.347	.423	.583
Ernie Banks	617	193	119	23	11	47	129	.313	.370	.614
Hank Aaron	601	196	109	34	4	30	95	.326	.387	.546

Aaron's team won the pennant, so that was a point in his favor. However, it must also be considered that he had a much better supporting cast in Milwaukee than either Mays had in San Francisco or Banks had in Chicago. Mays put up better numbers than Aaron, but the disparity was probably not great enough to overcome the Giants' third-place finish, 12 games off the pace. However, Banks' numbers were easily the most impressive. The Chicago shortstop finished with the lowest batting average and on-base percentage, and he posted comparable numbers to the other two players in most other categories. But Banks finished with far more home runs and runs batted in, and he compiled a much higher slugging percentage. He led the league in all three categories, while Mays only led the N.L. in one department, and Aaron failed to finish first in any. It is true that the Cubs finished sixth in the standings, 20 games behind the Braves, but they did finish ahead of two other teams, and it is doubtful that they even would have done that without Banks. His numbers were just too outstanding to overlook.

Banks' selection as the league's Most Valuable Player for the 1958 season would be hard to disagree with.

1959

AMERICAN LEAGUE

After two straight second-place finishes, the Chicago White Sox finally overcame New York and captured the American League pennant in 1959. Finishing last in the league with only 97 home runs, sixth in runs scored with 669, and sixth in batting average with a mark of just .250, the White Sox hardly overwhelmed their opposition with a powerful offense. Rather, they managed to prevail in many close games due to their outstanding pitching, excellent defense, and superior baserunning.

Chicago's pitching staff combined for a league-leading 3.29 team earned run average, and veteran righthander Early Wynn was the league's best pitcher. He finished 22-10 for the Sox, with a 3.17 earned run average and a league-leading 255 innings pitched. Wynn was rewarded at season's end by being named the major leagues' Cy Young Award winner.

On offense and in the field, the *Go-Go White Sox*, as they were frequently referred to, were led by the excellent double play combination of Luis Aparicio at shortstop and Nellie Fox at second. Aparicio batted only .257, but he scored 98 runs, led the league with 56 stolen bases, and was considered to be the finest defensive shortstop in the game. Fox hit only two home runs and knocked in just 70 runs, but he batted .306 and finished among the league leaders with 191 hits.

Several players on other teams posted numbers that were far superior to the figures compiled by Aparicio and Fox. Jim Lemon and Harmon Killebrew both put up impressive power numbers for Washington. Lemon hit 33 home runs and drove in 100 runs, while Killebrew tied for the league lead with 42 home runs and knocked in 105 runs. However, the Senators finished last, 31 games back, so neither player could be seriously considered for league MVP honors.

Harvey Kuenn and Al Kaline both had outstanding seasons for Detroit. Kuenn led the league with a .353 batting average, 198 hits, and 42 doubles, and he scored 99 runs. Kaline hit 27 homers, knocked in 94 runs, finished second to Kuenn with a .327 average, and led the A.L. with a .530 slugging percentage. However, their chances were both hurt by Detroit's distant fourth-place finish, 18 games off the pace.

Vic Power batted .289 and scored 102 runs for second-place Cleveland, and teammate Minnie Minoso hit 21 homers, drove in 92 runs, scored another 92, and batted .302. The Indians' most productive hitter, though, was outfielder Rocky Colavito, who tied Harmon Killebrew for the league lead with 42 homers and knocked in 111 runs. With Cleveland finishing just five games behind Chicago in the standings, Colavito was certainly a prime contender for the MVP trophy.

Let's look at his stats, along with those of Aparicio and Fox, the other leading candidates:

PLAYER	AB	HITS	RUNS	2B	3B	HR	RBI	AVG	OBP	SLG PCT
Luis Aparicio	612	157	98	18	5	6	51	.257	.319	.332
Nellie Fox	624	191	84	34	6	2	70	.306	.383	.389
Rocky Colavito	588	151	90	24	0	42	111	.257	.339	.512

With the exception of Colavito's home run and RBI totals, none of the three men posted particularly impressive numbers. Fox's overall numbers were better than Aparicio's, but the shortstop's greatest contributions were made in the field and on the basepaths, where he stole 56 bases. Colavito had much more power than Fox, and he was superior as a run-producer, but the second baseman finished with a much higher batting average and on-base percentage. More importantly, Fox possessed many intangible qualities that did not show up in the boxscores, and he contributed to his team's successful pennant-run in many other ways.

In addition to being a fine fielder and team leader, he provided the perfect complement to Aparicio at the top of the Chicago batting order. The White Sox did not have a great deal of power, and they had to scratch and claw their way to many of the runs they were able to put on the board. Batting number two in the White Sox lineup, behind leadoff hitter Aparicio, Fox was extremely patient at the plate. He took a lot of pitches, giving Aparicio ample opportunity to steal second base. In addition, the lefthanded hitting Fox was quite adept at pulling the ball through the right side of the infield. With Aparicio hitting only .257, compiling an on-base percentage of just .319, and collecting a total of only 29 extra-base hits, it was certainly Fox's patience, bat control, and ability to hit behind the runner that enabled the speedy shortstop to score 98 runs on the season.

Therefore, even though his offensive statistics were far from overwhelming, Fox's overall contributions to the success of his team were considerable. His selection over Aparicio, who finished second in the MVP voting, and Colavito, who finished fourth, was the appropriate one.

NATIONAL LEAGUE

The Dodgers won their first pennant in Los Angeles in 1959, finishing just two games ahead of the defending National League champion Milwaukee Braves. Despite capturing the N.L. flag, the Dodgers were without a truly outstanding MVP candidate. Most of the nucleus of the team that dominated the league for much of the previous ten seasons was gone by 1959. Jackie Robinson, Pee Wee Reese, and Ralph Branca all retired, Don Newcombe was traded away, and Roy Campanella was tragically paralyzed in an automobile accident. Duke Snider, Gil Hodges, and Carl Furillo still remained, but they were all in the twilight of their careers. As a result, the closest thing the Dodgers had to a legitimate MVP candidate was outfielder Wally Post, who hit 19 home runs, drove in 74 runs, scored 93 others, and batted .302. While those numbers were certainly respectable, they were not on a par with those compiled by several other players in the league, whose qualifications would have to be considered far more impressive.

In just his first full major league season, outfielder Vada Pinson had an outstanding year for the Reds, who finished tied with the Cubs for fifth place. Pinson hit 20 home runs, drove in 84 runs, batted .316, led the league with 131 runs scored, and finished second with 205 hits. Orlando Cepeda hit 27 homers, knocked in 105 runs, and batted .317 for the third-place Giants, who finished just four games out of first. Warren Spahn and Lew Burdette both won 21 games for Milwaukee, and Spahn led the league with 292 innings pitched and 21 complete games.

But there were five men who were clearly the most outstanding MVP candidates in the league. Let's look at their numbers to determine who was truly the most deserving:

PLAYER	AB	HITS	RUNS	2B	3B	HR	RBI	AVG	OBP	SLG PCT
Eddie Mathews	594	182	118	16	8	**46**	114	.306	.391	.593
Hank Aaron	629	**223**	116	46	7	39	123	**.355**	.406	**.636**
Willie Mays	575	180	125	43	5	34	104	.313	.385	.583
Ernie Banks	589	179	97	25	6	45	**143**	.304	.379	.596
Frank Robinson	540	168	106	31	4	36	125	.311	.397	.583

The Cubs finished tied for fifth in the league, 13 games out of first, thereby finishing seven games closer in the pennant race than they did the previous season. Ernie Banks had another huge year, leading the league with 143 runs batted in, and finishing second with 45 home runs. However, unlike the previous year, when his statistics were overwhelmingly superior to those of any other player in the league, the shortstop's numbers weren't much better than the figures posted by the other four men listed above.

Robinson's Reds finished tied with the Cubs for fifth place, and the Cincinnati outfielder's numbers were almost as good as those compiled by Banks. Yet, for some reason, while Banks was selected MVP of the league, Robinson finished ninth in the balloting.

Mays' overall numbers were also almost as impressive as those posted by Banks, with the latter's biggest edge being his league-leading RBI total. Yet, Mays scored many more runs, making the two men almost equal as run-producers. With the Giants finishing third, only four games behind the first-place Dodgers, a legitimate case could be made for selecting Mays over Banks. However, Willie finished just sixth in the voting.

Since Mathews and Aaron were teammates, they undoubtedly took some votes away from each other. Mathews finished second in the voting, and Aaron came in third. However, the Braves finished second, just two games behind the Dodgers, and both men had tremendous years. Mathews led the league in home runs and posted numbers that were extremely comparable to those put up by Banks. While the latter drove in 30 more runs, Mathews scored 20 more times, and their stat-line was almost identical in virtually every other category. Therefore, the Braves' slugger probably would have been a better choice for MVP.

However, even more deserving was Aaron. While Banks hit a few more homers and knocked in 20 more runs, Aaron scored 20 more times and compiled better numbers in every other statistical category. He led the league in three different departments and finished with a much higher batting average, on-base percentage, and slugging percentage than Banks. With his team barely losing out to the Dodgers, Aaron clearly should have been the writers' selection as the National League's Most Valuable Player in 1959.

EXPANSION HITS THE MAJORS

After having endured for almost 60 years with 16 teams, the major leagues expanded for the first time in 1961. Two new American League franchises were established, with one of those being the Angels, who were awarded to the city of Los Angeles. With team owner Calvin Griffith moving the original Washington Senators franchise to the city of Minnesota and renaming it the *Twins*, a new Senators franchise was established in the city of Washington. One year later, the National League followed suit, adding two new teams to its membership. Having lost both the Giants and Dodgers to the state of California just a few years earlier, the National League fans of New York, who never even considered rooting for the hated Yankees, hungered for the creation of a new team to represent them. Their wishes were fulfilled in 1962, when the New York Metropolitans joined the fraternity of National League clubs. The Houston Colt 45s, who were later renamed the *Astros*, were also added to the league's roster of teams.

Thus, in just two short years, the major leagues expanded from 16 to 20 teams. The four new franchises enabled a greater number of marginal pitchers to make it onto big league rosters. The end result was increased offensive productivity by most of the game's better hitters, and the compilation of some extremely impressive offensive numbers. The size of the strike zone was increased in 1963, shifting the balance of power back to the pitchers. But, in each of the prior two seasons, the pool of legitimate MVP candidates was comprised almost entirely of hitters.

	ACTUAL MVP WINNERS		SUGGESTED WINNERS	
	A.L.	**N.L.**	**A.L.**	**N.L.**
1960	Roger Maris	Dick Groat	Roger Maris	Hank Aaron/
				Eddie Mathews
1961	Roger Maris	Frank Robinson	Mickey Mantle	Frank Robinson
1962	Mickey Mantle	Maury Wills	Mickey Mantle	Willie Mays
1963	Elston Howard	Sandy Koufax	Elston Howard	Sandy Koufax

1960

AMERICAN LEAGUE

New York rebounded from a disappointing 1959 season to return to the top of the American League standings in 1960, finishing eight games in front of the second-place Baltimore Orioles. The Yankees infield was the best in the league, and its top two players were first baseman Moose Skowron and shortstop Tony Kubek. Skowron hit 26 home runs, knocked in 91 runs, and led the team with a .309 batting average. Kubek hit a career-high 14 homers, drove in 62 runs, scored 77 others, batted .273, and provided excellent defense up the middle. Yet, neither player could be seriously considered for MVP honors.

The runner-up Orioles had a viable candidate in Brooks Robinson, who knocked in 88 runs, batted .294, and led league third basemen in fielding. Although teammate Jim Gentile hit 21 home runs and drove in 98 runs in only 384 at-bats, Robinson was clearly Baltimore's best player, and he was the one most responsible for the team's strong showing. He finished a close third in the MVP voting.

The men who finished just ahead of Robinson were New York sluggers Mickey Mantle and Roger Maris. The latter was obtained from Kansas City for four players prior to the start of the season in the hope that he would provide the Yankees with another powerful bat in the middle of their lineup. Maris gave the Yankees everything they wanted, and more. In his first season in pinstripes, the lefthanded slugger led the American League in runs batted in, and he finished a close second to Mantle in home runs. Hitting fourth in New York's lineup, immediately behind Mantle, Maris also provided ample protection for the veteran centerfielder, helping him to improve greatly on the numbers he compiled the previous year.

A look at the statistics of both men reveals that the two players were quite evenly matched:

PLAYER	AB	HITS	RUNS	2B	3B	HR	RBI	AVG	OBP	SLG PCT
Mickey Mantle	527	145	119	17	6	40	94	.275	.402	.558
Roger Maris	499	141	98	18	7	39	112	.283	.374	.581

Mantle scored about 20 more runs and finished with a higher on-base percentage, but Maris knocked in approximately 20 more runs and compiled a higher slugging percentage. Their statistics were almost identical in every other category.

There really was very little separating the two men, and it would have been just as easy to name Mantle MVP. The writers gave Maris a total of 225 points, to Mantle's total of 222. We will not argue with their decision here. The Yankees failed to win the pennant for the first time in five seasons in 1959, but their new rightfielder's exceptional all-around play helped them return to the Fall Classic in 1960. Although Maris was known mostly for hitting home runs and driving in runs, he excelled in many aspects of the game. An outstanding outfielder, Maris possessed good speed and a strong throwing arm. In fact, he won a Gold Glove for his excellent outfield play in 1960. Maris also made a strong impression on his teammates with his aggressive baserunning, and with his ability to break up the double play at second base.

NATIONAL LEAGUE

While Maris and Mantle were clearly the top two candidates for A.L. MVP in 1960, there were several legitimate contenders for the National League honor. The Pittsburgh Pirates captured their first pennant in 35 years in 1960, finishing seven games ahead of the Milwaukee Braves, who came in second for the second consecutive season. The Pirates did not have any one player whose numbers were particularly overwhelming, but there were a number of men who contributed greatly to their success.

Vernon Law led the Pittsburgh pitching staff with a record of 20-9, a 3.08 earned run average, 271 innings pitched, and a league-leading 18 complete games. He was named the winner of the Cy Young Award at season's end. Roberto Clemente batted .314, led the team with 94 runs batted in, and played a brilliant right field. Third baseman Don Hoak drove in 79 runs, batted .282, and led the team with 97 runs scored. He finished second in the MVP balloting to teammate Dick Groat. The Pittsburgh shortstop led the league with a .325 batting average and provided considerable on-field leadership to his young Pirates teammates.

However, there were several other players in the league whose numbers were far more impressive than any member of the pennant-winning Pirates.

Let's look at their statistics, alongside those of Hoak, Groat, and Clemente:

PLAYER	AB	HITS	RUNS	2B	3B	HR	RBI	AVG	OBP	SLG PCT
Don Hoak	553	156	97	24	9	16	79	.282	.368	.445
Dick Groat	573	186	85	26	4	2	50	.325	.372	.394
Roberto Clemente	570	179	89	22	6	16	94	.314	.360	.458
Eddie Mathews	548	152	108	19	7	39	124	.277	.401	.551
Hank Aaron	590	172	102	20	11	40	126	.292	.359	.566
Ken Boyer	552	168	95	26	10	32	97	.304	.373	.562

Groat's numbers were actually the least impressive of the three Pittsburgh players. He finished with the highest batting average and on-base percentage, and he compiled the most doubles, but he hit only two home runs, drove in just 50 runs, and posted a much lower slugging percentage than either of his teammates. Groat was one of Pittsburgh's team leaders, but he had limited range at shortstop and he was not nearly as good an all-around player as Clemente. Yet, the rightfielder finished just eighth in the balloting, well behind Groat, Hoak, and Pirates pitcher Vernon Law. Clemente was clearly not a favorite of the writers.

Cardinals third baseman Ken Boyer put up even better numbers than Clemente, and he finished well ahead of Groat in most offensive categories. Boyer hit 32 homers, drove in almost twice as many runs as the Pirates shortstop, scored 10 more runs, and compiled a slugging percentage that was almost 200 points higher. St. Louis finished third in the league, nine games behind Pittsburgh, and, with Stan Musial nearing the end of his career, Boyer was the Cardinals' best player and team leader. Yet, he could do no better than sixth in the voting.

Even more disturbing were the poor showings of Mathews and Aaron, who finished tenth and eleventh, respectively, in the balloting. The two Milwaukee sluggers were the most productive hitters in the league. They finished first and second in runs batted in, second and third in home runs, and were also among the leaders in runs scored. Mathews drew 111 bases on balls and also finished among the league leaders with a .401 on-base percentage. With the Braves finishing second to the Pirates, it is inexplicable that both Aaron and Mathews did not receive more support. One or the other should have been named the league's Most Valuable Player.

With the two men posting numbers that were remarkably similar, we won't try to choose between them here. Instead, we'll give them each a share of the trophy.

1961

AMERICAN LEAGUE

If 1968 eventually became known as *The Year of the Pitcher*, then 1961 could just as easily be referred to as *The Year of the Hitter*. With the American League expanding to 10 teams, a far greater number of marginal pitchers received employment at the major league level. The result was an overall increase in offensive productivity, and the posting of some huge offensive numbers. Harmon Killebrew hit 46 home runs and knocked in 122 runs for the seventh-place Twins. Playing for the third-place Orioles, Jim Gentile slugged 46 homers, finished second in the league with 141 runs batted in, and batted .302. Both Rocky Colavito and Norm Cash had monstrous years for the second-place Tigers, who finished eight games behind the pennant-winning Yankees. Colavito hammered 45 homers, drove in 140 runs, scored another 129, and batted .290. Cash hit 41 round-trippers, knocked in 132 runs, scored 119 others, and led the league with a .361 batting average and 193 hits.

But the two most dominant players in the league were Mickey Mantle and Roger Maris, who played on baseball's dominant team— the New York Yankees. Still seething after their 1960 World Series defeat at the hands of the Pittsburgh Pirates, who New York outscored by a two-to-one margin over the course of the seven games, the Yankees took out their anger on the rest of the baseball world. First, they ravaged the American League during the regular season, compiling a record of 109-53, and establishing in the process a new major league record by hitting 240 home runs. They then trampled the Cincinnati Reds in the World Series, four games to one.

However, it should be noted that, while Mantle and Maris received most of the notoriety, the two sluggers received ample support from their Yankees teammates. Moose Skowron hit 28 home runs and drove in 89 runs. Elston Howard hit 21 four-baggers, knocked in 77 runs, and hit a career-high .348. Yogi Berra hit 22 homers in only 395 at-bats, and third-string catcher Johnny Blanchard hit 21 homers and knocked in 54 runs in only 243 at-bats.

The Yankees also had the best pitching in the league. Their staff was headed by Whitey Ford, who finished with a phenomenal 25-4 record, to lead the league in victories. He also led the circuit with 283 innings pitched, compiled a 3.21 earned run average, and struck out 209 batters. Ralph Terry compiled a record of 16-3 and a 3.15 earned run average, while Bill Stafford finished second in the league with a 2.68 earned run average and also won 14 games. New York even had the best relief pitcher in the league. Luis Arroyo appeared in a league-leading 65 games, compiled a record of 15-5 and a 2.19 earned run average, and led the A.L. with 29 saves.

But it was really the combination of Mantle and Maris, as well as their pursuit of Babe Ruth's home run record, that drove the Yankees to the pennant and made them the great team they were.

A look at their numbers reveals just how dominant they were:

PLAYER	AB	HITS	RUNS	2B	3B	HR	RBI	AVG	OBP	SLG PCT
Mickey Mantle	514	163	**132**	16	6	54	128	.317	.452	**.687**
Roger Maris	590	159	**132**	16	4	**61**	**142**	.269	.376	.620

Maris led the league in home runs and runs batted in, but Mantle wasn't far behind him in either category. They tied for the league lead in runs scored, and Mantle's .687 slugging percentage led the American League. In an extremely close vote, the writers selected Maris over Mantle as the league's Most Valuable Player, 202 points to 198. But, was he really more valuable? True, Maris established a new major league home run record and drove in 14 more runs than his teammate, but Mantle out-hit him by almost 50 points and finished with an on-base percentage that was some 75 points higher and a slugging percentage that was almost 70 points better. Mantle also led the league with 126 walks. In short, as great as Maris was, Mantle was even better.

Furthermore, Maris would never have been able to accomplish the things he did if he didn't have Mantle hitting behind him. Pitchers were more afraid of Mantle than they were of Maris. As a result, the latter did not receive one intentional walk all year. In addition, both Maris and the Yankees struggled during the season's first month. Maris hit only one home run through the end of April, as the team hovered around the .500-mark. During that period, it was Mantle who carried the team, enabling the Yankees to stay close to the first-place Tigers. When Maris and the rest of the team finally righted themselves, they were within striking distance of Detroit primarily because of Mantle.

In spite of Roger Maris' great accomplishment in 1961, Mickey Mantle should have been named the league's Most Valuable Player.

NATIONAL LEAGUE

The National League also featured several outstanding hitting performances in 1961. Roberto Clemente had an exceptional season for the sixth-place Pirates, hitting 23 home runs, driving in 89 runs, scoring another 100, and leading the league with a .351 batting average. Ken Boyer hit 24 homers, knocked in 95 runs, scored 109 others, and batted .329 for the fifth-place Cardinals. Hank Aaron, whose Braves finished fourth, hit 34 homers, drove in 120 runs, batted .327, and scored 115 runs. All three players finished in the top ten in the league MVP voting.

So, too, did Orlando Cepeda and Willie Mays of the third-place Giants. Both sluggers put up numbers that compared favorably to those compiled by any other player in the league. Cepeda led the N.L. with 46 home runs and 142 runs batted in, scored 105 runs, and batted .311. Mays hit 40 homers, knocked in 123 runs, batted .308, and led the league with 129 runs scored.

Finishing just out of the top ten in the balloting was Wally Moon, who was the second-place Dodgers' leading candidate. Moon hit 17 homers, drove in 88 runs, batted .328, and led the league with a .438 on-base percentage.

The pennant-winning Reds, who finished four games ahead of the Dodgers, placed four players in the top ten of the voting. Lefthander Jim O'Toole won 19 games and came in tenth, while righthander Joey

Jay led the N.L. with 21 victories and finished fifth in the balloting. Centerfielder Vada Pinson received the third highest vote total for finishing second in the league with a .343 batting average, scoring 101 runs, and leading the N.L. with 208 hits. But the league's Most Valuable Player was Frank Robinson, who led the Reds to their first pennant since 1940 with his brilliant play and fierce competitive spirit. Robinson finished among the league leaders with 37 home runs, 124 runs batted in, a .323 batting average, 117 runs scored, 22 stolen bases, and a .411 on-base percentage. He also led the N.L. with a .611 slugging percentage.

Looking beyond sheer numbers, Robinson was Cincinnati's team leader and one of the league's most aggressive baserunners, well known for his ability to break up the doubleplay.

1962

AMERICAN LEAGUE

Although the Yankees repeated as American League champions in 1962, they failed to dominate the rest of the league the way they did the previous year, finishing just five games ahead of the second-place Twins. Minnesota was led by sluggers Harmon Killebrew and Bob Allison, both of whom had extremely productive seasons. Killebrew led the league with 48 home runs and 126 runs batted in, and Allison hit 29 homers, drove in 102 runs, and scored another 102. However, with Killebrew batting only .243 and scoring just 85 runs, and with Allison hitting only .266, neither Twin could be seriously considered for MVP honors.

The same could be said for Minnesota's top two pitchers, both of whom had very solid seasons. Camilo Pascual finished 20-11 and led the league with 206 strikeouts, 18 complete games, and five shutouts. Jim Kaat finished 18-14 and tied Pascual for the league lead in shutouts.

Leon Wagner had an extremely productive year for the third-place Angels, hitting 37 home runs and knocking in 107 runs. Rocky Colavito put up equally impressive numbers for the fourth-place Tigers, hitting 37 homers and driving in 112 runs. However, the Angels finished 10 games off the pace, and the Tigers finished 10½ back. Also, Wagner batted just .268, while Colavito's average was only

.273. Therefore, it would be difficult to make a valid case for either man being the league's Most Valuable Player.

But, what of the pennant-winning Yankees? Surely they had at least one leading candidate. Well, righthander Ralph Terry, who surrendered Bill Mazeroski's World Series clinching home run just two years earlier, led the American League with 23 victories and 298 innings pitched. However, with an earned run average of 3.19 and only 14 complete games, his performance could hardly be described as dominant. Whitey Ford compiled a record of 17-8 and a 2.90 earned run average, but he had other seasons in which he was far more effective.

That leaves us with Mickey Mantle and Bobby Richardson—the top two vote-getters in the MVP balloting.

A look at their numbers is most revealing:

PLAYER	AB	HITS	RUNS	2B	3B	HR	RBI	AVG	OBP	SLG PCT
Mickey Mantle	377	121	96	15	1	30	89	.321	.488	.605
Bobby Richardson	692	209	99	38	5	8	59	.302	.338	.406

There are stark contrasts in the numbers posted by the two players. In 315 more official at-bats, Richardson collected almost twice as many hits and finished with far more doubles and triples. However, Mantle hit many more home runs, drove in far more runs, and compiled much higher on-base and slugging percentages. The only categories in which the teammates were fairly close were runs scored and batting average.

In spite of Mantle's vastly superior power numbers and on-base percentage, the first inclination is to go with Richardson because he was on the field much more than Mantle. The second baseman appeared in every game for New York, establishing a new club record in the process by totaling 692 official at-bats. He led the A.L. in hits, and he was one of the league's most durable players. Meanwhile, Mantle appeared in only 123 games, collecting just 377 official at-bats.

However, not shown in the numbers above are the walks compiled by the two players. Richardson, who hardly ever walked, drew only 37 bases on balls, while Mantle walked 122 times. That means Mantle essentially drew one walk per-game. As a result, he was able to lead the league with a .488 on-base percentage—a figure *150* points higher than the one compiled by Richardson. If one were to add Mantle's walks (122) to his hits (121), the total would amount to 243. Adding the same figures for Richardson results in a total of 246. Therefore, even though he appeared in almost 40 fewer games than Richardson, compiling 315 fewer official at-bats in the process, Mantle actually reached base only three fewer times.

It follows that, in spite of the fact that Richardson was far more durable than Mantle, appearing in many more games and collecting almost twice as many hits during the season, Mantle had a far more productive year. He was clearly New York's best player and was, therefore, most deserving of the MVP Award presented to him at season's end.

NATIONAL LEAGUE

The National League featured a three-team pennant race in 1962, between San Francisco, Los Angeles, and Cincinnati. With the Reds being eliminated in the season's final week, the Giants and Dodgers were left to battle it out right to the very end. In fact, since both teams concluded the regular season with identical 101-61 records, the two teams were forced to play a three-game playoff to determine the eventual champion. As was the case 11 years earlier when the arch-rivals last met in a three-game playoff, the Giants prevailed, thereby earning the right to represent the National League in the World Series.

There were several players who contributed greatly to the success of each of the pennant contenders, many of whom were pitchers. For Cincinnati, Bob Purkey finished 23-5, with a 2.81 earned run average, 288 innings pitched, and 18 complete games. Jack Sanford and Juan Marichal both had excellent seasons for the Giants. Sanford finished second in the league with 24 victories (against only 7 defeats), and threw 265 innings. Marichal had his first big year for San Francisco, finishing 18-11, with 262 innings pitched and 18 complete games. Sandy Koufax was extremely effective for the Dodgers, compiling a record of 14-7, leading the league with a 2.54 earned run average, and striking out 216 batters in only 184 innings of work. But the National League's best pitcher in 1962 was Koufax's teammate with the Dodgers, Don Drysdale. The big righthander led the league with 25 wins (against 9 losses), compiled a 2.83 earned run average, and led N.L. pitchers with 232 strikeouts and 314 innings pitched.

However, with two new expansion teams entering the league, most of the leading MVP candidates were offensive players. Vada Pinson hit 23 homers, knocked in 100 runs, scored another 107, and batted .292 for the third-place Reds. Frank Howard slugged 31 homers, drove in 119 runs, and batted .296 for the runner-up Dodgers. Even more effective was Hank Aaron, who had a brilliant year for Milwaukee. Aaron finished among the league leaders with 45 home runs, 128 runs batted in, 127 runs scored, and a .323 batting average. Unfortunately for Hank, the Braves finished fifth, 15½ games back, eliminating any chance he may have had of being selected league MVP.

Each of the top three teams had at least one leading candidate. The Reds had Frank Robinson. The Dodgers had Maury Wills and Tommy Davis. And the Giants had Willie Mays.

Let's take a look at the numbers posted by all four men:

PLAYER	AB	HITS	RUNS	2B	3B	HR	RBI	AVG	OBP	SLG PCT
Tommy Davis	665	230	120	27	9	27	153	.346	.379	.535
Maury Wills	695	208	130	13	10	6	48	.299	.349	.373
Willie Mays	621	189	130	36	5	49	141	.304	.385	.615
Frank Robinson	609	208	134	51	2	39	136	.342	.424	.624

A valid case could be made for any of the four men. Davis had a spectacular year, leading the league in batting, base hits, and runs batted in. Although Wills' overall numbers were not as impressive as those amassed by the other three men, he was the catalyst of the Dodgers' offense, establishing a new major league record by stealing 104 bases. Mays led the league in homers, finished second in runs batted in, and tied for second in runs scored. With the possible exception of Robinson, who led the N.L. in four different offensive categories and finished in the top five in four others, Mays was the league's best all-around player. After all, much of the credit for Tommy Davis' league-leading total of 153 runs batted in has to go to Maury Wills. The Dodgers' leadoff hitter was constantly in scoring position for his team's number three batter. Furthermore, even though he led the league in batting, Davis hardly ever walked. Therefore, both Mays and Robinson finished with higher on-base percentages.

As for Wills, he was most certainly the catalyst of the Dodgers' offense, and, with 104 steals, 208 hits, and 130 runs scored, he was well-deserving of serious consideration for MVP honors. However, with only six home runs, 48 runs batted in, and 13 doubles, his overall numbers were dwarfed by those of both Mays and Robinson. In addition, his on-base percentage was some 35 points lower than the mark posted by Mays, and 75 points less than Robinson's figure, while his slugging percentage was some 250 points lower than the figures compiled by both sluggers. Thus, while the writers' selection of Wills was not a particularly bad one, it was not the one that should have been made.

The National League's Most Valuable Player for the 1962 season should have been either Willie Mays or Frank Robinson. The latter actually put up slightly better numbers than he did in his MVP season of 1961. However, his team won the pennant that year. In 1962, they finished a close third.

Willie Mays, whose Giants won the league championship, would have been the best choice for MVP.

1963

AMERICAN LEAGUE

The Yankees captured their fourth consecutive American League pennant in 1963, finishing 10½ games in front of the second-place White Sox, and 13 games ahead of the third-place Twins. Interestingly, even though they ran away with the A.L. flag, New York did not possess either the best offense in the league, or the best pitching staff.

The league's best offense belonged to the Minnesota Twins, who led the A.L. with 767 runs scored, 225 home runs, and a .255 team batting average. Their attack was led by Harmon Killebrew, Bob Allison, and rookie centerfielder, Jimmie Hall. Although he batted only .258, Killebrew led the league with 45 home runs and knocked in 96 runs. Allison hit 35 homers, drove in 91 runs, batted .271, and led the league with 99 runs scored. Hall slugged 33 homers, knocked in 80 runs, and scored another 88.

The runner-up White Sox had the best pitching in the league. Combining for a league-leading team earned run average of 2.97, the Sox staff was headed by lefthanders Gary Peters and Juan Pizarro. Peters finished 19-8 with a league-leading 2.33 earned run average, and Pizarro finished second to his teammate with a 2.39 earned run average, while compiling a record of 16-8.

The Detroit Tigers had the best all-around player in the league. Al Kaline hit 27 home runs, finished second in the A.L. with 101 runs batted in, and also placed second with a .312 batting average. However, with Detroit finishing a distant fifth, 25 games off the pace, it would be difficult to select him as the league's Most Valuable Player.

As a result, we must look to pennant-winning New York for a viable candidate. While they possessed neither the league's top offense nor the circuit's best pitching, the Yankees were clearly the most well-balanced team in the A.L. They finished second in homers (188), runs scored (714), batting average (.252), and earned run average (3.07). Their pitching staff featured Jim Bouton, Al Downing, and Whitey Ford. Bouton, in his first full season, compiled a record of 21-7, with a 2.53 earned run average and 249 innings pitched. Downing, also in his first full year, finished 13-5, with a 2.56 earned run average and 171 strikeouts in only 175 innings of work. Ford was the ace of the staff. His record of 24-7 was the best in the American League, he compiled a 2.74 earned run average, and he threw a league-leading 269 innings. He certainly had to be considered a leading candidate for MVP honors.

On offense, New York was led by first baseman Joe Pepitone, outfielder Tom Tresh, and catcher Elston Howard. Pepitone hit 27 homers and knocked in 89 runs. Tresh hit 25 home runs and finished third in the league with 91 runs scored. Howard finished fifth in the league with 28 homers, drove in 85 runs, and batted .287.

In spite of those fairly modest numbers, the Yankee catcher was selected by the writers as the league's Most Valuable Player. At first glance, this might seem like a bit of a stretch. However, it bears mentioning that two of New York's top offensive players were lost to the team for much of the season. Mickey Mantle appeared in only 65 games and accumulated just 172 at-bats. Roger Maris played in only 90 games and came to the plate a total of just 312 times. Yet, even with those major losses, New York managed to win the pennant by 10½ games. There is little doubt that Howard had a great deal to do with that. In the absence of Mantle and Maris, he became the team's on-field leader. Whitey Ford was also a team leader, but he only played every fourth day. It was Howard who picked up much of the slack in the absence of Mantle and Maris. In the face of all those injuries, he helped to keep the team together.

With no other truly outstanding MVP candidate in the league, Howard was the best choice that could have been made.

NATIONAL LEAGUE

The Dodgers rebounded from their three-game playoff setback one year earlier by capturing the National League pennant in 1963. In doing so, they finished six games ahead of the second-place Cardinals, and 11 games in front of the third-place Giants.

With sluggers Willie McCovey, Orlando Cepeda, and Willie Mays comprising the middle of their lineup, San Francisco had one of the top offenses in the league. McCovey tied for the N.L. lead with 44 home runs, knocked in 102 runs, and scored another 103. Cepeda slugged 34 homers, drove in 97 runs, scored 100 others, and batted .316. As usual, Mays led the Giants' attack with 38 home runs, 103 runs batted in, 115 runs scored, and a .314 batting average.

San Francisco also received a brilliant performance from Juan Marichal. *The Dominican Dandy* finished with a record of 25-8, to tie for the league lead in victories, compiled a 2.41 earned run average, struck out 248 batters, and led N.L. hurlers with 321 innings pitched.

The second-place Cardinals also had several outstanding performers in 1963. First baseman Bill White hit 27 home runs, drove in 109 runs, scored another 106, batted .304, and collected 200 hits. Curt Flood batted .302, scored 112 runs, collected 200 hits, and played a brilliant centerfield. Although he hit only six home runs and knocked in just 73 runs, shortstop Dick Groat finished among the league leaders with a .319 batting average and 201 hits, and he led the N.L. with 43 doubles. Third baseman Ken Boyer hit 24 home runs, drove in 111 runs, and batted .285.

But the league's top offensive player in 1963 was Milwaukee's Hank Aaron, who led the N.L. in five different offensive categories and finished in the top five in two others. Aaron tied for the league lead with 44 home runs, finished first with 130 runs batted in, third in batting with a mark of .319, second with 31 stolen bases, and led the N.L. with 121 runs scored, 370 total bases, and a .586 slugging percentage. Even though the Braves finished sixth, they were 15 games back—close enough to keep Aaron in the running for MVP honors.

However, the pennant-winning Dodgers received a magnificent performance from Sandy Koufax. The lefthander finished 25-5, to tie Marichal for the league lead in victories. He also led N.L. pitchers with a 1.88 earned run average, 306 strikeouts, and 11 shutouts, and he finished second to Marichal with 311 innings pitched. Tommy Davis, Frank Howard, and Maury Wills all contributed to the Dodgers on offense. Davis knocked in 88 runs and led the league with a .326 batting average. Howard led the team with 28 homers, and Wills batted .302 and led the N.L. with 40 stolen bases.

But, with all three players experiencing significant drop-offs from their 1962 performances, it was the Dodgers' league-leading team earned run average of 2.85 that enabled them to capture the league championship. And it was Koufax who was the team's best player, and the driving force behind their pennant-run.

Therefore, as great a year as Hank Aaron had, with the Braves finishing sixth and the Dodgers winning the pennant, Koufax had to be considered the league's Most Valuable Player.

MVP INCONSISTENCIES

16

We earlier examined some of the more controversial MVP elections conducted over the years. We saw that the voters seemed to pay little attention to statistics in their assessment of the various candidates in some seasons. Instead, top priority was given to less tangible qualities such as fielding, baserunning, and leadership skills, and, also, to the final placement in the standings of a particular player's team. We also saw that, from one year to the next, there did not seem to be any set pattern as to how players with distinctly different styles of play were judged. This was particularly noticeable in those instances in which an outstanding pitcher was pitted against a superb hitter. We specifically focused on the National League elections of 1965 and 1966, and the American League elections of 1978 and 1986 to see just how unpredictable the thought process of the baseball writers can be. However, there were several other elections that equally demonstrate the level of inconsistency shown by the writers in some of their selections.

The Yankees won the American League pennant in 1932, finishing 13 games ahead of the second-place Athletics. New York was led by Lou Gehrig, who had an outstanding season. The first baseman hit 34 home runs, knocked in 151 runs, batted .349, and scored 138 runs. However, Gehrig was not the league's best player that year. Jimmie Foxx's incredible season enabled Philadelphia to finish second in the standings, albeit a distant second. Foxx led the A.L. in six different offensive categories, finishing with 58 home runs, 169 runs batted in, 151 runs scored, and a .364 batting average. Although Gehrig also had a great year, leading his team to the pennant in the process, the writers made the correct choice by selecting Foxx as the league's Most Valuable Player.

Just one year later, Foxx was again the league's dominant player, capturing the A.L. Triple Crown with 48 homers, 163 runs batted in, and a .356 batting average. However, his A's finished further back in the standings, coming in third, 19½ games behind the first-place Senators, who had a legitimate MVP candidate of their own. Shortstop Joe Cronin drove in 118 runs, batted .309, and led the league with 45 doubles. Yet, for the second straight year, the best player on the pennant-winning team finished second in the MVP balloting to the league's most dominant player, Jimmie Foxx.

It was a different story, though, in 1934. This time, the American League's dominant player was New York's Lou Gehrig, who captured the Triple Crown by hitting 49 home runs, driving in 165 runs, and batting .363. In fact, Gehrig's statistics that year were remarkably similar to those posted by Foxx the previous season. Gehrig's great year enabled the Yankees to finish second in the standings, seven games behind the pennant-winning Tigers. Yet, Detroit catcher Mickey Cochrane, who hit only two home runs and knocked in just 76 runs while batting .320, finished well ahead of Gehrig in the balloting. In fact, the Yankee first baseman amazingly finished *fifth* in the voting.

In 1952, the Chicago Cubs finished fifth in the National League, 19½ games behind the pennant-winning Brooklyn Dodgers. The Cubs' best player that year was the league's top offensive player as well. Outfielder Hank Sauer led the N.L. with 37 home runs and 121 runs batted in, and he was named the league's Most Valuable Player at the end of the year. Yet, while his overall numbers were not as impressive as Sauer's, the Dodgers' Jackie Robinson was certainly a legitimate MVP candidate. Even though his 19 home runs and 75 runs batted in fell far short of the totals compiled by the Cubs slugger, Robinson's .308 batting average was 38 points higher than Sauer's, and his 104 runs scored were 15 more than the 89 Sauer scored for Chicago. Nevertheless, the final voting wasn't even close. Sauer received 226 points, while Robinson totaled just 31. And what of Robin Roberts, whose 28 victories for the Phillies that year were 10 more than any other pitcher in the league compiled. He was clearly the National League's most dominant player, and his team finished one place and 10 games ahead of Sauer's Cubs in the standings. Yet, Roberts finished a close second to Sauer in the voting. Clearly the voters were impressed by the power numbers posted by the Cubs slugger.

However, just three years later, the writers' thinking changed. The Dodgers won the pennant in 1955, finishing 18½ games ahead of the third-place Giants, who had the league's best player in Willie Mays. The centerfielder led the N.L. with 51 home runs, finished second with 127 runs batted in and 123 runs scored, and batted .319. Yet, the player selected as the league's Most Valuable Player was Brooklyn catcher Roy Campanella, whose numbers were not nearly as impressive. While he batted .318, Campanella hit 32 homers, drove in 107 runs, and scored only 81 others. In fact, he wasn't even the best player on the Dodgers that year. Duke Snider, with 42 home runs, 136 runs batted in, 126 runs scored, and a .309 batting average was Brooklyn's top performer. If any Dodger player should have been selected over Mays as the league's MVP that year, it was Snider.

The Yankees won the American League pennant in 1958, finishing 10 games ahead of the second-place White Sox and 13 in front of third-place Boston. Mickey Mantle was the league's best player, leading the A.L. with 42 home runs and 127 runs scored, and batting .304. Yet, Red Sox outfielder Jackie Jensen was named league MVP, in spite of his team's distant third-place finish and Mantle's superior numbers. True, with a league-leading 122 runs batted in, Jensen drove in 25 more runs than Mantle. But the Yankee centerfielder scored 44 more runs than Jensen, and he finished well ahead of him in virtually every other offensive category. With his team finishing first in the standings, one would have thought that Mantle would have received more votes than Jensen.

Just one year later, in 1959, the White Sox captured the American League flag, beating out the Indians by just five games. Cleveland slugger Rocky Colavito led the league with 42 home runs and finished among the leaders with 111 runs batted in. With his team finishing a close second, and with no one on first-place Chicago posting numbers even close to those compiled by Mantle the prior year, it would seem that Colavito would have been the writers' choice for league MVP. However, they opted instead for White Sox second baseman Nellie Fox, who batted .306 but hit only two home runs and knocked in just 70 runs.

The Braves won their second consecutive National League pennant in 1958, and Hank Aaron was the team's best player. Aaron hit 30 homers, drove in 95 runs, scored another 109, and batted .326. Those were fine numbers, but they were not nearly as impressive as the figures posted by Chicago's Ernie Banks. The Cubs slugger led the N.L. with 47 home runs and 129 runs batted in, scored 119 runs, and batted .313. As a result, the writers selected Banks as the league's Most Valuable Player in spite of Chicago's sixth-place finish, 20 games off the pace.

The following season, Banks was selected again as the league's MVP, even though the Cubs finished tied for fifth, 13 games behind the pennant-winning Dodgers. Banks had another exceptional year, hitting 45 home runs and leading the league with 143 runs batted in. His numbers far exceeded those of Wally Post, the Dodgers' leading MVP candidate. Post batted .302, but he hit only 19 homers and drove in just 74 runs. Thus, it is quite clear that, in both those elections, the voters looked much more closely at Banks' impressive numbers than they did at his team's mediocre performance.

However, in 1960, the writers were of a completely different mind-set. Milwaukee finished second in the standings, seven games behind pennant-winning Pittsburgh. Braves teammates Hank Aaron and Eddie Mathews both had exceptional years. Aaron hit 40 homers, drove in a league-leading 126 runs, scored another 102, and batted .292. Mathews slugged 39 homers, knocked in 124 runs, scored 108 others, and batted .277. Yet, the writers opted instead for Pirates shortstop Dick Groat, who led the league with a .325 batting average, but hit only two home runs, knocked in just 50 runs, and scored only 85 others.

The Pirates finished first in the National League East in 1971, seven games ahead of the second-place Cardinals. Pittsburgh outfielder Willie Stargell had an excellent year, leading the league with 48 home runs, finishing second with 125 runs batted in, scoring 104 runs, and batting .295. But St. Louis third baseman Joe Torre had an even better season, leading the N.L. with 137 runs batted in, a .363 batting average, and 230 hits. In spite of the Pirates' first-place finish, Torre was able to out-poll Stargell in the MVP balloting by almost 100 points.

Just two years later, in 1973, Stargell had another superb season, leading the league with 44 home runs, 119 runs batted in, 43 doubles, and a .646 slugging percentage, scoring 106 runs, and batting .299. Pittsburgh finished a close third in the N.L. East, just 2½ games behind the first-place Mets. Pete Rose helped lead Cincinnati to the

Western Division title that year, leading the league with 230 hits and a .338 batting average, and scoring 115 runs. However, with only five home runs, 64 runs batted in, and a .437 slugging percentage, his overall numbers were dwarfed by Stargell's. Yet, Rose finished first in the MVP balloting, 24 points ahead of runner-up Stargell.

The Detroit Tigers finished third in the American League East in 1990, nine games behind first-place Boston. Tiger slugger Cecil Fielder was unquestionably the most imposing hitter in baseball that year, leading the majors with 51 home runs, 132 runs batted in, and a .592 slugging percentage. Yet, he finished a close second in the MVP balloting to Oakland's Rickey Henderson, who led the A's to the Western Division title. While not possessing Fielder's power numbers, Henderson excelled in other areas, batting .325, stealing 65 bases, and leading the A.L. with 119 runs scored and a .441 on-base percentage. Thus, in that instance, the voters looked more closely at Henderson's overall contributions to the success of a winning team than at Fielder's prodigious power totals.

Three years earlier, though, a similar situation presented itself in the National League. The Cardinals finished first in the N.L. East in 1987, just four games ahead of the third-place Expos. Montreal was led by speedy outfielder Tim Raines, who actually had a season quite similar to the one Henderson had for Oakland in 1990.

Let's look at Raines' 1987 statistics next to those compiled by Henderson in 1990:

PLAYER	AB	HITS	RUNS	2B	3B	HR	RBI	AVG	OBP	SLG PCT	SB
Tim Raines	530	175	123	34	8	18	68	.330	.431	.526	50
Rickey Henderson	489	159	**119**	33	3	28	61	.325	**.441**	.577	65

Meanwhile, the Cubs finished last in the N.L. East in 1987, 18½ games behind St. Louis. Chicago outfielder Andre Dawson posted numbers similar to those compiled by Fielder for Detroit three years later.

Let's take a look:

PLAYER	AB	HITS	RUNS	2B	3B	HR	RBI	AVG	OBP	SLG PCT
Andre Dawson	621	178	90	24	2	**49**	137	.287	.329	.568
Cecil Fielder	573	159	104	25	1	**51**	132	.277	.380	**.592**

Yet, in spite of his team's last-place finish, Dawson was selected as the league's MVP. Inexplicably, Raines finished seventh in the balloting. True, Henderson's A's won the division title when he was selected league MVP in 1990, while Raines' Expos finished third in 1987. But, when Fielder had his tremendous season, only to finish runner-up in the voting, the Tigers finished third in their division. Dawson's Cubs finished dead last when he was voted MVP.

These are only a few examples of the inconsistencies exhibited by the MVP voters throughout the years that have helped to create confusion among those who regularly follow the results of the balloting.

THE 1964-1968 SEASONS—

THE END OF BASEBALL AS WE KNEW IT

Following the extensive changes that occurred during the late 1950s and early 1960s, which included the migration of teams to the West Coast and the expansion of the major leagues from 16 to 20 teams, the next few seasons were relatively uneventful. However, baseball continued its expansion in 1969 when it added four more teams and devised a new four-division setup. A few years later, the American League instituted the use of a designated hitter in its games, and, shortly thereafter, free agency changed the face of baseball forever. Therefore, the 1964-1968 seasons essentially marked the end of baseball as we knew it.

Aside from the growing dominance of pitchers, the most significant changes that took place during this period involved the relocations of three more franchises. Prior to the start of the 1965 season, the Los Angeles Angels moved to the city of Anaheim and began calling themselves the *California Angels*. The Braves left Milwaukee for Atlanta the very next year, and Kansas City Athletics owner Charlie Finley moved his team to Oakland at the conclusion of the 1967 campaign.

Oh, yes. There was one other significant change that occurred. The New York Yankee dynasty, which ruled the baseball world for more than 40 years, crumbled at the end of the 1964 season. The team that won 16 of the previous 18 American League pennants failed to make another postseason appearance until 1976. The Yankees decline was also reflected in the A.L. MVP balloting since a New York player won the award every year from 1960 to 1963. It would be another 13 years before a member of the Yankees would be selected for the honor again.

ACTUAL MVP WINNERS		SUGGESTED WINNERS	
A.L.	**N.L.**	**A.L.**	**N.L.**
1964 Brooks Robinson	Ken Boyer	Brooks Robinson	Ken Boyer
1965 Zoilo Versalles	Willie Mays	Zoilo Versalles	Willie Mays
1966 Frank Robinson	Roberto Clemente	Frank Robinson	Sandy Koufax
1967 Carl Yastrzemski	Orlando Cepeda	Carl Yastrzemski	Orlando Cepeda
1968 Denny McLain	Bob Gibson	Denny McLain	Bob Gibson

1964

AMERICAN LEAGUE

The Yankees tied their own record by winning their fifth consecutive American League pennant in 1964, barely beating out the White Sox and Orioles, who finished just one and two games back, respectively. New York was again the most well-balanced team in the league, finishing second in the A.L. with 730 runs scored, and placing third in team earned run average, with a mark of 3.15. The New York pitching staff was headed by Whitey Ford, who finished 17-6, with an outstanding 2.13 earned run average. Jim Bouton compiled a record of 18-13, with a 3.02 earned run average and a team-leading 271 innings pitched. Al Downing finished 13-8 and led the league with 217 strikeouts. Rookie righthander Mel Stottlemyre, who joined the team in early August, went 9-3 with a 2.06 earned run average and was invaluable to New York over the season's final two months.

On offense, reigning MVP Elston Howard batted .313 and drove in 84 runs, while Joe Pepitone hit 28 homers and knocked in 100 runs. New York's best player was Mickey Mantle, who finished third in the league with 35 home runs and 111 runs batted in, fourth in batting with a mark of .303, and led the A.L. with a .426 on-base percentage. Mantle finished second in the MVP balloting.

For the second straight year, the Minnesota Twins possessed the league's most explosive offense. They led the A.L. with 737 runs scored and 221 home runs, and their lineup featured two of the league's top players. Harmon Killebrew topped the circuit in home runs with 49, and also knocked in 111 runs. Rookie rightfielder Tony Oliva hit 32 homers, drove in 94 runs, and led the league with a .323 batting average, 109 runs scored, 217 hits, and 43 doubles. Had the Twins not finished sixth, 20 games off the pace, he would have been a serious contender for league MVP honors.

The White Sox again boasted the league's best pitching, leading the A.L. with a team earned run average of 2.72. Gary Peters finished 20-8, with a 2.50 earned run average. Juan Pizarro's record was 19-9, and he pitched to a 2.56 earned run average. Righthander Joe Horlen won 13 games and finished second in the league with a 1.88 earned run average.

The American League's best pitcher was the Angels' Dean Chance, who was named the recipient of the Cy Young Award at season's end. The righthander tied Peters for the league lead with 20 victories (against 9 losses), and also finished first with a 1.65 earned run average, 278 innings pitched, and 11 shutouts. With the Angels finishing fifth, though, 17 games out of first, Chance could do no better than fifth in the MVP balloting.

Another of the league's top pitchers was Wally Bunker, who finished 19-5 with a 2.69 earned run average for the third-place Orioles. However, Baltimore's two most significant players were members of their everyday lineup. Splitting time between the outfield and first base, Boog Powell compiled only 424 official at-bats. Yet, he still managed to hit 39 home runs, drive in 99 runs, bat .290, and lead the league with a .606 slugging percentage. Brooks Robinson hit 28 homers, led the A.L. with 118 runs batted in, and finished second in the league with a .317 batting average, 194 hits, and 319 total bases. A great defensive third baseman as well, Robinson rivaled Tony Oliva as the American League's best all-around player in 1964. With the Orioles finishing only two games behind the Yankees in the pennant race, Robinson was clearly the best choice for league MVP.

NATIONAL LEAGUE

One of the great pennant races in National League history took place in 1964, with no fewer than five teams remaining in contention until the season's final two weeks. The Philadelphia Phillies had what seemed to be a comfortable 6½-game lead with just two weeks remaining in the season, but they collapsed down the stretch. Manager Gene Mauch attempted to eliminate the other pennant contenders from the race by starting his two best pitchers, Jim Bunning and Chris Short, on short rest during the season's final days. However, the strategy backfired, enabling the hard-charging Cardinals to overtake his squad and capture the N.L. flag. Philadelphia finished tied for second with Cincinnati, one game behind St. Louis. The Giants finished fourth, three games back, and the Braves finished fifth, just five games off the pace.

Several players made major contributions to each of those contending teams. Hank Aaron and Joe Torre both had outstanding seasons for the Braves. Aaron hit 24 homers, knocked in 95 runs, scored 103 others, and batted .328. Torre hit 20 homers, drove in 109 runs, and batted .321.

Orlando Cepeda hit 31 homers, knocked in 97 runs, and batted .304 for San Francisco. Juan Marichal won 21 games, pitched to a 2.48 earned run average, struck out 206 batters, and led N.L. hurlers with 22 complete games. San Francisco's best player was Willie Mays, who had another superb season. Mays led the league with 47 home runs, knocked in 111 runs, scored another 121, and batted .296. He certainly had to be considered a leading candidate for league MVP honors.

Another top contender was Cincinnati's Frank Robinson, who hit 29 homers, drove in 96 runs, scored 103 others, and batted .306.

Philadelphia's Chris Short and Jim Bunning were both among the league's best pitchers. Short finished 17-9 with a 2.20 earned run average, and Bunning compiled a record of 19-8, with a 2.63 earned run average and 284 innings pitched. Still, the team's top two MVP candidates were rookie third baseman Richie Allen and rightfielder Johnny Callison. Allen hit 29 homers, knocked in 91 runs, batted .318, and led the league with 125 runs scored and 13 triples. Callison led the Phillies with 31 homers and 104 runs batted in, and also scored 101 runs.

The pennant-winning Cardinals also featured several outstanding performers. Lefthander Ray Sadecki finished 20-11, while righty Bob Gibson won 19 games and led the team with 245 strikeouts, 287 innings pitched, and 17 complete games. First baseman Bill White hit 21 home runs, drove in 102 runs, and batted .303. Centerfielder Curt Flood batted .311, scored 97 runs, and led the N.L. with 211 hits.

After being acquired in a trade with the Cubs during the season's first half, leftfielder Lou Brock was the team's offensive catalyst the remainder of the year. In 103 games with the Cardinals, he batted .348, scored 81 runs, and stole 33 bases. Brock's totals for the year were a .315 batting average, 111 runs scored, 43 stolen bases, and 200 base hits. Those figures, coupled with the impact he had on both his team and the pennant race, should have made him a leading candidate for league MVP. But, for some reason, he finished just tenth in the balloting. Perhaps Brock's cause was hurt somewhat by the outstanding performance turned in by the captain of his team, third baseman Ken Boyer, who won the award.

Let's look at Boyer's numbers, along with those of the other leading candidates:

PLAYER	AB	HITS	RUNS	2B	3B	HR	RBI	AVG	OBP	SLG PCT
Hank Aaron	570	187	103	30	2	24	95	.328	.394	.514
Willie Mays	578	171	121	21	9	**47**	111	.296	.384	**.607**
Ken Boyer	628	185	100	30	10	24	**119**	.295	.367	.489
Richie Allen	632	201	**125**	38	**13**	29	91	.318	.383	.557
Johnny Callison	654	179	101	30	10	31	104	.274	.318	.492
Frank Robinson	568	174	103	38	6	29	96	.306	.399	.548

Based on their statistics and the final placement in the standings of their respective teams, it would seem that Mays, Boyer, Allen, and Robinson deserved the greatest amount of consideration. Yet, Callison finished second in the voting, while Allen came in seventh. Callison's higher finish in the balloting was perhaps due to the fact that Allen was not very popular with the press. In addition, he played in the city of Philadelphia, which had long been known for its racial intolerance towards black players. Callison was far more popular with the Philadelphia fans, and with the press as well. True, Callison was a fine defensive outfielder and an excellent all-around player. He also hit two more home runs than Allen and knocked in more runs than the rookie third baseman. But Allen finished well ahead of him in every other category. While he may not have been the league's Most Valuable Player in 1964, Allen was clearly the Phillies' MVP.

As for Mays, Boyer, and Robinson—any of the three men would have been a good choice. Mays put up the best numbers, and the figures Robinson posted were slightly better than Boyer's as well. On the other hand, Boyer led the league in runs batted in, and he was the

Cardinals' captain and team leader. In addition, his team won the pennant.

It would be difficult to find fault with Boyer's selection as the league's Most Valuable Player.

1965

AMERICAN LEAGUE

Minnesota ended New York's five-year reign as American League champions in 1965, compiling a regular-season record of 102-60 and finishing seven games in front of second-place Chicago. While the Twins had the most potent offense in the A.L., scoring a league-leading 774 runs (almost 100 more than the 680 scored by runner-up Detroit), it was largely their improved pitching that enabled them to jump five places in the standings from the prior year. Their staff was headed by lefthander Jim Kaat and righthander Jim "Mudcat" Grant. Kaat finished 18-11, with a 2.83 earned run average and 264 innings pitched. Grant had a career year, compiling a record of 21-7, with an earned run average of 3.30, 270 innings pitched, 14 complete games, and a league-leading six shutouts.

Despite leading all A.L. pitchers with 21 wins, Grant was not the league's best pitcher. Both Sam McDowell and Mel Stottlemyre were better. Pitching for the fifth-place Indians, who finished 15 games behind the Twins, McDowell compiled a record of 17-11 and a league-leading 2.18 earned run average and 325 strikeouts. Pitching for the sixth-place Yankees, who finished 25 games off the pace, Stottlemyre finished 20-9, with a 2.63 earned run average and a league-leading 291 innings pitched and 18 complete games. Neither McDowell nor Stottlemyre, though, merited serious consideration for league MVP honors.

Cleveland's Rocky Colavito was among the top offensive players in the league. He hit 26 home runs, led the A.L. with 108 runs batted in, scored 92 runs, and batted .287. Had the Indians finished higher in the standings, Colavito would have been a leading candidate. Willie Horton hit 29 home runs and knocked in 104 runs for the fourth-place Tigers, who finished 13 games back. Brooks Robinson hit 18 home runs, drove in 80 runs, and batted .297 for Baltimore. With the Orioles finishing third, just eight games off the pace, he deserved serious consideration.

However, let's not forget about the team with the best offense in the league—the pennant-winning Twins. Jimmie Hall hit 20 homers, knocked in 86 runs, and batted .285. Bob Allison hit 23 homers and drove in 78 runs. Despite missing almost one-third of the season and accumulating only 401 official at-bats, Harmon Killebrew finished the year with 25 homers and 75 runs batted in. But the Twins' two best players, and the top two candidates for league MVP, were shortstop Zoilo Versalles and rightfielder Tony Oliva.

Let's take a look at the statistics of both men:

PLAYER	AB	HITS	RUNS	2B	3B	HR	RBI	AVG	OBP	SLG PCT
Zoilo Versalles	666	182	126	45	12	19	77	.273	.322	.462
Tony Oliva	576	185	107	40	5	16	98	.321	.384	.491

In just his second season, Oliva won his second batting title and also led the league in hits for the second time. He finished well ahead of Versalles in both on-base and slugging percentage, and in runs batted in as well. However, the shortstop finished with more home runs and only three fewer hits, and he also led the league in doubles, triples, and runs scored. When it is considered that Versalles batted leadoff for Minnesota, while Oliva usually hit third, the RBI discrepancy becomes insignificant. Therefore, with almost 20 more runs scored, Versalles was actually the superior run-producer of the two. He also stole 27 bases, served as Minnesota's offensive catalyst, and played the more demanding position of the two. All things considered, the selection of Versalles as league MVP over Oliva, who finished second in the balloting, was a good one.

NATIONAL LEAGUE

For the second straight year the National League champion was decided in the season's final days, with the Dodgers finally prevailing over the Giants by a mere two games. While both San Francisco and fourth-place Cincinnati had more potent offenses, it was the Los Angeles pitching staff that enabled them to capture their second N.L. flag in three years. Sandy Koufax and Don Drysdale combined for 49 wins, forming the most formidable pitching duo in the big leagues. Drysdale finished 23-12, with a 2.77 earned run average, 210 strikeouts, 308 innings pitched, and 20 complete games. Koufax was even better, dominating the league's statistical categories for pitchers. He led the N.L. with 26 victories (against only 8 losses), a 2.04 earned run average, 382 strikeouts, 335 innings pitched, and 27 complete games, and he finished second with eight shutouts. Koufax was clearly the Dodgers' MVP, and he was a leading candidate for league honors as well.

Dodger shortstop Maury Wills also had an excellent year, batting .286, scoring 92 runs, and leading the league with 94 stolen bases. However, his numbers were not nearly as impressive as those compiled by several other players in the league.

The fourth-place Reds, who finished eight games behind the Dodgers, had the best offense in the N.L. Their team batting average of .273 was the best in the league, and their 825 runs scored were by far the most compiled by any team. In fact, the runner-up Cardinals scored 118 fewer runs, and the Dodgers scored 217 fewer times. Cincinnati's attack was led by Frank Robinson and Deron Johnson. Robinson hit 33 home runs, knocked in 113 runs, scored another 109, and batted .296. Johnson hit 32 homers and led the league with 130 runs batted in. They were joined by Tommy Harper, who led the league with 126 runs scored, and Pete Rose, who batted .312, scored 117 runs, and led the N.L. with 209 hits.

The second-place Giants also had a potent offense, and a good pitching staff to go along with it. Their staff was headed by Juan Marichal, who compiled a 22-13 record, with a 2.13 earned run average, 240 strikeouts, 295 innings pitched, 24 complete games, and a league-leading 10 shutouts. On offense, Willie McCovey finished second in the league with 39 home runs, drove in 92 runs, and scored 93 others. Third baseman Jim Ray Hart hit 23 homers, knocked in 96 runs, scored another 91, and batted .299. The Giants' top threat was again Willie Mays, who was also the best all-around player in the league. The centerfielder led the N.L. with 52 home runs, finished third with 112 runs batted in and a .317 batting average, and placed second with 118 runs scored. He also led the league with 360 total bases, a .399 on-base percentage, and a .645 slugging percentage. Mays was unquestionably the only player capable of mounting a serious challenge to Sandy Koufax for league MVP honors. But which one was more deserving?

Koufax had a slightly more dominant year, leading N.L. pitchers in five of the six major statistical categories, and finishing runner-up in the sixth. Mays finished first in four different offensive categories, and he placed in the top five in three others. Sandy's team also won the pennant, while Willie's squad finished second. However, the Giants finished only two games back of the Dodgers and remained in contention almost to the very end. Mays played every day, and he was unquestionably the Giants' leader and the primary reason why they almost beat out the Dodgers for the league championship.

While Koufax certainly would not have been a bad choice, the voters cannot be faulted for their selection of Mays as the National League's Most Valuable Player.

1966

AMERICAN LEAGUE

The Baltimore Orioles ran away with the American League pennant in 1966, finishing nine games ahead of the defending-champion Twins. Harmon Killebrew, Tony Oliva, and Jim Kaat all had outstanding seasons for Minnesota. Killebrew finished second in the league with 39 home runs and 110 runs batted in, batted .281, and led the league with 103 bases on balls. Oliva hit 25 homers, knocked in 87 runs, finished second in the A.L. with a .307 batting average and 99 runs scored, and led the league with 191 hits. Kaat was the American League's best pitcher, leading the league with 25 victories, 304 innings pitched, and 19 complete games, and compiling a 2.75 earned run average. However, with the Twins finishing nine games off the pace, and with three players on the pennant-winning Orioles having excellent years as well, neither Killebrew, Oliva, nor Kaat could be seriously considered for league MVP honors.

The three Baltimore players who performed at an extremely high level in 1966 were Boog Powell, Brooks Robinson, and Frank Robinson. Powell batted .287 and finished among the league leaders with 34 home runs and 109 runs batted in. Brooks hit 23 homers, drove in 100 runs, and scored another 91. But the best player in baseball in 1966 was unquestionably Frank Robinson. After being traded to Baltimore from Cincinnati for three players during the off-season, Robinson set out to prove just how wrong the Reds were when they said they made the deal because Robinson was "an old 30." And prove them wrong he did. All Robinson did was capture the league's Triple Crown by finishing first in home runs (49), runs batted in (122), and batting average (.316). He also led the league with 122 runs scored, 367 total bases, a .415 on-base percentage, and a .637 slugging percentage. Robinson punctuated his MVP season by hitting two home runs in the Orioles' four-game World Series sweep of the Dodgers.

NATIONAL LEAGUE

The Dodgers edged out the Giants for the second consecutive year, this time finishing just 1½ games ahead of their arch-rivals. The Pirates finished third, just three games back, the Phillies were fourth, eight games out, and the Braves finished fifth, 10 games back. Each of the contending teams had at least one outstanding MVP candidate.

Atlanta's offense was the best in the N.L. in 1966, scoring a league-leading 782 runs. Catcher Joe Torre hit 36 home runs, drove in 101 runs, and batted .315. Outfielder Felipe Alou hit 31 homers, finished second in the league with a .327 batting average, and led the N.L. with 122 runs scored and 218 hits. Outfield mate Rico Carty finished third in the league with a .326 batting average. But the Braves' top player was Hank Aaron, who led the league with 44 home runs and 127 runs batted in, finished second with 117 runs scored, and batted .279. He had to be considered a leading candidate for MVP.

So, too, did Richie Allen, who had a superb season for the fourth-place Phillies. Allen finished second to Aaron with 40 homers and also placed among the league leaders with 110 runs batted in, 112 runs scored, a .317 batting average, and a .398 on-base percentage. His .632 slugging percentage led the circuit.

The third-place Pirates finished second to the Braves with 759 runs scored. They were led by outfielders Willie Stargell and Roberto Clemente. Stargell hit 33 homers, knocked in 102 runs, and batted .315. Clemente hit 29 home runs and finished among the league leaders with 119 runs batted in, 105 runs scored, a .317 batting average, 202 hits, and 342 total bases. Along with Aaron and Allen, he had to be considered a prime MVP candidate.

The second-place Giants also featured their fair share of contenders. Willie McCovey hit 36 homers, drove in 96 runs, and batted .295. Jim Ray Hart hit 33 home runs, knocked in 93 runs, and batted .285. Willie Mays finished among the league leaders with 37 home runs and 103 runs batted in, scored 99 runs, and batted .288. Juan Marichal was absolutely brilliant for San Francisco, compiling a record of 25-6, with a 2.23 earned run average, 222 strikeouts, 307 innings pitched, and 25 complete games.

Amazingly, Marichal was not the National League's best pitcher in 1966. That distinction went to Sandy Koufax, who had another magnificent season for the pennant-winning Dodgers. Koufax led N.L. hurlers in all six major statistical categories, finishing first with a record of 27-9, a 1.73 earned run average, 317 strikeouts, 323 innings pitched, 27 complete games, and five shutouts. He was clearly the league's most dominant player, but, as a pitcher, was he most deserving of being named its Most Valuable Player?

Roberto Clemente was the choice of the writers, receiving a total of 218 points, to 208 for Koufax. However, while Clemente had a tremendous year, he was not nearly as dominant as Koufax. The Pirate outfielder failed to lead the league in any major statistical category, and it is even debatable as to whether or not he was the National League's top position player. While Pittsburgh finished higher in the standings than either Philadelphia or Atlanta, thereby making Clemente a more viable MVP candidate, both Richie Allen and Hank Aaron put up numbers that were comparable to those compiled by the Pittsburgh rightfielder.

Meanwhile, in spite of Juan Marichal's great year for the Giants, Koufax was clearly the league's top pitcher. Furthermore, he received little help from his Dodger teammates much of the year. Los Angeles finished eighth in the league in runs scored, providing Koufax little margin for error. Except for Maury Willis, who finished third in the league in stolen bases, Koufax was the only Dodger player to finish in the top five in any major statistical category. With both Wills and Don Drysdale suffering through sub-par seasons, it was Koufax who held the team together. Wills, who scored 92 runs and stole 94 bases the prior year, scored only 60 runs and stole just 38 bases in 1966. Drysdale, who finished 23-12 with a 2.77 earned run average a year earlier, finished the season with a record of only 13-16 and an earned run average of 3.42.

Without Koufax pitching as brilliantly as he did, the Dodgers probably would not have finished any higher than third or fourth in the standings. That being the case, he should have been the writers' choice as league MVP, over Clemente.

1967

AMERICAN LEAGUE

In a thrilling four-team race that went right down to the season's final day, the Boston Red Sox captured the American League pennant in 1967, finishing just one game ahead of the Twins and Tigers, and three games ahead of the White Sox. Boston defeated Minnesota on the last day of the regular season, then clinched their first A.L. championship in 21 years when the Angels defeated the Tigers later in the day.

While the Red Sox, Twins, and Tigers all boasted solid lineups, the fourth-place White Sox depended more on their strong pitching staff to remain in contention for most of the year. Chicago's team earned run average of 2.45 was almost 70 points lower than that of any other club in the league. Righthander Joe Horlen led all A.L. hurlers with a 2.06 earned run average and six shutouts, while compiling a record of 19-7 and throwing 258 innings. Lefthander Gary Peters placed second to Horlen with a 2.28 earned run average and finished 16-11, with 215 strikeouts and 260 innings pitched. Lefty Tommy John finished fourth in the league with a 2.47 earned run average.

However, Minnesota, Detroit, and Boston were all more balanced teams. The Twins' top offensive player was Harmon Killebrew, who tied for the league lead with 44 home runs and finished second with 113 runs batted in and 105 runs scored. Their best pitcher was Dean Chance, who finished 20-14, with a 2.73 earned run average and 220 strikeouts, and led the league with 283 innings pitched and 18 complete games.

On offense, the Tigers were led by veteran rightfielder Al Kaline, who hit 25 home runs and finished among the league leaders with a .308 batting average and 94 runs scored. Righthander Earl Wilson won 22 games for Detroit, compiling a 3.27 earned run average and throwing 264 innings.

The league's best pitcher, though, was Boston righthander Jim Lonborg, who tied Wilson for the league lead with 22 victories (against 9 losses), finished with a 3.16 earned run average, 273 innings pitched, and 15 complete games, and led the league with 246 strikeouts. George Scott contributed to the Red Sox offense, hitting 19 home runs, driving in 82 runs, and batting .303. Still, there can be no doubt as to who Boston's top player was, and as to who the league's Most Valuable Player was that year.

Carl Yastrzemski captured the A.L. Triple Crown by hitting 44 home runs, driving in 121 runs, and batting .326. He also led the league with 112 runs scored, 189 hits, 360 total bases, a .421 on-base percentage, and a .622 slugging percentage—all while playing a brilliant left field. Yastrzemski carried the Red Sox on his back down the stretch, batting .522, with five homers and 22 runs batted in during the final two weeks of the season. In the World Series, he continued his magnificent play by hitting .400, with three home runs.

NATIONAL LEAGUE

The Cardinals dominated the National League in 1967, finishing 10½ games ahead of the second-place Giants and 14 in front of the third-place Cubs. St. Louis was led by first baseman Orlando Cepeda, who was acquired from San Francisco during the off-season for pitcher Ray Sadecki. Cepeda hit 25 home runs, led the N.L. with 111 runs batted in, and finished among the league leaders with a .325 batting average, 91 runs scored, and 183 hits. At season's end, the writers made him the easy winner in the MVP balloting. However, there were several other players who deserved consideration.

Willie McCovey hit 31 home runs and drove in 91 runs for the runner-up Giants. Jim Ray Hart added 29 homers, 99 runs batted in, and 98 runs scored. San Francisco lefthander Mike McCormick was presented with the league's Cy Young Award at the end of the year for his 22-10 record, 2.85 earned run average, and 262 innings pitched.

The Cubs' two best players were third baseman Ron Santo and pitcher Ferguson Jenkins. Santo hit 31 homers, drove in 98 runs, scored another 107, and batted .300. Jenkins finished with a record of 20-13, an earned run average of 2.80, 236 strikeouts, 289 innings pitched, and a league-leading 20 complete games.

The two best players in the league were Pittsburgh's Roberto Clemente and Atlanta's Hank Aaron. Clemente hit 23 homers, drove in 110 runs, scored 103 others, and led the N.L. with a .357 batting average and 209 hits. Aaron drove in 109 runs, batted .307, and led the league with 39 home runs, 113 runs scored, and a .573 slugging percentage. The numbers posted by both Clemente and Aaron were slightly better than Cepeda's. However, the Pirates finished sixth, 20½ games back, and the Braves finished seventh, 24½ games out, so it would be difficult to make a valid case for either Clemente or Aaron being the league's Most Valuable Player.

In addition, the Cardinals' record, only 83-79 in 1966, improved to 101-60 in 1967. While St. Louis made several other roster changes during the off-season, including obtaining Roger Maris from the Yankees, Cepeda's acquisiton was the team's most noticeable move. It is quite clear, then, that he had a major impact on his new team, and that he was the primary reason why they were able to improve as much as they did. It also follows that his selection as the league's MVP cannot be questioned.

However, one thing that must be questioned was Tim McCarver's second-place finish in the balloting. While the St. Louis catcher had a solid season, it is inexplicable that he finished second, with a total of 136 points, while teammate Lou Brock came in seventh, with only 49 points. True, McCarver played the more demanding position of the two, but Brock was the finest leadoff hitter in the game, and he was the one who ignited the Cardinals' offense. He led the league with 52 stolen bases and 113 runs scored, and he put up much better numbers than McCarver. Brock hit more home runs (21 to 14), knocked in more runs (76 to 69), hit for a higher average (.299 to .295), scored many more runs (113 to 68), and collected far more hits (206 to 139). It is difficult to imagine what the writers were thinking when they gave more votes to McCarver than to Brock.

1968

AMERICAN LEAGUE

The 1968 season came to be known as *The Year of the Pitcher*, and with good reason. Pitchers dominated baseball that year, with several hurlers having truly remarkable seasons, and with numerous records being set. In the National League, Dodger righthander Don Drysdale established a new record for most consecutive scoreless innings pitched, and Cardinal great Bob Gibson compiled a mind-boggling 1.12 earned run average. In the A.L., Tiger righthander Denny McLain became the first major league pitcher in 34 years to win as many as 30 games in a season. Run production and batting averages were down in both leagues, with Carl Yastrzemski leading the American League with a mark of only .301. Nevertheless, there were a few players who were able to put up some fairly impressive offensive numbers.

Washington Senators slugger Frank Howard led the American League with 44 home runs and finished second with 106 runs batted in. Boston outfielder Ken Harrelson hit 35 homers and led the league with 109 runs batted in. However, with both the Senators and Red Sox finishing well out of contention, neither player could be seriously considered for league MVP honors.

The Detroit Tigers ran away with the A.L. pennant, finishing the regular season with a record of 103-59, 12 games in front of the second-place Orioles. Outfielder Willie Horton was their primary offensive threat, finishing second in the league with 36 home runs, driving in 85 runs, and batting .285. He was joined by catcher Bill Freehan, who hit 25 homers and knocked in 84 runs, and outfielder Jim Northrup, who hit 21 round-trippers and finished third in the league with 90 runs batted in. But, with such modest numbers, it would be difficult to consider any of the three Tiger batsmen as the league's Most Valuable Player.

Therefore, we must look to the circuit's top pitchers. Yankee righthander Mel Stottlemyre had an excellent year, compiling a record of 21-12, with a 2.45 earned run average, 278 innings pitched, and 19 complete games. But, New York finished fifth, well out of contention. Baltimore lefthander Dave McNally finished 22-10, with a 1.95 earned run average, 273 innings pitched, and 18 complete games. With the

Orioles finishing second, he would have to be given a certain amount of consideration. So, too, would Cleveland righthander Luis Tiant, who was absolutely brilliant all year. The Indians finished third, 16½ games off the pace, but Tiant compiled a record of 21-9, with a league-leading 1.60 earned run average and nine shutouts. He also struck out 264 batters and completed 19 games.

In a normal year, those numbers would have been good enough to gain Tiant recognition as the league's finest pitcher. However, he had to settle for second best in 1968 because Detroit's Denny McLain had a truly remarkable year. The righthander finished the season with a record of 31-6, a 1.96 earned run average, and 280 strikeouts, and he led the A.L. with 336 innings pitched and 28 complete games. As the central figure on the league's dominant team, McLain was the only logical choice for league MVP.

NATIONAL LEAGUE

While pitching dominated both leagues in 1968, National League hitters fared somewhat better than their American League counterparts. Cincinnati's Pete Rose led the N.L. with a .335 batting average, 210 hits, and a .394 on-base percentage, and he also finished second with 94 runs scored. San Francisco's Willie McCovey led the league with 36 home runs and 105 runs batted in. Lou Brock, whose Cardinals captured their second consecutive league championship by finishing nine games ahead of the second-place Giants, led the N.L. with 14 triples, 46 doubles, and 62 stolen bases. In so doing, he became the first National League player since Honus Wagner in 1908 to lead the league in all three categories in the same year.

But, as was the case in the A.L., pitchers were the dominant figures in the N.L. in 1968. Juan Marichal had a magnificent season for the second-place Giants. He led the league with 26 victories, compiling a record of 26-9, with a 2.43 earned run average and a league-leading 326 innings pitched and 30 complete games. However, Marichal was overshadowed by Bob Gibson, who didn't receive as much run support from his Cardinal teammates, but managed to compile a record of 22-9, with a league-leading 1.12 earned run average, 268 strikeouts, and 13 shutouts. He also finished second among N.L. hurlers with 28 complete games, and third with 304 innings pitched. Gibson was not only the best *pitcher* in baseball, but he was the game's most dominant *player*.

As such, and with his team winning the pennant, there is no question that Gibson was also the league's Most Valuable Player.

THE DOMINANCE OF THE BIG RED MACHINE

18

The major leagues underwent drastic changes in 1969, expanding from 20 to 24 teams and adopting a new four-division setup. For the first time, each league champion was not decided by which team finished with the best regular-season record. Instead, the regular season was used to determine the four division champions, and the two division champions in each league then squared off in a five-game series to determine the league champion. The league champions then met in the World Series.

The four new teams were the Kansas City Royals and Seattle Pilots in the American League, and the Montreal Expos and San Diego Padres in the National League.

The divisions were aligned as follows:

A.L. EAST	A.L. WEST	N.L EAST	N.L. WEST
Baltimore	Minnesota	Chicago	Atlanta
Detroit	Oakland	St. Louis	Cincinnati
Boston	California	Pittsburgh	San Francisco
New York	Chicago	Philadelphia	Los Angeles
Cleveland	Kansas City	New York	Houston
Washington	Seattle	Montreal	San Diego

Following the 1969 season, the Pilots moved from Seattle to Milwaukee and renamed themselves the *Brewers*. Just two years later, the Senators left Washington for Texas, leaving the nation's capital without a franchise of its own for the first time since the turn of the century. The new team in Texas was renamed the *Rangers*, and they switched places with the Brewers, with Milwaukee moving to the A.L. East and Texas taking over their spot in the A.L. West.

The new two-division setup in each league meant that twice as many teams remained in contention until late in the season. It also followed that the number of legitimate MVP candidates increased, since more players were involved in the pennant race.

Just a few years later, prior to the start of the 1977 campaign, two more teams were added—both in the American League. The Toronto Blue Jays became the A.L.'s first Canadian representative, taking up residence in the Eastern Division. In addition, a new franchise was established in the city of Seattle, with the Mariners joining the Western Division. The two new franchises increased to 14 the total number of teams in the American League.

Another development during this period was the emergence of Cincinnati's *Big Red Machine* as baseball's dominant team. Although they won only two world championships between 1969 and 1977, the Reds appeared in four World Series and five League Championship Series. They also featured one of the most formidable starting lineups in baseball history, with virtually all of their position players appearing in multiple All-Star games. The Reds also dominated the MVP voting, with six of the nine N.L. awards presented during the period going to Cincinnati players.

	ACTUAL MVP WINNERS		SUGGESTED WINNERS	
	A.L.	**N.L.**	**A.L.**	**N.L.**
1969	Harmon Killebrew	Willie McCovey	Harmon Killebrew	Willie McCovey
1970	Boog Powell	Johnny Bench	Boog Powell	Johnny Bench
1971	Vida Blue	Joe Torre	Vida Blue	Joe Torre
1972	Dick Allen	Johnny Bench	Dick Allen	Johnny Bench
1973	Reggie Jackson	Pete Rose	Reggie Jackson	Willie Stargell
1974	Jeff Burroughs	Steve Garvey	Jeff Burroughs	Mike Marshall
1975	Fred Lynn	Joe Morgan	Fred Lynn	Joe Morgan
1976	Thurman Munson	Joe Morgan	Thurman Munson	Joe Morgan
1977	Rod Carew	George Foster	Rod Carew	George Foster

1969

AMERICAN LEAGUE

The Minnesota Twins finished on top in the A.L. West in 1969, while the Baltimore Orioles prevailed in the East. Finishing nine games ahead of second-place Oakland, Minnesota featured a well-balanced offense with Cesar Tovar and Rod Carew providing speed at the top of the lineup, and Tony Oliva and Harmon Killebrew supplying much of the punch further down in the order. Leadoff hitter Tovar batted .288, scored 99 runs, and stole 45 bases. Number two hitter Carew led the American League with a .332 batting average. Oliva hit 24 homers, drove in 101 runs, batted .309, and led the league with 197 hits and 39 doubles. Killebrew led the league with 49 home runs, 140 runs batted in, and a .430 on-base percentage. He certainly had to be considered a leading candidate for league MVP.

Baltimore ran away with the A.L. East title, compiling the best regular-season record in baseball (109-53), and finishing 19 games in front of the defending champion Tigers. The Orioles were the most well-balanced team in baseball, possessing a solid lineup, excellent pitching, and good team speed and defense. The pitching staff was headed by lefthanders Mike Cuellar and Dave McNally, and righthander Jim Palmer. Cuellar finished 23-11, with a 2.38 earned run average, 290 innings pitched, and 18 complete games. McNally's record was 20-7, and he compiled a 3.22 earned run average in 268 innings of work. Palmer finished 16-4 with a 2.34 earned run average.

Defensively, third baseman Brooks Robinson and shortstop Mark Belanger made it virtually impossible to get anything through the left side of the Baltimore infield. They were joined by Paul Blair, the best centerfielder in the game. Blair also had a fine offensive season, hitting 26 home runs, batting .285, and scoring 102 runs. Leadoff hitter Don Buford batted .291 and scored 99 runs. Frank Robinson returned from an injury-plagued 1968 campaign to hit 32 home runs, drive in 100 runs, bat .308, and score 111 runs. He deserved MVP consideration. Baltimore's leading candidate, though, was first baseman Boog Powell, who hit 37 homers and knocked in 121 runs.

There were several other legitimate candidates as well. Although Detroit finished 19 games behind Baltimore, Denny McLain had another great year. The Tiger righthander compiled a record of 24-9, to lead the league in victories, and he also finished with a 2.80 earned run average, 23 complete games, and a league-leading 325 innings pitched and nine shutouts. Washington finished fourth in the East, 23 games out, but Senators outfielder Frank Howard had a monstrous season, hitting 48 home runs, knocking in 111 runs, scoring 111 others, and batting .296. Oakland teammates Sal Bando and Reggie Jackson both had big years. Bando hit 31 homers, drove in 113 runs, scored another 106, and batted .281. Jackson finished among the league leaders with 47 home runs and 118 runs batted in, batted .275, and led the A.L. with 123 runs scored and a .608 slugging percentage.

However, due to their fine seasons and the first-place finishes of their respective teams, Killebrew and Powell had to be considered the top two candidates.

Let's take a look at the numbers compiled by the two men:

PLAYER	AB	HITS	RUNS	2B	3B	HR	RBI	AVG	OBP	SLG PCT
Harmon Killebrew	555	153	106	20	2	**49**	**140**	.276	**.430**	.584
Boog Powell	533	162	83	25	0	37	121	.304	.388	.559

Overall, Killebrew's numbers were far more impressive. He led the league in three offensive categories, while Powell failed to finish first in any. Killebrew was far superior as a run-producer, both knocking in and scoring approximately 20 more runs than Powell. The only significant edge that Powell had was in batting average, since he out-hit his rival by almost 30 points. However, Killebrew led the league with 145 walks, as opposed to only 72 bases on balls for Powell. Therefore, the Minnesota slugger finished with a much higher on-base percentage.

True, Powell played on the league's best team, which had easily the best record in the circuit. But that is exactly what the Orioles were—a great *team*. Possessing no glaring weaknesses, they were a finely tuned machine. The Orioles were strong at every position, and they were not overly-dependent on any one player. The Twins were a very solid team as well, but they relied much more heavily on Killebrew. All things considered, the Minnesota slugger was clearly the American League's Most Valuable Player.

1969-1977

NATIONAL LEAGUE

The New York Mets shocked the baseball world in 1969, capturing the National League East title by finishing eight games ahead of the second-place Cubs. They then went on to sweep the Western Division champion Atlanta Braves in three games in the NLCS, before stunning the heavily-favored American League champion Baltimore Orioles in five games in the World Series. The Mets were not the most talented team in baseball, but they had excellent pitching, solid defense, and a team chemistry that made them extremely difficult to beat. Their top two offensive players were leftfielder Cleon Jones and centerfielder Tommie Agee. Jones had the finest season of his career, finishing third in the league with a .340 batting average. Agee led the team with 26 home runs and 97 runs scored. Both men placed in the top ten in the league MVP voting.

However, it was primarily New York's pitching that carried the team to the world championship. The leader of the Mets' pitching staff was unquestionably Tom Seaver. In just his third season, the righthander established himself as the best pitcher in the game by leading the N.L. with a record of 25-7, compiling a 2.21 earned run average, throwing 273 innings, completing 18 games, and striking out 208 batters. Seaver finished second in the MVP balloting.

Third baseman Ron Santo and pitcher Ferguson Jenkins both had outstanding years for second-place Chicago. Santo hit 29 home runs, finished second in the league with 123 runs batted in, scored 97 runs, and batted .289. Jenkins finished the season with a record of 21-15, an earned run average of 3.21, 311 innings pitched, 23 complete games, and a league-leading 273 strikeouts.

The Braves edged out the Giants by three games in the Western Division, with the third-place Reds finishing just four games back. Knuckleballer Phil Niekro led Atlanta's pitching staff with a record of 23-13, a 2.56 earned run average, 284 innings pitched, and 21 complete games. Hank Aaron led the offense with 44 home runs, 97 runs batted in, 100 runs scored, and a .300 batting average.

The third-place Reds had the strongest offense in the league. They led the N.L. with 798 runs scored, 171 home runs, and a team batting average of .277. First baseman Lee May hit 38 home runs and drove in 110 runs. Third baseman Tony Perez hit 37 homers, knocked in 122 runs, scored 103 others, and batted .294. Outfielder Pete Rose was the team's leading MVP candidate, finishing second in the league with 218 hits, and leading the N.L. with a .348 batting average and 120 runs scored.

The second-place Giants received fine seasons from both outfielder Bobby Bonds and pitcher Juan Marichal. Bonds hit 32 homers, drove in 90 runs, led the league with 120 runs scored, and stole 45 bases. Marichal finished 21-11, with a league-leading 2.10 earned run average and eight shutouts. He also placed among the leaders with 299 innings pitched and 27 complete games. However, San Francisco's best player was Willie McCovey, who was named National League MVP. In the finest season of his career, the big first baseman finished fifth in the batting race with a mark of .320, while leading the league with 45 home runs, 126 runs batted in, a .458 on-base percentage, and a .656 slugging percentage.

McCovey's exceptional year and San Francisco's close second-place finish clearly justified the slugger's selection as league MVP.

1970

AMERICAN LEAGUE

The Orioles continued their dominance of the American League in 1970, compiling a regular-season record of 108-54 and finishing 15 games ahead of second-place New York in the Eastern Division. Baltimore was once again the most well-balanced team in baseball, leading the A.L. with 792 runs scored and a team earned run average of 3.15. The Orioles also finished third in the league with 179 home runs and a .257 team batting average. Frank Robinson hit 25 home runs, knocked in 78 runs, and batted .306. Brooks Robinson hit 18 homers, drove in 94 runs, and batted .276. Paul Blair hit 18 homers and scored 79 runs, while Don Buford hit 17 homers and led the team with 99 runs scored. The team's top offensive performer for the second consecutive season was Boog Powell, who led the Birds with 35 home runs and 114 runs batted in, while batting .297. He had to be considered a leading candidate for league MVP honors for the second straight year.

Nevertheless, the Orioles' greatest strength may well have been their pitching. Dave McNally and Mike Cuellar tied for the league lead with 24 victories, finishing 24-9 and 24-8, respectively. McNally also pitched 296 innings, while Cuellar threw 297 frames and led the league with 21 complete games. Jim Palmer finished 20-10 with a 2.71 earned run average, and led A.L. pitchers with 305 innings pitched and five shutouts.

The third-place Red Sox, who finished 21 games behind Baltimore, had perhaps the most potent offense in the league, leading the A.L. with 203 home runs and a .262 team batting average, and finishing second with 786 runs scored. Centerfielder Reggie Smith hit 22 homers, scored 109 runs, and batted .303. Shortstop Rico Petrocelli hit 29 home runs and drove in 103 runs. Rightfielder Tony Conigliaro, still on the mend from his serious 1967 beaning, hit 36 home runs and finished second in the league with 116 runs batted in. Boston's best player was Carl Yastrzemski, who was the best all-around player in the league. Yaz hit 40 homers, knocked in 102 runs, finished second in the batting race with a .329 average, and led the league with 125 runs scored, 335 total bases, a .453 on-base percentage, and a .592 slugging percentage. He certainly deserved serious consideration for league MVP honors.

However, the same could not be said for Washington outfielder Frank Howard. Even though the mammoth slugger led the league with 44 home runs and 126 runs batted in, the Senators finished last in the A.L. East, 38 games behind Baltimore, thereby negating his chances of being selected for the award.

The Minnesota Twins repeated as Western Division champions, finishing nine games ahead of Oakland for the second consecutive year. Pitcher Jim Perry tied for the league lead with 24 victories, compiling a record of 24-12, with a 3.04 earned run average and 278 innings pitched. Cesar Tovar provided an offensive spark at the top of the batting order, hitting .300, finishing among the league leaders with 120 runs scored, 195 hits, and 30 stolen bases, and leading the A.L. with 36 doubles and 13 triples. Tony Oliva had a big year, hitting 23 home runs, driving in 107 runs, batting .325, and leading the league with 204 hits and 36 doubles. Reigning MVP Harmon Killebrew finished among the league leaders with 41 home runs and 113 runs batted in, while batting .271.

One of the finest all-around players in the league was Milwaukee's Tommy Harper. Although the Brewers finished fourth, 33 games behind the Twins, Harper had a tremendous year. Shifting between the outfield, third base, and second base, Milwaukee's leadoff hitter hit 31 home runs, knocked in 82 runs, batted .296, scored 104 runs, and finished second in the league with 38 stolen bases. Had the Brewers not finished so far behind Minnesota in the standings, Harper would have been a leading candidate for league MVP.

All things considered, the strongest contenders for the award were Boog Powell, Carl Yastrzemski, Harmon Killebrew, and Tony Oliva. Yastrzemski was the league's best player, but his team finished 21 games off the pace. Therefore, it would be difficult to justify his selection. Killebrew and Oliva both had fine seasons, and either man would have been a valid selection. Still, the feeling here is that the award should have gone to Powell. His overall numbers were slightly better than those of both Oliva and Killebrew, and he was clearly Baltimore's top player. Frank and Brooks Robinson both had solid years, but neither man was nearly as productive at the plate as Powell. In addition, Frank knocked in 22 fewer runs than he did the previous year, and Paul Blair scored 23 fewer times.

As a result, Powell's offensive productivity was far more essential to the success of the Birds in 1970 than it was the prior year. His selection by the writers was the correct one.

NATIONAL LEAGUE

The Pittsburgh Pirates captured the National League East title in 1970, finishing five games ahead of the second-place Chicago Cubs. Pittsburgh's lineup was one of the best in the N.L., featuring several of the league's top batsmen. Leadoff hitter Matty Alou batted .297, scored 97 runs, and collected 201 hits. Although he appeared in only 108 games, tallying just 412 official at-bats, Roberto Clemente batted .352. Willie Stargell led the team with 31 home runs and 85 runs batted in. Powerful first baseman Bob Robertson hit 27 home runs and drove in 82 runs in only 390 at-bats, and catcher Manny Sanguillen batted .325.

However, the best player in the Eastern Divison, and perhaps the top performer in the entire league, was Cubs outfielder Billy Williams. The leftfielder placed second in the N.L. with 42 home runs and 129 runs batted in, finished fourth in batting average, with a mark of .322, and led the league with 137 runs scored, 205 hits, and 373 total bases. With Chicago finishing second, only five games out of first, Williams had to be considered a leading candidate for league MVP.

The Cincinnati Reds rode their powerful offense to the N.L. West title, finishing 14½ games ahead of the runner-up Dodgers. Cincinnati's lineup was the best in the league, leading the N.L. with 191 home runs and a team batting average of .270. At the top of the order, outfielders Bobby Tolan and Pete Rose set the table for middle-of-the-lineup sluggers Tony Perez, Johnny Bench, and Lee May. Tolan hit 16 homers, drove in 80 runs, batted .316, scored 112 runs, and led the league with 57 stolen bases. Rose batted .316, scored 120 runs, and tied for the league lead with 205 hits. May hit 34 homers and drove in 94 runs. Perez had a tremendous year, finishing among the league leaders with 40 home runs and 129 runs batted in, hitting .317, and scoring 107 runs. Bench led the league with 45 home runs and 148 runs batted in, scored 97 runs, and batted .293, all while doing a superb job behind the plate. He and Perez both deserved serious consideration for MVP honors.

Another player who had an excellent year was Wes Parker, first baseman for the second-place Dodgers. The slick-fielding Parker drove in 111 runs, batted .319, and led the league with 47 doubles. Willie McCovey and Bobby Bonds both had exceptional seasons for the Giants, who finished third in the West, 16 games behind Cincinnati. McCovey followed up his 1969 MVP campaign by hitting 39 home runs, knocking in 126 runs, batting .289, scoring 98 runs, and leading the league with 137 walks and a .612 slugging percentage. Bonds hit 26 round-trippers, batted .302, scored 134 runs, and collected 200 hits. The fifth-place Braves, who finished 26 games off the pace, had the league's batting champion in Rico Carty. The outfielder hit 25 homers, drove in 101 runs, and led the N.L. with a .366 batting average and a .456 on-base-percentage. The MVP aspirations of Parker, McCovey, Bonds, and Carty were all greatly diminished, though, by the fact that their teams finished well out of contention.

That leaves us with Billy Williams, Johnny Bench, and Tony Perez. Let's take a look at the statistics of the three players:

PLAYER	AB	HITS	RUNS	2B	3B	HR	RBI	AVG	OBP	SLG PCT
Billy Williams	636	205	137	34	4	42	129	.322	.391	.586
Johnny Bench	605	177	97	35	4	45	148	.293	.345	.587
Tony Perez	587	186	107	28	6	40	129	.317	.401	.589

Bench and Perez played for the same team, and both men had fabulous years. Bench hit more home runs and drove in more runs, but Perez scored more times, hit for a higher average, and compiled a higher on-base percentage. Statistically, it's very close. Looking beyond the numbers, Perez was Cincinnati's number one team leader. Manager Sparky Anderson often stated that every other member of the Reds deferred to Perez. But Bench was also an outstanding leader and he did a marvelous job of handling Cincinnati's rather mediocre pitching staff. Furthermore, in just his third full season, Bench was already regarded as the best catcher in baseball, and he often drew favorable comparisons to the finest defensive receivers in the history of the game. The catcher's defensive prowess, along with the tremendous offensive contributions he offered the team from the most demanding position on the diamond, move him slightly ahead of Perez.

In comparing Bench to Williams, the Chicago outfielder posted better overall numbers. Bench hit three more homers and knocked in almost 20 more runs than Williams. The two men were extremely close in doubles, triples, and slugging percentage. But Williams scored 40 more runs than Bench, batted 30 points higher, collected almost 30 more hits, and compiled an on-base percentage that was some 45 points better. Williams also did not have as strong a supporting cast in Chicago as Bench had in Cincinnati. However, the Reds won the N.L. West, while the Cubs finished second in the Eastern Division. Furthermore, Bench played a far more demanding defensive position, and, even at the tender age of 22, he was already viewed as one of Cincinnati's team leaders. It's awfully close, but, all things considered, Bench was probably the best choice that could have been made.

1971

AMERICAN LEAGUE

The Orioles won their third consecutive A.L. East title in 1971, finishing 12 games ahead of the second-place Tigers. Reigning MVP Boog Powell had a subpar season, hitting only 22 home runs, driving in 92 runs, batting just .256, and scoring only 59 runs. Yet, Baltimore still managed to lead the league with 742 runs scored and a .261 team batting average. Frank Robinson led the team with 28 home runs, finished second in the league with 99 runs batted in, and batted .281. Brooks Robinson hit 20 homers and drove in 92 runs. Don Buford hit 19 homers, batted .290, and led the A.L. with 99 runs scored, and young outfielder Merv Rettenmund hit .318.

It was Baltimore's pitching, though, that truly separated them from the rest of the league. Their team earned run average of 2.99 was the lowest in the A.L., and their staff featured four 20-game winners. Dave McNally finished 21-5 with a 2.89 earned run average. He was joined by Jim Palmer, Mike Cuellar, and Pat Dobson. Palmer and Cuellar both finished with records of 20-9, and Dobson's record was 20-8. Palmer also compiled an earned run average of 2.68 in 282 innings of work, while throwing 20 complete games. Cuellar pitched to a 3.08 earned run average and completed 21 of his starts, while Dobson's earned run average was 2.90, and he threw 18 complete games.

However, the two best players in the A.L. East played for other teams. Detroit lefthander Mickey Lolich had a tremendous year, leading the league with 25 victories, against 14 defeats. He also compiled a 2.92 earned run average and led A.L. hurlers with 308 strikeouts, 376 innings pitched, and 29 complete games. With the Tigers finishing second in the division to the Orioles, Lolich was certainly a legitimate MVP candidate.

The league's top offensive player was New York outfielder Bobby Murcer. The Yankees centerfielder hit 25 home runs, finished among the league leaders with 94 runs batted in, placed second in the A.L. with a .331 batting average, 94 runs scored, and a .543 slugging percentage, and led the league with a .429 on-base percentage. However, with New York finishing fourth in the division, 21 games behind Baltimore, it would be difficult to make a valid case for Murcer being the league's Most Valuable Player.

In the Western Division, the Oakland A's replaced Minnesota at the top of the standings, finishing 16 games in front of the runner-up Kansas City Royals. Oakland's offense was led by third baseman Sal Bando and rightfielder Reggie Jackson. Bando hit 24 home runs and drove in 94 runs. Jackson hit 32 homers, knocked in 80 runs, and batted .277.

The A's had a couple of 20-game winners of their own in Catfish Hunter and Vida Blue. Hunter finished 21-11, with a 2.96 earned run average, 273 innings pitched, and 16 complete games. Blue's 24 victories (against only 8 losses) were the second most in the league, and he led the A.L. with a 1.82 earned run average and eight shutouts. He also finished among the leaders with 301 strikeouts, 312 innings pitched, and 24 complete games. Blue was the best pitcher in the league, the best player on his own team, and the league's most dominant player. Since his team won its division, he was the only logical choice for A.L. MVP.

NATIONAL LEAGUE

The Giants-Dodgers rivalry was renewed in 1971, with San Francisco beating out Los Angeles by just one game to capture the N.L. West title. Bobby Bonds was San Francisco's best player, hitting 33 home runs, finishing among the league leaders with 102 runs batted in and 110 runs scored, and batting .288. The Dodgers' top performers were outfielder Willie Davis and pitcher Al Downing. Davis batted .309 and collected 198 hits. Downing finished 20-9 with a 2.68 earned run average, 262 innings pitched, and a league-leading five shutouts.

The Western Division's best player was Atlanta's Hank Aaron. The 37-year-old Aaron finished among the league leaders with 47 home runs, 118 runs batted in, and a .327 batting average, and he led the N.L. with a .669 slugging percentage. With the Braves finishing third in the West, eight games out of first, Aaron had to be considered a leading candidate for league MVP.

The Pirates finished first in the N.L. East, beating out the second-place Cardinals by seven games. The Cubs, who finished fourth, 14 games out, had the National League's best pitcher in Ferguson Jenkins.

Jenkins finished 24-13, to lead N.L. hurlers in victories. He also compiled a 2.77 earned run average with 263 strikeouts, and he led the league with 325 innings pitched and 30 complete games. However, each of the top two teams in the division had MVP candidates who were more worthy than Jenkins.

The Pirates featured the league's most potent offense, with solid hitters up and down their batting order. Roberto Clemente batted .341 and drove in 86 runs. Bob Robertson hit 26 home runs, and Manny Sanguillen batted .319 and knocked in 81 runs. Pittstburgh's top offensive performer was Willie Stargell. The big leftfielder led the league with 48 home runs, finished second with 125 runs batted in, scored 104 runs, and batted .295. He was the team's dominant player and the one most responsible for Pittsburgh's first-place finish.

However, Joe Torre had an even better year for the runner-up Cardinals. The third baseman hit 24 homers, scored 97 runs, and led the N.L. with 137 runs batted in, a .363 batting average, and 230 hits.

Let's take a look at his stat-line, along with those of Stargell and Aaron, the other leading candidates:

PLAYER	AB	HITS	RUNS	2B	3B	HR	RBI	AVG	OBP	SLG PCT
Willie Stargell	511	151	104	26	0	48	125	.295	.401	.628
Joe Torre	634	230	97	34	8	24	137	.363	.424	.555
Hank Aaron	495	162	95	22	3	47	118	.327	.410	.669

The statistics of Stargell and Aaron were actually quite comparable, with both players hitting virtually the same number of home runs and collecting the same number of extra-base hits. Stargell knocked in and scored a few more runs, but Aaron hit for a higher average and compiled higher on-base and slugging percentages. But, with the Pirates finishing first in the East and the Braves coming in third in the West, it would be difficult to make a valid case for selecting Aaron over Stargell.

In comparing Torre and Stargell, the latter hit twice as many home runs, scored a few more runs, and finished with a much higher slugging percentage. Torre, though, knocked in more runs, out-hit Stargell by almost 70 points, finished with almost 80 more hits, and collected far more doubles and triples. Still, when one considers that, in spite of Torre's huge edge in batting average, his on-base percentage was only 23 points higher than Stargell's, his overall statistical advantage was a relatively small one. Since Stargell's team finished seven games ahead of Torre's, a legitimate case could be made for selecting the Pittsburgh slugger as the league's Most Valuable Player.

However, two other factors gave Torre a decided advantage. Firstly, Stargell had a much better supporting cast in Pittsburgh. The Pirates' lineup was loaded with other talented hitters such as Roberto Clemente, Bob Robertson, Al Oliver, Manny Sanguillen, Richie Hebner, and Dave Cash. Meanwhile, the only other quality offensive players the Cardinals had in 1971 were Lou Brock and Ted Simmons. True, Brock had an outstanding season, batting .313 with 200 hits, and leading the league with 126 runs scored and 64 stolen bases. But the Cepedas, Floods and Marises who were key components to the Cardinals' back-to-back league championships of 1967 and 1968 were long gone. Torre was the team's only big RBI man, and he was the focal point of the St. Louis offense. In addition, while the Pirates' 1971 record was eight games better than their previous year's mark, the Cardinals' 90 victories represented a 14-game improvement for them.

There is no question that Torre's fabulous year was the primary reason for the progress made by the team. He would have to be considered the league's Most Valuable Player.

1972

AMERICAN LEAGUE

Baltimore's dominance of the American League ended in 1972, as the Detroit Tigers edged out the Red Sox by a half game to capture the Eastern Division title. Prior to the start of the season, the Orioles traded away their best player and team leader, Frank Robinson. They were also victimized by sub-par seasons from Boog Powell, Paul Blair, Don Buford, Dave McNally, and an aging Brooks Robinson. As a result, Baltimore slipped to third place, five games behind the Tigers, who were the recipients of an outstanding year by portly lefthander Mickey Lolich. Lolich compiled a record of 22-14, with a 2.50 earned run average, 250 strikeouts, 327 innings pitched, and 23 complete games. He was Detroit's top MVP candidate.

Luis Tiant was second-place Boston's leading contender for the award. The veteran righthander finished 15-6 with a league-leading

1.91 earned run average. Neither Lolich nor Tiant was the best pitcher in the league, though. Pitching for the fifth-place Indians, who finished 14 games behind Detroit, Gaylord Perry compiled the most impressive stat-line among all A.L. hurlers. Although he also lost 16 games, Perry's 24 victories tied him for the league lead in wins. His 1.92 earned run average was the second lowest in the league, he finished second in the circuit with 342 innings pitched, and he struck out 234 batters and led A.L. hurlers with 29 complete games. At season's end, Perry was named the recipient of the American League's Cy Young Award. However, he was not the league's Most Valuable Player.

Others who deserved consideration were New York's Sparky Lyle and Bobby Murcer. While the Yankees finished fourth in the East, they were only 6½ games out of first, and Lyle and Murcer helped to keep them in the pennant race much of the year. Lyle compiled a record of 9-5, with a 1.92 earned run average, and he led the league with 35 saves. Murcer was one of the best all-around players in the A.L., finishing among the leaders with 33 home runs and 96 runs batted in, hitting .292, and leading the league with 102 runs scored and 314 total bases.

In the Western Division, the A's came out on top for the second straight year, finishing 5½ games ahead of second-place Chicago. Oakland's top two players were leftfielder Joe Rudi and pitcher Catfish Hunter. Rudi hit 19 home runs, knocked in 75 runs, batted .305, finished second in the league with 94 runs scored, and led the A.L. with 181 hits. Hunter compiled a record of 21-7, with a 2.04 earned run average, 295 innings pitched, and 16 complete games.

The runner-up White Sox got an outstanding performance from knuckleballer Wilbur Wood. The lefthander finished 24-17, to tie for the league lead in victories, compiled a 2.51 earned run average, threw 20 complete games, and led A.L. pitchers with 376 innings pitched.

However, Chicago's best player, and the league's top player in 1972, was first baseman Dick (formerly known as *Richie*) Allen. The enigmatic slugger led the American League with 37 home runs and 113 runs batted in, finished among the leaders with a .308 batting average and 90 runs scored, and topped the circuit with a .422 on-base percentage and a .603 slugging percentage. With the White Sox finishing just 5½ games behind the A's in the West, Allen was clearly the league's Most Valuable Player. No one else was even close.

NATIONAL LEAGUE

The Pirates captured their third straight N.L. East title in 1972, finishing 11 games ahead of the second-place Cubs. Once again, it was Pittsburgh's lineup that shouldered much of the burden, with the team featuring the league's top offense. Their lineup featured Roberto Clemente, who hit .312 in only 378 at-bats in his final season. He was joined by Al Oliver and Richie Hebner. Oliver also batted .312, drove in 89 runs, and scored 88 others. Hebner hit 19 home runs and batted .300. As was the case the previous year, Pittsburgh's top offensive player was Willie Stargell, who finished among the league leaders with 33 home runs and 112 runs batted in, while batting .293. He would have to be considered a legitimate MVP candidate.

Another leading contender was Steve Carlton, who had an absolutely brilliant year for the last-place Phillies. Carlton led N.L. starters in every major statistical category, finishing 27-10 with a 1.97 earned run average, 310 strikeouts, 346 innings pitched, and 30 complete games. His 27 victories represented an amazing 46 percent of his team's 59 wins, thereby establishing an all-time major league record. It seemed that the Phillies became a different team when Carlton pitched. Therefore, a strong case could be made for him being the league's Most Valuable Player. Carlton also had the most dominant season of anyone in the N.L. However, it must also be remembered that Philadelphia finished with a record of 59-97, 37½ games behind Pittsburgh. As a result, it would be difficult to select Carlton over someone who wasn't as dominant, but who played on a contending team.

Such a player was Chicago's Billy Williams, whose Cubs finished second to the Pirates in the N.L. East. Williams hit 37 home runs, knocked in 122 runs, and led the league with a .333 batting average and a .606 slugging percentage. He was the most legitimate MVP candidate from the league's Eastern Division.

Cincinnati finished first in the N.L. West, with Houston and Los Angeles both finishing 10½ games back. Tony Perez had a solid year for the Reds, hitting 21 home runs, driving in 90 runs, and batting .283. Joe Morgan, acquired during the off-season in a multi-player deal with the Astros, served as the team's offensive catalyst. The second baseman hit 16 home runs, batted .292, led the league with 122 runs scored, 115 walks, and a .419 on-base percentage, and finished second with 58 stolen bases. However, Morgan was not Cincinnati's most valuable player. Johnny Bench led the league with 40 home runs and 125 runs batted in.

Let's take a look at his stat-line, along with that of Billy Williams, the other leading MVP candidate:

PLAYER	AB	HITS	RUNS	2B	3B	HR	RBI	AVG	OBP	SLG PCT
Billy Williams	574	191	95	34	6	37	122	**.333**	.403	**.606**
Johnny Bench	538	145	87	22	2	**40**	**125**	.270	.386	.541

As was the case two years earlier when Bench finished just ahead of Williams in the voting, the Chicago outfielder posted better overall numbers. His biggest advantage was in batting average, since he out-hit Bench by 63 points. However, the Cincinnati catcher walked much more frequently than Williams, giving him an on-base percentage that was only 17 points lower. Nevertheless, the overall edge would have to go to Williams. Yet, when it is considered that his Cubs finished farther out of first place than they did in 1970, while Bench's Reds again won the Western Division, it becomes harder to make a valid case for the Chicago leftfielder. All things considered, the writers' selection of Bench was the correct one.

1973

AMERICAN LEAGUE

The Orioles returned to the top of the A.L. East standings in 1973, finishing eight games ahead of the second-place Red Sox. Baltimore's team was not as dominant as the one that won three straight division titles from 1969 to 1971, but Manager Earl Weaver's squad was still the most fundamentally sound unit in the league. The Birds relied heavily on strong pitching and solid defense to defeat their opponents. They had the American League's best pitcher in righthander Jim Palmer, who compiled a record of 22-9 with a league-leading 2.40 earned run average. He also threw 296 innings and 19 complete games. Palmer was one of the leading candidates for league MVP.

Detroit's John Hiller also had a fine year. The lefthanded reliever finished 10-5 with a 1.44 earned run average and a league-leading 38 saves. He also led A.L. pitchers with 65 appearances and struck out 124 batters in 125 innings.

The A's captured their third consecutive Western Division title, beating out the runner-up Kansas City Royals by six games. The Royals were an up-and-coming team that featured young stars such as centerfielder Amos Otis and first baseman John Mayberry. Otis hit 26 home runs, drove in 93 runs, scored 89 others, and batted .300. Mayberry also hit 26 homers, knocked in 100 runs, batted .278, and led the A.L. with 122 walks and a .420 on-base percentage.

The class of the division, though, was still Oakland. The A's had a solid lineup and the best pitching staff in baseball. That staff was headed by a trio of 20-game winners. The first was Catfish Hunter, who finished 21-5 with a 3.34 earned run average. He was joined by lefthanders Ken Holtzman and Vida Blue. Holtzman finished 21-13 with a 2.97 earned run average and 297 innings pitched. Blue's record was 20-9, and he pitched to a 3.28 earned run average in 263 innings of work.

Team captain Sal Bando was a major contributor on offense. The third baseman hit 29 home runs, drove in 98 runs, scored 97 others, and batted .287. But the A's best player, and the top player in the league, was Reggie Jackson. The slugging rightfielder batted .293 and led the A.L.with 32 home runs, 117 runs batted in, 99 runs scored, and a .531 slugging percentage. Oakland had other key players on offense, such as Bando, Joe Rudi, and Bert Campaneris, but Jackson was the team's dominant hitter and the league's Most Valuable Player.

NATIONAL LEAGUE

New York ended Pittsburgh's three-year dominance of the National League East in 1973, riding a late-season surge to finish 1½ games ahead of the second-place Cardinals. The Pirates finished third, 2½ games back.

While the Mets' lineup was hardly overpowering, they had perhaps the strongest pitching in the league. Their staff ace was Tom Seaver, who won his second Cy Young Award by finishing 19-10 with a league-leading 2.08 earned run average in 290 innings of work. He also led all N.L. pitchers with 251 strikeouts and 18 complete games.

The runner-up Cardinals got outstanding years from Ted Simmons and Lou Brock. Simmons hit .310, drove in 91 runs, and collected 192 hits. Brock batted .297, scored 110 runs, amassed 193 hits, and led the N.L. with 70 stolen bases.

Ken Singleton and Mike Marshall both had strong seasons for the fourth-place Expos, who finished just 3½ games out of first. Singleton hit 23 homers, drove in 103 runs, scored 100 others, batted .302, and led the league with a .429 on-base percentage. Marshall won 14 games in relief, pitched to a 2.66 earned run average, and led the league with 31 saves and 92 appearances, while pitching 179 innings.

The best player in the East was Pittsburgh's Willie Stargell. The Pirates slugger led the league with 44 home runs, 119 runs batted in, 43 doubles, and a .646 slugging percentage. Stargell was the league's dominant hitter, but he was not the writers' choice for league MVP.

They opted instead for Cincinnati outfielder Pete Rose, who helped lead the Reds to the Western Division title. Cincinnati finished 3½ games ahead of the second-place Dodgers. The Giants, who finished third, 11 games back, had a legitimate MVP candidate of their own in Bobby Bonds. Bonds hit 39 home runs, drove in 96 runs, batted .283, stole 43 bases, and led the league with 131 runs scored. But it was Rose who received the most points in the MVP balloting.

Let's look at his numbers, along with those of Stargell, who finished a close second in the voting:

PLAYER	AB	HITS	RUNS	2B	3B	HR	RBI	AVG	OBP	SLG PCT
Pete Rose	680	230	115	36	8	5	64	.338	.401	.437
Willie Stargell	522	156	106	43	3	44	119	.299	.395	.646

The statistics posted by the two players would seem to indicate that Stargell had the better year. While Rose finished with far more hits, scored a few more runs, and compiled a much higher batting average, Stargell hit many more home runs, drove in almost twice as many runs, and finished with a slugging percentage that was more than 200 points higher. In addition, in spite of Rose's superior batting average, he finished with an on-base percentage that was only six points higher than Stargell's. The Pittsburgh slugger clearly had a far more productive year than Rose, and he was the better player of the two.

Furthermore, Rose had much more help from the rest of the Cincinnati lineup than Stargell had with the Pirates. Roberto Clemente was tragically killed in a plane crash during the off-season, Bob Robertson had a poor year, and both Al Oliver and Manny Sanguillen had sub-par seasons. Meanwhile, Cincinnati's Big Red Machine was working in high gear for much of the year. Johnny Bench hit 25 home runs and knocked in 104 runs. Tony Perez hit 27 homers, drove in 101 runs, and batted .314. Joe Morgan hit 26 round-trippers, knocked in 82 runs, scored 116 others, and batted .290. In fact, it is even debatable as to whether or not Morgan was Cincinnati's most valuable player, instead of Rose.

Although it is true that the Reds won their division while the Pirates finished third in theirs, Pittsburgh finished only 2½ games out. They were in the pennant race for virtually the entire year. That should have been enough to earn Stargell MVP honors.

1974

AMERICAN LEAGUE

The Orioles won their second straight A.L. East title, and their fifth in six seasons in 1974, finishing just two games ahead of the second-place Yankees. Designated hitter Tommy Davis provided clutch hitting down the stretch, and second baseman Bobby Grich had a solid season for the Birds. But Mike Cuellar was Baltimore's most outstanding performer. The veteran lefthander compiled a record of 22-10, with a 3.11 earned run average and 20 complete games. Still, Cuellar wasn't the American League's top pitcher.

The man selected as the league's Cy Young Award winner was Jim "Catfish" Hunter. Pitching for the A's, who won their fourth consecutive A.L. West crown, Hunter finished with a record of 25-12, to tie for the league lead in victories. He also led A.L. hurlers with a 2.49 earned run average, and he finished among the leaders with 318 innings pitched and 23 complete games. Hunter received a considerable amount of support from an Oakland lineup that included Sal Bando, Joe Rudi, and Reggie Jackson. Bando batted only .243, but hit 22 home runs and finished second in the league with 103 runs batted in. Rudi also hit 22 homers, finished third with 99 runs batted in, batted

.293, and led the A.L. with 39 doubles. Jackson was Oakland's top MVP candidate. He finished second in the league with 29 home runs, drove in 93 runs, scored 90 others, and batted .289. However, there were three other legitimate MVP candidates from the A.L. West.

The Twins finished third in the division, eight games behind Oakland, and their lineup featured the league's batting champion, Rod Carew. Although he hit only three home runs and knocked in just 55 runs, Carew led the league with a .364 batting average and 218 hits, and he finished second with 38 stolen bases.

The Texas Rangers came in second in the A.L. West, just five games behind the A's. Ferguson Jenkins tied Catfish Hunter for the league lead with 25 victories, led the A.L. with 29 complete games, and also finished among the leaders with a 2.82 earned run average, 225 strikeouts, and 328 innings pitched. But the Rangers' top player was outfielder Jeff Burroughs. He led the American League with 118 runs batted in, batted .301, and finished among the league leaders with 25 home runs, a .405 on-base percentage, and a .504 slugging percentage. Burroughs helped the Rangers improve their record by a startling *27* games over the 57-105 mark they posted the previous year when they finished last in the A.L. West. The Rangers finished the 1974 campaign with a record of 84-76, and they placed second in the final standings. While other players made major contributions to the improved play of the Rangers, Burroughs was their best player and the man most responsible for the success they experienced. He was clearly deserving of the Most Valuable Player Award that was presented to him at season's end.

NATIONAL LEAGUE

After a one-year hiatus, the Pirates returned to the top of the N.L. East standings in 1974, barely edging out the Cardinals by just 1½ games. Pittsburgh was led by Al Oliver and Willie Stargell. Oliver batted .321, drove in 85 runs, scored 96 others, and collected 198 hits. Stargell hit 25 homers, knocked in 96 runs, scored another 90, and batted .301. Ted Simmons had a fine year for the second-place Cardinals. The St. Louis catcher hit 20 homers and drove in 103 runs. But the Cardinals' most outstanding performer was Lou Brock, who established a new single-season major league record by stealing 118 bases. He also batted .306, scored 105 runs, and collected 194 hits. Brock finished second in the MVP voting.

Perhaps the finest all-around season of anyone in the league was turned in by Philadelphia third baseman Mike Schmidt. Schmidt led the N.L. with 36 home runs and a .546 slugging percentage, and he also finished among the leaders with 116 runs batted in and 108 runs scored. Nevertheless, with the Phillies finishing third in the East, eight games back, Schmidt could do no better than sixth in the balloting.

In the Western Division, the Dodgers compiled baseball's best record (102-60), beating out second-place Cincinnati by four games in the process. Los Angeles was the league's most well-balanced team, finishing first in runs scored (798), home runs (139), and team earned run average (2.97), and placing second in team batting average (.272). The Dodger staff featured three of the National League's top starting pitchers. Andy Messersmith compiled a record of 20-6, with a 2.59 earned run average, 221 strikeouts, and 292 innings pitched. Don Sutton finished 19-9, with a 3.23 earned run average and 276 innings pitched, and Tommy John went 13-3 with a 2.59 earned run average.

The Dodgers also had the strongest lineup in the league from top to bottom. Leadoff hitter Davey Lopes scored 95 runs and stole 59 bases. Bill Buckner batted .314 and scored 83 runs. Ron Cey hit 18 homers, drove in 97 runs, and scored 88 others. Jim Wynn led the team with 32 home runs and 104 runs scored, knocked in 108 runs, and batted .271. But the man selected by the writers as the league's Most Valuable Player was Steve Garvey. The Dodger first baseman was a model of consistency all year, finishing the season with 21 home runs, 111 runs batted in, a .312 batting average, and 200 hits. Garvey had a very solid year, but was he truly deserving of being named league MVP?

Let's look at his numbers, alongside those of Mike Schmidt and the Reds' Johnny Bench, to get a better idea:

PLAYER	AB	HITS	RUNS	2B	3B	HR	RBI	AVG	OBP	SLG PCT
Mike Schmidt	568	160	108	28	7	**36**	116	.282	.398	**.546**
Steve Garvey	642	200	95	32	3	21	111	.312	.346	.469
Johnny Bench	621	174	108	38	2	33	**129**	.280	.365	.507

Garvey finished with the most hits and with the highest batting average. However, both Schmidt and Bench hit far more home runs, knocked in and scored more runs, and compiled much higher slugging percentages. The fact that Garvey hardly ever walked also enabled both Schmidt and Bench to finish with higher on-base percentages. Clearly, Schmidt and Bench were better players than the Dodger first baseman. But, were they more valuable to their respective teams? Well, the Phillies finished third in the East, eight games behind the Pirates. While Schmidt's numbers were better than Garvey's, they may not have exceeded them by a wide enough margin to overcome the Dodgers' first-place finish in the West.

Bench's numbers were extremely comparable to Schmidt's, and his Reds finished just four games behind Garvey's Dodgers. As was the case with Garvey in Los Angeles, Bench also had an excellent supporting cast in Cincinnati. Tony Perez hit 28 home runs and drove in 101 runs. Pete Rose led the league with 110 runs scored and 45 doubles, while batting .284 and compiling an excellent .388 on-base percentage. Joe Morgan hit 22 home runs, batted .293, scored 107 runs, and led the N.L. with a .430 on-base percentage. All things considered, it would seem that the vote could have gone either way, and that either Garvey or Bench would have been a good selection. However, the Dodgers had another player whose contributions have yet to be mentioned.

Los Angeles reliever Mike Marshall had a superb season for the Western Division champs. Pitching strictly in relief, the righthander appeared in a league-leading 106 contests, winning 15 games and saving another 21. His 21 saves led the National League, and he also compiled a 2.42 earned run average and struck out 143 batters in an amazing 208 innings of work. The numbers posted by Marshall were clearly atypical of those for a relief pitcher. His 106 appearances and 208 innings pitched were both extraordinary figures, and, with his 15 wins and 21 saves, Marshall was involved in 36 of his team's victories. Yet, he finished a distant third in the balloting. Perhaps Marshall's scruffy appearance, as opposed to Garvey's good-looking, clean-cut image, cost him the election. Or perhaps Marshall lost out because the voters were not yet prepared for the idea of a relief pitcher being named league MVP. But Marshall was most certainly the National League's Most Valuable Player in 1974.

1975

AMERICAN LEAGUE

The Oakland Athletics captured their fifth consecutive A.L. West title in 1975, finishing seven games ahead of the second-place Kansas City Royals. In spite of the loss of staff ace Jim "Catfish" Hunter to free agency during the off-season, the A's relied heavily on their pitching to hold off the hard-charging Royals. Vida Blue led the team with 22 victories (against 11 losses), pitched to a 3.01 earned run average, and struck out 189 batters in 278 innings of work. Ken Holtzman won 18 games and compiled a 3.14 earned run average in 266 innings pitched. Rollie Fingers won 10 games in relief and saved another 24, while appearing in a league-leading 75 games. Reggie Jackson paced the Oakland offense with a league-leading 36 home runs. He also drove in 104 runs and scored another 91. However, Jackson's .253 batting average prevented him from being seriously considered for league MVP honors.

The runner-up Royals had a legitimate candidate in slugging first baseman John Mayberry. He finished among the league leaders with 34 home runs and 106 runs batted in, while scoring 95 runs and batting .291. Mayberry placed second in the MVP balloting.

In the Eastern Division, the Red Sox beat out Baltimore by 4½ games to capture their first A.L. East title. The second-place Orioles had a leading candidate for league MVP in Cy Young Award winning righthander Jim Palmer. Palmer finished the year with a record of 23-11, led the A.L. with a 2.09 earned run average and 10 shutouts, and threw 323 innings and 25 complete games.

Catfish Hunter and Thurman Munson both had excellent years for the third-place Yankees, who finished 12 games behind the Red Sox. Hunter tied Palmer for the league-lead with 23 victories, while compiling a 2.58 earned run average and leading A.L. hurlers with 328 innings pitched and 30 complete games. Munson finished among the league leaders with 102 runs batted in, a .318 batting average, and 190 hits.

But the best team in the American League was the Boston Red Sox, who combined solid pitching with the most potent offense in the league. Their staff was headed by Luis Tiant, who finished 18-14, with 18 complete games and 260 innings pitched. He was joined by lefthander Bill Lee, who compiled a record of 17-9 with 17 complete games.

Boston's greatest strength was its offense, which led the A.L. with 796 runs scored and a team batting average of .275. Carl Yastrzemski scored 91 runs. Despite being injured for much of the year, Carlton Fisk batted .331, drove in 52 runs, and scored another 47 in only 263 official at-bats.

A great deal of the Red Sox success lay squarely on the shoulders of their two outstanding rookies. With his compact yet powerful swing, Jim Rice hit 22 home runs, knocked in 102 runs, scored 92 others, and batted .309. He finished third in the MVP balloting. Fellow rookie Fred Lynn won the award for his brilliant all-around play. Lynn hit 21 homers, finished among the league leaders with 105 runs batted in and a .331 batting average, and led the A.L. with 103 runs scored, 47 doubles, and a .566 slugging percentage. He also played a superb centerfield for the Sox.

In being named league MVP, Lynn became the first player to win both the Rookie of the Year Award and the Most Valuable Player Award in the same year.

NATIONAL LEAGUE

The Pirates won their fifth N.L. East title in six years in 1975, finishing 6½ games ahead of the runner-up Phillies. Pittsburgh had a capable pitching staff and one of the best lineups in the league. Their staff ace was Jerry Reuss, who finished 18-11 with a 2.54 earned run average. The Pirates were led on offense by MVP candidate Dave Parker, who hit 25 home runs, knocked in 101 runs, and batted .308. He was joined by Willie Stargell and Al Oliver. Stargell hit 22 homers, drove in 90 runs, and batted .295. Oliver hit 18 home runs, knocked in 84 runs, scored 90 others, and batted .280.

The second-place Phillies had a legitimate MVP candidate of their own in outfielder Greg Luzinski. The powerfully-built slugger finished third in the league with 34 home runs, led the N.L. with 120 runs batted in, and batted .300. Luzinski finished second in the MVP balloting.

The Cincinnati Reds dominated the league's Western Division, compiling a regular-season record of 108-54 and finishing 20 games ahead of the second-place Dodgers. While they had a solid bullpen and decent starting pitching, it was the Reds' offense that made them baseball's dominant team. Their 840 runs scored were 105 more than the 735 tallied by league runner-up Philadelphia, and 44 more than A.L. leader Boston. The fact that the Reds scored more runs than any American League team speaks to the explosiveness of their lineup when it is considered that the junior circuit employed a designated hitter.

At the top of the order, Pete Rose batted .317, collected 210 hits, and led the N.L. with 112 runs scored and 47 doubles. He was followed by Ken Griffey, who batted .305 and scored 95 runs. Further down in the lineup, Tony Perez hit 20 homers, knocked in 109 runs, and batted .282. Johnny Bench hit 28 home runs, finished second in the league with 110 runs batted in, and batted .283. George Foster added 23 homers and batted .300.

But the man who galvanized everything was second baseman Joe Morgan. Morgan hit 17 home runs, drove in 94 runs, finished among the league leaders with a .327 batting average, 107 runs scored, and 67 stolen bases, and led the N.L. with 132 bases on balls and a .471 on-base percentage. Morgan was Cincinnati's offensive catalyst and the best all-around player in the National League. He was clearly deserving of the MVP trophy that was presented to him at season's end.

1976

AMERICAN LEAGUE

The New York vs. Kansas City rivalry began in 1976, with the Yankees and Royals both winning the first of three consecutive division titles. New York finished first in the A.L. East, beating out second-place Baltimore by 10½ games. The Yankees' team earned run average of 3.19 was the lowest in the American League, and they also finished second in the league with a .269 team batting average, 120 home runs, and 730 runs scored.

New York's pitching staff was headed by Catfish Hunter, who won 17 games and finished among the league leaders with 298 innings pitched and 21 complete games. Ed Figueroa led the staff with 19 victories and compiled a 3.02 earned run average. Dock Ellis finished

17-8 and pitched to a 3.19 earned run average. In the bullpen, closer Sparky Lyle led the league with 23 saves, while compiling a 2.26 earned run average.

On offense, Roy White batted .286, stole 31 bases, and led the league with 104 runs scored. First baseman Chris Chambliss was a model of consistency, hitting 17 home runs, driving in 96 runs, and batting .293. After a slow start, third baseman Graig Nettles was the team's hottest hitter over the season's final two months. Nettles ended up leading the A.L. with 32 home runs, while driving in 93 runs. Speedy centerfielder Mickey Rivers provided a spark at the top of the batting order, hitting .312, scoring 95 runs, and stealing 43 bases in 50 attempts. But the man who held everything together was the Yankees' catcher and team captain, Thurman Munson. The gritty Munson hit 17 home runs, finished second in the league with 105 runs batted in, batted .302, and placed among the league leaders with 186 hits. He was New York's leading candidate for league MVP.

The second-place Orioles got fine seasons from first baseman Lee May and the newly-acquired Reggie Jackson. May hit 25 home runs and drove in a league-leading 109 runs. Jackson finished second in the A.L. with 27 home runs, knocked in 91 runs, and led the league with a .502 slugging percentage. However, with Baltimore finishing 10½ games behind New York in the East, neither May nor Jackson could be seriously considered for MVP honors.

In the Western Division, Kansas City ended Oakland's five-year reign as division champions by beating out the A's by just 2½ games. Joe Rudi, Sal Bando, Bill North, and Vida Blue all had solid seasons for the defending champs. Rudi scored 94 runs, Bando hit 27 home runs and drove in 84 runs, and North scored 91 runs and led the league with 75 stolen bases. Blue won 18 games and led the Oakland staff with a 2.35 earned run average, 298 innings pitched, and 20 complete games. But, with both Catfish Hunter and Reggie Jackson playing for other teams, the A's were unable to overcome Kansas City's combination of speed, timely hitting, and solid pitching. Although they hit only 65 home runs as a team, the Royals finished fourth in the league in runs scored. They also placed second in the A.L. with 218 stolen bases, while compiling the second lowest team earned run average (3.21).

Kansas City's best pitcher was righthander Dennis Leonard, who led the team with 17 victories, 259 innings pitched, and 16 complete games. On offense, diminutive shortstop Fred Patek stole 51 bases. John Mayberry knocked in 95 runs. Centerfielder Amos Otis hit 18 home runs, drove in 86 runs, scored 93 others, batted .279, stole 26 bases, and led the league with 40 doubles. Outfielder/designated hitter Hal McRae finished a close second in the A.L. batting race with a mark of .332, and also compiled an excellent .412 on-base percentage. Kansas City's best player was third baseman George Brett. Although he hit only seven home runs and knocked in just 67 runs, Brett scored 94 times and led the league with a .333 batting average, 215 hits, 14 triples, and 298 total bases. Along with Munson, he had to be considered the leading candidate for league MVP. But, who was more deserving—Brett or Munson?

A look at their numbers may help to answer that question:

PLAYER	AB	HITS	RUNS	2B	3B	HR	RBI	AVG	OBP	SLG PCT
George Brett	645	215	94	34	14	7	67	.333	.377	.462
Thurman Munson	616	186	79	27	1	17	105	.302	.337	.432

Brett's overall statistics were slightly better. While Munson hit more home runs and knocked in more runs, Brett compiled a higher batting average and finished ahead of Munson in doubles, triples, runs scored, base hits, and in both on-base and slugging percentage. Yet, it is difficult to ignore the Yankee catcher's superiority as a run-producer. Although Brett scored 15 more times, Munson drove in 38 more runs. That's a net difference of 23 in Munson's favor.

In addition, Brett did not have the overall impact on the Royals that Munson had on the Yankees at that point in their respective careers. The Kansas City third baseman was his team's best player, but he had yet to establish himself as the Royals' leader. Meanwhile, Munson was New York's captain and acknowledged team leader. He was admired and respected by everyone in the clubhouse. He was also a tremendous handler of pitchers. Furthermore, as a catcher, he played a more demanding defensive position than Brett, and he had a greater impact on the game.

All things considered, the writers made the correct choice when they named Munson league MVP.

NATIONAL LEAGUE

The Cincinnati Reds continued their dominance of the National League in 1976, easily capturing the Western Division title and leading the league in virtually every major offensive team category. They led the N.L. with 141 home runs, 210 stolen bases, and a team batting average of .280, and their 857 runs scored were 87 more than the 770 scored by runner-up Philadelphia. Their powerful offense enabled them to finish 10 games ahead of the second-place Dodgers and masked the fact that they also had a solid pitching staff. That staff finished fifth in the league in team earned run average, with a mark of 3.51. Cincinnati's best pitcher was oft-injured lefthander Don Gullett, who was limited to just 20 starts, but managed to compile an excellent 11-3 record and 3.00 earned run average. Pat Zachry finished 14-7 with a 2.74 earned run average. Reliever Rawly Eastwick led the N.L. with 26 saves and finished 11-5 with a 2.09 earned run average.

But it was Cincinnati's lineup that instilled fear in the opposition. In fact, the Reds' offense was so strong that their eighth-place hitter, centerfielder Cesar Geronimo, batted .307. Leadoff hitter Pete Rose batted .323 and led the N.L. with 130 runs scored, 215 hits, and 42 doubles. Number two hitter Ken Griffey batted .336, scored 111 runs, and stole 34 bases. Tony Perez hit 19 homers and drove in 91 runs in his final year in Cincinnati. Leftfielder George Foster hit 29 home runs, batted .306, and led the league with 121 runs batted in. The team's best player was Joe Morgan, who had another sensational season. Morgan hit 27 home runs and finished among the league leaders with 111 runs batted in, 113 runs scored, a .320 batting average, and 60 stolen bases. He also led the N.L. with a .453 on-base percentage and a .576 slugging percentage. Morgan was certainly a leading contender for league MVP honors.

In the Eastern Division, the Phillies overtook the Pirates, finishing nine games ahead of the prior year's division champions. Greg Luzinski hit 21 home runs, knocked in 95 runs, and batted .304. Garry Maddox batted .330, stole 29 bases, and was generally considered to be the finest defensive centerfielder in the game. Steve Carlton finished 20-7 with a 3.13 earned run average and 195 strikeouts. Mike Schmidt led the National League with 38 home runs, and also finished among the leaders with 107 runs batted in and 112 runs scored. He would have to be considered Philadelphia's top MVP candidate. However, Schmidt batted only .262, and he did not have nearly as good an all-around year as Joe Morgan. The second baseman finished ahead of Schmidt in every offensive category, except home runs, and he was his team's offensive catalyst.

The National League's best all-around player for the second consecutive season, Morgan was also unquestionably the league's Most Valuable Player once more.

1977

AMERICAN LEAGUE

The race in the American League East was much closer in 1977, with both the Orioles and Red Sox remaining in contention until the season's final days. However, the Yankees prevailed in the end, finishing 2½ games ahead of both Baltimore and Boston. All three contenders featured several players who had outstanding seasons.

Lee May hit 27 home runs and knocked in 99 runs for the Orioles. Rookie first baseman/designated hitter Eddie Murray also hit 27 homers, drove in 88 runs, and batted .283. Jim Palmer led the league with 20 victories (against 11 losses), compiled a 2.91 earned run average, and led A.L. pitchers with 319 innings pitched and 22 complete games. Baltimore's best player was outfielder Ken Singleton. The switch-hitting Singleton hit 24 home runs, knocked in 99 runs, scored 90 others, and finished among the league leaders with a .328 batting average and a .442 on-base percentage. He finished third in the MVP voting.

Boston's powerful lineup led the league with 213 home runs. First baseman George Scott hit 33 homers, drove in 95 runs, and scored 103 others. Third baseman Butch Hobson hit 30 homers and knocked in 112 runs. Catcher Carlton Fisk had perhaps his finest all-around season, hitting 26 home runs, driving in 102 runs, scoring another 106, and batting .315. Boston's most potent offensive weapon, though, was Jim Rice. In just his third season, Rice established himself as the league's most dangerous hitter. He led the A.L. with 39 home runs, finished among the leaders with 114 runs batted in, 104 runs scored, a .320 batting average, and 206 hits, and led the league with 382 total bases and a .593 slugging percentage. Rice finished fourth in the MVP balloting.

The Eastern Division champion Yankees finished second in the league with a team batting average of .281 and compiled the third lowest team earned run average (3.61) in the A.L. In just his first full season, lefthander Ron Guidry was an extremely pleasant surprise, finishing 16-7 with a 2.82 earned run average. Sparky Lyle led the league with 72 relief appearances, compiled a record of 13-5, pitched to a 2.17 earned run average, and saved 26 games. At season's end, he was named the winner of the A.L. Cy Young Award.

On offense, Chris Chambliss hit 17 home runs, both knocked in and scored 90 runs, and batted .287. Mickey Rivers batted .326 and led the team with 22 stolen bases. In his first year in pinstripes, Reggie Jackson hit 32 home runs, knocked in 110 runs, scored 93 others, and batted .286. Reigning MVP Thurman Munson hit 18 home runs, drove in 100 runs, and batted .308. Third baseman Graig Nettles finished second in the league with 37 home runs, knocked in 107 runs, and scored 99 others. He was the only Yankee who finished in the top five in the MVP balloting, coming in fifth.

The A.L. West was not nearly as competitive, with Kansas City finishing eight games ahead of second-place Texas. The Royals again relied more on speed and pitching than on power to defeat their opposition. They finished sixth in the league with 146 home runs, and their .277 team batting average was the fifth highest in the A.L. However, they finished second in the league with 170 stolen bases, and their team earned run average of 3.52 was the lowest in the A.L. Dennis Leonard was the ace of the pitching staff, tying Jim Palmer for the league lead with 20 victories, and finishing among the leaders with 244 strikeouts, 292 innings pitched, and 21 complete games. He was joined by Paul Splittorff, who chipped in with 16 victories.

Kansas City shortstop Fred Patek led the American League with 53 stolen bases. Hal McRae hit 21 home runs, drove in 92 runs, scored another 104, batted .298, and led the league with 54 doubles. George Brett hit 22 homers, knocked in 88 runs, batted .312, and finished among the league leaders with 105 runs scored. Kansas City's top player was rightfielder Al Cowens. Working extensively with batting instructor Charlie Lau, Cowens learned to use the entire ballfield, and also to "jerk" the inside pitch. The result was the finest season of his career, as Cowens hit 23 home runs, drove in 112 runs, scored 98 others, and batted .312. He finished runner-up in the MVP voting.

The man who finished first was Minnesota's Rod Carew. Always a superb hitter, Carew increased his offensive productivity in 1977 and ended up having the greatest season of his career. He hit 14 home runs (which was actually a lot for him), knocked in a career-high 100 runs, and led the league with a .388 batting average, 128 runs scored, 239 hits, 16 triples, and a .452 on-base percentage. Carew also finished second with 351 total bases and a .570 slugging percentage. Although the Twins finished 17½ games behind Kansas City in the A.L. West, they were able to come in fourth largely because of Carew. Had he not had such a great year, there is no telling where they would have finished. Al Cowens had an outstanding season for the Western Division champs, and Jim Rice had an even better one for contending Boston. But Rod Carew was clearly the league's best player, and he was the man most deserving of A.L. MVP honors. His statistics were just too overwhelming to overlook.

NATIONAL LEAGUE

The Phillies captured their second straight N.L. East title in 1977, finishing five games in front of the second-place Pirates. Philadelphia had the National League's best offense, leading the league with 847 runs scored and a .279 team batting average, and finishing second with 186 home runs. Their attack was led by Greg Luzinski and Mike Schmidt. Luzinski finished second in the league with 39 home runs and 130 runs batted in, scored 99 runs, and batted .309. Schmidt finished third in homers with 38, placed second with 114 runs scored, and knocked in 101 runs. Philadelphia also had the league's best pitcher in Steve Carlton, who compiled a record of 23-10 with a 2.64 earned run average, 283 innings pitched, and 17 complete games.

The runner-up Pirates had one of the finest all-around players in the game in young star Dave Parker. The rightfielder hit 21 homers, knocked in 88 runs, scored 107 others, and led the league with a .338 batting average, 215 hits, and 44 doubles. Like Luzinski, Schmidt, and Carlton, Parker had to be considered a leading candidate for the MVP Award.

Los Angeles turned the tables on Cincinnati in the N.L. West, beating out the Reds by 10 games to capture the division title. While Philadelphia's offense was more potent, the Dodgers were the league's best balanced team. They led the N.L. with 191 home runs, finished third with 769 runs scored, placed fifth with a team batting average of .266, and perhaps most importantly, they led the league with a team earned run average of only 3.22. Tommy John was the staff ace, compiling a record of 20-7 with a 2.78 earned run average.

On offense, Davey Lopes batted .283, scored 85 runs, and stole 47 bases. Dusty Baker hit 30 homers, both knocked in and scored 86 runs, and batted .291. Ron Cey hit 30 homers and drove in 110 runs. Reggie Smith hit 32 four-baggers, drove in 87 runs, scored 104 others, batted .307, and led the league with a .432 on-base percentage. Steve Garvey was the team's leading MVP candidate.

Let's look at his numbers, alongside those of the other top contenders:

PLAYER	AB	HITS	RUNS	2B	3B	HR	RBI	AVG	OBP	SLG PCT
Mike Schmidt	544	149	114	27	11	38	101	.274	.399	.574
Steve Garvey	646	192	91	25	3	33	115	.297	.337	.498
George Foster	615	197	124	31	2	52	149	.320	.386	.631
Greg Luzinski	554	171	99	35	3	39	130	.309	.399	.594
Dave Parker	637	215	107	44	8	21	88	.338	.399	.531

Overall, Garvey's numbers were the least impressive of anyone in the group. His home run and RBI totals were quite substantial, but he scored the fewest number of runs, and both his on-base and slugging percentages were much lower than the others. He played for the pennant-winning team, but, as we saw earlier, the Dodgers were a well-balanced club that provided Garvey with a great deal of support. All things considered, he was the least-deserving of the five men.

Dave Parker led the league in three different offensive categories, including batting average. But both Greg Luzinski and Mike Schmidt posted identical on-base percentages, finished with much higher slugging percentages, hit many more home runs, and were far superior as run-producers. In addition, the Phillies finished five games ahead of Parker's Pirates in the standings. As a result, the Pittsburgh outfielder was the next to go.

Luzinski and Schmidt played for the same team, and their overall numbers were actually quite comparable. They hit virtually the same number of home runs and, even though Luzinski out-hit Schmidt by 35 points, the two men finished with the same on-base percentage. Luzinski was the greater run-producer and the more consistent hitter of the two men. On the other hand, Schmidt was a more complete player, fielding his position and running the bases much better than Luzinski. Still, it is difficult to ignore the overall edge that Luzinski had on offense.

That leaves us with Luzinski and George Foster. In most years, the Philadelphia slugger would have walked away with the MVP trophy. The Phillies won their division and Luzinski had a fabulous season. However, Cincinnati's George Foster had an absolutely spectacular year. He led the National League in four different offensive categories, posting some extraordinary numbers in the process. Foster's 52 home runs were the most hit by a major leaguer since Willie Mays compiled the same total for the Giants in 1965. Foster's 149 runs batted in were the most in the majors since Tommy Davis knocked in 153 runs for the Dodgers in 1962. The Cincinnati outfielder finished well ahead of Luzinski in both categories. He also scored 25 more runs than Luzinski, while compiling a much higher slugging percentage as well. Luzinski finished slightly ahead in doubles, triples, and on-base percentage, but Foster's overall numbers were considerably better than Luzinski's. The Reds finished 10 games behind Los Angeles in the N.L. West, but they also finished a very respectable second. It would be difficult to find fault with the writers' selection of Foster as league MVP.

SLUGGERS REIGN ONCE MORE

19

The strong showings of young sluggers Jim Rice and Dave Parker in the MVP balloting of 1977 were a portent of things to come. Rice walked away with the A.L. award the following year, and Parker was named the winner in the National League. Their selections were just the first in a series of choices made over the next few years honoring players who compiled some rather prolific offensive numbers. In fact, in all but one of the 12 elections held between 1978 and 1983, the player chosen as his league's Most Valuable Player was among the top run-producers and offensive forces in baseball.

| | ACTUAL MVP WINNERS | | SUGGESTED WINNERS | |
	A.L.	N.L.	A.L.	N.L.
1978	Jim Rice	Dave Parker	Jim Rice	Dave Parker
1979	Don Baylor	Keith Hernandez/ Willie Stargell	Don Baylor	Keith Hernandez
1980	George Brett	Mike Schmidt	George Brett	Mike Schmidt
1981	Rollie Fingers	Mike Schmidt	Rickey Henderson	Mike Schmidt
1982	Robin Yount	Dale Murphy	Robin Yount	Dale Murphy
1983	Cal Ripken Jr.	Dale Murphy	Cal Ripken Jr.	Dale Murphy

1978

AMERICAN LEAGUE

The Kansas City Royals captured their third consecutive A.L. West title in 1978, finishing five games in front of both Texas and California. The Angels' top player was outfielder Don Baylor, who hit 34 home runs, knocked in 99 runs, and scored 103 others. Centerfielder Amos Otis led Kansas City's attack, hitting 22 home runs, driving in 96 runs, batting .298, and stealing 32 bases. The Royals also received strong efforts from two of their pitchers. Dennis Leonard won 21 games, threw 294 innings, and completed 20 of his starts. Larry Gura was the team's most effective starter, compiling a record of 16-4 and a 2.72 earned run average.

Most of the league's top players, though, resided in the Eastern Division. Eddie Murray, Doug DeCinces, and Jim Palmer all had outstanding seasons for the fourth-place Orioles, who finished nine games off the pace. Murray hit 27 home runs, drove in 95 runs, and batted .285. DeCinces, who had the unenviable task of trying to replace the great Brooks Robinson at third base for the Orioles, hit 28 homers, knocked in 80 runs, and batted .286. Palmer finished 21-12, with a 2.46 earned run average, 19 complete games, and a league-leading 296 innings pitched.

Mike Caldwell, who pitched for the third-place Brewers, had an even better year. The lefthander compiled a record of 22-9, to finish second among A.L. pitchers in victories. He also finished third with a 2.36 earned run average and 293 innings pitched, second with six shutouts, and first with 23 complete games. The Milwaukee offense was led by outfielder Larry Hisle, who finished among the league leaders with 34 home runs and 115 runs batted in, while batting .290 and scoring 96 runs. With the improving Brewers finishing just 6½ games out of first place, Hisle received the third highest point total in the MVP balloting.

The top two vote-getters came from the division's two best teams—New York and Boston. The Yankees mounted a furious second-half comeback to eventually catch the first-place Red Sox and force a one-game playoff at Fenway Park. The Yankees won the contest by a score of 5-4 to capture their third straight A.L. East crown. Several players contributed to New York's great comeback. Chris Chambliss knocked in 90 runs and Lou Piniella led the team with a .314 batting average. Second baseman Willie Randolph batted .279, scored 87 runs, and led New York with 36 stolen bases. Though injured much of the year, Thurman Munson batted .297, led the Yankees with 183 hits, and helped to hold the team together in spite of all the inner turmoil that plagued them throughout the year. Reggie Jackson hit 27 home runs and knocked in 97 runs. Graig Nettles tied Jackson for the team lead with 27 homers, drove in 93 runs, batted a career-high .276, and won his second straight Gold Glove for his tremendous work at third base. Ed Figueroa compiled a record of 20-9 and a 2.99 earned run average, and Rich Gossage led the league with 27 saves while pitching to a 2.01 earned run average.

However, New York's most valuable player was clearly Ron Guidry. The little lefthander from Louisiana dominated the statistical categories for pitchers almost as much as he dominated American League hitters. He finished the season with a remarkable record of 25-3, along with a league-leading 1.74 earned run average and nine shutouts. Guidry also finished among the leaders with 248 strikeouts, 273 innings pitched, and 16 complete games. He practically guaranteed the Yankees a victory every time he took the mound, almost singlehandedly keeping them within striking distance of Boston much of the year while the rest of the team struggled. In most seasons, Guidry would have been an easy winner in the league MVP voting.

The 1978 season was an exception, though, because Jim Rice had an equally phenomenal year for the Red Sox. Rice led the A.L. with 46 home runs, 139 runs batted in, 213 hits, 15 triples, 406 total bases, and a .600 slugging percentage. He also finished second with 121 runs scored and third with a .315 batting average. Rice had a great deal of help from his teammates. Carlton Fisk hit 20 home runs, drove in 88 runs, scored 94 others, and batted .284. Fred Lynn hit 22 four-baggers, knocked in 82 runs, and batted .298. Carl Yastrzemski drove in 81 runs and batted .277, while Dennis Eckersley led the pitching staff with a record of 20-8, a 2.99 earned run average, 268 innings pitched, and 16 complete games. But Rice was the focal point of the Boston offense throughout the year, and he was primarily responsible for the team's strong second-place finish.

The obvious question then is: who was most deserving of the league MVP trophy—Rice or Guidry? Both men had extraordinary seasons, and they were clearly the dominant figures in baseball that year. They were both the primary reasons why their respective teams fared as well as they did during the regular season. Guidry's team finished first in the division, but Rice's squad wasn't eliminated until the season's final day. Either player would have been a good selection. However, Rice had an edge in that he played in virtually all of his team's games, while Guidry appeared in only 35 of his team's contests.

That last fact was unquestionably the overriding factor in the minds of the writers, who selected Rice over Guidry by a margin of 352 to 291. We will not dispute that decision here.

NATIONAL LEAGUE

The Dodgers and Phillies repeated as division champions in the National League in 1978, but both by the slimmest of margins. Los Angeles captured the Western Division crown, finishing just 2½ games ahead of second-place Cincinnati, who featured the division's most dominant hitter in George Foster. The league's reigning MVP led the N.L. with 40 home runs and 120 runs batted in, while batting .281. Foster's teammate, Pete Rose, also had a fine year, batting .302, scoring 103 runs, leading the league with 51 doubles, and setting a new National League record by hitting in 44 consecutive games.

However, neither the efforts of Foster nor Rose were enough to overcome the overall team balance of the Dodgers. Los Angeles led the N.L. with 727 runs scored, 149 home runs, a .264 team batting average, and a team earned run average of 3.12. Their pitching staff featured three fine starters in lefthander Tommy John and righthanders Don Sutton and Burt Hooton. John won 17 games, Sutton another 15, and Hooten led the staff with a record of 19-10 and an earned run average of 2.71. On offense, leadoff hitter Davey Lopes was an excellent table-setter. The speedy second baseman hit 17 home runs, batted .278, scored 93 runs, and stole 45 bases in 49 attempts. Third baseman Ron Cey hit 23 homers and drove in 84 runs, while rightfielder Reggie Smith hit 29 round-trippers, knocked in 93 runs, and batted .295. The Dodgers' leading candidate for MVP, though, was first baseman Steve Garvey, who hit 21 home runs, drove in 113 runs, finished second in the league with a .316 batting average, and led the N.L. with 202 hits. For his outstanding season, Garvey finished second in the MVP balloting.

The Phillies repeated as Eastern Division champs, beating out the Pirates by just 1½ games. Philadelphia's main power source was Greg Luzinski, who finished second in the league with 35 home runs and knocked in 101 runs. However, Luzinski's .265 batting average greatly reduced his chances of being named league MVP. Mike Schmidt added 21 homers and 93 runs scored, while Garry Maddox batted .288 and stole 33 bases. The player who received more support than any other Phillie in the MVP balloting was Larry Bowa, who had the finest season of his career. Bowa batted .294, collected 192 hits, stole 27 bases, and led all N.L. shortstops with a .986 fielding percentage. He finished third in the voting.

The man who finished first was Pittsburgh Pirates outfielder Dave Parker, who was the league's best all-around player. Although his 30 home runs placed him 10 behind league-leader George Foster, Parker finished a close second to Foster with 117 runs batted in and won his second straight batting title, with a mark of .334. He also led the league with 340 total bases and a .585 slugging percentage, while placing among the leaders with 102 runs scored and 194 hits. Teammate Willie Stargell also had a fine year, hitting 28 home runs, driving in 97 runs, and batting .295 in just 390 official at-bats. But Stargell appeared in only 122 games for the Pirates, easily making Parker the team's most valuable player. He was the man most responsible for Pittsburgh's extremely close second-place finish. As the league's top player, Parker was also most deserving of the MVP trophy he was presented with at the end of the season.

1979

AMERICAN LEAGUE

Both New York and Kansas City were dethroned as division champions in the American League in 1979. Baltimore replaced New York at the top of the A.L. East standings, finishing eight games ahead of second-place Milwaukee. Gorman Thomas, Cecil Cooper, and Sixto Lezcano all had big years for the Brewers. Thomas led the league with 45 homers and knocked in 123 runs. Cooper hit 24 homers, drove in 106 runs, and batted .308. Lezcano hit 28 home runs, knocked in 101 runs, and batted .321.

The Orioles' offense was not as potent, but their pitching was easily the best in the league. In fact, their league-leading team earned run average of 3.26 was more than a-half-a-run per game better than the 3.83 mark posted by league runner-up New York. Baltimore's staff was headed by Cy Young Award winner Mike Flanagan, whose 23 victories and five shutouts led the American League. Baltimore's 757 runs scored were only eighth-best in the A.L., and their team batting average of .261 placed them eleventh in the league. However, they finished third with 181 home runs. Eddie Murray had another solid season, hitting 25 home runs, driving in 99 runs, scoring 90 others, and batting .295. Ken Singleton was the team's top offensive performer, hitting 35 homers, driving in 111 runs, and batting .295. He was among the leading contenders for league MVP honors.

The third-place Red Sox, who finished 11½ games behind the Orioles, had a couple of leading contenders as well. Jim Rice followed up his fabulous 1978 campaign with another brilliant season, hitting 39 homers, knocking in 130 runs, scoring another 117, and batting .325. Teammate Fred Lynn put up numbers that were just as impressive. The Boston centerfielder also hit 39 homers, drove in 122 runs, scored 116 others, and led the league with a .333 batting average. Along with Singleton, Rice and Lynn were the top candidates from the Eastern Division.

The California Angels used the league's top offense to beat out the Kansas City Royals by three games in the Western Division. While California's team earned run average of 4.34 was just the ninth best in the A.L., their 866 runs scored topped all American League teams. Brian Downing finished third in the league with a .326 batting average and scored 87 runs. Bobby Grich hit 30 home runs, drove in 101 runs, and batted .294. Carney Lansford hit 19 homers, batted .287, and scored 114 runs. But the Angels' top player was Don Baylor, who hit 36 home runs and led the A.L. with 139 runs batted in and 120 runs scored.

Let's look at his numbers, alongside those of Singleton, Rice, Lynn, and George Brett, who had an outstanding year for the runner-up Royals:

PLAYER	AB	HITS	RUNS	2B	3B	HR	RBI	AVG	OBP	SLG PCT
Ken Singleton	570	168	93	29	1	35	111	.295	.409	.533
Don Baylor	628	186	**120**	33	3	36	**139**	.296	.377	.530
Jim Rice	619	201	117	39	6	39	130	.325	.385	.596
Fred Lynn	531	177	116	42	1	39	122	**.333**	.426	**.637**
George Brett	645	**212**	119	42	**20**	23	107	.329	.378	.563

Lynn and Rice actually put up the best numbers, with the former leading the league in both batting average and slugging percentage. He also played a marvelous centerfield for the Red Sox. All things considered, Lynn was probably the best all-around player in the league. However, Boston finished third in the East, 11½ games behind the Orioles. Therefore, it would be difficult to select Lynn over Don Baylor, whose numbers were almost as good, and whose team finished first in the West. Singleton's team also won its division, but his overall statistics were not as impressive as Baylor's. Brett's stat-line was comparable to that of the Angels' slugger, but his team finished second in the West. In addition, Baylor was the league's top run-producer, leading the A.L. in both runs batted in and runs scored.

It's a close call, but we'll go along with the writers' selection of Baylor as the league's Most Valuable Player.

NATIONAL LEAGUE

For the second straight year, both divisional races in the National League went down to the season's final days. In the Western Division, Cincinnati beat out Houston by just 1½ games, overcoming outstanding seasons by the Astros' top two pitchers—Joe Niekro and J.R. Richard. Niekro finished 21-11, with a 3.00 earned run average and a league-leading five shutouts. Richard compiled a record of 18-13, with a league-leading 2.71 earned run average and 313 strikeouts.

The Reds had an outstanding pitcher of their own in Tom Seaver. The former New York Met finished 16-6 and tied Niekro for the league lead with five shutouts. Cincinnati also had a solid offense, with George Foster, Johnny Bench, and Ray Knight leading the way. Foster hit 30 homers, drove in 98 runs, and batted .302. Bench hit 22 home runs and knocked in 80 runs. Knight filled in admirably at third base for Pete Rose, who signed with Philadelphia during the off-season as a free agent. In his first season as the Reds' starting third baseman, Knight batted .318 and drove in 79 runs. But the Western Division's top player was San Diego Padres outfielder Dave Winfield, who hit 34 home runs, led the league with 118 runs batted in, and batted .308. The Padres, though, finished fifth in the West, 22 games off the pace, greatly diminishing Winfield's chances of being named league MVP.

In the Eastern Division, the Pirates finished just two games ahead of the second-place Expos, to end Philadelphia's three-year reign as division champions. However, while Pittsburgh and Montreal battled it out for the division title, two of the league's most productive hitters played for other teams. Mike Schmidt hit 45 home runs and knocked in 114 runs for Philadelphia, and Chicago's Dave Kingman led the N.L. with 48 home runs, drove in 115 runs, batted a career-high .288, and led the league with a .613 slugging percentage. But, with the Phillies finishing fourth and the Cubs fifth, both well out of contention, neither player could be seriously considered for league MVP honors.

The young and improving Expos featured young stars such as Ellis Valentine, Andre Dawson, and Gary Carter. Valentine hit 21 home runs, drove in 82 runs, batted .276, and had one of the strongest throwing arms in the league in right field. Dawson hit 25 homers, knocked in 92 runs, scored 90 others, and batted .275. Carter hit 22 round-trippers, drove in 75 runs, and batted .283.

Still, Montreal's youthful exuberance was not enough to overcome the "family" environment created on the division-winning Pirates. The patriarch of that "family", and Pittsburgh's emotional leader was Willie Stargell, who was the one remaining link to the outstanding Pirates teams of the late 1960s and early 1970s. The younger Pirates all looked to him for leadership, and Stargell helped to create a team chemistry that enabled Pittsburgh to eventually win the world championship. The writers recognized Stargell's contributions to his team by awarding him a share of the MVP trophy at season's end, in spite of the rather modest offensive numbers he posted during the regular season.

Let's look at those numbers, alongside those of Dave Winfield and Keith Hernandez—the other leading MVP candidates:

PLAYER	AB	HITS	RUNS	2B	3B	HR	RBI	AVG	OBP	SLG PCT
Dave Winfield	597	184	97	27	10	34	**118**	.308	.396	.558
Willie Stargell	424	119	60	19	0	32	82	.281	.357	.552
Keith Hernandez	610	210	**116**	48	11	11	105	**.344**	**.421**	.513

Stargell's home run total and slugging percentage were fairly impressive, but he didn't come close to either of the other two players in any other statistical category. Hernandez's batting average and on-base percentage were both more than 60 points higher than Stargell's, he knocked in 23 more runs, and he finished with almost twice as many runs scored. While Stargell didn't come close to leading the league in any statistical category, Hernandez topped the circuit in four. Furthermore, Stargell appeared in only 126 of his team's games, accumulating a total of just 424 official at-bats. Meanwhile, Hernandez played in 161 games for St. Louis. As a result of Stargell's somewhat limited playing time, it is even debatable as to whether or not he was Pittsburgh's most valuable player. Teammate Dave Parker put up much better numbers. He hit 25 home runs, knocked in 94 runs, scored another 109, batted .310, and collected 193 hits and 45 doubles.

True, Stargell was the Pirates' emotional leader, but he missed almost a quarter of their games and he was only the second best player on the team. Both Winfield and Hernandez had much better years. They were clearly the two best players in the National League. Their overall numbers were fairly comparable, but, with the Cardinals finishing a very respectable third in the East, 12 games out of first, Hernandez's claim to the MVP trophy was far more valid than Winfield's.

The St. Louis first baseman should not have had to share the MVP Award with Stargell. He should have been the writers' lone selection.

1980

AMERICAN LEAGUE

After a tumultuous 1979 season in which they tragically lost their team captain Thurman Munson in a plane crash, the Yankees regrouped under new manager Dick Howser in 1980 to win 103 games and finish with baseball's best record. New York finished near the top of the A.L. team rankings in numerous statistical categories. They were second in home runs (189), runs scored (820), and earned run average (3.58), and several players on the roster had seasons that were among the best of their careers.

One of those was Thurman Munson's replacement behind the plate, Rick Cerone, who established career-highs with 14 home runs, 85 runs batted in, and a .277 batting average. He also did a fine job of handling a pitching staff that included some of the top hurlers in the league. Tommy John led the team with a record of 22-9, 16 complete games, and six shutouts. Ron Guidry finished 17-10, and Rudy May compiled a record of 15-5 and led all A.L. starters with a 2.46 earned run average. In the bullpen, Rich Gossage finished 6-2 with a league-leading 33 saves, while pitching to a 2.27 earned run average and striking out 103 batters in 99 innings of work. His outstanding performance earned him a third-place finish in the MVP voting.

New York also received major contributions from first baseman Bob Watson and second baseman Willie Randolph. Watson batted .307 and Randolph hit .294, scored 99 runs, led the league with 119 walks, and finished second with a .429 on-base percentage. The Yankees' most valuable player, though, was Reggie Jackson, who finished second in the league MVP voting. In his finest season in New York, Jackson led the A.L. with 41 home runs, knocked in 111 runs, batted .300 for the only time in his career, and scored 94 runs. More than anyone, he was responsible for New York's superb season.

In order to win the A.L. East title, it was imperative for the Yankees to play as well as they did because second-place Baltimore won 100 games and finished only three games back. The Orioles had two of the league's finest pitchers in righthander Steve Stone and lefty Scott McGregor. Stone finished 25-7, to lead A.L. pitchers in victories, and he also compiled an earned run average of 3.23. At season's end, he was presented with the league's Cy Young Award. McGregor finished with a 20-8 record and a 3.32 earned run average. On offense, the Birds were led by Eddie Murray and Al Bumbry. Murray finished among the league leaders with 32 home runs and 116 runs batted in, batted .300, and scored 100 runs. Bumbry batted .318, scored 118 runs, collected 205 hits, and stole 44 bases.

Perhaps the Eastern Division's finest player was Milwaukee Brewers first baseman, Cecil Cooper. He hit 25 home runs, led the A.L. with 122 runs batted in, finished second with a .352 batting average and 219 hits, and scored 96 runs. Although the Brewers finished third, 17 games off the pace, Cooper's tremendous year earned him MVP consideration.

Kansas City returned to the top of the Western Division standings as well in 1980, winning 97 games and finishing 14 games ahead of runner-up Oakland. The A's had some of the best young talent in the league in players like Mike Norris, Tony Armas, and Rickey Henderson. Norris compiled a record of 22-9, and finished second in the league with a 2.53 earned run average, 24 complete games, and 284 innings pitched. Armas hit 35 home runs, drove in 109 runs, and batted .279. Henderson batted .303, scored 111 runs, and led the A.L. with 100 stolen bases.

In the end, though, Oakland was unable to contend with Kansas City's superior pitching, batting order, and team speed. The Royals' staff was headed by Dennis Leonard, who compiled a record of 20-11, and Larry Gura, who finished 18-10 with a 2.95 earned run average, 283 innings pitched, and 16 complete games. Dan Quisenberry won 12 games in relief, while tying Gossage for the league lead with 33 saves and appearing in a league-leading 75 games.

On offense, Kansas City's team batting average of .286 was the best in the American League, and they also finished first with 185 stolen bases. Designated hitter Hal McRae batted .297 and knocked in 83 runs. First baseman Willie Aikens hit 20 homers, drove in 98 runs, and batted .278. Centerfielder Willie Wilson provided exceptional speed at the top of the batting order, hitting .326, stealing 79 bases, and leading the A.L. with 133 runs scored, 230 hits, and 15 triples. But the Royals' best player, and unquestionably the league's Most Valuable Player, was George Brett, who had an absolutely phenomenal year. The third baseman hit 24 home runs, finished second in the league with 118 runs batted in, scored 87 runs, and led the A.L. with a .390 batting average, a .461 on-base percentage, and a .664 slugging percentage. Earlier in the year, there was some question as to whether Brett or Reggie Jackson would eventually earn MVP honors.

But, when Jackson slumped badly for an entire month during the season's second half while Brett continued to flirt with the .400-mark, it became obvious that the latter was the league's Most Valuable Player.

NATIONAL LEAGUE

As close as the divisional races were in the National League in 1979, they were even closer in 1980. The Astros finished just one game ahead of the second-place Dodgers in the Western Division. While the Astros had little in the way of power, they had good team speed and the best pitching staff in the league. In fact, their team earned run average of 3.10 was the best in the major leagues. Houston's top starter was Joe Niekro, who finished 20-12 with 256 innings pitched. The Astros were led on offense by their speedy outfield of Terry Puhl, Cesar Cedeno, and Jose Cruz. Puhl batted .282 and stole 27 bases. Cedeno hit .309 and finished among the league leaders with 48 steals. Cruz batted .302, drove in 91 runs, and stole 36 bases. He finished third in the league MVP voting.

The Dodgers took the Astros to the season's final day with their excellent team balance. Jerry Reuss led the pitching staff with a record of 18-6 and six shutouts, while compiling a 2.51 earned run average. Don Sutton finished 13-5 with a league-leading 2.20 earned run average. Dusty Baker and Steve Garvey wielded the most potent bats in the Los Angeles lineup. Baker hit 29 home runs, knocked in 97 runs, and batted .294. Garvey hit 26 homers, drove in 106 runs, batted .304, and led the league with 200 hits. Yet, neither man deserved serious consideration for league MVP honors.

The race in the Eastern Division was also an extremely close one, with the Phillies barely edging out the Expos by one game. Montreal outfielder Andre Dawson hit 17 home runs, drove in 87 runs, scored 96 others, batted .308, and stole 34 bases. But teammate Gary Carter was the Expos' leading MVP candidate. The Montreal catcher hit 29 home runs and knocked in 101 runs. For his efforts, Carter finished runner-up in the balloting.

The first-place Phillies got fine seasons from starter Dick Ruthven and reliever Tug McGraw. Ruthven finished 17-10, while McGraw saved 20 games and compiled a superb 1.46 earned run average. The leader of the Philadelphia pitching staff was Steve Carlton, who captured the third Cy Young Award of his career by leading all N.L. pitchers with a record of 24-9, 286 strikeouts, and 304 innings pitched, while pitching to a 2.34 earned run average.

Speedy Bake McBride provided an offensive spark by hitting .309 and driving in 87 runs. But there is little doubt that Mike Schmidt was Philadelphia's best player, and that he was also the league's most valuable player in 1980. The third baseman had the finest season of his career, carrying the Philadelphia offense on his back for much of the year. He led the National League with 48 home runs, 121 runs batted in, and a .624 slugging percentage, batted .286, and scored 104 runs. Schmidt was easily able to out-poll Carter in the MVP balloting.

1981

AMERICAN LEAGUE

With major league players striking for almost two months during the 1981 campaign, the regular season was split into two halves for the first time in history. As a result, the first round of the playoffs was designed to determine the two division winners in each league. The team with the best record in each division prior to the player walk-out met the team with the best record in the division after the players returned to their jobs. Once the division champions were determined, they faced each other in the traditional League Championship Series.

In the American League West, the Billy Martin-led Oakland A's compiled the division's best record during the season's first half, while the Kansas City Royals posted the best record during the season's second half. The A's played an aggressive style of ball known as *Billyball* that featured speed, bunting, hitting-and-running, and base-stealing. The symbol of that style of play was leadoff hitter Rickey Henderson. Playing in 108 of Oakland's 109 games, Henderson hit only six home runs and knocked in just 35 runs, but he finished fourth in the league with a .319 batting average and he led the A.L. with 89 runs scored, 135 hits, and 56 stolen bases. He was ably assisted by Tony Armas, who led the league with 22 home runs and finished second with 76 runs batted in. Steve McCatty led the A's pitching staff with a record of 14-7, a 2.33 earned run average, 16 complete games, and four shutouts. But it was Henderson who made Oakland the Western Division's strongest team—that division's eventual representative in the ALCS.

In the Eastern Division, New York compiled the best record during the season's first half, while Milwaukee was the second-half winner. Perhaps the division's finest player, though, was Eddie Murray, whose Orioles finished just one game behind the Brewers for the division's best overall record. Murray tied for the league lead with 22 home runs, led the A.L. with 78 runs batted in, and batted .294. Boston's Dwight Evans also had an excellent year, tying Murray for the league lead with 22 homers, knocking in 71 runs, hitting .296, and finishing second in the A.L. with 84 runs scored.

New York's best player was Dave Winfield, who batted .294 and drove in 68 runs. But it was the Yankees' pitching that enabled them to advance to the ALCS. Their team earned run average of 2.90 was easily the lowest in the American League. Rookie starter Dave Righetti finished 8-4 with a league-leading 2.05 earned run average. Ron Guidry compiled a record of 11-5 and a 2.76 earned run average. The team's toughest pitcher was reliever Goose Gossage, who was all but unhittable during the regular season. Gossage finished 3-2, with 20 saves and a 0.77 earned run average. He also surrendered only 22 hits in 46 innings of work, while striking out 48 batters.

Equally effective was Milwaukee's Rollie Fingers, who was the Brewers' leading candidate for league MVP. Fingers finished 6-3, with a 1.04 earned run average and a league-leading 28 saves. He surrendered 55 hits in 78 innings pitched, walked only 13 batters, and struck out 61. Milwaukee also got fine seasons from Pete Vukovich, who finished 14-4, and Cecil Cooper, who knocked in 60 runs, scored 70 others, and batted .320. But Fingers was the team's dominant player. The Brewers finished the regular season with a record of 62-47, and, with six wins and 28 saves, Fingers had a hand in 34 of the team's 62 victories. The writers acknowledged his importance to the Brewers by voting him the league's Most Valuable Player at season's end, in a very close ballot. Fingers received a total of 319 points, while Oakland's Rickey Henderson tallied 308 points.

The selection of Fingers was not a bad one. He had a dominant season, and he was the primary reason why the Brewers were able to advance into the postseason. However, Henderson played every day, and he was the catalyst of his team's offense. He led the league in stolen bases, runs scored, and base hits, and he placed fourth in the batting race.

Finishing with the league's best overall record (64-45), the A's were the Western Division's dominant team. Rickey Henderson was the man most responsible for their success. He should have been selected the league's Most Valuable Player.

NATIONAL LEAGUE

In the National League, the teams with the two best regular season records failed to make it into the postseason. In the Western Division, the Cincinnati Reds finished the regular season with a record of 66-42. That was four games better than the mark posted by the Dodgers, and six games better than the figure turned in by the Astros. However, Los

Angeles was the division's first-half winner, while Houston compiled the best record during the season's second half. Therefore, Cincinnati was left out in the cold.

Nevertheless, the Reds had three players worthy of MVP consideration. George Foster finished among the league leaders with 22 home runs and 90 runs batted in, while batting .295. Shortstop Dave Concepcion hit .306 and drove in 67 runs. Tom Seaver was the league's best pitcher. He finished 14-2, to lead all N.L. hurlers in victories, while also compiling a 2.54 earned run average.

Pitching was once again the key to Houston's success. The Astros' staff led the National League with a team earned run average of 2.66. Nolan Ryan finished 11-5 and led the league with a 1.69 earned run average. Bob Knepper compiled a record of 9-5 with a 2.18 earned run average. The Dodgers also had an excellent pitcher in lefty phenom Fernando Valenzuela. Valenzuela finished 13-7 with a 2.48 earned run average, and he led the league with 180 strikeouts, 192 innings pitched, 11 complete games, and eight shutouts. He was the Dodgers' leading MVP candidate.

In the Eastern Division, the Phillies were the first-half winner, while the Expos compiled the best second-half record. Therefore, those were the two teams that met in the playoff series to determine the division champion. Yet, it was the Cardinals that posted the best overall record in the division. They were led by Keith Hernandez, George Hendrick, and Bruce Sutter. Hernandez batted .306 and scored 65 runs. Hendrick hit 18 homers, drove in 61 runs, and scored another 67. Sutter led the league with 25 saves and compiled a 2.62 earned run average.

Montreal received a major contribution from young outfielder Tim Raines, who was called up early in the season. In just 88 games, Raines batted .304, scored 61 runs, and led the N.L. with 71 stolen bases. The Expos' best player was Andre Dawson, who finished runner-up in the MVP balloting. The centerfielder hit 24 home runs, drove in 64 runs, batted .302, scored 71 runs, and stole 26 bases.

Philadelphia's Steve Carlton had another outstanding year, finishing 13-4 with a 2.42 earned run average, 179 strikeouts, and 190 innings pitched. On offense, Pete Rose finished second in the league with a .325 batting average, while scoring 73 runs. Gary Matthews batted .301 and knocked in 67 runs. Mike Schmidt was the backbone of the Philadelphia attack and the league's dominant player for the second consecutive season. He led the N.L. in five different offensive categories, finishing first with 31 home runs, 91 runs batted in, 78 runs scored, a .439 on-base percentage, and a .644 slugging percentage. Schmidt also finished fourth in the league with a career-best .316 batting average. He was clearly the National League's Most Valuable Player.

1982

AMERICAN LEAGUE

Both divisions in the American League were extremely competitive in 1982, with the division winners being determined in the season's final week. In the A.L. West, the California Angels edged out the Kansas City Royals by three games to capture their second division title. The Angels' best pitcher was Geoff Zahn, who finished the season with a record of 18-8. On offense, California was led by Reggie Jackson and Doug DeCinces. Jackson led the American League with 39 home runs, knocked in 101 runs, and scored 92 others. DeCinces hit 30 homers, drove in 97 runs, scored 94 others, and batted .301. He was the Angels' leading candidate for league MVP.

The runner-up Royals had the division's best player in Hal McRae. In his most productive season, McRae hit 27 home runs, led the league with 133 runs batted in, scored 91 runs, and batted .308. He had to be considered a legitimate contender for MVP honors.

Oakland's Rickey Henderson also had a fine season. Although he batted only .267, Henderson scored 119 runs and established a new major league record by stealing 130 bases. However, the A's finished fifth in the division, 25 games behind the Angels, thereby making Henderson an MVP afterthought.

In the A.L. East, the Milwaukee Brewers barely edged out Baltimore by one game to capture their first division crown. Eddie Murray was the heart of the Orioles' offense, finishing the year with 32 home runs, 110 runs batted in, and a .316 batting average. But it was the Brewers who had the league's most potent offense. Managed by former A.L. batting champion Harvey Kuenn, the Milwaukee lineup came to be known as *Harvey's Wall-bangers* for its explosive nature. The Brewers led the American League with 891 runs scored and 216 home runs, and they finished second with a team batting average of .279. Although he batted only .245, centerfielder Gorman Thomas tied Reggie Jackson for the league lead with 39 home runs, while also driving in 112 runs. Second baseman Paul Molitor batted .302 and led the league with 136 runs scored. Cecil Cooper finished among the league leaders with 32 home runs, 121 runs batted in, a .313 batting average, and 205 hits.

Perhaps Milwaukee's best all-around player was shortstop Robin Yount. Let's look at his numbers alongside those of the other leading MVP candidates:

PLAYER	AB	HITS	RUNS	2B	3B	HR	RBI	AVG	OBP	SLG PCT
Eddie Murray	550	174	87	30	1	32	110	.316	.395	.549
Hal Mcrae	613	189	91	46	8	27	133	.308	.370	.542
Robin Yount	635	210	129	46	12	29	114	.331	.384	.578
Cecil Cooper	654	205	104	38	3	32	121	.313	.345	.528
Paul Molitor	666	201	136	26	8	19	71	.302	.368	.450
Doug Decinces	575	173	94	42	5	30	97	.301	.374	.548

All six men had outstanding seasons, but Murray, McRae, Yount, and Cooper would have to be considered the leading contenders. McRae loses points because he spent most of his time as a designated hitter. Yount had the best year of the three remaining players. He led the league in three different offensive categories, and he was the circuit's top run-producer, combining for a total of 243 runs batted in and runs scored. With Murray and Cooper both first basemen, Yount also played the most demanding defensive position of the three. Therefore, he was clearly deserving of the MVP Award that was bestowed upon him at the end of the year.

NATIONAL LEAGUE

The National League also featured a couple of close divisional races in 1982, with St. Louis capturing the Eastern Division title and Atlanta finishing on top in the West. The Cardinals finished three games ahead of the second-place Phillies, who were once again led by two-time league MVP Mike Schmidt and three-time Cy Young Award winner Steve Carlton. Schmidt finished among the league leaders with 35 home runs and 108 runs scored, batted .280, and led the N.L. with a .407 on-base percentage and a .547 slugging percentage. Carlton led N.L. pitchers with 23 wins (against 11 losses), 286 strikeouts, 295 innings pitched, 19 complete games, and six shutouts, while pitching to a 3.10 earned run average. He was rewarded for his efforts with his fourth Cy Young Award at season's end.

However, the first-place Cardinals had more depth on their roster. George Hendrick led the team with 19 home runs and 104 runs batted in, while batting .282. Keith Hernandez knocked in 94 runs, batted .299, and finished second in the league with a .404 on-base percentage. Lonnie Smith batted .307, led the N.L. with 120 runs scored, and stole 68 bases. Joaquin Andujar finished 15-10, with a 2.47 earned run average and 265 innings pitched. Bruce Sutter led the league with 36 saves.

The third-place Expos, who finished six games behind St. Louis, also had a deep squad. Andre Dawson hit 23 homers, batted .301, scored 107 runs, and stole 39 bases. Tim Raines scored 90 runs and led the league with 78 stolen bases. Gary Carter hit 29 home runs, knocked in 97 runs, scored another 91, and batted .293. Montreal's best player was Al Oliver, who hit 22 home runs, scored 90 runs, and led the league with 109 runs batted in, a .331 batting average, and 204 hits. Along with Lonnie Smith, he had to be considered the division's leading candidate for league MVP.

In the Western Division, Atlanta's hard-hitting lineup was able to overcome the Dodgers' superior pitching, as the Braves finished just one game ahead of runner-up Los Angeles, and just two in front of third-place San Francisco. The Dodgers had the league's best pitching, leading the N.L. with a team earned run average of 3.26. Their staff was led by Fernando Valenzuela and Jerry Reuss. Valenzuela finished among the league leaders with a record of 19-13, a 2.87 earned run average, 199 strikeouts, 285 innings pitched, and 18 complete games. Reuss finished 18-11 with a 3.11 earned run average. The Dodgers' primary offensive threat was Pedro Guerrero, who led the team with 32 home runs, 100 runs batted in, and a .304 batting average.

In the end, though, Atlanta's stronger lineup enabled them to barely edge out the Dodgers for the division title. Although their team earned run average of 3.82 was the third highest in the National League, the Braves led the league with 739 runs scored and 146 home runs. Third baseman Bob Horner was a major contributor, hitting 32 home runs and driving in 97 runs. The focal point of the team's offense was centerfielder Dale Murphy, who was the best all-around player in the league. Murphy finished second in the N.L. with 36 home runs and 113 runs scored, tied for the league lead with 109 runs batted in, batted .281, and won the first Gold Glove of his career for his outstanding centerfield play. Smith, Oliver, and Guerrero were worthy contenders, but Murphy was clearly the league's Most Valuable Player.

1983

AMERICAN LEAGUE

The Chicago White Sox ran away with the A.L. West title in 1983, finishing 20 games ahead of second-place Kansas City. The Sox were buoyed by the outstanding seasons turned in by several of their young and extremely talented players. Rookie Ron Kittle finished among the league leaders with 35 home runs and knocked in 100 runs. Harold Baines hit 20 homers, drove in 99 runs, and batted .280. Lamarr Hoyt finished 24-10, to lead all A.L. pitchers in victories. He was joined on the Sox staff by Rich Dotson, who compiled a record of 22-7. Veteran catcher Carlton Fisk did a fine job of handling the team's young staff, contributing to the offense as well by hitting 26 home runs, driving in 86 runs, and batting .289. His contributions to the team were acknowledged by the writers, who placed him third in the league MVP balloting.

George Brett and Dan Quisenberry both had fine years for the runner-up Royals. Brett hit 25 home runs, knocked in 93 runs, scored 90 others, batted .310, and led the league with a .563 slugging percentage. Quisenberry compiled a 1.94 earned run average and led the league with 45 saves and 69 relief appearances. But, with Kansas City finishing 20 games off the pace, it would be difficult to give either man serious consideration for MVP honors.

After coming up just one game short the prior year, Baltimore captured the A.L. East title in 1983, finishing six games in front of second-place Detroit. The runner-up Tigers got fine seasons from Lance Parrish, Jack Morris, and their doubleplay combination of second baseman Lou Whitaker and shortstop Alan Trammell. Parrish hit 27 home runs and drove in 114 runs. Morris won 20 games and led the league with 232 strikeouts and 293 innings pitched. Trammell hit .319, while Whitaker batted .320, scored 94 runs, and collected 206 hits. None of the four Tiger players, though, was even among the division's top performers.

Dave Winfield and Ron Guidry both had outstanding years for the third-place Yankees, who finished seven games behind Baltimore. Winfield hit 32 home runs, knocked in 116 runs, scored another 99, and batted .283. Guidry finished 21-9 and led the league with 21 complete games.

The Red Sox had perhaps the two finest offensive players in the league in Wade Boggs and Jim Rice. Boggs won the batting title with a mark of .361, scored 100 runs, and collected 210 hits. Rice led the A.L. with 39 home runs and 126 runs batted in, scored 90 runs, batted .305, and led the league with 344 total bases. However, neither man merited serious consideration for league MVP honors since Boston finished sixth in the division, 20 games behind Baltimore.

In the end, it came down to the Orioles' top two players—Cal Ripken Jr. and Eddie Murray. Both men had exceptional years for the league's best team. A look at their offensive numbers reveals just how closely matched the two players were:

PLAYER	AB	HITS	RUNS	2B	3B	HR	RBI	AVG	OBP	SLG PCT
Eddie Murray	582	178	115	30	3	33	111	.306	.398	.538
Cal Ripken Jr.	663	211	121	47	2	27	102	.318	.373	.517

The two men were essentially equal as run-producers, with Murray driving in nine more runs but Ripken scoring six more times. Murray had an edge in home runs, on-base percentage, and slugging percentage, but Ripken hit for a slightly higher average, collected far more doubles, and finished with many more hits. However, while Murray failed to lead the league in any statistical category, Ripken finished first in three. He also played every game for the Orioles at shortstop, a far more demanding position than first base. Therefore, it would be difficult to disagree with the writers' selection of Ripken over Murray as the league's Most Valuable Player.

NATIONAL LEAGUE

Los Angeles turned the tables on Atlanta in 1983, finishing first in the N.L. West in another extremely close pennant race. The Dodgers, who beat out the Braves by three games, were led by Pedro Guerrero and young second baseman Steve Sax. Guerrero hit 32 home runs, knocked in 103 runs, and batted .298. Sax batted .281, scored 94 runs, and finished third in the league with 56 stolen bases.

Atlanta got another superb season from reigning MVP Dale Murphy, who hit 36 home runs, led the league with 121 runs batted in, placed second in runs scored, with 131, batted .302, and won his second consecutive Gold Glove Award. He had to be considered a leading candidate for the honor once more.

Philadelphia replaced St. Louis at the top of the N.L. East standings, finishing six games in front of the runner-up Pirates and eight games ahead of the third-place Expos. The Phillies' John Denny was the league's best pitcher, compiling a record of 19-6, to lead N.L. hurlers in victories, while pitching to a 2.37 earned run average. Their top player, though, was Mike Schmidt, who led the N.L. with 40 home runs, knocked in 109 runs, and scored another 104.

The Pirates were paced by third baseman Bill Madlock, who led the league with a .323 batting average. Meanwhile, Montreal remained in contention for much of the year largely because of their two best players—Tim Raines and Andre Dawson. Raines batted .298 and led the league with 133 runs scored and 90 stolen bases. Dawson rivaled Dale Murphy as the National League's finest all-around player.

Let's look at his numbers, along with those of the other leading MVP candidates:

PLAYER	AB	HITS	RUNS	2B	3B	HR	RBI	AVG	OBP	SLG PCT
Andre Dawson	633	189	104	36	10	32	113	.299	.347	.539
Mike Schmidt	534	136	104	16	4	40	109	.255	.402	.524
Pedro Guerrero	584	174	87	28	6	32	103	.298	.377	.531
Dale Murphy	589	178	131	24	4	36	121	.302	.396	.540

Schmidt led the league in home runs and, despite batting only .255, his 128 bases on balls enabled him to also top the circuit in on-base percentage. His team also won its division. But his other numbers were not particularly overwhelming, and it would be difficult to give the MVP Award to a .255 hitter.

The Dodgers won their division, and Guerrero was their primary power threat. However, he was not a particularly good fielder, and his overall numbers did not come close to those of either Murphy or Dawson.

Murphy's numbers were better than Dawson's, and he was the league's top run-producer, finishing first in runs batted in, and placing a very close second in runs scored. Also, the Braves finished only three games out of first in the West, while the Expos finished eight games back in the East. In addition, Murphy had less of a supporting cast in Atlanta than Dawson had in Montreal. The Braves' centerfielder was clearly deserving of the second straight MVP trophy with which he was presented.

SOME HIGHLY QUESTIONABLE SELECTIONS

20

Between 1984 and 1988, the baseball writers demonstrated a great deal of inconsistency with some of their MVP selections. Players such as the Cardinals' Willie McGee and the Dodgers' Kirk Gibson were named the National League's Most Valuable Player in 1985 and 1988, respectively, based on their outstanding contributions to a pennant-winning team. Yet, while both outfielders had fine seasons, neither man posted the most impressive offensive numbers in the league. Meanwhile, Mike Schmidt and Andre Dawson were named MVP in 1986 and 1987, respectively, for being the league's most outstanding player even though their respective teams finished well out of contention. In fact, Dawson became the first player on a last-place team to receive the honor.

We will discover as we examine the selections made between 1984 and 1988 that the BBWAA made some highly questionable decisions during this period.

	ACTUAL MVP WINNERS		**SUGGESTED WINNERS**	
	A.L.	**N.L.**	**A.L.**	**N.L.**
1984	Willie Hernandez	Ryne Sandberg	Willie Hernandez	Ryne Sandberg
1985	Don Mattingly	Willie McGee	George Brett	Dave Parker
1986	Roger Clemens	Mike Schmidt	Don Mattingly	Mike Schmidt
1987	George Bell	Andre Dawson	George Bell	Jack Clark
1988	Jose Canseco	Kirk Gibson	Jose Canseco	Orel Hershiser

1984

AMERICAN LEAGUE

The Detroit Tigers were the American League's dominant team in 1984. Getting off to a torrid 35-5 start under manager Sparky Anderson, the Tigers never looked back, cruising to a 104-58 record and a 15-game margin of victory over the second-place Toronto Blue Jays in the A.L. East. Detroit had both the best offense and the most effective pitching staff in the A.L., leading the league with 829 runs scored, 187 home runs, and a team earned run average of 3.49.

On offense, leadoff hitter Lou Whitaker batted .289 and scored 90 runs. He was followed in the order by Alan Trammell, who batted .314 and scored 85 runs. Lance Parrish and Kirk Gibson provided power in the middle of the lineup. Although he batted just .237, Parrish hit 33 home runs and drove in 98 runs. Gibson was the team's best all-around player and spiritual leader. He hit 27 home runs, knocked in 91 runs, scored 92 others, and batted .282. Centerfielder Chet Lemon chipped in with 20 home runs and a .287 batting average.

The Detroit staff was led by a pair of fine righthanders—Jack Morris and Dan Petry. Morris finished 19-11 with a 3.60 earned run average, and Petry compiled a record of 18-8 and a 3.24 earned run average.

Detroit's leading MVP candidate was relief pitcher Willie Hernandez, who had the greatest season of his career. Hernandez won nine games, saved 32 others, compiled an earned run average of 1.92, and appeared in a league-leading 80 games out of the bullpen. Perhaps even more impressive is the fact that he went the entire season without blowing a single save opportunity. This truly made him invaluable to Detroit all year.

Still, there were several other fine players in the division who played for teams that finished behind Detroit in the standings. Boston also had a very strong offense, finishing second to the Tigers with 810 runs scored and 181 home runs, and leading the league with a team batting average of .283. Jim Rice hit 28 homers for the Sox and finished second in the league with 122 runs batted in. Wade Boggs batted .325, scored 109 runs, and collected 203 hits. Tony Armas led the A.L. with 43 home runs and 123 runs batted in, and scored 107 runs. Dave Winfield batted .340 for New York, hit 19 home runs, drove in 100 runs, and scored another 106.

Perhaps the league's finest hitter was Winfield's teammate with the Yankees—Don Mattingly. In just his first full season, Mattingly led the league with a .343 batting average, 207 hits, and 44 doubles. He also hit 23 home runs, drove in 110 runs, and scored 91 others. However, the Yankees finished third, 17 games behind Detroit, and the Red Sox came in fourth, 18 games back. Therefore, it would be difficult to justify the selection of any of these players as the league's MVP.

The Kansas City Royals were able to capture the Western Division title with a rather unimpressive record of 84-78. They finished three games ahead of both California and Minnesota. With George Brett injured for much of the year, Kansas City's top offensive players were Steve Balboni and Willie Wilson. Balboni led the team with 28 home runs and 77 runs batted in, while Wilson batted .301, scored 81 runs, and stole 47 bases. The division's top hitter played for the Twins. First baseman Kent Hrbek hit 27 home runs, drove in 107 runs, and batted .311 for Minnesota. He ended up finishing second in the MVP balloting.

Placing third in the voting was Kansas City's leading MVP candidate. Reliever Dan Quisenberry had a season that rivaled that of Detroit's Willie Hernandez. Let's look at the numbers of the two closers:

PITCHER	W	L	SAVES	ERA	G	IP	H	SO	BB
Willie Hernandez	9	3	32	1. 92	80	140	96	112	36
Dan Quisenberry	6	3	44	2. 64	72	129	121	41	12

Quisenberry finished with 12 more saves, leading the league in that department. He also walked far fewer batters than Hernandez in almost as many innings. However, the Tiger closer struck out almost three times as many hitters as Quisenberry. Furthermore, Hernandez won three more games, compiled a much lower earned run average, and finished with a much better hits-to-innings pitched ratio. In short, Hernandez was the much more effective pitcher. He was also the most important player on the league's dominant team. That should have been enough to justify his selection as the league's Most Valuable Player.

NATIONAL LEAGUE

The Chicago Cubs made it into the postseason for the first time in almost 40 years in 1984, finishing first in the N.L. East, 6½ games ahead of the second-place Mets, who were the league's most improved team. In fact, New York's 90-72 record represented a 22-game improvement over their 68-win, last-place finish in 1983. Young stars such as Darryl Strawberry and Dwight Gooden contributed greatly to the team's progression. Strawberry hit 26 home runs and drove in 97 runs, while Gooden finished 17-9, with a 2.60 earned run average and a league-leading 276 strikeouts. However, the team's most valuable player was first baseman Keith Hernandez, who hit 15 home runs, knocked in 94 runs, batted .311, and compiled a .415 on-base percentage. More importantly, Hernandez provided much-needed leadership to his young teammates. His contributions to the Mets were recognized by the writers, who placed him second in the league MVP voting.

Several players also made major contributions to the first-place Cubs. Former Dodger third baseman Ron Cey hit 25 home runs and drove in 97 runs. Catcher Jody Davis hit 19 homers and knocked in 94 runs. First baseman Leon Durham hit 23 four-baggers and drove in 96 runs. Outfielder Gary Matthews batted .291, scored 101 runs, and led the league with 103 walks and a .417 on-base percentage. Lee Smith won nine games in relief and finished second in the league with 33 saves. After coming over from Cleveland during the season's first half, righthander Rick Sutcliffe was the National League's best pitcher. Following a 4-5 start with the Indians, Sutcliffe subsequently posted a record of 16-1 and an earned run average of 2.69 with the Cubs. He finished fourth in the MVP balloting.

The man the writers selected as the league's MVP was Chicago second baseman Ryne Sandberg, who was among the finest all-around players in the circuit. Sandberg hit 19 homers, knocked in 84 runs, batted .314, and led the N.L. with 114 runs scored and 19 triples, all while playing a brilliant second base. Philadelphia's Mike Schmidt and Atlanta's Dale Murphy also had excellent years. Schmidt led the league with 36 home runs and 106 runs batted in, batted .277, and scored

93 runs. Murphy tied Schmidt for the league lead with 36 homers, knocked in 100 runs, scored 94 others, batted .290, and led the N.L. with a .547 slugging percentage. But Philadelphia finished fourth in the East, 15½ games back, and Atlanta finished 12 games back in the West. Therefore, while the overall numbers of both Schmidt and Murphy may have been slightly better than Sandberg's, Chicago's first-place finish made the second baseman a better choice for league MVP.

However, Tony Gwynn had an excellent year for San Diego, and the Padres captured their first Western Division title, finishing 12 games ahead of both Houston and Atlanta. Steve Garvey and Kevin McReynolds also had good seasons for the Padres. Garvey batted .284 and drove in 86 runs, while McReynolds hit 20 homers and knocked in 75 runs. But, Gwynn was clearly the team's best player. He led the league with a .351 batting average and 213 hits. Along with Sandberg, Gwynn had to be considered the leading candidate for league MVP.

Let's look at the numbers of both men:

PLAYER	AB	HITS	RUNS	2B	3B	HR	RBI	AVG	OBP	SLG PCT
Tony Gwynn	606	213	88	21	10	5	71	.351	.411	.444
Ryne Sandberg	636	200	114	36	19	19	84	.314	.369	.520

Gwynn led the league in batting average and hits, and he also compiled a much higher on-base percentage than Sandberg. However, the Chicago second baseman finished well ahead of Gwynn in every other statistical category. Sandberg hit almost four times as many home runs, compiled almost twice as many doubles and triples, drove in 13 more runs, scored 26 more, and posted a significantly higher slugging percentage than Gwynn.

Sandberg was also the leader of the Cubs' infield, and he was the superior defensive player of the two men. That is not to diminish in any way Gwynn's defensive ability. He was a fine outfielder. But Sandberg was a *great* second baseman. He was also unquestionably the league's Most Valuable Player in 1984.

1985

AMERICAN LEAGUE

The Toronto Blue Jays won their first A.L. East title in 1985, edging out the Yankees by just two games. While the Blue Jays had a solid lineup, posting the second-highest team batting average in the league (.269) and finishing fourth in runs scored (759), it was their superior pitching that enabled them to beat out New York for the division crown. Toronto's staff, which posted the lowest team earned run average in the league (3.31), was headed by righthander Dave Stieb and lefty Jimmy Key. Both Stieb and Key won 14 games, and the former's 2.48 earned run average was the lowest in the A.L.

On offense, the Blue Jays were led by their outstanding young outfield. Leftfielder George Bell led the team with 28 home runs and 95 runs batted in. Centerfielder Lloyd Moseby hit 18 homers and scored 92 runs, and rightfielder Jesse Barfield, who had as strong an arm as anyone in the league, hit 27 homers, knocked in 84 runs, scored 94 others, and batted .289. However, not one Toronto player finished in the top five in the league MVP voting.

Two players who received far more support in the balloting were Boston's Wade Boggs and Baltimore's Eddie Murray. Boggs scored 107 runs and led the league with a .368 batting average, 240 hits, and a .452 on-base percentage. Murray hit 31 homers, finished second in the league with 124 runs batted in, scored 111 runs, and batted .297. However, the Red Sox finished fifth, 18½ games out of first, while the Orioles could do no better than fourth, 16 games back. As a result, Boggs and Murray finished a distant fourth and fifth, respectively, in the voting.

Ron Guidry and Dave Winfield both had outstanding years for the second-place Yankees. Guidry compiled a record of 22-6, to lead A.L. pitchers in victories, while pitching to a solid 3.27 earned run average. Winfield hit 26 home runs, knocked in 114 runs, and scored another 105. But New York's two best players were Rickey Henderson and Don Mattingly, both of whom had dominant seasons. Henderson batted .314, compiled a .422 on-base percentage, and led the league with 146 runs scored and 80 stolen bases. Mattingly hit 35 home runs, batted .324, collected 211 hits, scored 107 runs, and led the league with 145 runs batted in and 48 doubles. Both players deserved serious consideration for league MVP honors.

In the A.L. West, Kansas City barely edged out California by one game to capture the division title. While the Angels got solid seasons from Brian Downing, Doug DeCinces, and Donnie Moore, they really did not have an outstanding MVP candidate. On the other hand, the Royals received excellent performances from Bret Saberhagen and Dan Quisenberry. Saberhagen finished 20-6 with an outstanding 2.87 earned run average, while Quisenberry compiled a 2.37 earned run average and led the league with 37 saves and 84 relief appearances.

Nevertheless, Kansas City's most valuable player was clearly George Brett, who had one of the finest seasons of his career. Let's look at his numbers, alongside those of Mattingly and Henderson, the other leading candidates for league MVP:

PLAYER	AB	HITS	RUNS	2B	3B	HR	RBI	AVG	OBP	SLG PCT
Rickey Henderson	547	172	146	28	5	24	72	.314	.422	.516
Don Mattingly	652	211	107	48	3	35	145	.324	.379	.567
George Brett	550	184	108	38	5	30	112	.335	.442	.585

The overall numbers would seem to favor both Mattingly and Brett over Henderson. Of course, not shown are the latter's 80 stolen bases, as well as the many intangible qualities he brought to his team. There is no way to quantifiably measure the degree to which Henderson helped the Yankees score runs by upsetting the opposing team's pitcher and infield defense. His presence on the basepaths also often enabled the hitters behind him to get better pitches to hit. Taking those factors into consideration, a strong case could certainly be made for naming Henderson the league's Most Valuable Player. The writers didn't feel that way, though, placing the speedy outfielder third in their balloting. As good as Henderson was, the superb performances of Mattingly and Brett made it extremely difficult to disagree with the outfielder's third-place finish.

In comparing Mattingly to Brett, the former's numbers were slightly better. Mattingly hit more home runs, collected more doubles, and finished with far more runs batted in. On the other hand, Brett had a slight edge in batting average and slugging percentage, and he compiled a much higher on-base percentage. Brett's 63-point advantage in the last category is actually quite revealing since it brings to light a number of factors not reflected in the above statistics.

First, the obvious—Brett walked far more frequently than Mattingly. In fact, the third baseman's 103 bases on balls placed him among the league leaders. But, why did Brett draw so many bases on balls? He was certainly a patient hitter with a keen batting eye. Also contributing greatly to Brett's high walk total was the lack of protection he received all year in the Kansas City lineup. Brett was usually followed in the Royals' batting order by either Steve Balboni or Frank White. Balboni hit 36 home runs and knocked in 88 runs, but he also batted only .243 and struck out 166 times. He was strictly a mistake hitter who most pitchers were not particularly afraid to pitch to. White hit 22 home runs and knocked in 69 runs, but he hit only .249 and compiled a poor .285 on-base percentage. The second baseman was clearly miscast as a cleanup hitter. As a result, Brett rarely saw a single decent pitch to hit when he came to the plate with men in scoring position.

Meanwhile, Mattingly was usually followed in the Yankee lineup by either Dave Winfield or Don Baylor. We saw earlier that Winfield hit 26 homers and knocked in 114 runs. Baylor was also extremely productive, hitting 23 home runs and driving in 91 runs. With such solid hitters batting behind him, Mattingly generally saw better pitches to hit than Brett.

Another huge factor was the great year Henderson had hitting ahead of Mattingly in the New York batting order. The leadoff hitter was constantly on-base—frequently in scoring position—when Mattingly came to the plate. Henderson's on-base percentage was an exceptional .422. Meanwhile, Willie Wilson, Kansas City's leadoff hitter, batted a respectable .278, but hardly ever walked. As a result, his on-base percentage was only .316—more than 100 points less than Henderson's. Wilson also scored only 87 runs—almost 60 fewer than Henderson tallied. Therefore, not taking anything away from Mattingly, who had a truly great year, Henderson had a huge hand in the 145 runs batted in he collected during the season.

In addition, New York's offense was far more potent than Kansas City's. The Yankees led the league with 839 runs scored. Kansas City scored only 687 runs—almost one less per-game than New York.

Therefore, as good as Mattingly was, he was not as important to New York's offense as Brett was to Kansas City's. In fact, it could be argued that Henderson was just as integral a part of the Yankees' attack as Mattingly. However, Kansas City's offense would have been feeble without Brett. There is no way the Royals would have come close to winning the A.L. West title without him.

The inevitable conclusion is that, while Mattingly may have been the league's best player, Brett was more valuable to his team. He should have been named the league's MVP.

NATIONAL LEAGUE

The N.L. East boiled down to a two-team race in 1985, with the Cardinals finally prevailing over the Mets by three games. Both teams had fine pitching, but the Cardinals eventually came out on top because of their superior run-production and team speed. Although the Cardinals finished next-to-last in the league with only 87 home runs, they led the N.L. with 747 runs scored, a .264 team batting average, and 314 stolen bases. They also finished second in the circuit with a team earned run average of 3.10. Their staff included two of the league's best pitchers in Joaquin Andujar and John Tudor. Andujar finished 21-12 and threw 269 innings. Tudor was the staff ace, compiling a record of 21-8 with a brilliant 1.93 earned run average. He also pitched 275 innings and led N.L. hurlers with 10 shutouts.

The Cardinals' speedy lineup included Vince Coleman at the top of the batting order. Coleman scored 107 runs and led the league with 110 stolen bases. Second baseman Tommy Herr had a career-year, knocking in 110 runs, scoring 97 others, and batting .302. Jack Clark provided what little power there was, leading the team with 22 home runs and 87 runs batted in, while batting .281. The Cards' best player was centerfielder Willie McGee, who stole 56 bases and led the league with a .353 batting average, 216 hits, and 18 triples. For his outstanding season, he was selected by the writers as the league's MVP. However, there were several other viable candidates.

The second-place Mets got an absolutely sensational season from sophomore righthander Dwight Gooden, who was their leading candidate. Gooden dominated the league's statistical categories for pitchers, compiling a record of 24-4, an earned run average of 1.53, 268 strikeouts, 276 innings pitched, and 16 complete games, while finishing second with eight shutouts. On offense, New York was led by Keith Hernandez, Gary Carter, and Darryl Strawberry. Hernandez knocked in 91 runs, batted .309, and continued to provide leadership to his Mets' mates. Carter led the team with 32 home runs and 100 runs batted in, while batting .281. In only 111 games and 393 official at-bats, Strawberry hit 29 home runs, drove in 79 runs, and scored another 78.

Perhaps the division's finest all-around player, though, was Montreal's Tim Raines. The speedy leftfielder finished second in the league with a .320 batting average, 115 runs scored, and 70 stolen bases. Had the Expos not finished 16½ games off the pace, Raines would have been a leading contender for MVP honors.

The Western Division's best all-around player may well have been Atlanta's Dale Murphy, who drove in 111 runs, batted .300, and led the league with 37 home runs and 118 runs scored. However, with the Braves finishing fifth, 29 games out of first, Murphy's chances of claiming his third MVP trophy were greatly diminished.

The Dodgers used their excellent pitching to claim the N.L. West title, finishing 5½ games ahead of the second-place Reds. The Los Angeles staff led the league with a team earned run average of 2.96 and featured three exceptional starters in Orel Hershiser, Fernando Valenzuela, and Bob Welch. Hershiser was the staff ace, compiling a record of 19-3 and a 2.03 earned run average. Valenzuela finished 17-10, with a 2.45 earned run average and a team-leading 208 strikeouts and 272 innings pitched. Welch finished 14-4 with a 2.31 earned run average.

The Los Angeles lineup, which finished fifth in the N.L. in runs scored, was not nearly as imposing. Yet, it managed to compile the second highest team batting average in the league, and it featured one of the circuit's top offensive players—Pedro Guerrero. Let's look at his statistics, alongside those of Willie McGee and Dave Parker, second-place Cincinnati's primary offensive threat:

PLAYER	AB	HITS	RUNS	2B	3B	HR	RBI	AVG	OBP	SLG PCT
Pedro Guerrero	487	156	99	22	2	33	87	.320	.425	.577
Willie Mcgee	612	216	114	26	18	10	82	.353	.387	.503
Dave Parker	635	198	88	42	4	34	125	.312	.367	.551

McGee was the selection of the writers, and he certainly had some outstanding credentials. He led the league in three different offensive categories, and his team won the pennant. His .353 batting average was considerably higher than either Guerrero's or Parker's. However, McGee hardly ever walked. As a result, his on-base percentage was only 20 points higher than Parker's, and almost *40 points lower* than Guerrero's. He also finished with a much lower slugging percentage than either player, and he hit far fewer home runs. McGee scored the most runs, but he also knocked in the fewest. Perhaps most important is the fact that the Cardinals had a well-balanced attack that was not overly-dependent on any one player. McGee was the team's best player, but he had a great deal of help from his teammates. Meanwhile, Guerrero and Parker had little help from their teammates in Los Angeles and Cincinnati, respectively. These were not the Dodger teams of the mid-to-late seventies that had players such as Steve Garvey, Ron Cey, Reggie Smith, Dusty Baker, Davey Lopes, and Rick Monday. Guerrero was the Dodgers' only real power threat, and he was the only big run-producer in their lineup.

Nor was this the *Big Red Machine* in Cincinnati, striking fear in the hearts of National League pitchers. Gone were Morgan, Bench, Perez, Foster, and Griffey. Dave Parker was forced to carry the offensive load for much of the season. Although the Reds finished 5½ games behind the Dodgers, it was Parker who kept them in the race for much of the year almost singlehandedly. He led the league in runs batted in, and his overall numbers were better than those of either Guerrero or McGee.

Parker should have been named league MVP. Either Guerrero or McGee, or perhaps even Dwight Gooden, who was actually the league's most dominant player, should have finished second.

1986

AMERICAN LEAGUE

After barely missing the playoffs the prior year, the Angels captured the A.L. West title in 1986, finishing five games ahead of the runner-up Rangers. While California also had a solid offense, it was their pitching that set them apart from the rest of the teams in their division. Their team earned run average of 3.84 was the second lowest in the American League, and their staff featured one of the league's best pitchers in Mike Witt. The lanky righthander compiled a record of 18-10 and a 2.84 earned run average, while striking out 208 batters and throwing 269 innings. Doug DeCinces and Brian Downing provided much of the power on offense. DeCinces hit 26 home runs and drove in 96 runs, while Downing hit 20 homers, knocked in 95 runs, and scored 90 others. Leadoff hitter Gary Pettis scored 93 runs and finished second in the league with 50 stolen bases. He also was the league's best defensive centerfielder. The team's top player was the American League's Rookie of the Year—Wally Joyner. The first baseman hit 22 home runs, knocked in 100 runs, and batted .290.

However, the best player in the division was Minnesota's Kirby Puckett, who hit 31 home runs, drove in 96 runs, and finished among the league leaders with a .328 batting average, 119 runs scored, and 223 hits. The Twins finished sixth, though, 21 games out of first, eliminating Puckett from serious MVP consideration.

Also adversely affected by the mediocre performances of their respective teams were Joe Carter, Jesse Barfield, and George Bell, all of whom had outstanding individual seasons for non-contending teams in the A.L. East. Carter hit 29 home runs, led the league with 121 runs batted in, batted .302, scored 108 runs, and collected 200 hits. But his Indians finished fifth in the division, 11½ games out of first. Barfield led the A.L. with 40 homers, knocked in 108 runs, scored 107 others, and batted .289. Teammate Bell hit 31 home runs, also drove in 108 runs, scored another 101, and batted .309. But the Blue Jays finished fourth, 9½ games off the pace.

The two teams that battled it out for the top spot in the A.L. East much of the year were Boston and New York. The Red Sox superior pitching eventually enabled them to secure first place by a comfortable 5½ game margin. Their staff, which finished tied for third in the league with a team earned run average of 3.93, featured two of the A.L.'s finest hurlers in Bruce Hurst and Roger Clemens. Hurst finished 13-8 with a 2.99 earned run average, and Clemens was the league's dominant pitcher. He finished the season with a record of 24-4, to lead the circuit in victories, and his 2.48 earned run average was the lowest in the league. He also finished among the leaders with 238 strikeouts and 254 innings pitched.

Boston also had a very strong offense that compiled the second highest team batting average in the A.L. (.271) and finished fifth in the league with 794 runs scored. Pesky Marty Barrett batted .286 and scored 94 runs. Bill Buckner hit 18 home runs and drove in 102 runs. Dwight Evans hit 26 homers and knocked in 97 runs. Don Baylor led the team with 31 homers, knocked in 94 runs, and scored 93 others. Wade Boggs led the league with a .357 batting average, 105 bases on balls, and a .455 on-base percentage. He also scored 107 runs and collected 207 hits. Jim Rice hit 20 homers, led the team with 110 runs batted in, batted .324, scored 98 runs, and collected 200 hits. He finished third in the MVP voting.

The man who finished second was New York's Don Mattingly. The Yankee first baseman followed up his outstanding 1985 season with another brilliant year. He hit 31 home runs, finished among the league leaders with 113 runs batted in, 117 runs scored, and a .352 batting average, and led the A.L. with 238 hits, 53 doubles, 388 total bases, and a .573 slugging percentage. Even though he hit four fewer home runs and knocked in 32 fewer runs than he did in his MVP season of 1985, it could be argued that Mattingly actually had a better overall year. He scored 10 more runs, batted almost 30 points higher, and finished with more hits and doubles, while also compiling a higher slugging percentage. Although Mattingly knocked in fewer runs than he did the previous season, the blame for that lay squarely on the shoulders of some of his teammates. Dave Winfield, who hit behind Mattingly much of the time, hit 24 home runs and knocked in 104 runs, but batted only .262.

Even more significant was the dropoff in Rickey Henderson's performance. The leadoff hitter improved slightly over his 1985 figures by hitting 28 home runs and driving in 74 runs. He also led the league with 130 runs scored and 87 stolen bases. But Henderson batted only .263 and compiled an on-base percentage of just .359. Those figures were down 51 and 63 points, respectively, from the marks he posted in 1985. As a result, Mattingly didn't come to the plate with Henderson on base nearly as often as he did the previous year.

It follows that the main question is this: Should Mattingly have been awarded the MVP trophy at season's end instead of Roger Clemens? The Red Sox won the pennant, and Clemens was their best player. However, he received a great deal of help from his teammates—Wade Boggs and Jim Rice, in particular. Mattingly's team wasn't as strong, but he managed to keep them in the division race for most of the year. Clemens was the league's best pitcher, leading A.L. hurlers in two categories and finishing among the leaders in two others. But Mattingly was clearly the circuit's top player, finishing first in four offensive categories and placing among the leaders in four others. He was a more dominant performer than Clemens. Furthermore, the Boston righthander pitched only every fifth day, while Mattingly played virtually every game for New York. A look at the results of the National League election from one year earlier makes an even stronger case on Mattingly's behalf.

Willie McGee was selected league MVP, receiving a total of 280 points from the writers. Dwight Gooden, with only 162 points, finished a distant fourth. Yet, Mattingly had a much better year for the Yankees in 1986 than McGee had for the Cardinals the prior year, and Gooden was more dominant for the Mets than Clemens was for the Red Sox. Mattingly finished well ahead of McGee in every offensive category, except for batting average, triples, runs scored, and stolen bases. At that, his batting average was just one point lower, and he scored three more runs. Meanwhile, Gooden put up much better numbers than Clemens. While the two hurlers compiled identical 24-4 records, Gooden's 1.53 earned run average was almost one run per-game less than Clemens' mark of 2.48. Gooden also struck out more batters (268 to 238), pitched more innings (276 to 254), completed more games (16 to 10), and threw more shutouts (8 to 1).

True, Gooden's numbers were aided by the fact that he pitched in a league that did not employ the designated hitter, but he had a more dominant season than Clemens. Gooden led N.L. hurlers in five different pitching categories, while Clemens led A.L. pitchers in only two.

It could be argued that McGee's team won the pennant, while Gooden's finished second. Meanwhile, Mattingly's team finished second, while Clemens' won the division. However, the Yankees finished a fairly close second, and Mattingly was the one primarily responsible. Had New York had a better pitching staff, the race would have been even closer. But the Yankees' team earned run average of 4.11 tied them for just eighth in the American League. The Cardinals' team earned run average (3.10) was one run per-game better, and it was the second lowest in the National League. Therefore, Mattingly was more important to New York than McGee was to St. Louis one year earlier.

If preference was shown for the everyday player in McGee's case, why was the same courtesy not extended to Mattingly? He should have been selected the league's Most Valuable Player, instead of finishing a distant second to Clemens, 339 points to 258.

NATIONAL LEAGUE

The Mets dominated the National League in 1986, finishing the regular season with a record of 108-54 and winning the Eastern Division title by 21½ games over the runner-up Phillies. Not only did the Mets compile the league's best record, but they finished first in several team statistical categories. While their 148 home runs were the third highest total in the N.L., New York led the league with 783 runs scored, a team batting average of .263, and a team earned run average of 3.11. Their pitching staff was the best and deepest in baseball. In fact, three of their starters finished in the top five in the league in earned run average. Dwight Gooden finished fourth with a mark of 2.84, while compiling a record of 17-6 and striking out 200 batters. Ron Darling placed third with an earned run average of 2.81, and he finished 15-6. Perhaps the team's most effective starter was lefthander Bob Ojeda, who compiled a record of 18-5, along with the second lowest earned run average in the league (2.57). Fourth starter, Sid Fernandez, finished 16-6 with 200 strikeouts.

On offense, third baseman Ray Knight had a fine year, batting .298 and driving in 76 runs. Darryl Strawberry led the team with 27 home runs and knocked in 93 runs. The Mets' two leading MVP candidates were Gary Carter and Keith Hernandez. Carter hit 24 home runs and knocked in 105 runs. Hernandez led the team with a .310 batting average, .a 414 on-base percentage, and 94 runs scored.

Neither Carter nor Hernandez was the division's best player, though. Mike Schmidt had an outstanding season for second-place

Philadelphia. He led the N.L. with 37 home runs, 119 runs batted in, and a .547 slugging percentage, and he batted .290. Along with Carter and Hernandez, he was a top contender for league MVP honors.

The Astros finished first in the N.L. West, beating out the runner-up Reds by 10 games. Houston's offense, which finished fourth in the league in batting average (.255), and eighth in both home runs (125) and runs scored (654), was hardly overwhelming. However, their pitching staff rivaled New York's as the best in the league, finishing a close second in team earned run average (3.15). Houston had three very strong starters in Mike Scott, Bob Knepper, and Nolan Ryan. Scott finished 18-10, and he led the league with a 2.22 earned run average, 306 strikeouts, 275 innings pitched, and five shutouts. Knepper compiled a record of 17-12 and an earned run average of 3.14 in 258 innings of work, and he tied Scott for the league lead with five shutouts. Ryan finished 12-8 with a 3.34 earned run average, and he struck out 194 batters in only 178 innings pitched.

Second baseman Bill Doran was a sparkplug on offense, batting .276, scoring 92 runs, and stealing 42 bases. He was joined by Kevin Bass, who hit 20 home runs, knocked in 79 runs, and batted .311. But the lineup's most imposing figure was first baseman Glenn Davis, who finished among the league leaders with 31 home runs and 101 runs batted in.

Let's look at his numbers, alongside those of the other leading MVP candidates:

PLAYER	AB	HITS	RUNS	2B	3B	HR	RBI	AVG	OBP	SLG PCT
Dave Parker	637	174	89	31	3	31	116	.273	.333	.477
Gary Carter	490	125	81	14	2	24	105	.255	.346	.439
Keith Hernandez	551	171	94	34	1	13	83	.310	.414	.446
Mike Schmidt	552	160	97	29	1	37	119	.290	.395	.547
Glenn Davis	574	152	91	32	3	31	101	.265	.348	.493

Dave Parker had another big year for the runner-up Reds in the West, but his numbers were down somewhat from the prior year. Also, Cincinnati finished much further off the pace in their division than they did in 1985, so Parker was the first to go. Both Carter and Hernandez had solid seasons for the Mets. Carter finished among the leaders in runs batted in, while Hernandez compiled the highest batting average and on-base percentage in the group, finished with the most doubles, and scored the second most runs. However, none of their other numbers were particularly impressive. In addition, the Mets were so much stronger than the rest of the N.L. East that they probably could have won the division handily even if either Carter or Hernandez missed an extensive amount of playing time.

That leaves us with Schmidt and Davis. Schmidt put up much better numbers. He finished well ahead in most offensive categories, and he was the far greater run-producer of the two. Both his on-base and slugging percentages were approximately 50 points higher than the figures posted by Davis. Schmidt was clearly the better player. Yet, the Astros won their division, while Philadelphia finished 21½ games behind New York in the East. Also, Davis was Houston's only real power threat. His 31 homers were one quarter of the team's total of 125, and he was the only Astros player to hit more than 20 home runs and knock in more than 80 runs. Davis was clearly the focal point of their attack.

Still, it is difficult to ignore the superiority of Schmidt's numbers, and the fact that he was easily the league's best player. While the Phillies finished well out of contention, they were able to come in second. Had Schmidt not had the type of year he did Philadelphia likely would have finished considerably further back in the standings. The writers' selection of Schmidt as the league's Most Valuable Player would have to be viewed as a good one.

1987

AMERICAN LEAGUE

The Minnesota Twins captured their first A.L. West title in 17 years in 1987, finishing first in a close, three-team pennant race. Kansas City finished second, just two games back, while Oakland came in third, four games out. Both the Royals and A's had a powerful hitter in the middle of their respective lineups around which their offenses were built. With George Brett once again injured for a good portion of the season, Danny Tartabull took over as Kansas City's primary offensive threat. The young outfielder led the team with 34 home runs, 101 runs batted in, 95 runs scored, and a .309 batting average. Oakland first baseman Mark McGwire established a new rookie record by hitting a league-leading 49 home runs. He also knocked in 118 runs, scored another 97, batted .289, and led the A.L. with a .618 slugging percentage. He finished sixth in the MVP balloting.

Meanwhile, the Western Division champion Twins were less dependent on any one player. They had several outstanding performers who helped put them over the top. Pitcher Frank Viola finished among the league leaders with 17 victories and a 2.90 earned run average. Outfielder Tom Brunansky hit 32 homers and knocked in 85 runs. Third baseman Gary Gaetti hit 31 home runs, led the team with 109 runs batted in, and scored 95 runs. Kent Hrbek hit 34 four-baggers, drove in 90 runs, and batted .285. Kirby Puckett was the team's leading MVP candidate. He hit 28 home runs, drove in 99 runs, scored another 96, batted .332, and led the league with 207 hits. Puckett finished third in the voting.

Many of the league's finest players resided in the Eastern Division. Don Mattingly had another outstanding year for New York, hitting 30 home runs, driving in 115 runs, and batting .327. Milwaukee's Paul Molitor finished second in the A.L. with a .353 batting average, stole 45 bases, and led the league with 114 runs scored and 41 doubles. However, the Yankees finished fourth in the East, nine games back, while the Brewers finished third, seven games off the pace, preventing both men from being among the leading MVP candidates.

Also excluded from serious MVP consideration were Boston's Dwight Evans and Wade Boggs, both of whom had exceptional seasons. Evans hit 34 home runs, finished second in the league with 123 runs batted in, batted .305, and scored 109 runs. Boggs established career highs with 24 home runs and 89 runs batted in, scored 108 runs, collected 200 hits, and led the league with a .363 batting average and a .467 on-base-percentage. But the Red Sox finished fifth, 20 games out of first.

The two teams that battled it out right down to the season's final days were Detroit and Toronto. The Tigers ended up winning the division by two games over the Blue Jays, due largely to their superior team balance. Detroit led the league with 225 home runs and 896 runs scored, and they finished third in both team batting average (.272) and team earned run average (4.02). Jack Morris was the team's best pitcher, finishing among the league leaders with 18 victories, a

3.38 earned run average, 208 strikeouts, and 266 innings pitched. On offense, Darrell Evans led the Tigers with 34 home runs, knocked in 99 runs, and scored 90 others. Chet Lemon hit 20 homers, drove in 75 runs, and batted .277. Kirk Gibson hit 24 round-trippers, knocked in 79 runs, scored another 95, and batted .277. Lou Whitaker scored 110 runs. Whitaker's doubleplay partner, Alan Trammell, had the finest season of his career. The Detroit shortstop hit 28 home runs, knocked in 105 runs, scored 109 others, and batted .343.

Toronto also had a very strong team. Jimmy Key was the ace of the pitching staff, finishing with a record of 17-8 and a league-leading 2.76 earned run average. Tony Fernandez played excellent defense at shortstop and contributed to the offense with 90 runs scored, 32 stolen bases, and a .322 batting average. Jesse Barfield hit 28 homers, drove in 84 runs, and scored 89 others. Lloyd Moseby hit 26 home runs, knocked in 96 runs, scored another 106, and batted .282. The team's best player, though, was George Bell, who rivaled Alan Trammell as the league's leading contender for MVP honors.

Let's look at the numbers of the two players:

PLAYER	AB	HITS	RUNS	2B	3B	HR	RBI	AVG	OBP	SLG PCT
Alan Trammell	597	205	109	34	3	28	105	.343	.406	.551
George Bell	610	188	111	32	4	47	134	.308	.357	.605

Trammell hit for a much higher average and compiled a much higher on-base percentage. However, Bell hit far more home runs, knocked in many more runs, and finished with a much higher slugging percentage. Trammell played the more demanding defensive position of the two, and he also played for the team that won the division. But Bell's Blue Jays finished only two games back, and they weren't eliminated until the season's final weekend. It's very close, and it really could have gone either way. But we'll opt for Bell because of his greater run production. The writers felt so too, since they selected him over Trammell by a narrow 21-point margin (332 to 311).

NATIONAL LEAGUE

Cincinnati finished runner-up in the N.L. West for the third consecutive year in 1987, losing out to the division-winning Giants by six games. The efforts of both teams were aided immeasurably by the presence of a young star on their respective rosters. Centerfielder Eric

Davis appeared in only 129 games for the Reds, but he hit 37 home runs, drove in 100 runs, scored another 120, batted .293, and stole 50 bases. First baseman Will Clark hit 35 homers for San Francisco, knocked in 91 runs, and batted .308.

The division's top two players played for non-contending teams. Although the Padres finished last, 25 games out of first, Tony Gwynn led the league with a .370 batting average and 218 hits, and he placed among the leaders with 119 runs scored and 56 stolen bases. Dale Murphy had an excellent year for the Braves, who finished fifth in the division, 20½ games back. Murphy hit 45 home runs, knocked in 105 runs, scored another 115, and batted .295. Had their teams fared a little better, both Gwynn and Murphy would have been serious contenders for league MVP honors.

In the Eastern Division, both Mike Schmidt and Juan Samuel had outstanding seasons for the fourth-place Phillies, who finished 15 games out of first. Schmidt hit 35 home runs, drove in 113 runs, and batted .293. Although Samuel struggled somewhat defensively at second base, he was one of the league's top offensive players. He hit 28 homers, drove in 100 runs, scored another 113, batted .272, led the N.L. with 15 triples, and finished among the leaders with 37 doubles, 35 stolen bases, and 329 total bases.

Most of the division's leading MVP candidates came from the three teams that contended for the division title. Tim Wallach and Tim Raines both had exceptional years for the Expos, who finished third, just four games out of first. Wallach hit 26 home runs, knocked in 123 runs, batted .298, and led the league with 42 doubles. Raines finished among the league leaders with a .330 batting average, a .431 on-base percentage, and 50 stolen bases, and he led the N.L. with 123 runs scored.

The Mets finished second, just three games back. Their top players were Darryl Strawberry and Howard Johnson. Strawberry hammered 39 homers, drove in 104 runs, scored 108 others, batted .284, and stole 36 bases. Johnson's numbers were almost as good. He hit 36 home runs, knocked in 99 runs, scored another 93, and stole 32 bases. Both men finished in the top ten of the voting.

The Cardinals, with their good pitching, solid defense, and well-balanced lineup, captured the division title for the second time in three seasons. Although they had little power, finishing last in the N.L. with only 94 home runs, the Cardinals led the league with 248 stolen bases, and they finished second with 798 runs scored. Vince Coleman batted .289, scored 121 runs, and led the league with 109 stolen bases. Willie McGee batted .285 and knocked in 105 runs. Ozzie Smith scored 104 runs, batted .303, stole 43 bases, and performed his usual wizardry at shortstop. Terry Pendleton knocked in 96 runs and batted .286. The team's most potent hitter was first baseman Jack Clark.

Let's look at his numbers, alongside those of three other players who also had superb seasons:

PLAYER	AB	HITS	RUNS	2B	3B	HR	RBI	AVG	OBP	SLG PCT
Tim Raines	530	175	123	34	8	18	68	.330	.431	.526
Jack Clark	419	120	93	23	1	35	106	.286	.461	.597
Andre Dawson	621	178	90	24	2	49	137	.287	.329	.568
Dale Murphy	566	167	115	27	1	44	105	.295	.420	.580

The numbers that jump out are Andre Dawson's league-leading home run and RBI totals. The writers certainly noticed them because they voted him the league's Most Valuable Player, in spite of the fact that his Cubs finished last in the East, 18½ games out of first. But, beyond those two figures, Dawson's numbers were not particularly impressive. He scored the fewest runs and had the lowest on-base percentage by far. In fact, Dawson's statistics were actually quite comparable to Murphy's. Dawson hit a few more home runs and knocked in 32 more runs, but Murphy scored 25 more times, finished with a slightly higher batting average and slugging percentage, and compiled a much higher on-base percentage. Murphy's Braves finished well out of contention in the West, 20½ games out of first, but that was only two games further back than Dawson's Cubs finished in the East. And at least the Braves finished fifth in their division, while Dawson's Cubs finished last in the East.

Yet, Dawson was named league MVP, while Murphy could do no better than 11th in the balloting.

Far more disturbing, though, were Clark's third-place finish and Raines' seventh-place showing. The Expos finished only four games behind the division-winning Cardinals in the East, and Raines was their offensive catalyst. He stole 50 bases, batted .330, and led the league in runs scored. Dawson hit more than twice as many home runs and knocked in almost 70 more runs, but Raines scored 33 more times, out-hit Dawson by more than 40 points, and compiled an on-base percentage that was more than *100* points higher. He should have received far more support.

Clark also should have fared much better in the voting. He was injured for part of the year and, therefore, appeared in only 131 games for the Cardinals, accumulating just 419 official at-bats. As a result, his home run and RBI totals fell well short of Dawson's. But Clark's numbers compared favorably to Dawson's in virtually every other department. Most noteworthy were the advantages he held in slugging percentage and on-base percentage—two categories in which he led the league. In fact, since Dawson walked only 32 times, Clark's league-leading 136 bases on balls enabled him to finish with an on-base percentage that was more than *130* points higher. The inordinately high number of walks Clark compiled was indicative of his status as the league's most feared hitter. He intimidated opposing pitchers, and he represented the Cardinals' only real power threat.

With St. Louis finishing last in the league with only 94 home runs, Clark's 35 homers represented a whopping 37 percent of the team's long balls. Therefore, his presence in the Cardinals' lineup was vital to the success of the team.

The same could not necessarily be said of Dawson, since his team finished last in spite of his outstanding year. In fact, even with Dawson leading the league in home runs and runs batted in, Chicago's won-lost record of 76-85 was only 5½ games better than it was the previous year. Therefore, how valuable could Dawson have been to Chicago? He should have finished no higher than third in the voting, behind both Clark and Raines.

Clark should have been named league MVP over Raines because his team won the division, and because his powerful bat was such an integral part of the St. Louis offense.

1988

AMERICAN LEAGUE

The Red Sox finished first in a close five-team race in the A.L. East in 1988, edging out the Tigers by only one game, the Blue Jays and Brewers by two, and the Yankees by 3½. Boston's offense was the best in the league, topping the circuit with 813 runs scored and a team batting average of .283. Dwight Evans hit 21 home runs, drove in 111 runs, scored 96 others, and batted .293. Centerfielder Ellis Burks hit 18 homers, knocked in 92 runs, scored another 93, batted .294, and stole 25 bases. Wade Boggs had one of his finest seasons, winning his fourth straight batting title with a mark of .366. He also led the league with 128 runs scored, 45 doubles, 125 bases on balls, and a .480 on-base percentage, while placing second with 214 hits. The man who the writers felt was Boston's most valuable player, though, was young outfielder Mike Greenwell, who replaced Jim Rice as the team's regular leftfielder. Greenwell hit 22 home runs, finished second in the A.L. with 119 runs batted in, and placed among the leaders with a .325 batting average and a .420 on-base percentage. He finished second in the league MVP voting.

The Red Sox also had solid pitching, with Bruce Hurst and Roger Clemens again heading the staff. Hurst finished 18-6, while Clemens also won 18 games, compiled a 2.93 earned run average, and led A.L. hurlers with 291 strikeouts, 14 complete games, and eight shutouts.

The other contending teams also featured players who had fine seasons. Toronto's Fred McGriff finished second in the league with 34 homers, scored 100 runs, and batted .282. Milwaukee's Robin Yount batted .306, knocked in 91 runs, and scored 92 others. Teammate Paul Molitor finished among the league leaders with a .312 batting average, 115 runs scored, and 41 stolen bases. New York's Rickey Henderson batted .305, scored 118 runs, and led the league with 93 stolen bases. Teammate Dave Winfield hit 25 home runs, drove in 107 runs, and batted .322. He finished fourth in the MVP balloting.

The man who finished third was Kirby Puckett, whose Twins finished second in the A.L. West, 13 games behind the division-winning Athletics. Puckett hit 24 home runs, finished second in the league with 121 runs batted in and a .356 batting average, scored 109 runs, and led the A.L. with 234 hits. Teammate Frank Viola was the league's best pitcher, compiling an A.L.-best record of 24-7, with a 2.64 earned run average, 193 strikeouts, and 255 innings pitched.

The American League's dominant team was the A's, who finished the regular season with a record of 104-58. They finished second in the league with 800 runs scored and 156 home runs, and their team earned run average of 3.44 was the best in the A.L. Dave Stewart led the staff with a 21-12 record, a 3.23 earned run average, 192 strikeouts, and a league-leading 275 innings pitched and 14 complete games. He was joined by Bob Welch, who finished the season with a 17-9 record. Dennis Eckersley was the league's top relief pitcher. He led the A.L. with 45 saves, compiled a 2.35 earned run average, and struck out 70 batters, while allowing only 52 hits in 72 innings of work.

On offense, centerfielder Dave Henderson hit 24 home runs, knocked in 94 runs, scored 100 others, and batted .304. Mark McGwire hit 32 homers and drove in 99 runs. But the team's dominant player was rightfielder Jose Canseco, who was named the American League's Most Valuable Player. The slugger led the league with 42 home runs, 124 runs batted in, and a .569 slugging percentage, while batting .307 and scoring 120 runs. He also stole 40 bases, to become the first player in major league history to hit 40 home runs and steal 40 bases in the same season.

NATIONAL LEAGUE

After failing to make the playoffs the prior year, the Mets dominated the N.L. East once more in 1988, finishing the regular season with a record of 100-60, 15 games ahead of the second-place Pirates. Pittsburgh actually had the league's best all-around player in centerfielder Andy Van Slyke. In addition to being a superb outfielder, Van Slyke was the Pirates' primary offensive threat, finishing the year with 25 home runs, 100 runs batted in, 101 runs scored, a .288 batting average, 30 stolen bases, and a league-leading 15 triples.

But the Mets were the division's dominant team, and the strongest overall team in the league. They led the N.L. with 703 runs scored, 152 home runs, and a team earned run average of 2.91, and their .256 team batting average was the second highest in the circuit. Their pitching staff featured three of the league's top hurlers in Dwight Gooden, Ron Darling, and David Cone. Gooden finished 18-9 with a 3.19 earned run average. Darling's record was 17-9, and he compiled a 3.25 earned run average. Cone was the staff ace, finishing among the league leaders with a 20-3 record, a 2.22 earned run average, 213 strikeouts, and 231 innings pitched.

On offense, Kevin McReynolds hit 27 home runs, knocked in 99 runs, batted .288, and was a perfect 21-for-21 in stolen base attempts. The team's dominant hitter was Darryl Strawberry, who led the league with 39 home runs and a .545 slugging percentage, while driving in 101 runs, scoring 101 others, and stealing 29 bases. He was clearly the leading MVP candidate in the division.

The Dodgers were not nearly as dominant in the N.L. West, finishing sixth in the league in runs scored, fifth in batting average, and eighth in home runs. But their team earned run average of 2.96 was second only to New York's, and it enabled them to finish seven games ahead of the Reds, who finished second in the division for the fourth straight year. Cincinnati featured one of the league's finest pitchers in lefthander Danny Jackson, who tied for the N.L. lead with 23 victories (against only 8 losses) and 15 complete games, while pitching to a 2.73 earned run average. The fourth-place Giants, who finished 11½ games off the pace, may well have had the division's top offensive player in Will Clark. The San Francisco first baseman hit 29 home runs, led the league with 109 runs batted in, batted .282, and scored 102 runs.

The first-place Dodgers' offense was sparked by leadoff hitter Steve Sax, who batted .277 and stole 42 bases. However, their top offensive threat was Kirk Gibson, who led the team with 25 home runs, 76 runs batted in, 106 runs scored, and a .290 batting average, while also stealing 31 bases. He edged out Strawberry by 36 points in the league MVP balloting.

Let's look at the numbers of the two players:

PLAYER	AB	HITS	RUNS	2B	3B	HR	RBI	AVG	OBP	SLG PCT
Darryl Strawberry	543	146	101	27	3	**39**	101	.269	.371	**.545**
Kirk Gibson	542	157	106	28	1	25	76	.290	.381	.483

Strawberry's statistics were clearly better. Gibson scored five more runs, hit for a higher average, and finished with a higher on-base percentage. But Strawberry hit far more home runs, knocked in many more runs, and compiled a much higher slugging percentage. Still, it could be argued that Gibson was more important to the Dodgers' offense than Strawberry was to that of the Mets. After all, New York's lineup was much stronger than the Dodgers' feeble attack. In addition,

Gibson was his team's emotional leader. That being said, a valid case could be made for either man.

However, something that must be considered is that it was not the Los Angeles offense that enabled them to win their division, but, rather, their pitching. While the Dodgers struggled to score runs, finishing sixth in the league in that department, their pitching staff compiled the second lowest team earned run average in the league. Tim Leary won 17 games and finished the year with a 2.91 earned run average.

Staff ace Orel Hershiser finished 23-8, to tie for the league lead in victories. He also finished third among N.L. pitchers with a 2.26 earned run average, struck out 178 batters, and led the league with 267 innings pitched, 15 complete games, and eight shutouts. In fact, six of those shutouts came in succession at the end of the regular season, enabling Hershiser to establish a new major league record by throwing 59 consecutive scoreless innings. The Dodgers didn't take over first place in the division until July, and it was Hershiser's amazing performance that allowed them to pull away from the rest of the pack and establish momentum going into the playoffs. Gibson may have been the team's emotional leader on an everyday basis, but the Dodgers knew they had an excellent chance of winning every time Hershiser took the mound. He was their security blanket down the stretch, and he was unquestionably their best player.

Hershiser should have been named the league's Most Valuable Player.

THE FINAL WINNERS UNDER THE OLD FORMAT

21

When baseball expanded to 24 teams in 1969, it adopted a new four-division setup. Eight years later, when the A. L. further expanded from 12 to 14 teams, the major leagues continued to function under the same four-division alignment. However, when the N.L. added two new teams to its membership prior to the start of the 1993 campaign, thoughts of realignment began entering into the minds of the baseball owners. The Colorado Rockies and Florida Marlins joined the fraternity of National League clubs, with the Rockies making the Western Division their home and the Marlins being slotted into the Eastern Division.

The presence of 14 teams in each league made the creation of additional divisions possible. This was an idea that appealed to the baseball hierarchy since more divisions not only meant more pennant races, but also increased revenue for the owners.

As a result, each league was split into three divisions in 1995, and a wild-card entry was added to the playoff picture for the first time. The MVP winners from the 1989 to 1994 seasons represent the last group of winners under the old format.

| | ACTUAL MVP WINNERS | | SUGGESTED WINNERS | |
	A.L.	N.L.	A.L.	N.L.
1989:	Robin Yount	Kevin Mitchell	Bret Saberhagen	Kevin Mitchell
1990:	Rickey Henderson	Barry Bonds	Rickey Henderson	Barry Bonds
1991:	Cal Ripken Jr.	Terry Pendleton	Frank Thomas	Terry Pendleton
1992:	Dennis Eckersley	Barry Bonds	Dennis Eckersley	Barry Bonds
1993:	Frank Thomas	Barry Bonds	Frank Thomas	Barry Bonds
1994:	Frank Thomas	Jeff Bagwell	Frank Thomas	Jeff Bagwell

1989

AMERICAN LEAGUE

Toronto finished first in the hotly-contested A.L. East in 1989, beating out second-place Baltimore by just two games. Boston finished third, six games back, and Milwaukee came in fourth, eight games out. The Blue Jays were led by the duo of George Bell and Fred McGriff. Bell hit 18 home runs, drove in 104 runs, and batted .297. McGriff led the league with 36 homers, knocked in 92 runs, and scored 98 others. Baltimore's top player was Cal Ripken Jr., who batted only .257 but hit 21 home runs and drove in 93 runs.

The Eastern Division's best player was Robin Yount, who moved from shortstop to centerfield a few years earlier. While he failed to lead the league in any statistical category, Yount finished among the leaders with 103 runs batted in, 101 runs scored, 195 hits, and a .318 batting average. He had to be considered the division's leading MVP candidate.

The A's captured their second straight A.L. West title, finishing seven games in front of the runner-up Royals. Oakland's primary power threat was Mark McGwire, who batted only .231, but hit 33 home runs and knocked in 95 runs. Third baseman Carney Lansford hit only two home runs and drove in just 52 runs, but he stole 37 bases and finished second in the league with a .336 batting average.

It was truly the Athletics' pitching that enabled them to finish first in the division. Their team earned run average of 3.09 was the lowest in the A.L., and their staff featured three of the league's top starters. Dave Stewart led the team with a record of 21-9, while also compiling a 3.32 earned run average. Mike Moore finished 19-11 with a 2.61 earned run average, and Storm Davis won 19 games, while losing only 7. Reliever Dennis Eckersley was brilliant all year, compiling a perfect 4-0 record with 33 saves, pitching to a 1.56 earned run average, and allowing only 32 hits in 57 innings of work. He finished fifth in the league MVP voting.

Second-place Kansas City got fine seasons from outfielder Bo Jackson and pitcher Bret Saberhagen. Jackson finished among the league leaders with 32 home runs and 105 runs batted in, while Saberhagen led A.L. hurlers with a 23-6 record, a 2.16 earned run average, 262 innings pitched, and 12 complete games. He also finished second with four shutouts, and he placed third with 193 strikeouts.

The division's top position player came from the fourth-place Rangers, who finished 16 games behind the A's. Ruben Sierra led the league in three different offensive categories, and he ended up finishing second to Robin Yount in the MVP voting.

Let's look at the numbers of the two players:

PLAYER	AB	HITS	RUNS	2B	3B	HR	RBI	AVG	OBP	SLG PCT
Ruben Sierra	634	194	101	35	14	29	119	.306	.352	.543
Robin Yount	614	195	101	38	9	21	103	.318	.387	.511

Sierra's overall numbers were slightly better than Yount's. He hit more home runs, knocked in more runs, and led the A.L. in three statistical categories, while Yount failed to lead the league in any. Yet, Yount's Brewers finished only eight games back in the East, and they remained in contention for much of the year. Meanwhile, Sierra's Rangers finished 16 games back in the West, and they were not in the pennant race for most of the season. Therefore, with Sierra holding only a small statistical advantage, a valid case could be made for placing Yount ahead of him in the MVP balloting.

However, Saberhagen's Royals finished only seven games behind the A's in the West. Furthermore, they placed second in the division, while Yount's Brewers could do no better than fourth in the East. In addition, Saberhagen had a far more dominant year than Yount. He led A.L. pitchers in four statistical categories, and he finished in the top three in two others. His 2.16 earned run average was 41 points lower than that of any other starting pitcher in the league. While it is highly questionable as to whether or not Yount was the league's top position player, Saberhagen was clearly the A.L.'s best pitcher, and he was also its most dominant player. As such, he should have been selected its Most Valuable Player. His eighth-place finish in the balloting was a travesty.

NATIONAL LEAGUE

The Chicago Cubs beat out both previous N.L. East champions in 1989, finishing six games ahead of the runner-up Mets and seven in front of the third-place Cardinals. The Cubs featured two fine pitchers in righthanders Greg Maddux and Mike Bielecki. Maddux finished

19-12 with a 2.95 earned run average, while Bielecki compiled a record of 18-7 and a 3.14 earned run average. On offense, Chicago was led by Mark Grace and Ryne Sandberg. Grace batted .314 and drove in 79 runs. Sandberg hit 30 homers, knocked in 76 runs, batted .290, and led the N.L. with 104 runs scored. He finished fourth in the league MVP voting.

Third baseman Howard Johnson had a big year for the Mets. He hit 36 home runs, knocked in 101 runs, batted .287, stole 41 bases, and tied Sandberg for the league lead with 104 runs scored. He finished right behind the Chicago second baseman in the MVP balloting.

Finishing just ahead of Sandberg was the Cardinals' best player, Pedro Guerrero. The outfielder hit 17 home runs, finished among the league leaders with 117 runs batted in and a .311 batting average, and led the N.L. with 42 doubles.

The top two MVP candidates came from the N.L. West, where the Giants edged out the Padres by three games to capture their first division title in 18 years. San Diego was led by Tony Gwynn, who won the N.L. batting crown with a mark of .336 and also led the league with 203 hits. But San Francisco had a more balanced team. Their pitching staff was headed by Rick Reuschel, who finished 17-8 with a 2.94 earned run average. Righthander Scott Garrelts compiled an excellent 14-5 record and led all N.L. starters with a 2.28 earned run average. On offense, centerfielder Brett Butler batted .283, scored 100 runs, and stole 31 bases.

Yet, there is little doubt as to which two players carried the team to the division title. Leftfielder Kevin Mitchell and first baseman Will Clark finished one-two in the league MVP voting, and with good reason.

A look at their numbers clearly indicates that they were the league's two best players:

PLAYER	AB	HITS	RUNS	2B	3B	HR	RBI	AVG	OBP	SLG PCT
Will Clark	588	196	**104**	38	9	23	111	.333	.412	.546
Kevin Mitchell	543	158	100	34	6	**47**	**125**	.291	.392	**.635**

Clark tied for the league lead in runs scored, and he finished among the leaders in batting average, runs batted in, hits, and doubles. Mitchell led the league in home runs, runs batted in, and slugging percentage, and he finished near the top in runs scored as well. Clark had a fine season and he was a worthy contender. But Mitchell was the league's dominant player, and he was the one most deserving of the MVP trophy. He doubled Clark's home run output, drove in 14 more runs, and compiled a slugging percentage that was some 90 points higher.

1990

AMERICAN LEAGUE

In finishing the regular season with a major-league leading 103 victories, the Oakland A's won their third consecutive A.L. West title in 1990. The Chicago White Sox finished second, nine games back. Oakland's pitching staff once again posted the lowest team earned run average in the league, with a mark of 3.18. Bob Welch led the majors with 27 victories, against only 6 losses, while pitching to a 2.95 earned run average. He was rewarded at season's end by being named the recipient of the A.L. Cy Young Award. Still, Welch may not have been the A's best pitcher since teammate Dave Stewart also had a superb year. He finished 22-11 with a 2.56 earned run average, and he led the league with 267 innings pitched, 11 complete games, and four shutouts. Even though Chicago's Bobby Thigpen established a new major league record by saving 57 games, the A's also had baseball's best reliever in Dennis Eckersley. He finished 4-2, with 48 saves and a miniscule 0.61 earned run average. Eckersley also struck out 73 batters in 73 innings of work, while allowing only 41 hits.

Much of the A's offensive firepower was supplied by *The Bash Brothers*—Mark McGwire and Jose Canseco. Despite batting only .235, McGwire finished second in the league with 39 home runs, knocked in 108 runs, and led the A.L. with 110 walks. Canseco finished right behind McGwire with 37 homers, and he drove in 101 runs.

Nevertheless, Oakland's most valuable player was unquestionably Rickey Henderson, who was the team's offensive catalyst. Henderson hit 28 home runs, batted .325, and led the A.L. with 119 runs scored, 65 stolen bases, and a .441 on-base percentage. More than anyone, he was responsible for the Athletics' outstanding season.

In the A.L. East, Boston finished just ahead of second-place Toronto, capturing the division title by a slim two-game margin. The Blue Jays got solid seasons from pitcher Dave Stieb, first baseman Fred McGriff, and third baseman Kelly Gruber. Stieb finished 18-6 with a 2.93 earned run average. McGriff finished among the league leaders with 35 home runs, and he also drove in 88 runs, scored another 91, and batted .300. Gruber had a career year, hitting 31 home runs and finishing second in the A.L. with 118 runs batted in. Those figures were good enough to place him fourth in the league MVP voting.

Finishing just ahead of Gruber in third place was the league's best pitcher. In compiling a record of 21-6, Roger Clemens won six fewer games than Bob Welch, but his league-leading 1.93 earned run average was one run-per-game better. He also finished among the leaders with 209 strikeouts.

On offense, the Red Sox were led by Wade Boggs, Ellis Burks, and Mike Greenwell. Boggs batted .302, scored 89 runs, and finished second in the league with 187 hits. Burks hit 21 home runs, knocked in 89 runs, scored 89 others, and batted .296. Greenwell batted .297 and finished fourth in the A.L. with 181 hits.

The division's top offensive player, though, was Detroit's Cecil Fielder. After an earlier stint with the Blue Jays, Fielder spent a year in Japan honing his offensive skills. He returned to American baseball in 1990 and proceeded to ravage A.L. pitching for a league-leading 51 home runs and 132 runs batted in. The Tigers finished nine games behind Boston in the East, but they also finished a very respectable third. Detroit finished dead last the previous season, 30 games off the pace. Therefore, Fielder had to be considered Rickey Henderson's primary competition for league MVP honors.

Let's look at the statistics of the two players:

PLAYER	AB	HITS	RUNS	2B	3B	HR	RBI	AVG	OBP	SLG PCT	SB
Rickey Henderson	489	159	119	33	3	28	61	.325	.441	.577	65
Cecil Fielder	573	159	104	25	1	51	132	.277	.380	.592	0

It is extremely difficult to compare the numbers of Henderson to those of Fielder, since the two men were polar opposites in terms of their styles of play. Henderson was the consummate leadoff hitter whose primary objective was to get on base, upset the opposing team's defense, and score runs. Meanwhile, it was Fielder's job to hit home runs and drive in a lot of runs.

Nevertheless, an examination of the statistics compiled by the two players reveals that Fielder, not surprisingly, hit many more home runs, drove in more than twice as many runs, and compiled a higher slugging percentage. On the other hand, Henderson finished ahead of the Tiger slugger in every other offensive category. He scored more runs, outhit Fielder by almost 50 points, and compiled an on-base percentage that was some 60 points higher. In addition, while Fielder failed to steal a single base, Henderson swiped 65 bags. Furthermore, although Fielder led the league in slugging percentage, Henderson finished only 15 points behind him, in second place. Statistically, it's really very close. True, Henderson had a better supporting cast around him in Oakland. As we saw earlier, it is also true that Fielder had a profound impact on the Tigers' fortunes.

But, it is difficult to ignore the fact that the A's were the league's dominant team, and that Henderson was the main reason for their success. Not only was he a major distraction to opposing teams when he was on the basepath—upsetting both their pitchers and their defense—but he frequently got the hitters batting behind him better pitches to hit. In so doing, Henderson made the players around him better.

As brilliant a year as Fielder had, he would have to be rated just behind Henderson when evaluating the MVP contenders. The writers felt so too, awarding Henderson a total of 317 points, to 286 for Fielder.

NATIONAL LEAGUE

The surprising Cincinnati Reds finished first in the N.L. West in 1990, beating out the runner-up Dodgers by five games, and the third-place Giants by six. San Francisco had the division's most potent offensive weapon in Matt Williams. The Giants' third baseman hit 33 home runs, batted .277, and led the league with 122 runs batted in. Williams was ably assisted by Brett Butler and reigning MVP Kevin Mitchell. Butler batted .309, scored 108 runs, stole 51 bases, and led the N.L. with 192 hits. Mitchell hit 35 home runs, knocked in 93 runs, and batted .290.

Eddie Murray had a solid season for the second-place Dodgers. The former Oriole hit 26 home runs, knocked in 95 runs, scored 96 others, and finished second in the league with a .330 batting average.

The Reds, who eventually went on to upset the heavily-favored A's in the World Series, were the league's surprise team. Without a true superstar, they combined solid pitching and defense with a deep lineup to wear down the opposition. Their best pitcher was hard-throwing righthander Jose Rijo, who compiled a record of 14-8 and finished among the league leaders with a 2.70 earned run average. The Cincinnati offense was led by Chris Sabo, Eric Davis, and Barry Larkin. Third baseman Sabo led the team with 25 home runs and 95 runs scored, while also stealing 25 bases. Davis hit 24 homers and drove in 86 runs. Larkin batted .301, scored 85 runs, stole 30 bases, and provided leadership in the infield. He was the only Cincinnati player to finish in the top ten in the league MVP balloting.

The top four vote-getters all came from the N.L. East, where the Pirates beat out the Mets by four games to capture their first division title in more than a decade. Perhaps the league's finest all-around player was Cubs second baseman Ryne Sandberg, who finished fourth in the balloting. Sandberg led the N.L. with 40 home runs, 116 runs scored, and 344 total bases, and he finished among the leaders with 100 runs batted in and a .306 batting average. But Chicago finished fifth in the division, 18 games off the pace, preventing Sandberg from winning his second MVP trophy.

The second-place Mets got fine seasons from Dave Magadan, Dwight Gooden, and Frank Viola. Magadan finished third in the league with a .328 batting average, and he led the N.L. with a .425 on-base percentage. Gooden compiled a record of 19-7, and Viola finished the season with a 20-12 record, a 2.67 earned run average, and a league-leading 249 innings pitched. New York's leading MVP candidate, though, was Darryl Strawberry, who finished among the league leaders with 37 home runs and 108 runs batted in.

Division-winning Pittsburgh had the league's best pitcher in Doug Drabek. The righthander led N.L. hurlers with a record of 22-6, and he pitched to an outstanding 2.76 earned run average. However, Pittsburgh's top two MVP candidates were outfielders Bobby Bonilla and Barry Bonds. Let's look at their numbers, alongside those of Strawberry:

PLAYER	AB	HITS	RUNS	2B	3B	HR	RBI	AVG	OBP	SLG PCT	SB
Darryl Strawberry	542	150	92	18	1	37	108	.277	.364	.518	15
Barry Bonds	519	156	104	32	3	33	114	.301	.410	**.565**	52
Bobby Bonilla	625	175	112	39	7	32	120	.280	.329	.518	4

The numbers of Strawberry and Bonilla were fairly comparable, with the latter holding the overall statistical edge due to his superior run-production. However, it could be argued that Bonilla was only the second best player on his own team. In comparing his numbers to those of Bonds, the teammates compiled similar totals in several statistical categories. Bonds hit one more home run, but Bonilla finished with a few more doubles and triples. Bonilla also drove in six more runs and scored eight more times than Bonds. However, Bonds compiled a slugging percentage that was almost 50 points higher, and he posted an on-base percentage that was some 80 points better. In addition, he was a far more complete player than Bonilla, being both a better defensive outfielder and a superior baserunner, as can be evidenced by his 52-to-4 advantage in stolen bases.

Even though he held only a slight statistical advantage, Bond's superior all-around ability enabled him to contribute to the Pirates in more ways than Bonilla. It follows that he was the correct choice as the league's Most Valuable Player.

1991

AMERICAN LEAGUE

After a close, second-place finish the prior year, Toronto captured the A.L. East title in 1991, finishing seven games ahead of both Detroit and Boston, and eight games in front of fourth-place Milwaukee. Toronto's balanced attack had a blend of both speed and power. Centerfielder Devon White and second baseman Roberto Alomar provided much of the speed at the top of the batting order. White batted .282, scored 110 runs, and stole 33 bases. Alomar batted .295, scored 88 runs, and finished among the league leaders with 53 steals. Joe Carter supplied much of the power in the Blue Jay lineup. He hit

33 home runs, knocked in 108 runs, and scored 89 runs. Toronto's best pitcher was lefthander Jimmy Key, who finished 16-12 with a 3.05 earned run average.

Paul Molitor had an outstanding year for the fourth-place Brewers. Serving primarily as a designated hitter, Molitor batted .325 and led the A.L. with 133 runs scored, 216 hits, and 13 triples.

Red Sox righthander Roger Clemens was the league's finest pitcher. Clemens compiled a record of 18-10, and he led A.L. hurlers with a 2.62 earned run average, 241 strikeouts, 271 innings pitched, and four shutouts.

The top two offensive players in the division were Detroit's Cecil Fielder and Baltimore's Cal Ripken Jr. Fielder led the league in home runs and runs batted in for the second consecutive year, finishing with 44 homers and 133 runs batted in. Ripken placed among the league leaders with 34 home runs, 114 runs batted in, and a .323 batting average. He was the writers' MVP selection in spite of the fact that his Orioles finished sixth, 24 games behind the Blue Jays.

Minnesota finished first in the A.L. West, beating out second-place Chicago by eight games. The Twins had the league's winningest pitcher in righthander Scott Erickson, who finished 20-8 with a 3.18 earned run average. Kirby Puckett led the Minnesota offense, driving in 89 runs, scoring another 92, and finishing among the league leaders with a .319 batting average and 195 hits.

However, the top two MVP candidates in the division came from the runner-up White Sox and the third-place Rangers, who finished 10 games behind the Twins. Chicago's Frank Thomas and Texas' Ruben Sierra were both among the league's most productive hitters.

Let's look at their numbers, alongside those of Ripken and Fielder:

PLAYER	AB	HITS	RUNS	2B	3B	HR	RBI	AVG	OBP	SLG PCT
Ruben Sierra	661	203	110	44	5	25	116	.307	.361	.502
Frank Thomas	559	178	104	31	2	32	109	.318	**.454**	.553
Cal Ripken Jr.	650	210	99	46	5	34	114	.323	.379	.566
Cecil Fielder	624	163	102	25	0	**44**	**133**	.261	.349	.513

Ripken's overall numbers were slightly better than those of the other three players, and it could be argued that he was the league's best all-around player. However, his team finished next-to-last in the East, 24 games out of first, while the teams of each of the other leading candidates fared much better. In addition, Ripken failed to lead the league in any offensive category. Therefore, it could be said that he did not have a truly dominant season. With the Orioles finishing so far out of contention, Ripken would only have been worthy of serious consideration had he stood head and shoulders above the other leading contenders. Since that was not the case, it would be difficult to justify his selection by the writers.

The numbers of the other three players were all fairly comparable, with those of Thomas and Fielder being slightly superior to Sierra's. Fielder finished well ahead of Thomas in both home runs and runs batted in, but the latter had an edge in every other statistical category. The writers placed Fielder a close second in the balloting, with Thomas finishing a distant third. But, in the end, it was Thomas' huge advantage in both on-base and slugging percentage that earned him the nod here as my choice. His slugging percentage was 40 points higher than Fielder's, and his league-leading .454 on-base percentage was more than 100 points higher than the Tiger first baseman's. As a result, Fielder must settle for an honorable mention for the second consecutive year.

NATIONAL LEAGUE

The Pirates repeated as N.L. East champions in 1991, finishing 14 games ahead of the second-place Cardinals. Pittsburgh's top pitcher was lefthander John Smiley, who tied for the league lead with 20 victories (against only 8 losses) and compiled a 3.08 earned run average. Pittsburgh's offense was once again paced by Bobby Bonilla and Barry Bonds. Bonilla hit 18 homers, knocked in 100 runs, scored 102 others, batted .302, and led the league with 44 doubles. Bonds was the league's finest all-around player, finishing with 25 home runs, 116 runs batted in, 95 runs scored, 43 stolen bases, and a league-leading .419 on-base percentage. He was the division's leading MVP candidate.

Howard Johnson had a big year for the Mets, leading the N.L. with 38 home runs and 117 runs batted in, and finishing second with 108 runs scored. However, with New York finishing fifth, 20½ games out of first, he could not be seriously considered for league MVP honors.

The Braves edged out the Dodgers by just one game in the West, largely on the strength of their outstanding pitching. Atlanta's staff was led by Cy Young Award winning lefthander Tom Glavine, who topped N.L. pitchers with a record of 20-11 and nine complete games, while also finishing among the leaders with a 2.55 earned run average and 246 innings pitched. Glavine was joined by Steve Avery, who compiled a record of 18-8 with a 3.38 earned run average.

On offense, Atlanta was led by outfielder Ron Gant and third baseman Terry Pendleton. Although he batted only .251, Gant hit 32 homers, drove in 105 runs, scored 101 others, and stole 34 bases. Pendleton was the team's top offensive player, leading the league with a .319 batting average and 187 hits.

The runner-up Dodgers got solid seasons from Brett Butler and Darryl Strawberry. Butler batted .296 and led the N.L. with 112 runs scored and 108 walks. Strawberry hit 28 homers and drove in 99 runs. But Pendleton was unquestionably the division's top contender for league MVP honors.

Let's look at his numbers, along with those of Bonds, the other leading candidate:

PLAYER	AB	HITS	RUNS	2B	3B	HR	RBI	AVG	OBP	SLG PCT	SB
Terry Pendleton	586	**187**	94	34	8	22	86	**.319**	.367	.517	10
Barry Bonds	510	149	95	28	5	25	116	.292	**.419**	.514	43

Pendleton had a fine year, leading the league in two offensive categories and finishing with numbers that were comparable to those posted by Bonds in most areas. However, Bonds' overall numbers were better. He knocked in 30 more runs and stole 33 more bases. In addition, although Pendleton led the league in batting, Bonds walked much more frequently, thereby compiling a much higher on-base percentage.

Bonds was clearly the better player. But, was he more valuable to his team? The Pirates had little trouble disposing of the rest of the N.L. East, finishing 14 games ahead of their nearest competitor. Meanwhile, the Braves were just barely able to edge out the Dodgers by one game. Therefore, it would seem that Pendleton's contributions to the Braves were absolutely essential to their first-place finish. Furthermore, Pendleton had previously been through tight pennant races with the Cardinals in both 1985 and 1987. Atlanta was still a very young and inexperienced team in 1991, and there is little doubt that Pendleton provided a great deal of leadership to his less-experienced teammates down the stretch.

Taking that factor into consideration as well, it is clear that he was most deserving of the MVP Award that was presented to him at season's end.

1992

AMERICAN LEAGUE

Toronto repeated as A.L. East champs in 1992, finishing four games ahead of second-place Milwaukee. The Blue Jays were the most well-balanced team in the league, possessing both solid pitching and a strong offense. Their staff was led by Jack Morris, who led all A.L. hurlers with 21 victories, against only 6 losses. He was joined by Juan Guzman, who compiled a record of 16-5 and finished among the league leaders with a 2.64 earned run average. On offense, Roberto Alomar batted .310, scored 105 runs, and stole 49 bases. Designated hitter Dave Winfield hit 26 homers, drove in 108 runs, scored 92 others, and batted .290. Joe Carter hit 34 home runs, finished second in the league with 119 runs batted in, and scored 97 runs. He finished third in the league MVP balloting.

Finishing just behind Carter, in fourth place, was Mark McGwire, whose A's returned to the top of the A.L. West standings after failing to make the playoffs the previous year. Oakland finished six games ahead of second-place Minnesota, and McGwire was the team's primary offensive threat. He hit 42 home runs, knocked in 104 runs, and led the league with a .585 slugging percentage. Still, McGwire was not the division's best offensive player.

Frank Thomas had another outstanding year for the White Sox, who finished third in the division, 10 games behind the A's. Thomas hit 24 home runs, finished among the league leaders with 115 runs batted in, 108 runs scored, and a .323 batting average, and led the A.L. with 46 doubles, 122 bases on balls, and a .446 on-base percentage. Minnesota's Kirby Puckett hit 19 homers, drove in 110 runs, scored 104 others, finished second in the league with a .329 batting average, and led the A.L. with 210 hits. He placed second in the MVP voting.

The man who finished just ahead of Puckett was the league's dominant player in 1992—Dennis Eckersley. The Oakland closer compiled a brilliant 7-1 record and 1.91 earned run average, and he led the league with 51 saves. He also struck out 93 batters, while walking only 11 men and surrendering just 62 hits in 80 innings of work. Eckersley appeared in 69 games for the A's and, by winning seven games and saving 51 others, he had a hand in 58 of Oakland's 96 victories. He was clearly the league's Most Valuable Player.

NATIONAL LEAGUE

The Pirates won their third consecutive N.L. East title in 1992, finishing nine games ahead of second-place Montreal. The Expos got fine seasons from young outfielders Marquis Grissom and Larry Walker. Grissom batted .276, scored 99 runs, and led the league with 78 stolen bases. Walker hit 23 homers, knocked in 93 runs, and batted .301. But, in the end, Montreal was no match for the Pirates, who were led by the outfield duo of Andy Van Slyke and Barry Bonds, and by the pitching of Doug Drabek. Drabek won 15 games and compiled a fine 2.77 earned run average. In addition to playing a superb centerfield, Van Slyke batted .324, knocked in 89 runs, scored another 103, and led the league with 199 hits and 45 doubles. He finished fourth in the league MVP voting.

Bonds won his second MVP trophy for hitting 34 home runs, driving in 103 runs, batting .311, and leading the league with 109 runs scored, a .461 on-base percentage, and a .624 slugging percentage.

The Braves also repeated as champs in the N.L. West, beating out second-place Cincinnati by eight games. The Reds' top player was outfielder Bip Roberts, who batted .323, scored 92 runs, and stole 44 bases. However, the division's finest offensive player may well have been San Diego's Gary Sheffield, who hit 33 home runs, knocked in 100 runs, and led the league with a .330 batting average. Although the Padres finished third, 16 games back, Sheffield managed to place third in the MVP balloting.

Once again, the Braves were the division's strongest team. Their team earned run average of 3.14 was the lowest in the N.L., and they featured two of the league's top starters. Tom Glavine finished 20-8, to lead all N.L. pitchers in victories. He also compiled a 2.76 earned run average, and he led league hurlers with five shutouts. John Smoltz won 15 games, pitched to a 2.85 earned run average, and led the league with 215 strikeouts.

On offense, Ron Gant hit 17 home runs and drove in 80 runs. David Justice hit 21 homers and knocked in 72 runs. The team's best player was once again Terry Pendleton, who rivaled Barry Bonds as the league's Most Valuable Player for the second year in a row.

Let's look at the numbers of the two players:

PLAYER	AB	HITS	RUNS	2B	3B	HR	RBI	AVG	OBP	SLG PCT	SB
Terry Pendleton	640	199	98	39	1	21	105	.311	.349	.473	5
Barry Bonds	473	147	109	36	5	34	103	.311	.461	.624	39

The statistical comparison once again favors Bonds, except the discrepancy is even greater this time. In addition to hitting several more home runs, scoring more runs, and stealing many more bases than Pendleton, Bonds finished with much higher on-base and slugging percentages. Leading the league in both categories, Bonds compiled an on-base percentage that was *112* points higher and a slugging percentage that was *151* points better. He was clearly a much more effective player than Pendleton. In addition, both the Pirates and Braves won their respective divisions rather handily. Therefore, unlike the prior year, it could not legitimately be said that Pendleton's performance was more essential to Atlanta's success than Bonds' was to the fortunes of the Eastern division champions.

The writers made the proper decision by selecting Bonds over Pendleton as the league's Most Valuable Player.

1993

AMERICAN LEAGUE

The Toronto Blue Jays captured their third consecutive A.L. East title in 1993, finishing seven games in front of second-place New York. Toronto was clearly the class of the American League, combining solid pitching with the league's most potent offense. Pat Hentgen was the team's top starter, finishing 19-9 with a 3.87 earned run average. Juan Guzman compiled an outstanding 14-3 record and finished among the league leaders with 194 strikeouts. Reliever Duane Ward led the A.L. with 45 saves while pitching to a 2.13 earned run average.

On offense, the Blue Jays had the most balanced attack in the league. Devon White placed among the A.L. leaders with 116 runs scored, 42 doubles, and 34 stolen bases. Roberto Alomar hit 17 home runs, drove in 93 runs, and finished near the top of the league rankings with a .326 batting average, 109 runs scored, and 55 stolen bases. Joe Carter led the team with 33 home runs and 121 runs batted in. Toronto's top two players were John Olerud and Paul Molitor. First baseman Olerud hit 24 homers, knocked in 107 runs, scored 109 others, and led the league with a .363 batting average, a .473 on-base percentage, and 54 doubles. Serving primarily as a designated hitter, Molitor hit 22 home runs, drove in 111 runs, scored another 121, batted .332, and led the league with 211 hits. Both men were leading contenders for league MVP honors.

Cleveland also had a powerful offense, with Albert Belle, Kenny Lofton, and Carlos Baerga all having outstanding seasons. Belle hit 38 home runs, batted .290, and led the league with 129 runs batted in. Lofton finished among the leaders with a .325 batting average and 116 runs scored, and he led the A.L. with 70 stolen bases. Baerga rivaled Alomar as the league's top second baseman, finishing the year with 21 home runs, 114 runs batted in, 105 runs scored, a .321 batting average, and 200 hits. However, with the Indians finishing 19 games behind Toronto, none of the Cleveland players was worthy of MVP consideration.

Chicago finished first in the West, beating out second-place Texas by eight games. The Rangers had two of the league's most productive hitters in Juan Gonzalez and Rafael Palmeiro. Gonzalez led the A.L. with 46 home runs and a .632 slugging percentage, while driving in 118 runs, batting .310, and scoring 105 runs. Palmeiro hit 37 round-trippers, knocked in 105 runs, batted .295, and led the league with 124 runs scored.

Seattle's Ken Griffey Jr. was also among the circuit's top offensive performers. He hit 45 home runs, knocked in 109 runs, scored 113 others, and batted .309. But Griffey's MVP chances were hurt by the Mariners' fourth-place finish in the West, 12 games off the pace.

The division-winning White Sox had the league's best pitcher in Jack McDowell. The Cy Young Award winning righthander finished 22-10, to lead A.L. hurlers in victories. He also compiled a 3.37 earned run average, threw 257 innings and 10 complete games, and led league pitchers with four shutouts. Wilson Alvarez gave the team a second strong starter by compiling a record of 15-8 and finishing second in the league with a 2.95 earned run average.

On offense, centerfielder Lance Johnson batted .311, stole 35 bases, and led the A.L. with 14 triples. Third baseman Robin Ventura hit 22 home runs and drove in 94 runs. But the team's most valuable player was unquestionably first baseman Frank Thomas.

Let's look at the numbers he posted, alongside those of Olerud and Molitor, the other leading MVP candidates:

PLAYER	AB	HITS	RUNS	2B	3B	HR	RBI	AVG	OBP	SLG PCT
John Olerud	551	200	109	54	2	24	107	.363	.473	.599
Frank Thomas	549	174	106	36	0	41	128	.317	.426	.607
Paul Molitor	636	211	121	37	5	22	111	.332	.402	.509

A valid case could be made for any of the three men. Molitor scored the most runs, collected the most hits, and was easily the best baserunner in the group. Thomas put up the best power numbers, and Olerud finished with the highest batting average and on-base percentage. Molitor loses some points, though, because he rarely played the field. He played first base in only 48 games, while serving as a designated hitter in 108 contests. Therefore, he was the first to be eliminated from consideration.

The statistics of Olerud and Thomas were fairly even. The former scored a few more runs, collected more hits, and finished with the higher batting average and on-base percentage. However, Thomas hit far more home runs and was the greater run-producer of the two. In addition, he was more important to the Chicago offense than Olerud was to the Toronto attack. While the Blue Jay first baseman was his team's best player, Toronto was a veritable collection of All-Stars. From Alomar, to Molitor, Carter, and White, the Blue Jays had the most formidable lineup in baseball. Chicago's batting order was not nearly as imposing. Therefore, Thomas was more valuable to his team than Olerud was to his. That being the case, the selection of Thomas by the writers as the league's MVP was a good one.

NATIONAL LEAGUE

Philadelphia ended Pittsburgh's three-year reign as N.L. East champs in 1993, winning their first division title in a decade by finishing three games ahead of second-place Montreal. Marquis Grissom and Larry Walker once again had solid seasons for the Expos. Grissom hit 19 home runs, drove in 95 runs, scored 104 others, batted .298, and stole 53 bases. Walker hit 22 homers, knocked in 86 runs, and scored 85 others. Even better was the Cardinals' Gregg Jefferies, who finished third in the N.L. with a .342 batting average, knocked in 83 runs, scored 89 others, and stole 46 bases. However, St. Louis finished third in the division, 10 games out of first, hurting Jefferies' chances of being named league MVP.

The first-place Phillies got an outstanding effort from ace righthander Curt Schilling, who compiled a record of 16-7 and finished among the league leaders with 186 strikeouts. Catcher Darren Daulton led the team with 24 home runs and 105 runs batted in, and first baseman John Kruk batted .316 and scored 100 runs. But Philadelphia's best player was leadoff hitter and centerfielder Len Dykstra. Dykstra was the team's offensive catalyst, batting .305, compiling an excellent .420 on-base percentage, stealing 37 bases, and leading the league with 143 runs scored and 194 hits. He was clearly the Eastern Division's leading MVP candidate.

In the West, the Braves captured their third straight division title, winning a major-league best 104 games but still just barely edging out the second-place Giants by one game. Atlanta's offense was led by David Justice, who finished second in the league with 40 home runs and 120 runs batted in. He was joined by speedy centerfielder Otis Nixon, who stole 47 bases, shortstop Jeff Blauser, who batted .305 and scored 110 runs, Terry Pendleton, who drove in 84 runs and scored 81 others, and Ron Gant, who finished among the league leaders with 36 home runs, 117 runs batted in, and 113 runs scored.

But, it was Atlanta's pitching that enabled them to finish just ahead of San Francisco in the divisional race. Their staff featured four of the best starting pitchers in the league. Tom Glavine finished 22-6, to lead N.L. hurlers in victories. In his first year in Atlanta after leaving the Cubs via free agency, Greg Maddux won his second straight Cy Young Award. Maddux finished 20-10, with a league-leading 2.36 earned run average, 267 innings pitched, and eight complete games. John Smoltz won 15 games, and Steve Avery compiled a record of 18-6 and a 2.94 earned run average.

Two of the division's top performers played for non-contending teams. Dodger catcher Mike Piazza hit 35 home runs, knocked in 112 runs, and batted .318. Andres Galarraga had a big year for the expansion Colorado Rockies. Galarraga hit 22 home runs, drove in 98 runs, and led the league with a .370 batting average. However, Los Angeles and Colorado both finished so far out of contention that it would have been impossible to give either player serious consideration for MVP honors.

On the other hand, the Giants won 103 games, and they finished just one game behind the first-place Braves. San Francisco had two fine pitchers in John Burkett and Billy Swift. Burkett tied Glavine for the league lead with 22 victories, while losing only 7. Swift compiled a record of 21-8 and a 2.82 earned run average. Third baseman Matt Williams was a major contributor on offense, hitting 38 home runs, driving in 110 runs, scoring another 105, and batting .294. The team's best player was Barry Bonds, who signed with the Giants as a free agent during the off-season.

Let's look at his numbers, along with those of Len Dykstra, the other leading MVP candidate:

PLAYER	AB	HITS	RUNS	2B	3B	HR	RBI	AVG	OBP	SLG PCT	SB
Len Dykstra	637	194	143	44	6	19	66	.305	.420	.482	37
Barry Bonds	539	181	129	38	4	46	123	.336	.458	.677	29

Dykstra finished slightly ahead of Bonds in hits, runs scored, doubles, triples, and stolen bases. He also established himself as the league's best leadoff hitter, and as one of the circuit's best players. However, Bonds was the best player in the National League. He led the league in home runs, runs batted in, and slugging percentage, finishing well ahead of Dykstra in each category. In fact, his .677 slugging percentage was almost *200* points higher than Dykstra's. Of course, it should be noted that Dykstra's role as leadoff hitter for the Phillies was far different than the one Bonds had for the Giants. Still, it is difficult to ignore the overall superiority of Bonds' numbers. The San Francisco outfielder's batting average was more than 30 points higher than Dykstra's, and his on-base percentage was almost 40 points better. He was clearly the better player of the two.

In addition, San Francisco finished fifth in the division the previous season, with a record of only 72-90. Correspondingly, their 103 victories and second-place finish in 1993 represented a remarkable improvement. While other factors certainly contributed to the team's progression, Bonds' presence was unquestionably the most important one. There can be no doubt that he was the league's Most Valuable Player.

1994

AMERICAN LEAGUE

The 1994 season ended prematurely due to a players' strike that left a bitter taste in the mouths of most fans, and that perhaps did more to hurt the game than any single occurrence since the *Black Sox* scandal of 1919. It took baseball several seasons to recover, with the 1998 home run race waged between Mark McGwire and Sammy Sosa, as well as the Yankees' incredible record-setting season finally able to lure back much of the fan base. However, 1994 was a sad year for baseball, with only slightly more than two-thirds of the regular-season schedule being completed, and with no World Series being played for the first time since the turn of the last century. Yet, a Most Valuable Player was selected in each league, with several players compiling some rather impressive statistics prior to the walk-out.

In the A.L. East, the Yankees' 70-43 record placed them four games ahead of the second-place Indians prior to the player strike. Lefthander Jimmy Key was New York's best pitcher, compiling a record of 17-4, to lead all A.L. hurlers in victories. On offense, Don Mattingly batted .304, Bernie Williams hit .289 and scored 80 runs, Mike Stanley hit 17 home runs and batted .300, and Wade Boggs finished among the league leaders with a .342 batting average and a .433 on-base percentage. Outfielder Paul O'Neill was New York's best player, though. He hit 21 home runs, drove in 83 runs, led the league with a .359 batting average, and finished among the leaders with a .461 on-base percentage and a .603 slugging percentage.

Even more impressive were the numbers posted by Albert Belle for second-place Cleveland. Belle finished among the league leaders with 36 home runs, 101 runs batted in, a .357 batting average, 90 runs scored, and a .714 slugging percentage. Teammate Kenny Lofton batted .349, scored 105 runs, and led the league with 160 hits and 60 stolen bases.

In the West, Chicago's record of 67-46 left them four games ahead of runner-up Kansas City. The Royals had the league's finest pitcher in David Cone, who compiled a record of 16-5 and a 2.94 earned run average. The Twins and Mariners, who finished 14 and 17½ games behind, respectively, each featured one of the league's top players. Minnesota's Kirby Puckett hit 20 home runs, led the league with 112 runs batted in, scored 79 runs, and batted .317. Seattle's Ken Griffey Jr. led the A.L. with 40 home runs, knocked in 90 runs, scored 94 others, and batted .323.

Yet, the White Sox were the division's strongest team. Robin Ventura hit 18 home runs, drove in 78 runs, and batted .282. Lance Johnson batted .277 and led the league with 14 triples. Designated hitter Julio Franco hit 20 home runs, drove in 98 runs, and batted .319. But, for the second year in a row, the league's dominant hitter was Frank Thomas. The big first baseman finished among the A.L. leaders with 38 home runs, 101 runs batted in, and a .353 batting average, and he led the circuit with 106 runs scored, a .487 on-base percentage, and a .729 slugging percentage. With the White Sox leading their division at the time of the strike, there is little doubt that Thomas was the league's Most Valuable Player.

NATIONAL LEAGUE

In the N.L. East, the Montreal Expos sported baseball's best record prior to the start of the player strike. Their 74-40 record left them six games ahead of the second-place Braves, who were shifted to the National League's Eastern Division prior to the start of the season. The Expos had the best young outfield in baseball in Moises Alou, Marquis Grissom, and Larry Walker. Alou hit 22 home runs, drove in 78 runs, scored 81 others, and batted .339. Grissom batted .288 and finished among the league leaders with 96 runs scored and 36 stolen bases. Walker hit 19 home runs, knocked in 86 runs, and batted .322. Reliever John Wetteland finished among the league leaders with

25 saves. In compiling a record of 16-5, Ken Hill finished tied for the league lead in victories. He was joined by Pedro Martinez, who compiled a record of 11-5 and finished among the league leaders with 142 strikeouts.

The National League's best pitcher, though, was Atlanta's Greg Maddux, who won his third straight Cy Young Award. Maddux finished 16-6, to tie for the league lead in wins, and he led the N.L. with a 1.56 earned run average, 202 innings pitched, 10 complete games, and three shutouts. On offense, the runner-up Braves were led by Fred McGriff, who finished among the league leaders with 34 home runs and 94 runs batted in, batted .318, and scored 81 runs.

In the West, Cincinnati's 68-46 record left them just one-half game ahead of the second-place Astros. The Reds' most dominant player was Kevin Mitchell, who hit 30 home runs, drove in 77 runs, and batted .326. He was joined by first baseman Hal Morris, who knocked in 78 runs and finished among the league leaders with a .325 batting average. Cincinnati's best pitcher was Jose Rijo, who won nine games, compiled a 3.08 earned run average, and struck out 171 batters in 172 innings of work.

One of the division's top offensive players was San Diego's Tony Gwynn, who led the league with a .394 batting average. However, the Padres were 18½ games behind the Reds in the standings. Both Barry Bonds and Matt Williams had big years for the Giants, who were 11½ games behind first-place Cincinnati. Bonds batted .312 and was among the league leaders with 37 home runs, 81 runs batted in, and 89 runs scored. Williams led the N.L. with 43 home runs and finished second with 96 runs batted in.

The second-place Astros, though, had the league's best player in Jeff Bagwell. The first baseman finished right behind Williams with 39 home runs, he placed second to Gwynn with a .368 batting average, and he led the N.L. with 116 runs batted in, 104 runs scored, 300 total bases, and a .750 slugging percentage.

With Houston only a half-game behind Cincinnati in the standings, Bagwell was clearly the league's Most Valuable Player.

POST-REALIGNMENT WINNERS AND THE IMPACT OF STEROIDS ON THE ELECTIONS

22

Baseball underwent its first major realignment in more than a quarter of a century in 1995 when each league was split into three divisions for the first time. Under the new setup, the three division winners in each league would automatically advance to the playoffs, and they would be joined by the second-place team with the best regular-season record.

With four teams in each league now making it into the postseason, an additional round of playoffs was added. The team with the best record in each league would square off against that circuit's wild-card entry in the first round, while the other two division winners would face each other in the opening series. The only exception would be if the wild-card team came from the same division as the division champion with the best record. It would not be possible for those two teams to meet until the final round of the playoffs. Following are the initial division setups in both leagues:

A.L. EAST	A.L. CENTRAL	A.L. WEST
Baltimore	Minnesota	Oakland
Detroit	Chicago	California
Boston	Kansas City	Seattle
New York	Cleveland	Texas
Toronto	Milwaukee	

N.L. EAST	N.L. CENTRAL	N.L. WEST
Philadelphia	Chicago	San Diego
New York	St. Louis	San Francisco
Montreal	Houston	Los Angeles
Atlanta	Cincinnati	Colorado
Florida	Pittsburgh	

Prior to the start of the 1997 campaign, the California Angels renamed themselves the *Anaheim Angels*. Just one year later, two additional franchises were awarded, with the Tampa Bay Devil Rays joining the A.L. East, and the Arizona Diamondbacks taking up residence in the N.L. West. To make things more equitable, Detroit moved from the A.L. East to the A.L. Central, and Milwaukee moved out of the A.L. Central into the N.L. Central.

More divisions meant more pennant races and an increased level of competition. The addition of a wild-card entry in each league enabled more teams to remain in contention until late in the season. The result was not only an increase in fan interest but, also, an increase in the number of viable MVP candidates in each league.

Another interesting development during this period was the growing use of performance-enhancing drugs in baseball. In an effort to increase the popularity of the sport following the player strike that drove away much of the fan base at the end of the aborted 1994 campaign, those entrusted with running the game chose to ignore this growing epidemic that severely threatened the sanctity of the national pastime. The lords of baseball saw fans heading out to the ballparks in droves to watch the home-run hitting exploits of sluggers such as Mark McGwire and Sammy Sosa, and they turned a blind man's eye to the problem. To make matters worse, casual fans of the game either feigned ignorance, or didn't seem to care that long-standing records were being shattered. But, baseball purists greatly resented the lack of integrity demonstrated by some of the sport's greatest stars, and the devious methods they used to greatly alter the record books.

The use of performance-enhancing drugs also had a profound impact on the outcomes of several MVP elections held during this period. Indeed, roughly 50 percent of the players named MVP between 1996 and 2004 were either known or suspected steroid-users. Ken Caminiti, the 1996 National League winner, Jason Giambi, the

A.L. Winner in 2000, and Alex Rodriguez, the junior circuit's winner in 2003, all later admitted to using performance-enhancing drugs. And others, such as Juan Rodriguez, the A.L. winner in both 1996 and 1998, Miguel Tejada, that league's winner in 2002, Sammy Sosa, the N.L. winner in 1998, and Barry Bonds, who took home the award from 2001 to 2004, are widely believed to be steroid-users as well. As a result, several of the Most Valuable Player Awards presented during this period do not carry with them the same historical significance typically associated with the honor.

Still, in reviewing each of these elections, the assumption here will be that the playing field was even for everyone involved, since that was the assumption made by the various members of the BBWAA when they cast their ballots.

	ACTUAL MVP WINNERS		SUGGESTED WINNERS	
	A.L.	**N.L.**	**A.L.**	**N.L.**
1995	Mo Vaughn	Barry Larkin	Mo Vaughn	Greg Maddux
1996	Juan Gonzalez	Ken Caminiti	Alex Rodriguez	Ken Caminiti
1997	Ken Griffey Jr.	Larry Walker	Ken Griffey Jr.	Mike Piazza
1998	Juan Gonzalez	Sammy Sosa	Juan Gonzalez	Sammy Sosa
1999	Ivan Rodriguez	Chipper Jones	Pedro Martinez	Chipper Jones
2000	Jason Giambi	Jeff Kent	Jason Giambi	Jeff Kent
2001	Ichiro Suzuki	Barry Bonds	Bret Boone	Barry Bonds
2002	Miguel Tejada	Barry Bonds	Miguel Tejada	Barry Bonds
2003	Alex Rodriguez	Barry Bonds	Carlos Delgado	Barry Bonds
2004	Vladimir Guerrero	Barry Bonds	Vladimir Guerrero	Barry Bonds
2005	Alex Rodriguez	Albert Pujols	Alex Rodriguez	Albert Pujols
2006	Justin Morneau	Ryan Howard	Justin Morneau	Ryan Howard
2007	Alex Rodriguez	Jimmy Rollins	Alex Rodriguez	Jimmy Rollins
2008	Dustin Pedroia	Albert Pujols	Dustin Pedroia	Albert Pujols
2009	Joe Mauer	Albert Pujols	Joe Mauer	Albert Pujols

1995

AMERICAN LEAGUE

The 1995 season began in ominous fashion, with the players still on strike and with the owners refusing to budge an inch in their negotiations with the players' union. Fortunately, though, about three weeks into the scheduled start of the regular season, both sides came to their senses and reached a compromise that allowed the games to get under way. However, the schedule was to be an abbreviated one, with the number of regular-season contests reduced from the normal total of 162 to just 144.

Once the season began, the Seattle Mariners and California Angels waged a thrilling divisional race in the A.L. West that ended with the two teams tied for first place at the end of play on the season's final day. A one-game playoff was needed to decide the division champion, and it was truly an all-or-nothing proposition for both teams since the Yankees already clinched a playoff spot as the league's initial wild-card entry. The Mariners prevailed in the decisive game to claim their first A.L. West title. The winning pitcher was Randy Johnson, who was the American League's dominant hurler all year. *The Big Unit* finished the season with a superb 18-2 record, and he led the league with a 2.48 earned run average and 294 strikeouts.

Seattle also received strong performances from first baseman Tino Martinez, third baseman Mike Blowers, and rightfielder Jay Buhner. Martinez hit 31 home runs, drove in 111 runs, scored 92 others, and batted .293. Blowers hit 23 homers and knocked in 96 runs. Buhner finished among the league leaders with 40 home runs and 121 runs batted in. Seattle's top player was Edgar Martinez, who hit 29 home runs, drove in 113 runs, and led the A.L. with 121 runs scored, 52 doubles, a .356 batting average, and a .479 on-base percentage.

The runner-up Angels got excellent years from outfielders Jim Edmonds and Tim Salmon. Edmonds hit 33 home runs, drove in 107 runs, finished third in the league with 120 runs scored, and batted .290. Salmon hit 34 homers, knocked in 105 runs, scored 111 others, and finished among the league leaders with a .330 batting average.

The Cleveland Indians dominated the newly-formed A.L. Central, compiling baseball's best record (100-44) and finishing 30 games in front of the second-place Royals. Cleveland's best pitcher was Dennis Martinez, who finished with a record of 12-5 and a 3.08 earned run average. Reliever Jose Mesa led the league with 46 saves.

But it was the Indians' potent offense that enabled them to distance themselves from the rest of the division. Leadoff hitter Kenny Lofton batted .310, scored 93 runs, and led the league with 54 stolen bases. Carlos Baerga drove in 90 runs, scored 87 others, and batted .314. Newly-acquired Eddie Murray hit 21 home runs, drove in 82 runs, batted .323, and provided his teammates with veteran leadership. The team's most dominant performer was Albert Belle, who posted the most impressive offensive numbers of any player in the league. The powerful leftfielder batted .317 and led the circuit with 50 home runs and a .690 slugging percentage. He also tied for the league lead with 126 runs batted in, 121 runs scored, and 52 doubles. He was clearly the division's leading MVP candidate.

Boston claimed the Eastern Division title, finishing seven games ahead of second-place New York. However, the Yankees finished with the best regular-season record among the second-place teams, thereby advancing to the playoffs as a wild-card. New York's best pitcher was David Cone, who joined the team during the season after spending the first part of the year with the Blue Jays. Cone went 9-2 for New York, and he finished the season with an overall record of 18-8 and an earned run average of 3.57. On offense, the Yankees were led by Paul O'Neill, Wade Boggs, and Bernie Williams. O'Neill hit 22 home runs, drove in 96 runs, and batted .300. Boggs finished among the league leaders with a .324 batting average. Williams hit 18 homers, knocked in 82 runs, scored 93 others, and batted .307.

Boston was the division's strongest team. Their top pitcher was Tim Wakefield, who finished 16-8 with a 2.95 earned run average. On offense, Jose Canseco hit 24 home runs, drove in 81 runs, and batted .306. Mike Greenwell knocked in 76 runs and batted .297. John Valentin hit 27 home runs, drove in 102 runs, scored another 108, and batted .298. Still, there is little doubt that first baseman Mo Vaughn was Boston's most valuable player.

Let's look at his statistics, alongside those of Edgar Martinez and Albert Belle, the other leading candidates for league MVP:

PLAYER	AB	HITS	RUNS	2B	3B	HR	RBI	AVG	OBP	SLG PCT
Mo Vaughn	550	165	98	28	3	39	**126**	.300	.388	.575
Albert Belle	546	173	**121**	**52**	1	**50**	**126**	.317	.401	**.690**
Edgar Martinez	511	182	**121**	**52**	0	29	113	**.356**	**.479**	.628

Based strictly on statistics, it is difficult to defend the writers' selection of Vaughn as the league's Most Valuable Player. He finished well behind the other two players in most offensive categories. Vaughn was a league-leader in only one category, while Martinez led the league in four, and Belle topped the circuit in five. On the surface, it would seem that either Belle or Martinez would have been a better choice, with each man holding certain statistical advantages over the other. However, other factors must be considered as well.

With Ken Griffey Jr. missing much of the season due to injury, Martinez helped to pick up much of the slack in the Mariners offense. In fact, he was probably the finest all-around hitter in baseball. But that is all Martinez was—a superb hitter. He was totally one-dimensional, since he was a full-time DH who never played the field. While Vaughn was far from an outstanding defensive first baseman, he at least gave his team a full nine innings every game. This clearly influenced the thinking of the writers, who placed Martinez third in the voting.

Albert Belle was a far more dominant hitter than Vaughn. While the two players tied for the league lead in runs batted in, Belle finished well ahead of Vaughn in most other offensive categories. However, Belle's positive influence on his team ended once he left the batter's box. He was a brooding man who had little or nothing to do with most of his teammates. In fact, he had a confrontation with teammate Eddie Murray at one point during the season after the first baseman grew increasingly weary of Belle's surliness and self-absorption as the year progressed.

Meanwhile, Vaughn was Boston's team leader. He had a positive effect on his teammates, and he used his competitive spirit and fiery temperament to bring out the best in them. The Boston lineup was not nearly as talented as that of either the Indians or the Mariners. Yet, under Vaughn's leadership, it managed to score 791 runs, only five fewer than Seattle, and 50 less than league-leading Cleveland.

All things considered, it is not too difficult to understand why the writers selected Vaughn as the American League's Most Valuable Player.

NATIONAL LEAGUE

The Atlanta Braves ran away with the N.L. East in 1995, finishing the regular season with a record of 90-54. Atlanta was clearly the class of the division, essentially using the regular season as a tune-up for the playoffs. On offense, the Braves were led by the duo of Fred McGriff and David Justice. McGriff hit 27 home runs, knocked in 93 runs, scored 85 others, and batted .280. Justice hit 24 homers and drove in 78 runs.

It was the Braves' pitching, though, that established them as the division's dominant team. Tom Glavine finished 16-7 with a 3.08 earned run average. John Smoltz was 12-7, with a 3.18 earned run average and 193 strikeouts. Greg Maddux was the staff ace, compiling a brilliant 19-2 record, to lead N.L. pitchers in victories. He also led the league with a 1.63 earned run average and 10 complete games in capturing his fourth consecutive Cy Young Award.

Los Angeles had a far more difficult time capturing the N.L. West title, edging out second-place Colorado by just one game. The Rockies were the league's wild-card representative. They had the league's most potent offense, with sluggers Andres Galarraga, Larry Walker, and Dante Bichette comprising the middle of their batting order. Galarraga hit 31 home runs, drove in 106 runs, and batted .280. Walker hit 36 homers, knocked in 101 runs, scored another 96, and batted .306. Bichette posted the most impressive offensive numbers in the league, leading the N.L. with 40 home runs, 128 runs batted in, 197 hits, and a .620 slugging percentage, and finishing among the leaders with a .340 batting average and 102 runs scored. The writers placed him second in the MVP voting.

The first-place Dodgers did not have nearly as potent an offense as their division rivals, but their pitching was among the best in the league. Ramon Martinez finished 17-7, and Hideo Nomo compiled a record of 13-6, placed second in the league with a 2.54 earned run average, and led the N.L. with 236 strikeouts. On offense, first baseman Eric Karros hit 32 home runs, drove in 105 runs, and batted .298. Rightfielder Raul Mondesi hit 26 homers, knocked in 88 runs, scored 91 others, stole 27 bases, and batted .285. Second baseman Delino DeShields finished among the league leaders with 39 stolen bases. The Dodgers' best player was catcher Mike Piazza, who hit 32 home runs, drove in 93 runs, and finished second in the league with a .346 batting average. Piazza finished fourth in the league MVP voting.

The Cincinnati Reds finished nine games ahead of Houston in the N.L. Central, to capture their first division title since their world championship year of 1990. Craig Biggio was Houston's top player, hitting 22 home runs, batting .302, stealing 33 bases, and leading the league with 123 runs scored. But, with Jeff Bagwell missing a month of the year with an injury, the Reds were able to take advantage of the slugger's absence and distance themselves from the second-place Astros. Cincinnati's best pitcher was Pete Schourek, who finished 18-7 with a 3.22 earned run average. Ron Gant led the team with 29 home runs, and he also drove in 88 runs and batted .276. Reggie Sanders hit 28 homers, knocked in 99 runs, scored another 91, and batted .306. Cincinnati's best all-around player was shortstop Barry Larkin, who was the writers' choice for league MVP.

Let's look at his numbers, alongside those of runner-up Dante Bichette:

PLAYER	AB	HITS	RUNS	2B	3B	HR	RBI	AVG	OBP	SLG PCT
Barry Larkin	496	158	98	29	6	15	66	.319	.394	.492
Dante Bichette	579	197	102	38	2	40	128	.340	.364	.620

The writers certainly showed a great deal of restraint by not being overwhelmed by Bichette's gaudy offensive numbers. They knew he compiled them playing in Colorado's Coors Field—a noted bandbox. Looking strictly at the numbers, there really was no comparison. Bichette hit almost three times as many home runs as Larkin, drove in almost twice as many runs, and compiled a slugging percentage that was almost 130 points higher. He led the league in four different offensive categories, while Larkin didn't come close to leading the circuit in any. However, Bichette's statistics were greatly inflated by his home ballpark, and the writers knew that.

Therefore, they opted instead for Larkin, whose offensive numbers were far more modest. They were aware that the Cincinnati shortstop was his team's best player, and that he played a major role in leading them to the Central Division title. But, was Larkin truly worthy of being named league MVP?

The feeling here is that the answer to that question is *no*, since, even though Larkin was a fine all-around player, there was someone else who was far more deserving. Atlanta's Greg Maddux was clearly the league's dominant player. His 19-2 record was easily the best in the National League, and his 1.63 earned run average was almost one run per-game less than the next lowest in the league. Although his Braves hardly had to struggle to win their division, they advanced into the postseason and Maddux was more responsible for their first-place finish than anyone else. He was the best player in the league, and he should have been named its Most Valuable Player, instead of finishing third in the voting.

1996

AMERICAN LEAGUE

The Yankees captured their first A.L. East title in 15 years in 1996, finishing four games ahead of the second-place Orioles, who were the league's wild-card entry. Baltimore's offense, which was aided immeasurably by playing in tiny Camden Yards, was among the best in the league. Roberto Alomar hit 22 home runs, drove in 94 runs, scored 132 others, and batted .328. Bobby Bonilla hit 28 homers, knocked in 116 runs, scored another 107, and batted .287. Rafael Palmeiro finished among the league leaders with 39 home runs, 142 runs batted in, and 110 runs scored. Centerfielder Brady Anderson had a career year, hitting 50 home runs, driving in 110 runs, scoring 117 others, and batting .297.

However, the impact that playing in Camden Yards had on the Oriole hitters can be evidenced by the inordinately high earned run averages posted by the team's pitchers. In fact, their best hurler, Mike Mussina, finished the year with an unseemly 4.81 earned run average despite compiling a fine 19-11 record during the regular season.

New York's offense was not as potent as Baltimore's, but it nevertheless featured several solid performers. In his first year in pinstripes, first baseman Tino Martinez hit 25 home runs, drove in 117 runs, and batted .292. A.L. Rookie of the Year Derek Jeter batted .314 and scored 104 runs. Paul O'Neill hit 19 homers, drove in 91 runs, and batted .302. Bernie Williams batted .305, knocked in 102 runs, and led the team with 29 home runs and 108 runs scored.

New York's pitching staff was led by Andy Pettitte, who was among the league's finest hurlers. Pettitte compiled a record of 21-8 and an earned run average of 3.87. His 21 victories were the most in the American League. Yet, the key to the Yankees' success lay in the strength of their bullpen, which enabled them to essentially turn their games into six-inning contests. With Mariano Rivera serving as setup man for closer John Wetteland, the team was practically guaranteed a victory if it had a lead after six innings. Rivera finished 8-3 with a 2.09

earned run average. In 108 innings of work, he struck out 130 batters, while walking only 34 and allowing just 73 base hits. Wetteland led the league with 43 saves.

The division's best player, though, was Boston's Mo Vaughn, who followed up his 1995 MVP season with an even better year in 1996. Vaughn finished among the league leaders with 44 home runs, 143 runs batted in, 118 runs scored, and a .326 batting average. With the Red Sox finishing third in the division, only seven games behind the Yankees, Vaughn deserved consideration for league MVP honors once more.

Cleveland dominated the A.L. Central for the second straight season, finishing 14½ games ahead of second-place Chicago. Charles Nagy was the Indians' best pitcher, compiling a record of 17-5 and an earned run average of 3.41. Jose Mesa finished second to Wetteland in the A.L. with 39 saves. On offense, Kenny Lofton had an outstanding year, finishing among the league leaders with 132 runs scored, 210 hits, and a .317 batting average, and leading the A.L. with 75 stolen bases. Third baseman Jim Thome had a breakout season, hitting 38 home runs, driving in 116 runs, scoring 122 others, and batting .311. But Albert Belle was once again the team's dominant player, leading the league with 148 runs batted in, batting .311, and finishing among the leaders with 48 home runs and 124 runs scored.

Still, Belle was rivaled by Chicago's Frank Thomas as the division's top player. The White Sox first baseman hit 40 home runs, knocked in 134 runs, scored another 110, and finished second in the league with a .349 batting average. However, with Chicago finishing 14½ games behind the Indians, it would be difficult to make a valid case for selecting Thomas over the Cleveland slugger.

It would also be hard to make a strong argument on behalf of Mark McGwire, who had a big year for Oakland in the A.L. West. McGwire led the league with 52 home runs, drove in 113 runs, scored 104 others, and batted a career-high .312. But the A's finished 12 games behind the division-winning Rangers, hurting his chances of being named league MVP.

First-place Texas had one of the league's top offenses. Their exceptional lineup included catcher Ivan Rodriguez, who had his first big offensive season. Rodriguez hit 19 homers, drove in 86 runs, scored another 116, and batted .300. Third baseman Dean Palmer hit 38 home runs, drove in 107 runs, and scored 98 others. Leftfielder Rusty Greer batted .332, drove in 100 runs, and scored another 96. The Rangers' top player was Juan Gonzalez, who finished among the league leaders with 47 home runs and 144 runs batted in, while batting .314. He was the writers' choice for league MVP.

However, the second-place Mariners, who finished only 4½ games behind Texas, had several legitimate candidates of their own. Edgar Martinez had another outstanding season, batting .327, hitting 26 home runs, driving in 103 runs, and scoring 121 others. Even better were shortstop Alex Rodriguez and centerfielder Ken Griffey Jr., both of whom posted numbers that compared quite favorably to the figures compiled by Gonzalez and Albert Belle, the two other leading candidates:

PLAYER	AB	HITS	RUNS	2B	3B	HR	RBI	AVG	OBP	SLG PCT
Alex Rodriguez	601	215	141	54	1	36	123	.358	.414	.631
Albert Belle	602	187	124	38	3	48	148	.311	.410	.623
Juan Gonzalez	541	170	89	33	2	47	144	.314	.368	.643
Ken Griffey Jr.	545	165	125	26	2	49	140	.303	.392	.628

Although the numbers compiled by Gonzalez were quite good, they were actually the least impressive in the group. Gonzalez finished with the highest slugging percentage, and he fared well in most other offensive categories. However, his on-base percentage was much lower than that of the other three players since he rarely walked. He also scored far fewer runs. Therefore, it would seem that either Belle, Rodriguez, or Griffey might have been a better choice. Belle finished third in the balloting, behind both Gonzalez and Rodriguez, but his lack of popularity with the sportswriters, to whom he refused to speak, may have prevented many of them from voting for him. Gonzalez and Belle had an edge over the two Seattle stars in that their teams won their respective divisions. But the Mariners finished a close second to Texas, and Rodriguez and Griffey were the most complete players in the group since they were better fielders and baserunners than Belle and Gonzalez.

Griffey's and A-Rod's stats were quite comparable, but the latter's overall numbers were slightly better. He led the league in three different offensive categories, and he played the more demanding defensive position of the two. It's a close call, but Alex Rodriguez is the choice here for league MVP.

NATIONAL LEAGUE

The Braves finished atop the N.L. East standings for the second consecutive season in 1996, beating out the second-place Expos by eight games. On offense, Atlanta was led by the trio of Fred McGriff, Marquis Grissom, and Chipper Jones. McGriff hit 28 home runs, drove in 107 runs, and batted .295. Grissom hit 23 homers, scored 106 runs, batted .308, collected 207 hits, and stole 28 bases. Jones led the team with 30 home runs, 110 runs batted in, 114 runs scored, and a .309 batting average. Nevertheless, it was once again the Braves' pitching that carried them to the division title. John Smoltz was named the league's Cy Young Award winner for leading N.L. hurlers with a 24-8 record, 276 strikeouts, and 254 innings pitched, while finishing among the leaders with a 2.94 earned run average. Smoltz was joined by Greg Maddux and Tom Glavine, both of whom won 15 games and finished in the top five in the league in earned run average. Maddux's mark of 2.72 was the second lowest in the N.L., and Glavine's 2.98 figure placed him fifth.

St. Louis was the N.L. Central champ, finishing six games ahead of the runner-up Astros, and seven games in front of third-place Cincinnati. The Reds' Barry Larkin actually had a better year than he did one year earlier when he was named league MVP. Larkin established career highs with 33 home runs, 89 runs batted in, and 117 runs scored, while batting .298 and stealing 36 bases. Houston's Jeff Bagwell was the division's top player. The Astros first baseman hit 31 home runs, knocked in 120 runs, scored 111 others, batted .315, and led the N.L. with 48 doubles.

In spite of the efforts of Larkin and Bagwell, it was the Cardinals who claimed the division title. Their best pitcher was Andy Benes, who finished 18-10 with a 3.83 earned run average. On offense, their top player was Brian Jordan, who drove in 104 runs and batted .310.

All of the league's leading MVP candidates came from the Western Division, where the Padres edged out the Dodgers by just one game to capture their first division crown in a dozen years. Los Angeles was the league's wild-card entry. The Dodgers again had one of the league's best pitching staffs. Hideo Nomo won 16 games, compiled a 3.19 earned run average, and finished second in the league with 234 strikeouts. Ramon Martinez went 15-6 with a 3.42 earned run average, and Todd Worrell led the league with 44 saves. On offense, the Dodgers were led by the same foursome that carried them to the division title one year earlier. Eric Karros hit 34 home runs and drove in 111 runs. Raul Mondesi hit 24 homers, knocked in 88 runs, scored 98 others, and batted .297. Although he hit only .224, Delino DeShields finished among the league leaders with 48 stolen bases. Mike Piazza hit 36 home runs, drove in 105 runs, and batted .336. He finished second in the MVP voting.

The first-place Padres got fine seasons from Steve Finley, Tony Gwynn, and Trevor Hoffman. The latter finished among the league leaders with 42 saves. Finley hit 30 homers, drove in 95 runs, batted .298, and finished second in the league with 126 runs scored. Gwynn appeared in only 116 games, accumulating just 451 official at-bats, but he batted .353.

The player who had more of an impact than anyone else on the team's fortunes, though, was third baseman Ken Caminiti, who finished among the league leaders with 40 home runs, 130 runs batted in, and a .326 batting average. Let's look at his numbers, alongside those of Piazza and Ellis Burks, who had a big year for the Rockies, who finished eight games behind San Diego in the West:

PLAYER	AB	HITS	RUNS	2B	3B	HR	RBI	AVG	OBP	SLG PCT
Ellis Burks	613	211	**142**	45	8	40	128	**.344**	.408	**.639**
Ken Caminiti	546	178	109	37	2	40	130	.326	.408	.621
Mike Piazza	547	184	87	16	0	36	105	.336	.422	.563

Statistically, Burks would have to be ranked number one. Although his numbers in most categories were extremely comparable to Caminiti's, the Colorado outfielder scored many more runs. However, as was the case one year earlier with Dante Bichette, Burks' statistics were inflated by playing his home games at Coors Field. In fact, two of Burks' own teammates compiled statistics that were almost as impressive as his own. Andres Galarraga led the league with 47 home runs and 150 runs batted in, he scored 119 runs, and he batted .304. Dante Bichette hit 31 homers, drove in 141 runs, scored 114 others, and batted .313. Thus, in spite of his impressive stat-line, Burks' third-place finish in the MVP balloting was quite appropriate.

As for Caminiti and Piazza, the two men compiled fairly similar numbers in most offensive categories, but the Padre third baseman was the greater run-producer by far, knocking in 25 more runs than Piazza, and surpassing the Dodger catcher by 22 runs scored. Since his team also edged out Piazza's for the division title, Caminiti was clearly deserving of MVP honors.

1997

AMERICAN LEAGUE

Baltimore turned the tables on New York in 1997, finishing two games ahead of the Yankees in the race for the A.L. East title. The Yankees entered the postseason as the league's wild-card entry. New York had one of the league's deepest pitching staffs. Andy Pettitte compiled a record of 18-7, and he finished among the league leaders with a 2.88 earned run average. David Cone was 12-6, and his 2.82 earned run average and 222 strikeouts both placed him among the league leaders. David Wells won 16 games and, after replacing John Wetteland as the team's closer, Mariano Rivera won six games, compiled a 1.88 earned run average, and finished second in the league with 43 saves. On offense, Derek Jeter batted .291 and finished near the top of the league rankings with 116 runs scored and 190 hits. Paul O'Neill batted .324 and drove in 117 runs. Bernie Williams knocked in 100 runs, scored 107 others, and batted .328.

Tino Martinez was New York's primary power threat. He finished second in the league with 44 home runs and 141 runs batted in, scored 96 runs, and batted .296. Martinez ended up finishing second in the league MVP voting.

The first-place Orioles also had an extremely well-balanced attack. Rafael Palmeiro hit 38 home runs and drove in 110 runs. Although he appeared in only 112 games, Roberto Alomar batted .333. In his first year at third base, Cal Ripken Jr. hit 17 home runs and drove in 84 runs. B.J. Surhoff knocked in 88 runs and batted .284. Brady Anderson scored 97 runs and batted .288. Mike Mussina was once again Baltimore's top starter, finishing the season with a 15-8 record, a 3.20 earned run average, and 218 strikeouts. Reliever Randy Myers led the A.L. with 45 saves.

The league's best pitcher was Toronto's Roger Clemens, who led A.L. hurlers with a 21-7 record, a 2.05 earned run average, and 292 strikeouts. Unfortunately for Clemens, the Blue Jays finished 22 games behind Baltimore in the East.

The Indians won their third straight Central Division title, but they received competition this time from the second-place White Sox, who finished only six games back. Chicago featured two of the league's top sluggers in Frank Thomas and Albert Belle, who left Cleveland via free agency during the off-season. Belle hit 30 homers and knocked in 116 runs. Thomas hit 35 home runs, drove in 125 runs, scored 110 others, and led the A.L. with a .347 batting average. He finished third in the league MVP voting.

The first-place Indians had several offensive weapons. David Justice hit 33 home runs, knocked in 101 runs, and finished third in the league with a .329 batting average. Moving over from third base to replace Eddie Murray as the team's regular first baseman, Jim Thome hit 40 homers, knocked in 102 runs, and scored 104 others. Manny Ramirez hit 26 long balls, scored 99 runs, and finished fourth in the batting race, with a mark of .328. Omar Vizquel batted .280, scored 89 runs, stole 43 bases, and won his fifth consecutive Gold Glove for his brilliant work at shortstop. Catcher Sandy Alomar Jr. had the finest season of his career, hitting 21 home runs, driving in 83 runs, and batting .324.

The only team in the league with a lineup capable of rivaling that of the Indians was the Mariners, who won their second Western Division title in three years. Seattle finished six games ahead of the runner-up Angels. Anaheim got a big year from Tim Salmon, who hit 33 homers, batted .296, and finished among the league leaders with 129 runs batted in. But the Mariners had a more balaced attack, featuring one of the most potent offenses in baseball. Jay Buhner hit 40 home runs, drove in 109 runs, and scored another 104. Edgar Martinez hit 28 round-trippers, drove in 108 runs, scored 104 others, and finished second in the league with a .330 batting average. Alex Rodriguez hit 23 homers, scored 100 runs, and batted .300.

Seattle's top player was Ken Griffey Jr., who was also the best player in the American League. Junior led the circuit with 56 home runs, 147 runs batted in, 125 runs scored, 393 total bases, and a .646

slugging percentage, while batting .304 and winning a Gold Glove for his outstanding centerfield play. Seattle also had pretty good pitching, with Randy Johnson having another outstanding season. *The Big Unit* finished second to Roger Clemens, with a record of 20-4, a 2.28 earned run average, and 291 strikeouts. He was joined by Jamie Moyer, who won 17 games.

But it was Seattle's offense that carried them to the division title, and Ken Griffey Jr. was the team's best player. He clearly deserved to be named league MVP.

NATIONAL LEAGUE

The Braves continued their dominance of the N.L. East in 1997, finishing nine games ahead of the second-place Marlins, who made it into the postseason as a wild card in only their fifth year in the league. Florida received fine seasons from pitcher Kevin Brown and outfielder Moises Alou. Brown compiled a record of 16-8, and he finished near the top of the league rankings with a 2.69 earned run average and 205 strikeouts. Alou led the Marlin offense with 23 home runs, 115 runs batted in, and a .292 batting average.

Atlanta's offense was led by the quartet of Kenny Lofton, Fred McGriff, Javy Lopez, and Chipper Jones. Lofton batted .333 and scored 90 runs. McGriff hit 22 homers and drove in 97 runs. Lopez hit 23 homers and batted .295. Jones was the team's top offensive threat, hitting 21 homers, driving in 111 runs, scoring 100 others, and batting .295.

But it was the Braves' fine quartet of starters that enabled them to capture their third straight division title. Lefthander Denny Neagle finished 20-5, to lead the league in victories. He also compiled a fine 2.97 earned run average. Tom Glavine finished 14-7, while pitching to a 2.96 earned run average. John Smoltz won 15 games and finished among the league leaders with 241 strikeouts and 256 innings pitched.. Greg Maddux was the team's best pitcher, compiling a record of 19-4 and an earned run average of 2.20.

Maddux was not the league's top pitcher, though. Montreal's Pedro Martinez finished 17-8, with a league-leading 1.90 earned run average and 13 complete games. He also finished second among N.L. starters with 305 strikeouts and four shutouts. However, the Expos finished 23 games behind Atlanta in the standings.

The Astros claimed their first Central Division title, beating out the runner-up Reds by eight games. Houston featured two of the league's best pitchers in Darryl Kile and Mike Hampton. Kile finished 19-7, with a 2.57 earned run average, 205 strikeouts, and four shutouts. Hampton finished 15-10 with a 3.83 earned run average. On offense, the Astros were led by the duo of Craig Biggio and Jeff Bagwell. Biggio hit 22 home runs, drove in 81 runs, batted .309, led the league with 146 runs scored, and finished among the leaders with 47 stolen bases. Bagwell scored 109 runs, stole 31 bases, and placed second in the league with 43 home runs and 135 runs batted in. By surpassing 30 homers and 30 stolen bases, he became the first full-time first baseman in major league history to top both marks in the same season. He placed third in the league MVP voting.

The Western Division was the most competitive in the league, with San Francisco edging out Los Angeles by just two games. The Giants had one of the league's top pitchers in Shawn Estes, who finished 19-5 with a 3.18 earned run average. Rod Beck finished second in the N.L. with 37 saves. On offense, J.T. Snow hit 28 homers and drove in 104 runs. Jeff Kent went deep 29 times and knocked in 121 runs. But the team's most valuable player was Barry Bonds, who hit 40 homers, drove in 101 runs, scored 123 others, and led the league with 145 walks. He deserved serious consideration for league MVP honors.

Another player who had to be considered a leading candidate for the award was the Dodgers' Mike Piazza. The Los Angeles catcher hit 40 homers, knocked in 124 runs, scored another 104, and finished third in the league with a .362 batting average. Piazza finished runner-up in the balloting.

In spite of Piazza's great season, San Diego had the division's top hitter. Having perhaps the finest season of his career, Tony Gwynn hit 17 home runs, drove in 119 runs, and led the league with a .372 batting average and 220 hits. The Padres, though, finished fourth in the West, 14 games off the pace.

Faring somewhat better were the Rockies, who came in third, just seven games back. The team's competitive showing enabled Larry Walker to earn league MVP honors. The Colorado outfielder posted the most impressive stat-line of anyone in the league.

Let's look at his numbers, along with those of the other leading candidates:

PLAYER	AB	HITS	RUNS	2B	3B	HR	RBI	AVG	OBP	SLG PCT
Jeff Bagwell	566	162	109	40	2	43	135	.286	.425	.592
Barry Bonds	532	155	123	26	5	40	101	.291	.446	.585
Mike Piazza	556	201	104	32	1	40	124	.362	.431	.638
Larry Walker	568	208	143	46	4	49	130	.366	.452	.720

The statistics of Bagwell and Bonds were actually quite comparable. Neither man finished with a particularly high batting average, but Bonds led the league with 145 walks, and Bagwell finished right behind him with 127 bases on balls. Therefore, they both posted extremely high on-base percentages. Each man also played on a division-winning team. However, Piazza's Dodgers finished only two games behind the Giants in the West, and the catcher's overall numbers were slightly better than those of either Bagwell or Bonds. He also played a more demanding position in the field. Therefore, Piazza would have to be given the nod over either of those two sluggers.

As for Walker, his numbers were clearly the best. He finished ahead of Piazza in every statistical category, and he was also a very good outfielder. However, with the exception of runs scored and slugging percentage, the Dodger catcher wasn't very far behind Walker in any area. Furthermore, both Walker's runs scored total and slugging percentage were greatly inflated by the ballpark in which he played. Piazza's numbers were attained under much more normal conditions, and he had an absolutely fabulous offensive year. As a catcher, he also played the most demanding defensive position on the diamond. With his team remaining in contention in the Western Division race the entire season, Piazza would have been the best choice for league MVP.

1998

AMERICAN LEAGUE

The Yankees dominated the American League East and the rest of the baseball world in 1998, establishing a new league record by winning 114 games during the regular season. Their tremendous performance left them 22 games ahead of the second-place Red Sox, who had a very respectable season themselves, winning 92 games and making it into the postseason as the league's wild-card representative. Boston got another big year from Mo Vaughn, who hit 40 home runs, knocked in 115 runs, scored 107 others, and finished among the league leaders with a .337 batting average and 205 hits. In just his second full season, shortstop Nomar Garciaparra also had a fine year for the Sox. He hit 35 homers, drove in 122 runs, scored another 111, and batted .323. Pedro Martinez was among the league's best pitchers, compiling a record of 19-7, with a 2.89 earned run average and 251 strikeouts.

But New York's extraordinary team balance overwhelmed the Red Sox, and everyone else for that matter. Although the Yankees didn't have any one player who was recognized as being a true superstar, they were a collection of extremely talented and selfless players who all had the same ultimate goal of winning a championship. And that they did, with several individuals contributing greatly to the success of the team.

Paul O'Neill hit 24 homers, knocked in 116 runs, scored 95 others, and batted .317. Bernie Williams homered 26 times, drove in 97 runs, scored another 101, and led the league with a .339 batting average. Tino Martinez led New York with 28 home runs and 123 runs batted in. Although he struggled in the field, leadoff hitter Chuck Knoblauch scored 117 runs. Third baseman Scott Brosius had the finest season of his career, hitting 19 home runs, driving in 98 runs, and batting .300. Derek Jeter led the A.L. with 127 runs scored, and he finished among the leaders with a .324 batting average and 203 hits. He finished third in the league MVP voting.

New York also had the deepest pitching staff in the league. David Cone led the team with a record of 20-7, and he finished among the league leaders with 209 strikeouts. David Wells posted an outstanding 18-4 record, and Andy Pettitte finished 16-11. But the team's best pitcher was closer Mariano Rivera, who compiled a record of 3-0, with a 1.91 earned run average and 36 saves. Once again, though, the league's top pitcher was Toronto's Roger Clemens, who led all A.L. hurlers with a 20-6 record, a 2.65 earned run average, and 271 strikeouts. Unfortunately, the Blue Jays finished well out of contention for the second consecutive year, limping home 26 games behind first-place New York.

Cleveland remained the only team to ever capture an A.L. Central title, beating out the runner-up White Sox by nine games. Albert Belle posted huge numbers for Chicago, finishing near the top of the league rankings with 49 home runs, 152 runs batted in, 113 runs scored, a .328 batting average, 200 hits, and 48 doubles, and leading the A.L. with a .655 slugging percentage. But Belle struggled during the first half of the season and compiled most of those numbers during the second half of the campaign, after the divisional race was all but over. Therefore, he could not be seriously considered for league MVP honors.

Meanwhile, the Indians ran away with the division title for the fourth consecutive year. Their two best pitchers were Charles Nagy and Bartolo Colon. Nagy won 15 games, and Colon added another 14 victories. Manny Ramirez was the team's big gun on offense, finishing among the league leaders with 45 home runs and 145 runs batted in, scoring 108 runs, and batting .294. Returning to Cleveland after spending the previous year in Atlanta, Kenny Lofton scored 101 runs and stole 54 bases. Third baseman Travis Fryman hit 28 homers and knocked in 96 runs. Jim Thome hit 30 home runs, drove in 85 runs, scored 89 others, and batted .293.

The Rangers won their second A.L. West title in three seasons, finishing three games ahead of the second-place Angels. Jim Edmonds was Anaheim's best player, finishing the year with 25 homers, 91 runs batted in, 115 runs scored, and a .307 batting average. But the Rangers were the division's strongest team. Their top pitchers were Rick Helling and Aaron Sele. Helling finished 20-7, and Sele's record was 19-11. On offense, Will Clark hit 23 homers, drove in 102 runs, scored 98 others, and batted .305. Rusty Greer knocked in 108 runs, scored another 107, and batted .306. Ivan Rodriguez hit 21 homers, drove in 91 runs, and batted .321. The Rangers' dominant player, just as he was during their last title season, was Juan Gonzalez. The slugging outfielder finished among the league leaders with 45 home runs, and he led the circuit with 157 runs batted in and 50 doubles.

Let's take a look at his numbers, alongside those of the other top two players in the league, Alex Rodriguez and Ken Griffey Jr, both of whom played for Seattle:

PLAYER	AB	HITS	RUNS	2B	3B	HR	RBI	AVG	OBP	SLG PCT	SB
Alex Rodriguez	686	213	123	35	5	42	124	.310	.360	.560	46
Juan Gonzalez	606	193	110	50	2	45	157	.318	.366	.630	2
Ken Griffey Jr.	633	180	120	33	3	56	146	.284	.365	.611	20

Gonzalez finished with slightly better numbers than Rodriguez, in spite of the fact that the latter scored more runs and stole many more bases. In fact, Rodriguez became just the third player in major league history to hit 40 home runs and steal 40 bases in the same season. However, Gonzalez knocked in many more runs, leading the league in that department, and he finished with a much higher slugging percentage.

Griffey's overall numbers were quite comparable to the figures posted by Gonzalez. But the Mariners finished third in the division, 11½ games behind Texas. Gonzalez was the driving force behind the Rangers' first-place finish, and he was the league's most imposing figure at the plate. He deserved the MVP honor that was bestowed upon him at the end of the year.

NATIONAL LEAGUE

The division races took a backseat to the thrilling home run race waged between Mark McGwire and Sammy Sosa in the National League in 1998. The nation focused much of its attention on the two sluggers as they approached, and eventually surpassed, Roger Maris' 37-year-old single-season home run record of 61. Yet, there were three division winners to be determined, and there were several other fine players on the teams that contended for those division titles.

One of those players was Andres Galarraga, whose Atlanta Braves captured their fourth straight N.L. East crown. The Braves finished 18 games ahead of the runner-up Mets, whose fine first baseman John Olerud finished second in the league with a .354 batting average and a .447 on-base percentage. Galarraga's overall numbers were even more impressive, since he finished among the league leaders with 44 home runs and 121 runs batted in, while scoring 103 runs and batting .305. Galarraga was joined by Javy Lopez and Chipper Jones, both of whom also had fine seasons for Atlanta. Lopez hit 34 homers and knocked in 106 runs, while Jones also hit 34 round-trippers, drove in 107 runs, scored 123 others, and batted .313.

Atlanta lefthander Tom Glavine won the second Cy Young Award of his career for posting a 20-6 record and a 2.47 earned run average. Teammate Greg Maddux finished 18-9, with a league-leading 2.22 earned run average and five shutouts.

San Diego replaced San Francisco as Western Division champs, beating out the runner-up Giants by 9½ games. San Francisco had two of the league's top players in Jeff Kent and Barry Bonds. Kent hit 31 homers, drove in 128 runs, and batted .297. Bonds went deep 37 times, knocked in 122 runs, scored another 120, and batted .303.

The Rockies, who finished well out of contention in the West, also had some of the league's top offensive performers. Larry Walker scored 113 runs and led the N.L. with a .363 batting average. Dante Bichette knocked in 122 runs and finished near the top of the league rankings with a .331 batting average and 219 hits. Vinny Castilla batted .319 and finished among the league leaders with 46 home runs and 144 runs batted in.

But it was the Padres who prevailed in the West. Their top pitcher was Kevin Brown, who finished 18-7, with a 2.38 earned run average and 257 strikeouts. Closer Trevor Hoffman led the N.L. with 53 saves. On offense, Tony Gwynn batted .321, while Steve Finley scored 92 runs. San Diego's leading MVP candidate, though, was outfielder Greg Vaughn, who supplied much of the team's power. Vaughn hit 50 homers, knocked in 119 runs, scored 112 others, and batted .272. He finished fourth in the MVP voting.

The top three finishers in the balloting all came from the N.L. Central, where Houston posted a record of 102-60 to finish 12 games ahead of the second-place Cubs. Chicago advanced to the postseason as the league's wild-card entry.

Houston's best pitcher was Shane Reynolds, who finished 19-8 with a 3.51 earned run average. On offense, Craig Biggio hit 20 homers, knocked in 88 runs, and finished among the league leaders with 123 runs scored, 210 hits, a .325 batting average, and 50 stolen bases. Jeff Bagwell hit 34 four-baggers, drove in 111 runs, scored another 124, and batted .304. Houston's top player was former Montreal Expo outfielder Moises Alou, who hit 38 homers, knocked in 124 runs, scored another 104, and batted .312. Alou finished third in the league MVP voting.

The men who placed first and second in the balloting were, to no one's surprise, Sammy Sosa and Mark McGwire. A look at their numbers shows how dominant the two sluggers were:

PLAYER	AB	HITS	RUNS	2B	3B	HR	RBI	AVG	OBP	SLG PCT
Sammy Sosa	643	198	**134**	20	0	66	**158**	.308	.377	.647
Mark Mcgwire	509	152	130	21	0	**70**	147	.299	**.470**	**.752**

The two men finished first and second in the league in all the power-related statistical categories. McGwire topped the circuit in home runs and slugging percentage, with Sosa finishing second in both departments. Sosa led the league in runs batted in and runs scored, and McGwire finished right behind him in both categories.

Comparing the numbers of the two players, they were relatively close in most statistical categories. However, McGwire held a huge advantage in both on-base and slugging percentage. Although Sosa actually finished with a slightly higher batting average, he walked only 73 times. Meanwhile, McGwire's 162 bases on balls were easily the most in the National League. As a result, his league-leading .470 on-base percentage was almost 100 points higher than Sosa's. Based purely on statistics, the edge would have to go to McGwire. He had a slightly more dominant season.

However, McGwire's Cardinals finished third in the division, 19 games behind Houston, while Sosa's Cubs came in second, 12 games back. More importantly, Chicago made it into the postseason, something St. Louis didn't come close to doing. It is true that Sosa had a slightly better supporting cast in Chicago than McGwire had in St. Louis. Cubs first baseman Mark Grace batted .309, knocked in 89 runs, and scored 92 others. Outfielder Henry Rodriguez hit 31 homers and drove in 85 runs. Pitcher Kevin Tapani won 19 games, and rookie righthander Kerry Wood won another 13, while compiling 233 strikeouts in only 26 starts. Meanwhile, aside from McGwire, Brian Jordan and Ray Lankford were really the only other quality players the Cardinals had on their roster. Jordan hit 25 homers, drove in 91 runs, scored another 100, and batted .316. Lankford hit 31 homers, knocked in 105 runs, and batted .293. Nevertheless, the fact remains that the games the Cubs played at the end of the regular season were meaningful ones, while the Cardinals' contests were relatively insignificant.

Many of McGwire's home runs, while important from a historical perspective, had no bearing on the playoff picture. On the other hand, every home run Sosa hit, and every run he knocked in, helped draw his team closer to the playoffs. He was clearly more valuable to the Cubs than McGwire was to the Cardinals, and he was more deserving of being named league MVP.

1999

AMERICAN LEAGUE

The Yankees claimed the A.L. East title for the second consecutive season in 1999, this time finishing 3½ games ahead of the second-place Red Sox, who made it into the postseason as a wild-card. New York was again the most well-balanced team in baseball, possessing both a solid lineup and a very deep pitching staff. That staff included four strong starting pitchers in David Cone, Roger Clemens, Andy Pettitte, and Cuban refugee Orlando "El Duque" Hernandez. Cone won 12 games and finished second in the league with a 3.44 earned run average. Clemens, acquired from Toronto during the off-season for a package of players that included David Wells, added 14 victories. Pettitte also won 14 games, while Hernandez was the team's big winner, finishing the regular season with a record of 17-9. New York also had one of the league's top bullpens, headed by baseball's premier closer, Mariano Rivera, who led the league with 45 saves. Rivera also won four games, compiled a 1.83 earned run average, and allowed only 43 hits in 69 innings of work.

On offense, Tino Martinez led the team with 28 home runs, while knocking in 105 runs and scoring 95 others. Paul O'Neill knocked in 110 runs, and Bernie Williams hit 25 homers, drove in 115 runs, scored another 116, and finished among the league leaders with a .342 batting average and 202 hits. New York's best all-around player was shortstop Derek Jeter, who hit 24 homers, knocked in 102 runs, placed second in the league with 134 runs scored and a .349 batting average, and led the A.L. with 219 hits.

The Red Sox were not nearly as talented, but they managed to stay close to New York for much of the season, largely on the strength of the tremendous performances turned in by their top two players—Nomar

Garciaparra and Pedro Martinez. Garciaparra hit 27 home runs, knocked in 104 runs, scored 103 others, and won the A.L. batting title with a mark of .357. Martinez won the pitcher's version of the Triple Crown by leading the league with a record of 23-4, an earned run average of 2.07, and 313 strikeouts.

The third-place Blue Jays, who finished 14½ games off the pace, featured two of the league's top players in first baseman Carlos Delgado and outfielder Shawn Green. Delgado finished among the league leaders with 44 home runs and 134 runs batted in, while scoring an additional 113 runs. Green was equally productive, hitting 42 homers, driving in 123 runs, scoring 134 others, and batting .309.

The Indians continued their dominance of the A.L. Central Division, using their powerful offense to create a 21-game margin between themselves and second-place Chicago. Kenny Lofton batted .301 and scored 110 runs. Jim Thome hit 33 homers, knocked in 108 runs, and scored 101 others. Richie Sexson hit 31 long balls and knocked in 116 runs. Manny Ramirez finished among the league leaders with 44 home runs, 131 runs scored, and a .333 batting average, and he led the A.L. with 165 runs batted in and a .663 slugging percentage. Roberto Alomar was perhaps the league's finest all-around player, driving in 120 runs, scoring 138 others, batting .323, stealing 37 bases, and winning the eighth Gold Glove of his career.

Cleveland also had an improved pitching staff that featured three solid starters. Dave Burba won 15 games, Charles Nagy compiled 17 victories, and Bartolo Colon led the Tribe with a record of 18-5.

Texas was also a repeat-winner in the A.L. West, this time beating out the second-place A's by nine games. Third-place Seattle had two of the league's best players in Ken Griffey Jr. and Alex Rodriguez. Junior led the A.L. with 48 home runs, and he finished among the leaders with 134 runs batted in and 123 runs scored. Rodriguez hit 42 homers, knocked in 111 runs, and scored another 110. But, with the Mariners finishing 16 games behind Texas, neither player was worthy of serious consideration for league MVP honors.

Aaron Sele was the division-winning Rangers' top starter, finishing the regular season with a record of 18-9. Reliever John Wetteland finished second in the league to former teammate Mariano Rivera, with 43 saves. On offense, Rusty Greer batted .300, drove in 101 runs, and scored another 107. Juan Gonzalez had another big year, hitting 39 home runs, driving in 128 runs, scoring 114 others, and batting .326. However, he was only the third best player on Texas. Both Ivan Rodriguez and Rafael Palmeiro had huge offensive years for the Rangers.

Let's look at their numbers, alongside those of the other leading MVP candidates:

PLAYER	AB	HITS	RUNS	2B	3B	HR	RBI	AVG	OBP	SLG PCT
Derek Jeter	627	219	134	37	9	24	102	.349	.438	.552
Manny Ramirez	522	174	131	34	3	44	165	.333	.442	.663
Roberto Alomar	563	182	138	40	3	24	120	.323	.422	.533
Ivan Rodriguez	600	199	116	29	1	35	113	.332	.356	.558
Rafael Palmeiro	565	183	96	30	1	47	148	.324	.420	.630

Each of these five men had tremendous years, and a legitimate case could be made for selecting any of them. All five MVP candidates played for division-winning teams. Jeter, Alomar, and Rodriguez were the most complete players in the group, but Ramirez and Palmeiro posted huge offensive numbers. Palmeiro was the first to be eliminated from consideration, though, because he spent the year almost exclusively as a designated hitter.

Ramirez actually had the most impressive stat-line, but he was a liability, both in the field and on the basepaths. He posted better numbers than his teammate, Roberto Alomar, but the latter was a better all-around player, and he was much more of a team leader. Yet, it would have been difficult to name Alomar league MVP since one of his own teammates had numbers that were far more impressive. The writers seemed to agree, placing Ramirez third in the balloting and slotting Alomar right behind him in the fourth spot.

Jeter's numbers were extremely comparable to Alomar's, and he was clearly his team's best player. Yet, the New York shortstop finished sixth in the voting.

The man the writers opted for instead was Ivan Rodriguez, who was the Rangers' most complete player. He was a fine hitter, a good baserunner, and a superb defensive catcher. But Rodriguez's overall numbers were the least impressive in the group. His total run production (i.e. runs batted in + runs scored) was less than that of any of the other candidates, and his .356 on-base percentage was the lowest by far. It is even somewhat debatable as to whether or not he was his own team's most valuable player, since both Palmeiro and Juan Gonzalez put up numbers that were superior to his.

Therefore, it would seem that not one of these five players had a distinct advantage over the other four. They were all very evenly matched, and one would have been as good a choice as any of the others. However there was one player who stood above all others as the league's most dominant performer during the regular season. Boston ace Pedro Martinez not only dominated the A.L. statistical categories for pitchers, but no one else was even close to him. His 23 victories exceeded his nearest rival's total by five; his 2.07 earned run average was almost 1.5 runs per-game less than the second lowest earned run average posted by a starting pitcher (3.44); and his 313 strikeouts were 113 more than the 200 compiled by the league runner-up. It is true that his Red Sox failed to win their division, but they finished only 3½ games out of first and made it into the playoffs as a wild-card.

Without Martinez, they wouldn't even have come close. He should have been selected as the league's Most Valuable Player, instead of finishing second in the voting.

NATIONAL LEAGUE

The Braves captured their fifth straight N.L. East title in 1999, but this time they received far more competition from the ever-improving Mets. New York compiled a regular-season record of 97-65, to finish just six games behind Atlanta and advance into the postseason as the league's wild-card entry. Mets catcher Mike Piazza hammered 40 home runs, drove in 124 runs, scored another 100, and batted .303. Second baseman Edgardo Alfonzo hit 27 homers, knocked in 108 runs, and led the team with 123 runs scored and a .304 batting average. John Olerud added 19 homers, 96 runs batted in, 107 runs scored, and a .298 batting average.

Yet, New York was unable to overcome Atlanta's superior team pitching. Greg Maddux won 19 games, and he was joined by Kevin Millwood, who compiled a record of 18-7 and finished among the league leaders with a 2.68 earned run average and 205 strikeouts. Tom Glavine chipped in with 14 victories, and John Smoltz added another 11. John Rocker led the bullpen with 38 saves.

The Braves also had a solid lineup that featured the newly-acquired Brian Jordan. The former St. Louis Cardinal hit 23 homers, knocked in 115 runs, scored another 100, and batted .283. Centerfielder Andruw Jones went deep 26 times and scored 97 runs. Chipper Jones was the team's best player. The third baseman finished third in the league with 45 home runs, drove in 110 runs, scored 116 others, and batted .319. He had to be considered a leading MVP candidate.

Perhaps the division's finest all-around player was Vladimir Guerrero, who had a huge year for the Expos. The young outfielder hit 42 home runs, knocked in 131 runs, scored 102 others, and batted .316. Unfortunately for Guerrero, Montreal finished 35 games behind Atlanta, ruining any chance he might have had of being named league MVP.

The Astros claimed their third consecutive N.L. Central title, edging out second-place Cincinnati by just 1½ games. The Reds, who finished with a record of 96-67, also barely missed making it into the playoffs as a wild-card. Their top players were first baseman Sean Casey and outfielder Greg Vaughn. Casey hit 25 homers, drove in 99 runs, scored 103 others, and batted .332. Vaughn hit 45 homers, knocked in 118 runs, and scored another 104.

While the Astros had a solid lineup, it was largely their superior pitching that enabled them to finish just ahead of the Reds in the division. Mike Hampton was among the league's best pitchers. The lefthander finished 22-4, to lead N.L. hurlers in victories. He also finished among the leaders with a 2.90 earned run average. Hampton was joined by Jose Lima and Shane Reynolds. Lima won 21 games, and Reynolds was victorious 16 times. Reliever Billy Wagner saved 39 games.

On offense, Craig Biggio batted .294, scored 123 runs, and led the league with 56 doubles. Carl Everett hit 25 homers, knocked in 108 runs, and batted .325. Jeff Bagwell was one of the N.L.'s most productive batters, hitting 42 home runs, driving in 126 runs, and leading the circuit with 143 runs scored. He certainly deserved serious consideration for league MVP honors.

Even more devastating than Bagwell were Mark McGwire and Sammy Sosa, who waged a thrilling home run race for the second consecutive season. McGwire ended up leading the N.L. with 65 home runs and 147 runs batted in, while scoring 118 runs and compiling a .697 slugging percentage. Sosa finished second to McGwire with 63 homers, knocked in 141 runs, and scored another 114. However, the Cardinals finished fourth in the division, 21½ games out of first, while the Cubs finished last, 30 games off the pace. Therefore, neither player was a serious MVP candidate.

In just their second year in existence, the Arizona Diamondbacks captured the Western Division crown, finishing 13½ games ahead of the runner-up Giants. Yet, the division's top offense belonged to the Colorado Rockies, who featured three of the league's best players. Larry Walker hit 37 home runs, drove in 115 runs, scored 108 others, and led the N.L. with a .379 batting average and a .710 slugging percentage. Dante Bichette homered 34 times, knocked in 133 runs, and scored another 104. Todd Helton hit 35 homers, drove in 113 runs, scored 114 others, and batted .320. But the Rockies finished 27½ games off the pace in the West.

Therefore, the division's only legitimate MVP candidate came from the first-place Diamondbacks, who had several players that made huge contributions. Steve Finley hit 34 homers, knocked in 103 runs, and scored another 100. Tony Womack scored 111 runs and led the league with 72 stolen bases. Randy Johnson was the circuit's top pitcher, compiling a record of 17-9, and leading N.L. hurlers with a 2.48 earned run average, 364 strikeouts, 271 innings pitched, and 12 complete games. Second baseman Jay Bell hit 38 homers, drove in 112 runs, scored another 132, and batted .289. Outfielder Luis Gonzalez went deep 26 times, knocked in 111 runs, scored 112 others, finished second in the league with a .336 batting average, and led the N.L. with 206 hits. The team's top player was third baseman Matt Williams, who finished third in the MVP voting.

Let's look at his numbers, alongside those of the other leading candidates:

PLAYER	AB	HITS	RUNS	2B	3B	HR	RBI	AVG	OBP	SLG PCT
Chipper Jones	567	181	116	41	1	45	110	.319	.441	.633
Jeff Bagwell	562	171	143	35	0	42	126	.304	.454	.591
Matt Williams	627	190	98	37	2	35	142	.303	.344	.536

As impressive as his numbers were, Williams was the first to be eliminated. He drove in the most runs, but he finished well behind both Jones and Bagwell in most other statistical categories. Bagwell's numbers were slightly better than those compiled by Jones. The latter held his own in most areas, but Bagwell was far superior as a run-producer, knocking in 16 more runs and scoring 27 more times. However, Jones was forced to operate under more difficult conditions than Bagwell, since two of Atlanta's top offensive players were missing from the Braves' lineup much of the year. Plagued by a serious illness, Andres Galarraga missed the entire campaign, and Javy Lopez missed half the season with an injury.

Therefore, Jones' offensive productivity was absolutely essential to the Braves all year. Although Brian Jordan and Andruw Jones were fine players, Chipper was the one player in the Atlanta lineup who opposing pitchers feared. Jordan, who batted right behind him in the batting order, led the team with 115 runs batted in. However, he drove in as many runs as he did because opposing pitchers refused to give Jones anything good to hit when he came to the plate with men in scoring position. Furthermore, Jones absolutely destroyed the pitching staff of the archrival Mets, peppering them for several key hits when the teams squared off during the regular season.

If not for Jones, the Eastern Division race would have been considerably closer than it was. All things considered, the writers made the correct choice by selecting Jones as the league's Most Valuable Player over Bagwell, who finished second in the balloting.

2000

AMERICAN LEAGUE

The Yankees won their third straight A.L. East title and their third consecutive world championship in 2000, finishing the regular season 2½ games ahead of the second-place Red Sox. New York was again the most well-balanced team in baseball, possessing both solid hitting and strong pitching. Their staff was led by Andy Pettitte, who won 19 games, while losing only nine. Roger Clemens added 13 victories, and Mariano Rivera won another seven in relief, while also compiling 36 saves.

On offense, Paul O'Neill drove in 100 runs and Tino Martinez knocked in another 91. Catcher Jorge Posada had his breakout season, hitting 28 homers, driving in 86 runs, scoring another 92, and batting .287. The team's top two players, though, were Bernie Williams and Derek Jeter. Williams led New York with 30 homers and 121 runs batted in, scored 108 runs, and batted .307. Jeter finished among the league leaders with a .339 batting average, 119 runs scored, and 201 hits.

The runner-up Red Sox failed to advance to the postseason as a wild-card for the first time in three years. Yet their two best players had fabulous seasons. Nomar Garciaparra hit 21 homers, drove in 96 runs, scored 104 others, and led the A.L. with a .372 batting average. Pedro Martinez was the league's best pitcher, finishing 18-6, with a league-leading 1.74 earned run average, 284 strikeouts, and four shutouts. He received help out of the Boston bullpen from Derek Lowe, who led the A.L. with 42 saves. Garciaparra was aided on offense by Carl Everett, who led the Sox with 34 homers and 108 runs batted in, while batting .300.

Although they finished third in the A.L. East, 4½ games behind first-place New York, the Blue Jays featured the division's best offensive player. First baseman Carlos Delgado placed among the league leaders with 41 home runs, 137 runs batted in, 115 runs scored, and a .344 batting average, and he led the A.L. with 57 doubles. Toronto also had one of the circuit's best pitchers in David Wells, who led the league with 20 victories and nine complete games.

Chicago ended Cleveland's five-year reign as A.L. Central champs by finishing five games ahead of the second-place Indians. Cleveland still had a very strong offense that was led by Manny Ramirez, Jim Thome, and Roberto Alomar. Ramirez hit 38 homers, drove in 122 runs, finished third in the league with a .351 batting average, and led the A.L. with a .697 slugging precentage. Thome went deep 37 times, knocked in 106 runs, and scored 106 others. Alomar drove in 89 runs, scored 111 others, batted .310, and finished second in the league with 39 stolen bases.

But the White Sox had an offense to match Cleveland's, and they also had a better pitching staff. Their top starter was Mike Sirotka, who won 15 games. On offense, shortstop Jose Valentin hit 25 homers, drove in 92 runs, and scored 107 others. Second baseman Ray Durham batted .280, stole 25 bases, and finished near the top of the league rankings with 121 runs scored. First baseman Paul Konerko hit 21 homers, knocked in 97 runs, and batted .298. Outfielder Carlos Lee hit 24 round-trippers, drove in 92 runs, scored another 107, and batted .301. Chicago's best all-around player was outfielder Magglio Ordonez, who went deep 32 times, knocked in 126 runs, scored 102 others, and batted .315. But the team's most imposing figure at the plate was Frank Thomas, who finished among the league leaders with 43 home runs, 143 runs batted in, 115 runs scored, and a .328 batting average. Thomas finished second in the league MVP voting.

Someone who didn't receive nearly as much support in the balloting was the division's other top offensive player—Mike Sweeney, first baseman for the third-place Royals. Sweeney hit 29 homers, finished second in the league with 144 runs batted in, scored 105 runs, and finished near the top of the league rankings with a .333 batting average and 206 hits. Kansas City also got fine seasons from outfielders Jermaine Dye and Johnny Damon. Dye hit 33 homers, drove in 118 runs, scored 107 others, and batted .321. Damon batted .327, finished second in the league with 214 hits, and led the A.L. with 136 runs scored and 46 stolen bases. However, with the Royals finishing 18 games off the pace in the A.L. Central, none of their top three players even made it into the top ten in the voting.

The league's closest divisional race was waged out west, where the A's just barely edged out the Mariners by one-half game to claim the Western Division title. Seattle made it into the playoffs as a wild-card. The Mariners' top pitcher was Aaron Sele, who won 17 games. On offense, Mike Cameron hit 19 homers, scored 96 runs, and stole 24 bases. John Olerud, acquired via free agency during the off-season, drove in 103 runs and batted .285. The team's top two players were Edgar Martinez and Alex Rodriguez. Martinez hit 37 home runs, drove in a league-leading 145 runs, and batted .324. Rodriguez finished near the top of the league rankings with 41 homers, 132 runs batted in, 134 runs scored, and a .316 batting average.

The third-place Angels also got exceptional years from their top two players. Young third baseman Troy Glaus led the American League with 47 home runs, knocked in 102 runs, scored another 120, and batted .284. Outfielder Darin Erstad hit 25 homers, drove in 100 runs, scored 121 others, finished second in the league with a .355

batting average, and led the circuit with 240 hits. However, Anaheim finished 9½ games behind the first-place A's, who had both a solid lineup and the division's best pitching.

Oakland's top pitcher was young righthander Tim Hudson, who tied for the league lead with 20 victories. He was joined by veterans Gil Heredia and Kevin Appier, both of whom won 15 games. The A's also had the best left side of the infield in baseball in youngsters Eric Chavez and Miguel Tejada. Third baseman Chavez hit 26 homers, knocked in 86 runs, scored 89 others, and batted .277. Shortstop Tejada collected 30 round-trippers, drove in 115 runs, crossed the plate 105 times himself, and batted .275. Still, Oakland's top player was unquestionably Jason Giambi, who led the team in most offensive categories. More than any other player, the slugging first baseman was responsible for the A's making it into the playoffs.

Let's look at his numbers, alongside those of the other leading MVP candidates:

PLAYER	AB	HITS	RUNS	2B	3B	HR	RBI	AVG	OBP	SLG PCT
Carlos Delgado	569	196	115	57	1	41	137	.344	.470	.664
Frank Thomas	582	191	115	44	0	43	143	.328	.436	.625
Jason Giambi	510	170	108	29	1	43	137	.333	.476	.647
Alex Rodriguez	554	175	134	34	2	41	132	.316	.420	.606
Edgar Martinez	556	180	100	31	0	37	145	.324	.423	.579

Thomas and Martinez were the first two to be eliminated from consideration. Their statistics were certainly on the same level as those posted by the other three players, but Thomas served primarily as a DH all year, while Martinez was a full-time designated hitter. Rodriguez, who finished third in the voting, played a more demanding defensive position than either Delgado or Giambi, and he was also more of a complete player. In addition, he scored more runs than either of the first basemen. However, both Giambi and Delgado drove in slightly more runs, compiled higher batting averages, and finished with much higher on-base and slugging percentages. Thus, Rodriguez was the next to be eliminated.

In comparing Delgado to Giambi, the two men finished relatively close in most offensive categories. However, Giambi had a distinct advantage in that his A's won the Western Division title, while Delgado's Blue Jays finished third in the East. Furthermore, Giambi was largely responsible for Oakland being able to chase down Seattle during the season's final month. He hit 13 home runs, knocked in 31 runs, and batted .405 in September. His clutch hitting down the stretch clearly earned Giambi the MVP trophy the writers awarded him at season's end.

NATIONAL LEAGUE

The Mets came very close to ending Atlanta's reign as N.L. East champs in 2000, but they fell just one game short. As a result, the Braves captured their sixth consecutive division title, while New York had to settle for the wild-card. However, the division's top player was neither a Brave nor a Met, but, rather, the Expos' Vladimir Guerrero. The Montreal rightfielder finished among the league leaders with 44 home runs, 123 runs batted in, and a .345 batting average, while scoring 101 runs. Unfortunately for Guerrero, the Expos finished 28 games behind the Braves, making him a mere afterthought when it came time for the MVP voting.

In spite of their first-place finish, the Braves began to show signs of vulnerability. Front-line starters Tom Glavine and Greg Maddux both had fine years. Glavine led the league with 21 victories, and Maddux won another 19. But Kevin Millwood, who was so effective the previous year, finished just 10-13, and John Smoltz missed the entire campaign with an arm ailment.

Fortunately for Atlanta, their offense was buoyed by the returns of Andres Galarraga and Javy Lopez. Galarraga hit 28 homers, knocked in 100 runs, and batted .302. Lopez added 24 round-trippers and 89 runs batted in. Young shortstop Rafael Furcal added speed to the Atlanta lineup, batting .295, scoring 87 runs, and stealing 40 bases. Brian Jordan hit 17 homers and knocked in 77 runs. Both Andruw and Chipper Jones had big years as well. Andruw hit 36 homers, drove in 104 runs, scored 122 others, and batted .303. Chipper also hit 36 long balls, scored 118 runs, and led the team with 111 runs batted in and a .311 batting average.

Still, the Mets continued to close the gap between the two teams. Mike Hampton improved New York's pitching by winning 15 games and compiling a 3.14 earned run average. Al Leiter led New York starters with a record of 16-8 and 200 strikeouts, while pitching to a 3.20 earned run average. On offense, Edgardo Alfonzo was perhaps the team's most reliable hitter. The second baseman hit 25 home runs, drove in 94 runs, scored 109 others, and batted .324. Mike Piazza was the lineup's most serious power threat, hitting 38 homers, driving in 113 runs, and batting .324. He finished third in the league MVP voting.

St. Louis ended Houston's three-year reign as N.L. Central champs, finishing 10 games ahead of second-place Cincinnati. The Astros and Cubs, both of whom finished well out of contention, each had one of the league's most potent offensive weapons. Houston's Jeff Bagwell finished among the league leaders with 47 home runs and 132 runs batted in, led the N.L. with 152 runs scored, and batted .310. Teammate Richard Hidalgo also put up some very impressive numbers. Hidalgo hit 44 homers, knocked in 122 runs, scored another 118, and batted .314. Meanwhile, Chicago's Sammy Sosa led the National League with 50 home runs, drove in 138 runs, scored 106 others, and batted .320. However, the Astros finished 23½ games out, and the Cubs finished 30 games back.

The division-winning Cardinals also had one of the league's top players in centerfielder Jim Edmonds. After spending his first seven seasons with the Angels, Edmonds feasted on National League pitching, hitting 42 home runs, driving in 108 runs, scoring another 129, and batting .295. The Cardinals had several other players who contributed to their first-place finish. In only 236 at-bats, Mark McGwire hit 32 homers, drove in 73 runs, and batted .305. J. D. Drew hit 18 homers and batted .295. Second baseman Fernando Vina batted .300 and scored 81 runs. Shortstop Edgar Renteria scored 94 runs, batted .278, and stole 21 bases. Pitcher Darryl Kile won 20 games. But Edmonds was clearly the Cardinals' most valuable player, and he was the one most responsible for the team claiming the division title. The writers placed him fourth in the league MVP voting.

The Giants finished first in the N.L. West, beating out the Dodgers by 11 games. Los Angeles had the division's best pitching, with both Chan Ho Park and Kevin Brown having particularly strong seasons. Park finished 18-10 with a 3.27 earned run average, and he struck out 217 batters. Brown's won-lost record was only 13-6, but he struck out 216 batters and he led N.L. starters with a 2.58 earned run average. The Dodgers also had one of the league's top offensive players in Gary Sheffield, who hit 43 homers, drove in 109 runs, scored 105 others, and batted .325. Equally impressive were the numbers posted by Luis Gonzalez of the third-place Diamondbacks, who finished 12 games behind the Giants in the West. Gonzalez went deep 31 times, drove in 114 runs, scored another 106, and batted .311.

The National League's top offensive player, though, was Colorado's Todd Helton, who continued that team's rich tradition of producing outstanding hitters. Helton hit 42 home runs, scored 138 times, and led the league with 147 runs batted in, a .372 batting average, 216 hits, 59 doubles, a .463 on-base percentage, and a .698 slugging percentage. With the Rockies finishing reasonably close to the top of the division, in fourth place, 15 games back, Helton deserved consideration for league MVP honors.

Livan Hernandez and Shawn Estes were the top two starters for the division champion Giants. Hernandez finished 17-11, and Estes posted a record of 15-6. Rob Nen finished among the league leaders with 41 saves. On offense, although he accumulated only 393 official at-bats, Ellis Burks hit 24 homers, knocked in 96 runs, and batted .344. First baseman J. T. Snow hit 19 long balls, drove in 96 runs, and batted .284. But San Francisco's two most valuable players were unquestionably Jeff Kent and Barry Bonds. Let's look at their numbers, along with those of the other leading contenders:

PLAYER	AB	HITS	RUNS	2B	3B	HR	RBI	AVG	OBP	SLG PCT
Mike Piazza	482	156	90	26	0	38	113	.324	.398	.614
Jim Edmonds	525	155	129	25	0	42	108	.295	.411	.583
Jeff Kent	587	196	114	41	7	33	125	.334	.424	.596
Barry Bonds	480	147	129	28	4	49	106	.306	.440	.688
Todd Helton	580	216	138	59	2	42	147	.372	.463	.698

Helton's statistics were considerably better than the figures posted by the other four men. He was easily the top run-producer in the group, and he led the league in six different offensive categories. However, it must be remembered that his statistics were greatly inflated by playing in Colorado. Furthermore, the other four candidates all played for teams that either won or seriously contended for their division titles. Meanwhile, Helton's Rockies finished fourth in the West, 15 games back. Thus, it would be difficult to select him as the league's Most Valuable Player.

Piazza played the most demanding defensive position of all the remaining players, but he was a liability behind the plate, at least when it came to throwing out attempted base stealers. In addition, his overall offensive numbers did not stack up to those of the other three players. Although he fared relatively well in most categories, Piazza scored far fewer runs and compiled a much lower on-base percentage.

A valid case could be made on Edmonds' behalf, since Kent and Bonds had each other for offensive support. But the St. Louis slugger's numbers were slightly inferior to those posted by both Giants players.

That leaves us with Bonds and Kent. The two men were virtually equal as run-producers, with Bonds scoring more often, but Kent driving in more runs. They were fairly close in most other statistical categories, with Bonds holding an overall edge due to his considerably higher slugging percentage. But, it must be taken into consideration that Kent was a second baseman, and that the numbers he posted were unusually prolific for a man who played his position. When that fact is considered, it becomes difficult to find fault with his selection by the writers as the league's Most Valuable Player.

2001

AMERICAN LEAGUE

The Yankees finished atop the A.L. East standings for the fourth consecutive year in 2001, finishing 13½ games in front of the second-place Red Sox. New York's Roger Clemens won his record sixth Cy Young Award for posting a brilliant 20-3 record, while compiling a 3.51 earned run average and 213 strikeouts. Clemens was joined in the starting rotation by newcomer Mike Mussina, who won 17 games and led New York starters with a 3.15 earned run average and 214 strikeouts. Andy Pettitte added 15 victories. Closer Mariano Rivera compiled a 2.34 earned run average and led the league with 50 saves.

The Yankees instilled some new blood into their offense in the person of Alfonso Soriano, who replaced Chuck Knoblauch as the team's regular second baseman. Soriano hit 18 homers and stole 43 bases. Veterans Tino Martinez and Paul O'Neill had solid seasons. Martinez led the team with 34 home runs and 113 runs batted in, while batting .280. O'Neill hit 21 homers and stole 22 bases in his final season in pinstripes. Jorge Posada hit 22 four-baggers and drove in 95 runs. Bernie Williams homered 26 times, knocked in 94 runs, scored another 102, and batted .307. Derek Jeter hit 21 homers, led New York with 110 runs scored and a .311 batting average, and was successful on 27 of 30 stolen base attempts.

The division's top offensive player, though, was Boston's Manny Ramirez, who hit 41 homers, drove in 125 runs, and batted .306. But, with the Red Sox finishing well out of contention, Ramirez was not a viable MVP candidate.

After a one-year absence, Cleveland returned to the postseason as A.L. Central champs, finishing six games ahead of the runner-up Twins. Rookie lefthander C. C. Sabathia improved the Indians' starting pitching, leading the staff with a record of 17-5. Bartolo Colon added 14 victories and struck out 201 batters. Reliever Bob Wickman finished a perfect 5-0, with a 2.39 earned run average and 32 saves.

Jim Thome and the newly-acquired Juan Gonzalez were the team's big guns on offense. Thome finished second in the league with 49 home runs, knocked in 124 runs, scored another 101, and batted .291. Gonzalez hit 35 round-trippers, finished second in the A.L. with 140 runs batted in, and batted .325. They were joined by Roberto Alomar, who hit 20 homers, knocked in 100 runs, scored 113 times, and finished among the league leaders with a .336 batting average.

The American League's dominant team during the regular season was the Seattle Mariners, who captured the Western Division title by finishing 14 games ahead of the second-place Athletics. The A's actually had an exceptional season themselves, finishing the year with a record of 102-60 and making it into the playoffs as a wild-card. However, Seattle's 116 regular-season victories established a new league record and enabled them to bring the division race to an early end.

The Mariners' winning formula was quite different than the one they employed during the latter portion of the 1990s. They earlier depended largely on the big bats of superstars Ken Griffey Jr., Alex Rodriguez, and Edgar Martinez, and on the left arm of Randy Johnson. The philosophy of that team was essentially to outscore and overpower the opposition. But Griffey, Rodriguez, and Johnson were all gone by 2001. In fact, Rodriguez had a banner year for Texas, leading the league with 52 home runs and 133 runs scored, driving in 135 runs, and batting .318. In spite of his efforts, though, the Rangers finished last in the division, 43 games behind the Mariners. Meanwhile, Martinez was the only "superstar" player who remained from the earlier Mariner squads. This Seattle team had a much deeper pitching staff, and it relied far more on solid defense, timely-hitting, speed, and baserunning to defeat the opposition.

Seattle's pitching staff was as deep as any in the league. Freddy Garcia was the most talented of the starters. He finished 18-6 with a 3.05 earned run average. Veteran lefthander Jamie Moyer led the staff with a record of 20-6, while pitching to a 3.43 earned run average. Paul Abbott finished 17-4, and Aaron Sele compiled a record of 15-5. Japanese import Kazuhiro Sasaki helped to stabilize the bullpen, finishing among the league leaders with 45 saves.

On offense, centerfielder Mike Cameron hit 25 home runs, drove in 110 runs, and scored another 99. John Olerud hit 21 homers, knocked in 95 runs, and batted .302. Edgar Martinez homered 23 times, drove in 116 runs, and batted .306. But the team's top two players were second baseman Bret Boone and rightfielder Ichiro Suzuki. Boone hit 37 homers, led the league with 141 runs batted in, scored 118 runs, and batted .331. Suzuki represented Seattle's new style of play more than anyone else on the team. He had great speed, he was an exceptional hitter and an aggressive baserunner, and he had a powerful throwing arm in the outfield. Suzuki ended up leading the American League with a .350 batting average, 242 hits, and 56 stolen bases. His efforts earned him the league's Most Valuable Player Award at the end of the season. Teammate Boone finished third in the voting.

The man who finished second was the American League's reigning MVP, Jason Giambi. The A's finished a distant second, but they still managed to win 102 games and compile the league's second-best regular-season record. And Giambi had another sensational year.

Let's look at his stat-line, along with those of Suzuki and Boone:

PLAYER	AB	HITS	RUNS	2B	3B	HR	RBI	AVG	OBP	SLG PCT
Ichiro Suzuki	692	242	127	34	8	8	69	.350	.381	.457
Bret Boone	623	206	118	37	3	37	141	.331	.372	.578
Jason Giambi	520	178	109	47	2	38	120	.342	.477	.660

It could be argued that Giambi actually had the best year of the three. His power numbers greatly exceeded those of Suzuki, and he also finished with a much higher on-base percentage. Although Suzuki led the league in batting, he walked only 30 times. Meanwhile, Giambi led the A.L. with 129 bases on balls. Also, while Boone produced more runs, Giambi finished with much higher on-base and slugging percentages. However, it is difficult to ignore the fact that Seattle was the league's dominant team, and that they finished 14 games ahead of Oakland in the West. It should also be noted that the A's were a considerably stronger team than the one that captured the division title the previous year. They had the league's best starting threesome in Mark Mulder, Barry Zito, and Tim Hudson. Mulder finished 21-8 with a 3.45 earned run average. Zito was 17-8, with a 3.49 earned run average and 205 strikeouts. Hudson compiled a record of 18-9 with a 3.37 earned run average. Oakland's two young infielders also had outstanding seasons. Miguel Tejada hit 31 homers, drove in 113 runs, and scored 107 others. Eric Chavez homered 32 times, knocked in 114 runs, and batted .288.

Weighing all these factors, and considering that Oakland finished well behind Seattle in the West, it would be difficult to make a case for selecting Giambi as the league's Most Valuable Player over either Suzuki or Boone.

Suzuki was the choice of the writers, and he was not a bad selection. After all, he led the league in batting, hits, and stolen bases, and he brought a new dimension to the Mariners' offense. Suzuki was also a terrific outfielder, committing only one error all year and intimidating opposing baserunners with his powerful throwing arm. But, was he more deserving than Boone? The Mariner second baseman hit almost five times as many home runs as Suzuki, and he was far superior to his teammate as a run-producer. Ichiro crossed the plate nine more times than Boone, but the latter knocked in more than twice as many runs as the rightfielder, leading the league with a total of 141 runs batted in. Boone's on-base percentage was only nine points lower than Suzuki's, and his slugging percentage was 121 points higher. He also did a tremendous job in the field, showing good range at second and committing only 10 errors all year.

Therefore, it would seem that Boone's credentials were every bit as impressive as Suzuki's. Yet, the writers selected the latter instead. Perhaps they were influenced by all the media attention given to the

Japanese superstar. As the first position player to come over to the U.S. from the Far East, Suzuki became an instant celebrity in this country—something he already was in his native land. His every move was scrutinized, and the different style of play he brought with him made him a fascinating figure to observe. Suzuki's iconic-like status may have swayed the writers to his side.

However, the bottom line is that Bret Boone had a more productive year. He put up prodigious offensive numbers, especially for a second baseman. That should have been enough to earn him MVP honors, in a close call over Suzuki.

NATIONAL LEAGUE

The Braves won their seventh straight N.L. East title in 2001, but this time their closest rival was the Philadelphia Phillies, who finished only two games back in the standings. The Phillies were an up-and-coming team that featured several young stars. Third baseman Scott Rolen hit 25 home runs, drove in 107 runs, scored 96 others, batted .289, and won the third Gold Glove of his young career for his excellent defensive work at the hot corner. Outfielder Pat Burrell hit 27 homers and knocked in 89 runs. Shortstop Jimmy Rollins crossed the plate 97 times and led the league with 46 stolen bases. Perhaps the team's finest all-around player was outfielder Bobby Abreu, who hit 31 homers, drove in 110 runs, scored another 118, batted .289, and stole 36 bases. Philadelphia's best pitcher was Robert Person, who finished the season with a record of 15-7. Reliever Jose Mesa saved 42 games.

Still, the young Phillies fell just short in the end, losing out to the Braves, who made it into the postseason with the fewest victories (88) of any playoff team in either league. Though not as strong as they were in seasons past, Atlanta still had the same veteran nucleus whose experience helped them ward off the talented, but less-seasoned Phillies. Greg Maddux won 17 games, and Tom Glavine was victorious 16 times. Brian Jordan hit 25 homers, drove in 97 runs, and batted .295. Andruw Jones homered 34 times, knocked in 104 runs, and scored another 104. Chipper Jones went deep 38 times, drove in 102 runs, scored 113 others, and batted .330.

An even closer race took place in the N.L. Central, where Houston and St. Louis finished with identical 93-69 records. The Astros ended up winning the division on a tiebreaker, leaving the Cardinals as the league's wild-card entry.

The Astros had one of the league's top offenses, along with an improved pitching staff. Their top two starters were Wade Miller and Roy Oswalt. Miller finished 16-8 with a 3.40 earned run average. Rookie Oswalt made only 20 starts, but he compiled an outstanding 14-3 record and 2.73 earned run average. Reliever Billy Wagner was successful in 39 of his 41 save opportunities.

On offense, Jeff Bagwell hit 39 homers, knocked in 130 runs, scored another 126, and batted .288. In his first full season, Lance Berkman hammered 34 homers, drove in 126 runs, scored 110 others, and batted .331. Moises Alou homered 27 times and knocked in 108 runs, while Craig Biggio hit 20 four-baggers, scored 118 runs, and batted .292.

The Cardinals' offense was almost as potent. N.L. Rookie of the Year Albert Pujols hit 37 homers, knocked in 130 runs, scored 112 times, and batted .329. He finished fourth in the league MVP voting. Jim Edmonds hit 30 home runs, drove in 110 runs, scored 95 others, and batted .304. J. D. Drew homered 27 times and batted .323. Fernando Vina batted .303 and scored 95 runs. The Cards' best pitcher was Matt Morris, who finished 22-8 to tie for the league lead in victories. He also compiled a fine 3.16 earned run average. Teammate Darryl Kile added 16 wins, while pitching to a 3.09 earned run average.

The division's top player was Sammy Sosa, whose Cubs finished third, five games off the pace. Sosa hit 64 home runs, led the league with 160 runs batted in and 146 runs scored, and batted .328. With those numbers, he certainly deserved serious consideration for league MVP honors.

Another close race was waged out West, where Arizona edged out San Francisco by two games. The Dodgers, who finished third, only six games back, had one of the league's best all-around players in Shawn Green. The outfielder hit 49 home runs, drove in 125 runs, scored another 121, and batted .297. But both the Diamondbacks and the Giants had players who posted numbers that were even more impressive.

Arizona actually had three legitimate MVP candidates. While Mark Grace, Reggie Sanders, and Steve Finley all had solid seasons as well, the team was carried for much of the year by the extraordinary pitching of Curt Schilling and Randy Johnson, and by the slugging of Luis Gonzalez. Schilling and Johnson were baseball's most intimidating hurlers all year, dominating the league's statistical categories for pitchers. Schilling's 22 victories (against only 6 losses) tied him for the league lead in that department. He also finished second in the N.L. with a 2.98 earned run average and 293 strikeouts, while leading the league with 256 innings pitched and six complete games. Johnson's record was 21-6, and he led N.L. starters with a 2.49 earned run average and 372 strikeouts, while finishing second to Schilling with 249 innings pitched. Gonzalez batted .325 and finished among the league leaders with 57 home runs, 142 runs batted in, and 128 runs scored. He finished third in the league MVP voting.

The man who the writers voted number one was Barry Bonds, whose Giants finished two games behind the Diamondbacks in the standings. Although the Giants failed to make the playoffs, Bonds did all he could to extend their season. A look at his numbers, alongside those of the other leading candidates, indicates how dominant he was throughout the year:

PLAYER	AB	HITS	RUNS	2B	3B	HR	RBI	AVG	OBP	SLG PCT
Sammy Sosa	577	189	**146**	34	5	64	**160**	.328	.437	.737
Barry Bonds	476	156	129	32	2	**73**	137	.328	**.515**	**.863**
Luis Gonzalez	609	198	128	36	7	57	142	.325	.429	.688

All three players had fabulous years. In fact, Sosa and Gonzalez put up numbers that most certainly would have gained them MVP honors in almost any other year. Their statistics were quite comparable to the figures Bonds compiled in most offensive categories, and they were slightly better in some areas. Sosa finished with more runs batted in and runs scored than Bonds, leading the league in both departments.

However, while all three players finished with virtually the same batting average, Bonds compiled an on-base percentage that was approximately 80 points higher than either of the other two men. The reason for that lay in the fact that opposing pitchers simply refused to pitch to him with men on base. As a result, Bonds established a new single-season major league record by walking 177 times. The inordinate number of walks Bonds received greatly limited his RBI opportunities, enabling him to knock in "only" 137 runs. Bonds also set new single-season marks for most home runs and highest slugging percentage.

Furthermore, the presence of Bonds in the middle of San Francisco's lineup caused opposing managers to alter their style of managing. They often made unconventional moves in an attempt to avoid pitching to him with men on base. As a result, Bonds also made the players around him better. Shortstop Rich Aurilia, who preceded Bonds in the San Francisco batting order, had the finest season of his career, hitting 37 home runs, driving in 97 runs, scoring another 114, batting .324, and leading the league with 206 hits. Aurilia's success was rooted in the fact that he was able to look for fastballs in most situations, knowing that opposing pitchers did not want to walk him with Bonds coming up next.

As outstanding as Sosa and Gonzalez were, Barry Bonds was unquestionably the National League's Most Valuable Player.

2002

AMERICAN LEAGUE

The Yankees finished the 2002 season with a major-league best 103-58 record to capture their fifth consecutive A.L. East title. The Red Sox finished a distant second, 10½ games back. David Wells led the New York staff with 19 victories, against only 7 defeats, and Mike Mussina won another 18 games. On offense, Jorge Posada hit 20 homers and drove in 99 runs. Derek Jeter scored 124 times, batted .297, and stole 32 bases. Bernie Williams drove in 102 runs and scored 102 others, collected 204 hits, and finished third in the league with a .333 batting average. The team's two primary power threats were Jason Giambi and Alfonso Soriano. After coming over from Oakland as a free agent, Giambi led the Yankees with 41 home runs and 122 runs batted in, scored 120 runs, and batted .314. Soriano came within one home run of becoming a member of the exclusinve 40-40 club, hitting 39 homers and leading the league with 41 stolen bases. Soriano also knocked in 102 runs, batted .300, and led the A.L. with 128 runs scored and 209 hits. He finished third in the league MVP voting.

The second-place Red Sox had two of the league's finest pitchers in Derek Lowe and Pedro Martinez. Lowe finished 21-8 with a 2.58 earned run average, while Martinez compiled a record of 20-4 and led A.L. hurlers with a 2.26 earned run average and 239 strikeouts. Nomar Garciaparra and Manny Ramirez also had outstanding seasons for Boston. Garciaparra hit 24 homers, knocked in 120 runs, scored 101 others, and batted .310. Ramirez went deep 33 times, drove in 107 runs, and led the league with a .349 batting average.

Minnesota surprised everyone in the A.L. Central, winning 94 games and finishing 13½ games in front of the runner-up White Sox. The Twins got fine seasons from pitchers Rick Reed and Eric Milton. Reed led the staff with 15 victories, while Milton added another 13 wins. Reliever Eddie Guardado led the league with 45 saves. On offense, Minnesota was led by outfielders Jacque Jones and Torii Hunter. Jones hit 27 homers, drove in 85 runs, scored 96 others, and batted .300. Hunter led the team with 29 home runs and 94 runs batted in, scored 89 runs, batted .289, and was awarded a Gold Glove for his outstanding centerfield play.

The second-place White Sox had the division's best player in Magglio Ordonez. The Chicago rightfielder hit 38 home runs, drove in 135 runs, scored 116 others, and batted .320. Another top player was the Indians' Jim Thome, who finished second in the league with 52 homers, knocked in 118 runs, batted .304, and led the A.L. with a .677 slugging percentage. However, Cleveland slumped to third, 20½ games behind Minnesota.

The American League's strongest division was the West, where three teams won more than 90 games. Seattle's record of 93-69 was only the third best in the division, and it left them a full 10 games back in the standings. Their best players were once again Ichiro Suzuki and Bret Boone. Suzuki batted .321 and finished among the league leaders with 111 runs scored, 208 hits, and 31 stolen bases. Boone homered 24 times and drove in 107 runs. They were joined by John Olerud, who hit 22 long balls, knocked in 102 runs, and batted .300.

The Anaheim Angels finished second in the division, four games out of first, but they advanced to the playoffs as a wild-card with a record of 99-63. The Angels had one of the league's top starters in Jarrod Washburn, and they also boasted the circuit's top closer in Troy

Percival. Washburn compiled a record of 18-6 and a 3.15 earned run average. Percival finished 4-1, with a 1.92 earned run average and 40 saves. He also struck out 68 batters in 56 innings of work.

The Angels also had a very strong lineup. Darin Erstad batted .283 and scored 99 runs. Shortstop David Eckstein batted .293 and scored 107 times. Tim Salmon homered 22 times, drove in 88 runs, and batted .286. Troy Glaus hit 30 homers, knocked in 111 runs, and scored 99 others. Anaheim's best all-around player was outfielder Garret Anderson, who hit 29 home runs, drove in 123 runs, scored another 93, batted .306, and led the league with 56 doubles. He finished fourth in the league MVP voting.

The team that finished just ahead of Anaheim in the A.L. West was the Oakland A's. Their regular-season record of 103-59 left them just one-half game behind the Yankees in their quest for the best record in baseball. Despite the loss of team leader Jason Giambi to New York via free agency, the A's managed to win the division largely on the strength of their outstanding starting pitching. Lefthander Barry Zito was named the league's Cy Young Award winner for leading A.L. pitchers with 23 victories, against only 5 losses. He also compiled an outstanding 2.75 earned run average and struck out 182 batters. Zito was joined in the Oakland rotation by Mark Mulder and Tim Hudson. Mulder finished 19-7 with a 3.47 earned run average, and Hudson went 15-9 with a 2.98 earned run average. On offense, Jermaine Dye hit 24 home runs and drove in 86 runs. Eric Chavez homered 34 times and knocked in 109 runs. But the man the writers selected as the American League's Most Valuable Player was shortstop Miguel Tejada.

Let's look at his numbers, alongside those of the other top vote-getters:

PLAYER	AB	HITS	RUNS	2B	3B	HR	RBI	AVG	OBP	SLG PCT	SB
Alex Rodriguez	624	187	125	27	2	57	142	.300	.392	.623	9
Alfonso Soriano	696	209	128	51	2	39	102	.300	.332	.547	41
Miguel Tejada	662	204	108	30	0	34	131	.308	.354	.508	7
Garret Anderson	638	195	93	56	3	29	123	.306	.332	.539	6

All four players had outstanding seasons, but Anderson's numbers fell just a bit short of the rest. Rodriguez finished second in the balloting, and his stat-line was the most impressive of anyone in the group. However, his Rangers finished last in the West, 25 games out of first, with a record of 71-91. Therefore, it would be impossible to consider him the league's Most Valuable Player.

As a result, we are left with Soriano and Tejada. The numbers posted by the two men were extremely comparable. They were virtually equal as run-producers, with Soriano scoring 20 more times and Tejada driving in 29 more runs. Of course, it must be remembered that Soriano batted leadoff the entire year, while Tejada usually batted third or fourth in the Oakland lineup. Therefore, the Oakland shortstop had more opportunities to drive in runs. Looking at their other numbers, it would seem that Soriano actually held a slight statistical advantage. However, he also had far more support in the New York lineup than Tejada had in Oakland. With Jason Giambi having left the A's during the off-season, Tejada became the most important player in Oakland's everyday lineup. He helped to pick up much of the slack in Giambi's absence. In addition, he performed at an extremely high level down the stretch for Oakland, coming up with many huge hits that enabled the A's to clinch the division title. During the month of September, Tejada batted .359, with five home runs and 17 runs batted in.

The shortstop's outstanding performance during the season's final month helped solidify his position as the league's Most Valuable Player.

NATIONAL LEAGUE

After a far more competitive 2001 season, the Braves resumed their dominance of the National League's Eastern Division in 2002, winning a league-best 101 games and finishing 19 games in front of the second-place Expos. Montreal's Vladimir Guerrero was once again among the league's best players. The Expos rightfielder hit 39 home runs, drove in 111 runs, scored 106 others, batted .336, led the league with 206 hits, and stole 40 bases. However, the Braves' improved pitching enabled them to run away with the division title.

Tom Glavine finished 18-11 with a 2.96 earned run average. Greg Maddux compiled a record of 16-6 and finished among the league leaders with a 2.62 earned run average. Kevin Millwood returned to his form of 2000, winning 18 games and compiling a 3.24 earned run average. Perhaps the staff's most important pitcher, though, was John Smoltz. After missing the entire 2000 campaign and a portion of 2001 as well, Smoltz established himself as one of the game's finest closers, compiling a league-leading 55 saves in 59 save opportunities. For his efforts, Smoltz was placed eighth in the league MVP voting by the writers.

On offense, Atlanta was led by Andruw and Chipper Jones. Andruw hit 35 home runs, knocked in 94 runs, and scored 91 others. Chipper went deep 26 times and led the team with 100 runs batted in and a .327 batting average. They were joined by Gary Sheffield and Rafael Furcal. Sheffield hit 25 homers, drove in 84 runs, and batted .307. Furcal scored 95 runs and stole 27 bases.

St. Louis captured the Central Division title for the second time in three years, beating out the runner-up Astros by 13 games. The Cardinals' best pitcher was Matt Morris, who finished the season with a record of 17-9 and an earned run average of 3.42. Veteran Tino Martinez replaced the retired Mark McGwire as the team's regular first baseman and contributed to the offense with 21 home runs and 75 runs batted in. Edgar Renteria drove in 83 runs, batted .305, and stole 22 bases. Jim Edmonds hit 28 home runs, knocked in 83 runs, scored 96 others, and batted .311. But the Cardinals' most valuable player was unquestionably Albert Pujols. In just his second major-league season, Pujols established himself as one of the game's finest hitters, amassing 34 home runs, 127 runs batted in, and 118 runs scored, while batting .314. He finished second in the league MVP voting.

Finishing just behind Pujols, in third place, was Houston's Lance Berkman. The young slugger finished among the league leaders with 42 home runs, led the circuit with 128 runs batted in, scored 106 runs, and batted .292. Equally impressive were the numbers posted by Sammy Sosa. The Chicago outfielder drove in 108 runs, batted .288, and led the N.L. with 49 home runs and 122 runs scored. However, Chicago finished fifth in the division, 30 games behind St. Louis.

The Western Division featured the league's most competitive race, with three teams vying for the division title most of the year. The Dodgers were the first to fall out of contention, having their title hopes dashed with one week remaining in the season. Their 92 victories left them in third-place, six games out of first. Los Angeles' best player was outfielder Shawn Green, who carried the team's rather anemic offense for much of the season. Green ended up with 42 home runs, 114 runs batted in, 110 runs scored, and a .285 batting average. He finished fifth in the MVP voting.

Arizona and San Francisco battled down to the season's final days, with the Diamondbacks finally prevailing. Their 98 victories left them 2½ games ahead of the Giants, who had to settle for the wild-card. Arizona's top offensive player was Luis Gonzalez, who led the team with 28 home runs and 103 runs batted in, while scoring 90 times himself and batting .288. Steve Finley added 25 homers and 89 runs batted in. Second baseman Junior Spivey led the D'backs with a .301 batting average and 103 runs scored, while shortstop Tony Womack scored 90 times and stole 29 bases.

But the team's two dominant performers were again pitchers Curt Schilling and Randy Johnson. Schilling finished second in the league to Johnson with a 23-7 record, 316 strikeouts, and 259 innings pitched, while compiling a 3.23 earned run average. Johnson led all N.L. starters with a 24-5 record, a 2.32 earned run average, 334 strikeouts, 260 innings pitched, and eight complete games. At season's end, he was presented with his fourth straight Cy Young Award, and the fifth of his career.

While not possessing anyone as dominant as either Schilling or Johnson, the runner-up Giants also had a solid pitching staff. Kirk Rueter won 14 games and compiled a 3.23 earned run average. Russ Ortiz won another 14, and Jason Schmidt added 13 victories. Closer Rob Nen finished 6-2, with a 2.20 earned run average and 43 saves. On offense, Jeff Kent hit 37 home runs, drove in 108 runs, scored another 102, and batted .313. Reggie Sanders hit 23 long balls and knocked in 85 runs.

There can be no doubt, though, as to who was San Francisco's best player. Barry Bonds followed up his record-setting 2001 season with another brilliant year in 2002. In addition to hitting 46 home runs, driving in 110 runs, and scoring 117 others in only 403 official at-bats, Bonds led the league with a career-best .370 batting average, while establishing new single-season major-league records by walking 198 times and compiling a .582 on-base percentage. A look at his numbers, alongside those of MVP runner-up Albert Pujols, gives a clear indication of just how dominant Bonds was:

PLAYER	AB	HITS	RUNS	2B	3B	HR	RBI	AVG	OBP	SLG PCT
Albert Pujols	590	185	118	40	2	34	127	.314	.394	.561
Barry Bonds	403	149	117	31	2	46	110	**.370**	**.582**	**.799**

Bonds compiled a much higher batting average, on-base percentage, and slugging percentage, and he also hit more home runs in far fewer at-bats. The two men scored virtually the same number of times, and Pujols knocked in 17 more runs. However, he did so in almost 200 more official at-bats. Opposing pitchers simply refused to pitch to Bonds with men in scoring position, greatly limiting his opportunities to drive in runs. Among his record-setting 198 bases on balls were a new single-season record 68 intentional walks. Taking all this into consideration, Bonds' overall numbers were far more impressive than those compiled by Pujols. He also led his team into the playoffs, albeit as a wild-card.

Bonds was unquestionably the National League's Most Valuable Player.

2003

AMERICAN LEAGUE

The Yankees established a new American League record by winning their sixth consecutive division title in 2003, finishing six games ahead of the second-place Red Sox in the A.L. East. Boston made it into the postseason as the league's wild-card entry.

New York's pitching staff was as deep as any in baseball. Andy Pettitte led the starters with a record of 21-8. He was joined by Roger Clemens, Mike Mussina, and David Wells. Clemens and Mussina both won 17 games, while Wells added 15 victories. Mariano Rivera won five games in relief, while pitching to a 1.66 earned run average and saving 40 games. On offense, former Japanese star Hideki Matsui knocked in 106 runs and batted .287. Derek Jeter batted .324 and scored 87 runs, despite missing more than a month of the season with a shoulder injury. Jason Giambi led the team with 41 home runs and 107 runs batted in. Alfonso Soriano hit 38 homers, drove in 91 runs, scored another 114, batted .290, and stole 35 bases. But the man perceived by the writers as the team's most valuable player was

Jorge Posada. The catcher hit 30 home runs, knocked in 101 runs, batted .281, and showed tremendous growth behind the plate, both as a receiver and as a handler of pitchers. Posada finished third in the league MVP voting.

Second-place Boston featured two of the league's better pitchers in Derek Lowe and Pedro Martinez. Lowe compiled a record of 17-7, and Martinez finished 14-4 with a league-best 2.22 earned run average. It was the Red Sox offense, though, that carried them into the playoffs. The Boston lineup was the best in baseball, with nary an easy out among the nine regulars. Kevin Millar hit 25 home runs and drove in 96 runs. Catcher Jason Veritek hit 25 long balls and knocked in 85 runs. Rightfielder Trot Nixon went deep 28 times, drove in 87 runs, and batted .306. Centerfielder Johnny Damon brought the team much-needed speed at the top of the batting order, scoring 103 times and stealing 30 bases. Third baseman Bill Mueller had the finest season of his career, hitting 19 home runs, driving in 85 runs, and leading the league with a .326 batting average. Manny Ramirez led the team with 37 home runs, knocked in 104 runs, scored 117 others, and batted .325. He finished sixth in the MVP voting. Coming in right behind Ramirez, in seventh place, was Nomar Garciaparra. The Boston shortstop homered 28 times, led the Sox with 105 runs batted in and 120 runs scored, and batted .301.

The team's top vote-getter was first baseman David Ortiz. Ortiz's 31 home runs, 101 runs batted in, and .288 batting average were not the most impressive numbers compiled by a Red Sox player, but he had many huge hits over the course of the season, many of which came against Boston's chief rival—New York. The writers acknowledged that fact by placing him fifth in the balloting.

While New York and Boston dominated the A.L. East, the division's best player came from third-place Toronto. Although the Blue Jays finished 15 games behind New York, first baseman Carlos Delgado placed among the league leaders with 42 home runs, 117 runs scored, a .426 on-base percentage, and a .593 slugging percentage. He also batted .302 and led the A.L. with 145 runs batted in. Delgado finished runner-up in the MVP voting.

The Twins captured their second consecutive Central Division title, beating out the second-place White Sox by four games, and topping third-place Kansas City by seven games. The Royals had the division's best all-around player in Carlos Beltran. The outfielder hit 26 home runs, knocked in 100 runs, scored 102 others, batted .307, and stole 41 bases in 45 attempts. But Minnesota and Chicago both had more balanced teams. Minnesota's offense was led by outfielders Jacque Jones and Torii Hunter. Jones batted .304 and scored 76 runs. Hunter hit 26 home runs and drove in 102 runs. First baseman Doug Mientkiewicz batted .300, and catcher A. J. Pierzynski hit .312. Minnesota's top two starters were Brad Radke and Johan Santana. Radke won 14 games, and Santana compiled an outstanding 12-3 record and a 3.07 earned run average. Reliever Eddie Guardado saved 41 games.

Chicago's offense was led by the threesome of Magglio Ordonez, Carlos Lee, and Frank Thomas. Ordonez hit 29 home runs, drove in 99 runs, scored 95 others, and batted .317. Lee hit 31 four-baggers, knocked in 113 runs, scored another 100, and batted .291. Thomas batted only .267, but he hit 42 homers and drove in 105 runs.

Oakland edged out Seattle by three games for the A.L. West title, and for the final playoff spot. Once again, the A's big three of Hudson, Mulder, and Zito gave the team as formidable a group of starters as anyone in the game. Hudson's 16 victories and 2.70 earned run average led the team. Mulder won 15 games and compiled a 3.13 earned run average, while Zito posted 14 victories while pitching to a 3.30 earned run average. Oakland's lineup was headed by Eric Chavez and reigning league MVP Miguel Tejada. Chavez hit 29 home runs, drove in 101 runs, scored another 94, and batted .282. Tejada homered 27 times, knocked in 106 runs, scored 98 others, and batted .278.

The runner-up Mariners had one of the league's best pitchers in veteran lefthander Jamie Moyer, who finished with an outstanding 21-7 record, while compiling an earned run average of 3.27. On offense, Ichiro Suzuki batted .312, scored 111 runs, and finished among the league leaders with 212 hits and 34 stolen bases. Bret Boone hit 35 homers, knocked in 117 runs, and scored 111 others.

The best player in the division was the Rangers' Alex Rodriguez, who was selected by the writers as the league's Most Valuable Player. Let's look at his statistics, alongside those of some of the other top vote-getters:

PLAYER	AB	HITS	RUNS	2B	3B	HR	RBI	AVG	OBP	SLG PCT
Jorge Posada	481	135	83	24	0	30	101	.281	.405	.518
David Ortiz	448	129	79	39	2	31	101	.288	.369	.592
Nomar Garciaparra	658	198	120	37	13	28	105	.301	.345	.524
Manny Ramirez	569	185	117	36	1	37	104	.325	**.427**	.587
Carlos Delgado	570	172	117	38	1	42	**145**	.302	.426	.593
Bret Boone	622	183	111	35	5	35	117	.294	.366	.535
Alex Rodriguez	607	181	**124**	30	6	**47**	118	.298	.396	**.600**

The statistics of Posada and Ortiz were extremely similar, with the only major discrepancies being the former's much higher on-base percentage and the latter's huge advantage in slugging percentage. Their overall numbers were also the least impressive in the group, due largely to the relatively low number of runs they both scored. Yet, both players finished in the top five in the MVP balloting. The writers must have been impressed with the impact Posada had on his team, both as a hitter and as a catcher. They also must have placed a great deal of importance on the many big hits Ortiz got over the course of the season. But it would be difficult to consider either man the league's Most Valuable Player.

Garciaparra and Ramirez both put up good numbers for Boston, but that was where their impact on the team ended. Garciaparra was not particularly popular in the clubhouse, and he was actually viewed by many of his teammates as being a bit of an annoyance. Ramirez drew criticism not only from the Boston press, but also from some of his teammates, for sitting out several important games with relatively minor injuries. Therefore, it would seem that neither of the two players could be viewed as being indispensable to the team.

Bret Boone had a fine year for Seattle, and his team narrowly missed making the playoffs. But his numbers were not nearly as impressive as those compiled by Delgado, who helped lead his undermanned Blue Jays to a very respectable third-place finish. The writers placed Delgado second in the balloting, behind Rodriguez. They undoubtedly frowned upon the fact that the Toronto first baseman compiled fewer than 50 runs batted in during the season's second half, after posting close to 100 runs batted in by the All-Star break. Yet he still managed to lead the league in that category, finishing with almost 30 more runs batted in than Rodriguez. It is true that Delgado was far less productive during the season's second half, but he carried the Blue Jays on his back during the first half of the campaign, keeping them in the pennant race far longer than they otherwise would have remained. His team ended up winning 86 games and finishing 10 games over .500. Meanwhile, Rodriguez's Rangers finished last in the West, 25 games out of first, with a record of only 71-91. At no point during the season was Texas even remotely in contention for the playoffs.

Therefore, one has to wonder what the writers were thinking when they named Rodriguez the league's Most Valuable Player. Ranger management seemed to agree since it dealt him away prior to the start of the subsequent season. Rodriguez may have been the league's *best* player, but he certainly was not the most *valuable* player in the American League. That honor should have gone to Carlos Delgado.

NATIONAL LEAGUE

The Atlanta Braves won their major-league record ninth consecutive National League East title in 2003, finishing 10 games ahead of the runner-up Florida Marlins. Florida made it into the playoffs as a wild-card with 91 victories. The young Marlins featured N.L. Rookie of the Year Dontrelle Willis, who finished 14-6 with a 3.30 earned run average. He was joined by fireballing righthander Josh Beckett, who became a regular member of the Marlins rotation during the course of the season. Beckett won only nine games, but he compiled a fine 3.04 earned run average and struck out 152 batters in only 142 innings of work. Speedy centerfielder Juan Pierre batted .305, scored 100 runs, collected 204 hits, and led the league with 65 stolen bases. Second baseman Luis Castillo batted .314 and scored 99 runs, while third baseman Mike Lowell led the team with 32 home runs and 105 runs batted in.

Perhaps the Marlins' most important player was catcher Ivan Rodriguez, who joined the team during the off-season as a free agent. Rodriguez drove in 85 runs and scored 90 others, but he more importantly provided veteran leadership to the many young players on the Florida roster.

The division-winning Braves got a fine season from veteran righthander Russ Ortiz, who finished the year with a record of 21-7. Greg Maddux pitched to an unusually high 3.96 earned run average, but he still managed to win 16 games. John Smoltz finished second in the league with 45 saves and compiled a superb 1.12 earned run average. On offense, Rafael Furcal batted .292, stole 25 bases, and finished near the top of the league rankings with 130 runs scored. Andruw Jones hit 36 home runs, knocked in 116 runs, scored 101 times, and batted .277. Chipper Jones hit 27 homers, drove in 106 runs, scored another 103, and batted .305. Gary Sheffield was clearly the team's best player, though. The rightfielder led Atlanta with 39 home runs, 132 runs batted in, and a .330 batting average, and he scored 126 runs. Sheffield finished third in the league MVP voting.

Another top player was Philadelphia first baseman Jim Thome, who joined the team during the off-season via free agency. Thome led the N.L. with 47 home runs, knocked in 131 runs, and scored another 111. However, the Phillies finished third in the division, 15 games behind the Braves.

The Cubs were the league's most improved team, winning 88 games—21 more than they won the prior year—and edging out Houston for the Central Division title by just one game. Sammy Sosa was Chicago's top offensive threat, leading the team with 40 home runs, 103 runs batted in, and 99 runs scored, while batting .279. Free agent acquisition Moises Alou chipped in with 22 homers and 91 runs batted in. But it was the Cubs' improved pitching that enabled them to leap four places in the standings. Finally healthy, Kerry Wood won 14 games, compiled a 3.20 earned run average, and led all N.L. hurlers with 266 strikeouts. Even better was Mark Prior, who finished among the league leaders with a record of 18-6, a 2.43 earned run average, and 245 strikeouts.

The second-place Astros were led on offense by Jeff Bagwell. The veteran first baseman hit 39 home runs, drove in 100 runs, and scored another 109. Lance Berkman hit 25 homers, knocked in 93 runs, and scored 110 others. Richard Hidalgo added 28 four-baggers, 88 runs batted in, and 91 runs scored, while batting .309. Roy Oswalt was Houston's top starter, finishing 10-5 with a 2.97 earned run average. Closer Billy Wagner saved 44 games and compiled an outstanding 1.78 earned run average.

The third-place Cardinals also remained in the division race for most of the season, finishing only three games behind the Cubs. Jim Edmonds hit 39 homers, knocked in 89 runs, and scored 89 others. Scott Rolen went deep 28 times, drove in 104 runs, scored 98 others, and batted .286. The Cardinals' leading MVP candidate was Albert Pujols, who compiled the most impressive statistics of anyone in the league. Pujols finished among the league leaders with 43 home runs and 124 runs batted in, and he led the N.L. with a .359 batting average, 137 runs scored, 212 hits, and 51 doubles. The writers placed him second in the MVP voting.

Another player who posted extremely impressive numbers was Colorado's Todd Helton. The young first baseman hit 33 home runs, drove in 117 runs, and finished second in the league with a .358 batting average, 135 runs scored, 209 hits, and a .458 on-base percentage. However, with the Rockies finishing fourth in the West, 26½ games out of first, Helton did not merit serious consideration for league MVP honors.

The Western Division champions were the San Francisco Giants, who met little resistance as they built up a 15½ game margin of victory over the runner-up Dodgers. The Giants had one of the league's best pitchers in Jason Schmidt, who finished 17-5 with a league-leading 2.34 earned run average. Schmidt also finished near the top of the league rankings with 208 strikeouts. On offense, San Francisco was hardly overwhelming. Benito Santiago batted .279, Rich Aurilia hit .277, and Edgardo Alfonzo finished second on the team with 81 runs batted in.

However, the Giants had one player who legitimized their offense. Although he appeared in only 130 games, compiling a total of just 390 official at-bats, Barry Bonds had another great year. Bonds hit 45 home runs, knocked in 90 runs, scored 111 others, batted .341, and led the N.L. with a .529 on-base percentage and a .749 slugging percentage. For his efforts, Bonds was selected by the writers for the third consecutive year, and for the sixth time in his career, as the league's Most Valuable Player. But, was he more deserving than Albert Pujols and Gary Sheffield, the players who finished second and third in the balloting? Perhaps a look at the numbers of the three players will provide the answer:

PLAYER	AB	HITS	RUNS	2B	3B	HR	RBI	AVG	OBP	SLG PCT
Albert Pujols	591	212	137	51	1	43	124	.359	.439	.667
Barry Bonds	390	133	111	22	1	45	90	.341	.529	.749
Gary Sheffield	576	190	126	37	2	39	132	.330	.419	.604

The overall numbers posted by both Pujols and Sheffield were superior to those of Bonds. Each man knocked in and scored many more runs, and they also collected far more hits and doubles. Pujols also compiled a higher batting average. However, much of the discrepancy in the numbers stems from the fact that Pujols and Sheffield accumulated many more at-bats than Bonds. In addition to appearing in only 130 games for the Giants, Bonds walked a total of 148 times. This again illustrates the unwillingness of opposing pitchers to give him an opportunity to hit with men on base, which explains his relatively low total of 90 runs batted in. It also explains his extremely high on-base percentage of .529, which was approximately 100 points higher than that of either Pujols or Sheffield. He also finished with a much higher slugging percentage than either player. Even more important is the fact that Bonds was the primary reason why San Francisco was able to run away with the Western Division title. San Francisco's offense totally revolved around Bonds, and, without him, the team would have had a difficult time scoring runs. There was no one else in their lineup who instilled fear in opposing pitchers.

Meanwhile, both Pujols and Sheffield had other good players surrounding them in their respective lineups. The overall numbers posted by Pujols and Sheffield may have been slightly more impressive, but Bonds was more valuable to his team. Therefore, his selection by the writers cannot be questioned.

2004

AMERICAN LEAGUE

The Yankees compiled the American League's best record in 2004, finishing 101-61, to capture their seventh consecutive A.L. East title. The Red Sox finished three games back in the standings, with a record of 98-64, thereby advancing to the playoffs as the league's wild-card entry.

In spite of their first-place finish, the Yankees' 2004 squad did not possess the overall team balance that characterized most of its immediate predecessors. The 2004 version depended far more on hitting to defeat the opposition, since its pitching staff was merely average. Ranking sixth in the American League with a team earned run average of 4.69, the unit's top winners were newcomers Javier Vazquez and Jon Leiber, each of whom posted only 14 victories while compiling earned run averages well in excess of 4.00. The staff's two most reliable pitchers were set-up man Tom Gordon and closer Mariano Rivera. Gordon finished 9-4, with four saves, a 2.21 earned run average, and 96 strikeouts in 90 innings of work. Rivera led the league with 53 saves, while compiling a record of 4-2 with an outstanding 1.94 earned run average.

With New York's starting pitchers displaying a great deal of mediocrity much of the time, it was the Yankees' offense that carried them to the division title. The Yankees led the league with 242 home runs, and they placed second with 897 runs scored. Derek Jeter had another solid season, hitting 23 home runs, batting .292, and scoring 111 runs. Hideki Matsui hit 31 homers, knocked in 108 runs, scored another 109, and batted .298. Jorge Posada finished the season with 21 home runs and 81 runs batted in. In his first season in pinstripes, Alex Rodriguez clubbed 36 homers, drove in 106 runs, scored 112 others, batted .286, and did a commendable job in the field in his first year as a third baseman. Wielding an even more potent bat was the team's leading candidate for league MVP honors, Gary Sheffield. After signing on as a free agent during the off-season, Sheffield hammered 36 home runs, batted .290, and placed among the league-leaders with 121 runs batted in and 117 runs scored. He ended up finishing second in the MVP voting.

Although they finished three games behind New York in the standings, the Red Sox were a better-balanced team. The Sox led the A.L. with 949 runs scored, and they tied for first in the league with a .282 team batting average. They also placed fourth in the circuit with 222 home runs, while posting the third-lowest team earned run average—a mark of 4.18. Their pitching staff was led by the duo of Curt Schilling and Pedro Martinez. Schilling finished 21-6, with a 3.26 earned run average and 203 strikeouts. Martinez went 16-9, with an earned run average of 3.90 and 227 strikeouts. Closer Keith Foulke saved 32 games.

On offense, Boston was paced by the trio of Johnny Damon, Manny Ramirez and David Ortiz. Centerfielder Damon hit 20 homers, knocked in 94 runs, batted .304, and finished second in the league with 123 runs scored. Ramirez led the A.L. with 43 home runs and a .613 slugging percentage, while also finishing third with 130 runs batted in, scoring 108 times, and batting .308. Ortiz batted .301, scored 94 runs, and placed among the league leaders with 41 homers, 139 runs batted in, and a .603 slugging percentage. Ramirez finished third in the MVP balloting, while Ortiz came in fourth.

Somewhat surprisingly, two of the league's most outstanding offensive performances were turned in by men who played for the Orioles, who finished a distant third in the division, 23 games off the pace. Third baseman Melvin Mora had the greatest season of his career, hitting 27 home runs, driving in 104 runs, scoring another 111, finishing second in the A.L. with a .340 batting average, and leading the circuit with a .419 on-base percentage. Right beside Mora, at shortstop, Miguel Tejada had a huge year after coming over from Oakland via free agency during the off-season. In his first year in Baltimore, Tejada hit 34 homers, knocked in a league-leading 150 runs, scored 107 times, and batted .311. But, with the Orioles out of contention most of the year, Tejada did well to finish as high as he did in the MVP voting, coming in fifth.

The Minnesota Twins won their third straight Central Division title, compiling a record of 92-70, to finish nine games ahead of second-place Chicago. The White Sox featured the division's most dynamic offensive player in Paul Konerko, who finished among the league leaders with 41 home runs and 117 runs batted in. But, in the end, Minnesota's superior team balance and outstanding pitching enabled them to pull away from Chicago in the divisional race.

On offense, the Twins were led by the quartet of Lew Ford, Jacques Jones, Torii Hunter, and Corey Koskie. Playing all three outfield positions, Ford batted .299, drove in 72 runs, and led the team with 89 runs scored. Jones hit 24 homers and knocked in 80 runs. Hunter went deep 23 times, collected 81 runs batted in, scored 79 runs, and won his fourth consecutive Gold Glove for his outstanding centerfield play. Third baseman Koskie drove in 71 runs and led the team with 25 long balls.

It was the Twins' pitching that set them apart from the rest of the division. Minnesota's team earned run average of 4.03 was the best in the American League, and their staff featured the league's most dominant starting pitcher, and also one of its best closers. Joe Nathan finished among the league leaders with 44 saves, while compiling an outstanding 1.62 earned run average and striking out 89 batters in only 72 innings of work. Meanwhile, lefthander Johan Santana established himself as the league's best pitcher in just his second full season. Santana finished 20-6, with a league-leading 2.61 earned run average and 265 strikeouts, to capture the A.L. Cy Young Award. Santana also received a great deal of support in the MVP balloting, coming in sixth.

The eventual winner of that coveted honor came out of the A.L. West, which was the league's most competitive division. The Anaheim Angels finished 92-70, to edge out the Oakland A's by just one game, and the Texas Rangers by only three. Yet, the Seattle Mariners, who finished last in the division, received a historical performance from Ichiro Suziki. The Seattle rightfielder not only led the league with a .372 batting average, but he also established a new major league record by amassing an astounding 262 hits. Had the Mariners not finished 29 games off the pace, Ichiro undoubtedly would have received serious consideration for league MVP honors, instead of finishing seventh in the voting.

Meanwhile, the third-place Rangers featured three players who deserved a certain amount of consideration as well. Third baseman Hank Blalock hit 32 home runs, drove in 110 runs, and scored another 107. First baseman Mark Teixeira led the team with 38 home runs and 112 runs batted in, while also scoring 101 runs and batting .281. And shortstop Michael Young homered 22 times, knocked in 99 runs, scored 114 others, batted .313, and finished second in the league with 216 hits. He finished eighth in the MVP balloting.

Mark Mulder won 17 games for the second-place A's, but his record was tarnished somewhat by his rather high 4.43 earned run average. The Oakland offense was led by centerfielder Mark Kotsay, leftfielder Eric Byrnes, third baseman Eric Chavez, and designated hitter Erubiel Durazo. Kotsay batted .314 and led the team with 190 hits. Byrnes hit 20 homers, batted .283 and scored 91 runs. Chavez homered 29 times, drove in 77 runs, and scored 87 others. Durazo hit 22 homers, knocked in 88 runs, and finished among the league leaders with a .321

batting average. But none of those players could be considered serious MVP candidates.

The division champion Anaheim Angels possessed rather mediocre starting pitching, with all but one member of their rotation finishing with an earned run average well in excess of 4.00. Even Bartolo Colon, who led the staff with 18 victories, struggled much of the time, finishing the year with an unimpressive 5.01 earned run average. One of the team's greatest strengths, though, was its bullpen, which featured two of the league's best relievers.

Fireballing setup man Francisco Rodriguez finished 4-1, with 12 saves, an outstanding 1.82 earned run average, and an amazing 123 strikeouts in 84 innings of work. Closer Troy Percival saved 33 games while pitching to a 2.90 earned run average.

The Anaheim offense, which finished seventh in the league in runs scored (836), and also placed tenth in the circuit in home runs (162), was far from imposing. But the Angels tied Boston for the highest team batting average (.282), and their lineup included several role players who contributed greatly to the success of the team. Versatile Chone Figgins played numerous positions in the field, batted .296, scored 83 runs, and stole 34 bases. Pesky shortstop David Eckstein batted .276 and scored 92 runs. First baseman Darin Erstad hit .295 and crossed the plate 79 times. Outfielder Jose Guillen provided much needed power in the middle of the lineup, hitting 27 home runs and driving in 104 runs.

But Anaheim's most valuable player was unquestionably Vladimir Guerrero, who was also the league's MVP. Leading the team in virtually every offensive category, the big rightfielder finished among the league leaders with 39 home runs, 126 runs batted in, 206 hits, a .337 batting average, and a .598 slugging percentage, and he led the A.L. with 124 runs scored and 366 total bases. It was largely Guerrero's great season that enabled the Angels to overcome numerous injuries that beset them over the course of the regular season. Those injuries greatly limited the availability of some of their other star players. Slugging third baseman Troy Glaus appeared in only 58 games and knocked in just 42 runs, while leftfielder Garret Anderson, who drove in 116 runs the previous year, knocked in only 75 runs in 112 games. Guerrero further solidified his MVP credentials by leading the Angels to the division title with an epic performance down the stretch. He hit 11 home runs, knocked in 25 runs, scored another 25, and batted .363 during the season's final month.

Guerrero's exceptional play over the final few weeks of the campaign most certainly justified his selection by the writers as the league's Most Valuable Player over New York's Gary Sheffield, who finished second in the balloting.

NATIONAL LEAGUE

The Atlanta Braves captured the National League East title for the tenth consecutive year in 2004, winning 96 games, to finish 10 games ahead of second-place Philadelphia. The defending world champion Florida Marlins finished a disappointing third in the division, 13 games behind Atlanta. Yet the Marlins featured one of the game's brightest young stars in 21-year-old Miguel Cabrera. In his first full major league season, Cabrera hit 33 home runs, drove in 112 runs, scored 101 others, and batted .294.

In spite of their distant second-place finish, the Phillies boasted the division's top offense. Their 215 home runs were the second most in the league, and their 840 runs scored represented the third highest total. Philadelphia's attack was led by the trio of Jimmy Rollins, Bobby Abreu, and Jim Thome. Rollins batted .289, stole 30 bases, and placed among the league leaders with 119 runs scored. Abreu hit 30 homers, knocked in 105 runs, batted .301, and finished near the top of the league rankings with 118 runs scored and 127 walks. Thome homered 42 times, drove in 105 runs, and scored 97 others.

Yet it was the Braves who came out on top in the division, due largely to their superior pitching. Atlanta's staff posted a league-best 3.74 team earned run average, and it featured four solid starters. Jaret Wright and Russ Ortiz each won 15 games, John Thomson chipped in with 14 victories, and Mike Hampton added another 13 wins. Atlanta's top pitcher, though, was John Smoltz, who saved 44 games coming out of the bullpen.

Still, the Braves were not without their fair share of offensive weapons. Chipper Jones hit 30 home runs and knocked in 96 runs. Catcher Johnny Estrada batted .314 and drove home 76 runs. Rafael Furcal batted .279, scored 103 runs, and stole 29 bases. Andruw Jones hit 29 homers and knocked in 91 runs. However, the most important man in the Atlanta lineup was J.D. Drew, who replaced the departed Gary Sheffield in right field and helped to fill his spot in the batting order. Drew hit 31 homers, drove in 93 runs, batted .305, and finished among the league leaders with 118 runs scored and 118 bases on balls. For his efforts, the writers placed Drew sixth in the MVP balloting at the end of the year.

The Western Division was easily the most competitive in the league, with three teams remaining in contention most of the year. With 93 victories, the Dodgers eventually prevailed, finishing two games ahead of the runner-up Giants and six games in front of third-place San Diego. San Francisco also just missed out on the wild-card, finishing just one game behind the Astros in the race for the final playoff spot.

The third-place Padres featured one of the league's best pitchers in young righthander Jake Peavy, who finished 15-6 with a league-leading 2.27 earned run average. Also outstanding was veteran righthander Jason Schmidt, who compiled a record of 18-7 and a 3.20 earned run average for the Giants. But San Francisco's most valuable player was unquestionably Barry Bonds. In only 373 official at-bats, Bonds hit 45 home runs, drove in 101 runs, and scored 129 others, while leading the league with a .362 batting average, an .812 slugging percentage, and an unbelievable .609 on-base percentage. Bonds also established a new major league record by walking 232 times over the course of the season. He certainly had to be considered a leading candidate for league MVP honors.

The first-place Dodgers had the league's best closer in Eric Gagne. The hard-throwing righthander finished 7-3 with a 2.19 earned run average, and he converted 45 of his 47 save opportunities. Gagne also struck out 114 batters in only 82 innings of work. The Los Angeles lineup featured shortstop Cesar Izturis and first baseman Shawn Green. Izturis batted .288, scored 90 runs, and stole 25 bases. Green hit 28 homers, knocked in 86 runs, and scored another 92. The Dodgers' dominant player was third baseman Adrian Beltre, who carried the team's offense much of the year. Beltre led the league with 48 homers, finished among the leaders with 121 runs batted in, a .334 batting average, and a .629 slugging percentage, scored 104 runs, and collected 200 hits. He clearly deserved serious MVP consideration as well.

The Cardinals dominated the N.L. Central, finishing the year with a major-league best 105-57 record, 13 games in front of the second-place Astros. Houston, with 92 victories, advanced into the postseason as the league's wild-card entry. The Cubs, who finished third in the division with a record of 89-73, featured several of the division's top performers. Righthander Carlos Zambrano was one of the league's better pitchers, compiling a record of 16-8, with a 2.75 earned run average. Outfielder Moises Alou and third baseman Aramis Ramirez led Chicago's offense. Alou hit 39 home runs, knocked in 106 runs, scored another 106, and batted .293. Ramirez clubbed 36 homers, drove in 103 runs, scored 99 others, and batted .318.

The second-place Astros possessed the best tandem of pitchers in the league in Roy Oswalt and Roger Clemens. Oswalt led all N.L. hurlers with 20 wins, against 10 losses, while pitching to a 3.49 earned run average and striking out 206 batters. Clemens was even better, compiling a record of 18-4, with an earned run average of 2.98 and 218 strikeouts. For his efforts, Clemens was presented with his record seventh Cy Young Award at season's end. He also finished eighth in the league MVP voting. Finishing just ahead of Clemens, in seventh place, was Houston outfielder Lance Berkman, who led the team in most offensive categories. Berkman hit 30 home runs, knocked in 106 runs, scored 104 others, batted .316, and walked 127 times.

Nevertheless, the Cardinals were the division's strongest team, and they were the league's prohibitive favorite heading into the playoffs. Possessing solid pitching and the N.L.'s top offense, St. Louis was easily the N.L.'s most well-balanced team. The St. Louis pitching staff posted the second lowest team earned run average in the league (3.75), and it featured the circuit's deepest starting rotation, with all five members finishing in double-digits in victories. Jeff Suppan led the team with 16 wins, while Jason Marquis, Matt Morris, and Chris Carpenter each won 15 games. Woody Williams chipped in with 11 victories. Meanwhile, closer Jason Isringhausen tied for the league lead, with 47 saves.

On offense, the Cardinals led the league in runs scored (855) and team batting average (.278), and they finished third in home runs (214).

Their attack was led by the formidable threesome of Jim Edmonds, Scott Rolen, and Albert Pujols. Edmonds hit 42 home runs, knocked in 111 runs, scored another 102, batted .301, and collected the seventh Gold Glove of his career for his outstanding play in centerfield. Rolen, despite missing 20 games due to injury, hit 34 homers, drove in 124 runs, scored 109 others, and batted .314, all while playing a Gold Glove caliber third base. Edmonds finished fifth in the MVP voting, while Rolen came in just ahead of him, in fourth place.

The Cardinals' leading MVP candidate was Albert Pujols. Let's look at his numbers, alongside those of the other top two contenders, Adrian Beltre and Barry Bonds:

PLAYER	AB	HITS	RUNS	2B	3B	HR	RBI	AVG	OBP	SLG PCT
Albert Pujols	592	196	**133**	51	2	46	123	.331	.415	.657
Barry Bonds	373	135	129	27	3	45	101	**.362**	**.609**	**.812**
Adrian Beltre	598	200	104	32	0	**48**	121	.334	.388	.629

The overall numbers of Pujols were slightly superior to those compiled by Beltre. Although the two men were extremely close in most statistical categories, Pujols had a decided advantage in runs scored and doubles. Yet, he finished third in the balloting, while Beltre came in second. The writers undoubtedly factored into the equation the better supporting cast Pujols had in St. Louis, as well as the ease with which the Cardinals captured their division title. Therefore, it would be difficult to argue with their placement of the two players.

Although Bonds collected approximately 200 fewer official at-bats than both Pujols and Beltre, he posted numbers that compared quite favorably to the figures compiled by the other two players in most offensive categories. While he finished with far fewer hits and scored 20 fewer runs than either of his nearest competitors, Bonds hit approximately the same number of home runs, hit for a higher average, and scored almost as many runs as Pujols, while scoring 25 more times than Beltre. Bonds' .812 slugging percentage was almost *200* points higher than the marks posted by Pujols and Beltre, and his record-setting 232 bases on balls enabled him to finish with an on-base percentage that was also some 200 points better than the figures compiled by the other two men.

It is true that both Pujols and Beltre played for division-winning teams, while Bonds' Giants failed to make the playoffs. But Bonds kept his team in the playoff picture until the season's final days, in spite of the fact that he represented the only real threat they had on offense. That last fact more than justifies his selection by the writers as the National League's Most Valuable Player.

2005

AMERICAN LEAGUE

The Chicago White Sox replaced Minnesota atop the American League Central standings in 2005, finishing with a league-best 99-63 record. The Twins, with 83 victories, slumped to third in the division, with the vastly improved Cleveland Indians claiming the second spot, with a record of 93-69.

The young Indians possessed one of the league's best pitching staffs, and also one of the circuit's more potent offenses. Their team earned run average of 3.61 was the lowest in the American League, and their rotation featured four solid starters. Lefthander Cliff Lee compiled a record of 18-5 and a 3.79 earned run average. C.C. Sabathia and Jake Westbrook each won 15 games, and Kevin Millwood posted a league-best 2.86 earned run average, even though he finished just 9-11. Veteran closer Bob Wickman tied for the A.L. lead with 45 saves.

On offense, Cleveland's 207 home runs were the third most in the league, and the team's 790 runs scored represented the fourth highest total. The Indians' attack was led by catcher Victor Martinez, centerfielder Grady Sizemore, and designated hitter Travis Hafner. Martinez hit 20 homers, drove in 80 runs, and batted .305. Sizemore went deep 22 times, knocked in 81 runs, scored 111 others, and batted .289. Hafner led the team with 33 home runs and 108 runs batted in, scored 94 runs, and batted .305. He finished fifth in the league MVP voting.

While possessing a less potent offense than Cleveland, the division champion White Sox boasted an equally impressive pitching staff. Matching the Indians with a league-leading 3.61 team earned run average, Chicago featured the A.L.'s deepest starting rotation. Righthander John Garland led the team with 18 victories, against 10 losses. Mark Buehrle finished 16-8 with an outstanding 3.12 earned run average. Cuban righthander Jose Contreras resurrected himself after an earlier failure with the Yankees, going 15-7 with a 3.61 earned run average. Freddy Garcia won 14 games, and Orlando Hernandez chipped in with another nine victories.

Although not overpowering on offense, the White Sox were extremely well-balanced, featuring seven players with at least 15 home runs, as well as one of the league's top base stealers. Outfielder Scott Podsednik failed to hit a home run during the regular season, but he scored 80 runs and finished second in the A.L. with 59 stolen bases. Aaron Rowand scored 77 runs and played brilliantly in centerfield. Second baseman Tadahito Iguchi hit 15 long balls, drove in 71 runs, and scored another 74. Designated hitter Carl Everett finished with 23 home runs and 87 runs batted in. Rightfielder Jermaine Dye hit 31 homers and knocked in 86 runs. Chicago's primary power threat was first baseman Paul Konerko, who led the team with 40 home runs, 100 runs batted in, and 98 runs scored. Konerko ended up finishing sixth in the MVP voting.

The Los Angeles Angels of Anaheim captured the Western Division title for the second straight year, finishing 95-67, seven games ahead of runner-up Oakland. Yet, the third-place Rangers, who finished 16 games off the pace, had the division's top offense, leading the American League with 260 home runs and placing third in runs scored, with 865. Texas featured two of the league's best hitters in shortstop Michael Young and first baseman Mark Teixeira. Young hit 24 home runs, drove in 91 runs, scored 114 others, and led the circuit with 221 hits and a .331 batting average. Teixeira batted .301, scored 112 runs, and placed among the league leaders with 43 homers and 144 runs batted in. Teixeira finished seventh in the MVP balloting.

The second-place Athletics were not nearly as strong as the Rangers on offense. Their primary threat was third baseman Eric Chavez, who led the team with 27 home runs, 101 runs batted in, and 92 runs scored. But Oakland's deep pitching staff enabled them to remain in the divisional race much of the year. Barry Zito and Dan Haren led the starters with 14 victories apiece. Joe Blanton won another 12 games, and Kirk Saarloos and Rich Harden each chipped in with 10 victories. A.L. Rookie of the Year Huston Street saved 23 games, won another five, and compiled a brilliant 1.72 earned run average.

The division-winning Angels were really no stronger than Oakland on offense. In fact, they hit eight fewer home runs and scored 11 fewer runs over the course of the season. But, they too had a great deal of depth in their starting rotation, as well as the league's best bullpen. Promoted to the role of closer during the off-season, Francisco Rodriguez struck out 91 batters in 67 innings of work, and he tied for the league lead with 45 saves. He was ably assisted by setup man Steve Shields, who won 10 games, while pitching to a 2.75 earned run average, and Brendan Donnelly, who picked up another nine victories in relief. Among the starters, Ervin Santana and Paul Byrd each won 12 games, while John Lackey finished 14-5 with a 3.44 earned run average. The Angels' best pitcher was Bartolo Colon, who compiled a record of 21-8, to lead all A.L. hurlers in victories, while pitching to a 3.48 earned run average. For his efforts, Colon was presented with the league's Cy Young Award at the end of the season.

In spite of his outstanding performance, Colon was not the Angels' most valuable player during the regular season. That distinction fell to rightfielder Vladimir Guerrero for the second consecutive year. There were certainly others who made major offensive contributions to the team over the course of the season. Chone Figgins batted .290, scored 113 runs, and stole 62 bases. Garret Anderson hit 17 homers and drove in 96 runs. But Guerrero once again drove the Angels to the division title, leading them in most offensive categories in the process. Guerrero hit 32 home runs, knocked in 108 runs, scored 95 others, and batted .317. Yet, those numbers were only good enough to earn him a third-place finish in the MVP balloting.

The top two vote-getters came from the American League East, which featured the circuit's closest divisional race. New York and Boston battled right down to the wire, with both teams finishing with identical 95-67 records. But, since the Yankees fared slightly better in the head-to-head competition between the two teams, they clinched the division on the next-to-last day of the regular season. The Red Sox had to settle for the wild-card.

The two squads were extremely similar in that they possessed outstanding offenses, but only mediocre pitching staffs. New York's team earned run average of 4.52 was just the ninth best in the league, while Boston's mark of 4.74 placed them eleventh in the rankings.

However, the Yankees finished second in the circuit in runs scored (886), batting average (.276), and home runs (229), while the Red Sox led the A.L. with 910 runs scored and a .281 team batting average, while placing fifth in home runs, with 199.

With Curt Schilling injured much of the year, Boston's most effective starters were Tim Wakefield and David Wells. The knuckleballing Wakefield led the team with 16 victories, against 12 losses, while Wells compiled a record of 15-7.

On offense, catcher Jason Varitek hit 22 homers and drove in 70 runs for the Sox. Shortstop Edgar Renteria batted .276 and scored 100 runs. Centerfielder Johnny Damon batted .316, scored 117 runs, and collected 197 hits. Leftfielder Manny Ramiriz finished among the league leaders with 45 home runs and 144 runs batted in, batted .292, and scored 112 runs. Ramirez placed fourth in the MVP voting.

Finishing two spots ahead of Ramirez in the balloting was the man considered by many to be the league's Most Valuable Player in 2005. David Ortiz had a monstrous year for the Red Sox, not only putting up prolific offensive numbers, but clearly establishing himself as the league's best clutch hitter. Ortiz led the A.L. with 148 runs batted in, finished among the leaders with 47 home runs, 119 runs scored, and a .604 slugging percentage, and batted an even .300. Furthermore, he provided numerous clutch hits over the course of the season, excelling in "close and late-game" situations. Those were situations in which Ortiz came to bat in the seventh inning or later, with either the score tied, his team ahead by one run, or the potential tying run on-deck. In 78 such instances, Ortiz batted .346, with 11 home runs, 33 runs batted in, and a .447 on-base percentage.

During the season's final month, Ortiz hit 11 homers, knocked in 30 runs, and batted .321, and he batted .352 with runners in scoring position over the course of the season. Supporters of Ortiz felt those numbers should have been good enough to earn him the MVP Award at season's end.

Still, there were others who pointed to the fact that Ortiz rarely played the field, since he served primarily as Boston's designated hitter. They also noted that a member of the division-winning Yankees had an equally impressive year.

Like Boston, New York had a plethora of talent on its roster. Lefthander Randy Johnson, acquired from Arizona during the off-season, led the staff with 17 victories and 211 strikeouts. Closer Mariano Rivera saved 43 games and won another seven, while compiling a brilliant 1.38 earned run average and allowing only 50 hits in 78 innings of work. On offense, Jason Giambi hit 32 homers and drove in 87 runs. Jorge Posada homered 19 times and knocked in 71 runs. Rookie second baseman Robinson Cano batted .297 and scored 78 runs. Derek Jeter batted .309 and finished among the league leaders with 202 hits and 122 runs scored. Hideki Matsui hit 23 homers, knocked in 116 runs, scored 108 others, and batted .305. Gary Sheffield hit 34 long balls, drove in 123 runs, amd scored another 104. He finished eighth in the league MVP voting.

But the man considered by most people to be the Yankees' most valuable player was Alex Rodriguez, who the writers named the American League's MVP at the end of the year. Let's look at his numbers, alongside those of David Ortiz, his main competition:

PLAYER	AB	HITS	RUNS	2B	3B	HR	RBI	AVG	OBP	SLG PCT
David Ortiz	601	180	119	40	1	47	**148**	.300	.397	.604
Alex Rodriguez	605	194	**124**	29	1	**48**	130	.321	.421	**.610**

In virtually the same number of at-bats, the two men finished extremely close in most statistical categories. The only decided advantages went to Ortiz in doubles and runs batted in, and to Rodriguez in batting average and on-base percentage. While Rodriguez held an edge in most other areas, the discrepancy was relatively minor.

Ortiz, though, built a huge reputation during the season as the league's best clutch hitter. Rodriguez also hit well under pressure, batting .290 with runners in scoring position, including a .302 average with two outs. But Ortiz's average in such situations was 62 points higher, and his success in late-game pressure situations has already been documented. Therefore, even though Rodriguez led the league in more statistical categories, Ortiz was the superior hitter of the two.

Yet, the Yankees won the division, doing so in their 161st game by defeating the Red Sox 8-4 at Fenway Park. Rodriguez went 4-for-5 in that contest, with a home run, to cap off an outstanding final month of the season in which he hit eight home runs, knocked in 25 runs, scored 26 others, and batted .330. A-Rod also stole 21 bases over the course of the year, as compared to the one that Ortiz swiped for Boston. Therefore, even though Ortiz was perhaps the slightly better hitter of the two, it is extremely debatable as to whether or not he was the superior all-around offensive player. Even more significant is the fact that Ortiz played the field in only 34 of the 159 games in which he appeared. Meanwhile, Rodriguez played 155 games at third base for New York, commiting a total of only 13 errors. Since Rodriguez also played the field, he was a far more complete player than Ortiz, and he was also more valuable to his team. The writers felt the same way, giving Rodriguez a total of 331 points in the MVP balloting, to the total of 307 they awarded Ortiz.

NATIONAL LEAGUE

The San Diego Padres were the best of a weak National League West in 2005, capturing the division title despite finishing the regular season with a record of just 82-80. The Arizona Diamondbacks, with 77 victories, finished five games back, while the San Francisco Giants, who had to play without Barry Bonds for virtually the entire year, came in third, seven games off the pace.

Bonds' impact on the Giants became more apparent than ever when the injured superstar sat out all but 14 games during the 2005 campaign. San Francisco finished second in the league the previous year, with 850 runs scored. But, without Bonds in their lineup, the otherwise feeble Giants' offense managed to score only 649 runs—the second lowest total in the N.L.

The absence of Bonds from San Francisco's lineup, along with the failure of the defending division champion Dodgers to win more than 71 games, enabled the decidedly mediocre Padres to sneak into the playoffs. The Padres finished just 13th in the league in runs scored (684), and they placed sixth in team earned run average (4.13). Jake Peavy was the team's most effective starting pitcher, finishing the year with a 13-7 record and a 2.88 earned run average. Closer Trevor Hoffman had a hand in more than half the team's victories, saving 43 games and winning another one. Outfielder Brian Giles was easily San Diego's most productive player on offense, leading the team with 83 runs batted in, 92 runs scored, and a .301 batting average. He finished ninth in the league MVP voting.

While the teams out west struggled the entire year, the N.L. East was the league's strongest division from top-to-bottom. Not one team finished below .500 and, with first-place Atlanta compiling a record of 90-72, virtually every squad remained in contention until the final two weeks of the season. The runner-up Phillies, with 88 victories, finished just two games back, with both Florida and New York finishing seven games off the pace.

The Marlins featured two of the league's best young players in pitcher Dontrelle Willis and leftfielder Miguel Cabrera. Willis compiled a record of 22-10, to lead all N.L. hurlers in victories. He also led the league with seven complete games and five shutouts, while pitching to an outstanding 2.63 earned run average. Willis ended up finishing second in the Cy Young balloting. Cabrera hit 33 home runs and placed among the league leaders with 116 runs batted in, 106 runs scored, 198 hits, and a .323 batting average. He finished fifth in the league MVP voting. Veteran first baseman Carlos Delgado also had a big year for the Marlins. In his only season in Florida, Delgado hit 33 homers, knocked in 115 runs, and batted .301. He finished right behind Cabrera in the balloting, coming in sixth.

The second-place Phillies had one of the league's top offenses, finishing second in the circuit with 807 runs scored and a .270 team batting average. In his first full season, second baseman Chase Utley hit 28 home runs, drove in 105 runs, scored 93 others, and batted .291. Bobby Abreu homered 24 times, knocked in 102 runs, scored another 104, batted .286, and drew 117 bases on balls. In only 88 games, N.L. Rookie of the Year Ryan Howard hit 22 homers and drove in 63 runs. Shortstop Jimmy Rollins batted .290, scored 115 runs, and stole 41 bases. Outfielder Pat Burrell batted .281 and led the team with 32 homers and 117 runs batted in. Burrell finished seventh in the MVP voting, while Rollins came in tenth.

The Braves were again the division's most well-balanced team, finishing sixth in the league in team earned run average (3.98), while placing fourth in runs scored (769) and home runs (184). Inserted back into the starting rotation, John Smoltz headed the pitching staff, compiling a record of 14-7 and a 3.06 earned run average. Tim Hudson, acquired from Oakland during the off-season, finished 14-9 with a 3.52 earned run average. Atlanta also received a huge lift from righthander Jorge Sosa, who they acquired from Tampa Bay prior to the start of the campaign. Entering the season with a career record of 11-26 and an earned run average well in excess of 5.00, Sosa compiled a record of 13-3, while pitching to an outstanding 2.55 earned run average.

Although not particularly imposing, Atlanta's offense also performed admirably, especially considering the numerous injuries it suffered during the season. Chipper Jones was limited to 109 games at third base, but he still managed to hit 21 home runs, drive in 72 runs, and bat .296. First baseman Adam LaRoche homered 20 times and knocked in 78 runs. Rookie outfielder Jeff Francoeur hit 14 home runs and drove in 45 runs, in just 257 at-bats. Second baseman Marcus Giles batted .291 and scored 104 runs. Shortstop Rafael Furcal batted .284, crossed the plate 100 times, and stole 46 bases. The most potent weapon in Atlanta's arsenal was centerfielder Andruw Jones, who had the most productive season of his career. Jones led the National League with 51 home runs and 128 runs batted in, and he finished among the leaders with a .575 slugging percentage. He also collected his eighth consecutive Gold Glove at the end of the year. Jones' fine season earned him a close second-place finish in the MVP balloting.

The league' Most Valuable Player ended up coming out of the Central Division, where the Cardinals repeated as champions, compiling the best record in the major leagues for the second straight year in the process. Finishing 100-62, St. Louis easily outdistanced the Astros, who became the league's wild-card entry for the second consecutive year by posting a record of 89-73. Yet, the circuit's most dominant player was Chicago first baseman Derrek Lee, who led the National League with a .335 batting average, a .662 slugging percentage, 199 hits, 50 doubles, and 393 total bases. He also placed among the leaders in home runs (46), runs batted in (107), runs scored (120), and on-base percentage (.418). But, with the Cubs finishing fourth in the division, 21 games behind the first-place Cardinals, Lee could do no better than third in the MVP balloting.

Finishing fourth in the voting was Houston third baseman Morgan Ensberg, who helped lead the Astros into the playoffs despite their rather anemic offense. In fact, Houston finished 11th in the league in runs scored (693), ninth in home runs (161), and 14th in batting average (.256). Therefore, Ensberg's 36 homers, 101 runs batted in, 86 runs scored, and .283 batting average were vital to the success of his team.

Perhaps even more important, though, was the presence of three of the league's best pitchers in the Houston starting rotation. Receiving very little in the way of run-support, Roger Clemens posted a record of only 13-8, despite compiling a league-best 1.87 earned run average. Andy Pettitte finished 17-9, with an outstanding 2.39 earned run average. Roy Oswalt led the staff with 20 wins, against 12 losses, while pitching to a 2.94 earned run average.

However, the league's best hurler was Chris Carpenter, who pitched for the division-winning Cardinals. St. Louis had the N.L.'s best pitching staff, leading the circuit with a team earned run average of 3.49, which was slightly better than the mark of 3.51 posted by Houston. Mark Mulder and Jeff Suppan each won 16 games, and Matt Morris contributed another 14 victories. But Carpenter was the staff ace, compiling a brilliant 21-5 record and an outstanding 2.83 earned run average. Those figures earned him the N.L. Cy Young Award at the end of the season and an eighth-place finish in the MVP balloting.

As good as Carpenter was, he was not the Cardinals' most valuable player during the season. Albert Pujols led the team in virtually every offensive category, finishing among the league leaders in several departments as well. Let's look at his numbers, alongside those of the other leading MVP candidates:

PLAYER	AB	HITS	RUNS	2B	3B	HR	RBI	AVG	OBP	SLG PCT
Albert Pujols	591	195	**129**	38	2	41	117	.330	.430	.609
Andruw Jones	586	154	95	24	3	**51**	128	.263	.347	.575
Derrek Lee	594	**199**	120	**50**	3	46	107	**.335**	.418	**.662**

Lee's overall numbers were quite comparable to those compiled by Pujols. The Cubs first baseman held a slight statistical edge in most categories, although Pujols was the slightly better run-producer. But, with Chicago finishing 21 games behind St. Louis in the standings, it would be difficult to consider Lee the more valuable player of the two men.

Jones led the league in home runs and runs batted in, but Pujols posted significantly better numbers in virtually every other category. He scored 34 more runs, collected 40 more hits, and hit almost 70 points higher. Pujols also finished with an on-base percentage that was some 80 points better, and he compiled a slugging percentage that exceeded Jones' by some 35 points. In short, Pujols was the much better player of the two.

It could be argued that Jones led the Braves to the Eastern Division title, in spite of the numerous injuries that befell them during the regular season. But the Cardinals were ravaged by injuries as well. Third baseman Scott Rolen, so productive one year earlier, appeared in only 56 games due to lingering back problems. In 196 at-bats, he managed only five home runs and 28 runs batted in. Centerfielder Jim Edmonds played through pain much of the year, hitting 29 home runs, but driving in only 89 runs, and batting just .263. As a result, Pujols was the one constant threat in the middle of the St. Louis lineup for most of the year. He was the best player on the best team in the league. As such, he was also the National League's Most Valuable Player. The writers felt so too, awarding him a total of 378 points in the MVP voting. Jones finished second, with 351 total points, while Lee placed third, with 263 points.

2006

AMERICAN LEAGUE

Posting an American League best 97-65 record during the regular season, the Yankees captured their ninth consecutive Eastern Division title in 2006. The Toronto Blue Jays finished a distant second, 10 games back in the standings, with the Boston Red Sox coming in third, 11 games off the pace.

Although the Blue Jays finished well behind New York, their 87 victories represented a seven-game improvement over their win total from the previous season. Contributing greatly to the team's progression were Toronto's three best players. Closer B.J. Ryan, signed as a free agent during the off-season, saved 38 games, while compiling a brilliant 1.37 earned run average and allowing just 42 hits in 72 innings of work. Starter Roy Halladay finished 16-5 with a 3.19 earned run average. Centerfielder Vernon Wells, one of the American League's finest all-around players, hit 32 home runs, drove in 106 runs, scored 91 others, and batted .303. Third baseman Troy Glaus also had a big year for the Blue Jays, knocking in 104 runs and leading the team with 38 home runs and 105 runs scored.

The third-place Red Sox stood atop the division standings much of the year. But they fell well out of contention after numerous injuries caused them to slump badly during the season's final two months. Still, they received outstanding performances from several key players. Jonathan Papelbon established himself as one of the game's best closers, finishing the campaign with 35 saves and a remarkable 0.92 earned run average. Manny Ramirez hit 35 homers, drove in 102 runs, and batted .321. Boston's most dominant player was DH David Ortiz, who batted .287, led the league with 54 home runs and 137 runs batted in, and also placed among the leaders with 115 runs scored and a .636 slugging percentage. Ortiz ended up finishing third in the MVP balloting.

Division-winning New York was also hit hard by injuries that would have devastated a lesser team. Starting outfielders Hideki Matsui and Gary Sheffield both went down during the first six weeks of the season, and they were lost to the team most of the year. Nevertheless, the Yankees led the league with 930 runs scored, and they placed second in the circuit in both home runs (210) and batting average (.285). The Yankees also received a huge lift from second-year pitcher Chien-Ming Wang. The Taiwanese righthander finished 19-6 with a 3.63 earned run average, to place second in the Cy Young voting at season's end.

Overcoming the loss of two of their top hitters, the Yankees' offense carried them much of the year. Jason Giambi hit 37 homers and drove in 113 runs. Jorge Posada homered 23 times and knocked in 93 runs. Johnny Damon provided outstanding productivity out of the leadoff spot, hitting 24 homers, driving in 80 runs, scoring 115 others, and batting .285. Although he frequently struggled in pressure situations, Alex Rodriguez compiled excellent numbers by the end of the year. The third baseman hit 35 homers, led the team with 121 runs batted in, scored 113 times, and batted .290. Despite missing more than a month of the season with a pulled hamstring, second baseman Robinson Cano hit 15 home runs, knocked in 78 runs, and finished third in the A.L. batting race, with an average of .342.

Finishing just ahead of Cano, in second place, was the Yankees' most consistent performer all year, Derek Jeter. The shortstop had perhaps his finest all-around season, batting .343, driving in 97 runs, stealing 34 bases, placing among the league leaders with 118 runs scored and 214 hits, and winning his third straight Gold Glove Award for his outstanding play in the field. Jeter finished a close second in the league MVP balloting.

In the A.L. West, Oakland captured the division title after finishing runner-up to Anaheim the previous two seasons. The A's finished the year 93-69, four games ahead of the second-place Angels. Yet, it was again the Texas Rangers who had the division's best offense. Their lineup featured Michael Young, Mark Teixeira, and Gary Matthews Jr. Young batted. 314, knocked in 103 runs, and finished second in the league with 217 hits. Teixeira led the team with 33 home runs and 110 runs batted in. Matthews batted .313 and led the Rangers with 102 runs scored. But, with Texas finishing third in the division, 13 games out of first, none of the three players could be considered a serious MVP candidate.

Since the Angels finished out of the playoffs for the first time in three years, it would also be difficult to make a strong case for Vladimir Guerrero, even though his numbers were among the most impressive in the league. Guerrero hit 33 home runs, drove in 116 runs, scored another 92, batted .329, and collected 200 hits. But there were other players, some of whom performed for teams that advanced into the postseason, whose numbers were equally impressive. Therefore, Guerrero could do no better than ninth in the MVP voting.

The first-place A's featured one of the league's better pitching staffs, placing fourth in the circuit with a team earned run average of 4.21. Barry Zito and Joe Blanton each won 16 games, while Dan Haren contributed 14 victories. Huston Street saved 37 games coming out of the bullpen.

The Oakland offense was less effective, finishing ninth in the A.L. in runs scored (771) and home runs (175), and placing 13th in batting average (.260). Outfielder Jay Payton batted .296 and scored 78 runs. Catcher Jason Kendall batted .295 and crossed the plate 76 times. Third baseman Eric Chavez batted only .241, but he hit 22 home runs and drove in 72 runs. First baseman Nick Swisher hit 35 homers, knocked in 95 runs, and scored 106 others. Frank Thomas was the team's most productive hitter, and he was certainly its most viable MVP candidate. After coming over from Chicago during the off-season, he provided the A's with a much-needed power bat in the middle of their lineup. Thomas led the team with 39 home runs and 114 runs batted in, while batting .270. For his efforts, the writers placed him fourth in the league MVP balloting.

The eventual winner of that honor came from the A.L. Central— the league's most competitive division. Minnesota, Detroit, and Chicago all won at least 90 games, with the Twins capturing the division title for the fourth time in five years by compiling a record of 96-66. The Tigers remained in first place most of the year, but they faltered down the stretch to finish one game behind the Twins with a record of 95-67. Still, Detroit advanced into the postseason as the league's wild-card entry. The White Sox finished third, six games off the pace, with a 90-72 record.

The disappointing Cleveland Indians, who finished fourth with only 78 wins, had the division's best offense for the second straight year. Placing second in the league with 870 runs scored, Cleveland's attack was led by centerfielder Grady Sizemore and designated hitter Travis Hafner. Sizemore hit 28 homers, drove in 76 runs, batted .290, and led the A.L. with 134 runs scored and 53 doubles. Hafner led the circuit with a .659 slugging percentage, and he also placed among the leaders with 42 home runs and 117 runs batted in, while batting .308 and scoring 100 runs despite missing almost a month of the season with an injury. He finished eighth in the MVP voting.

The defending champion White Sox slipped to third in the division due to their ineffective pitching. In fact, Chicago's team earned run average of 4.61 was exactly one run per-game higher than the mark of 3.61 the staff posted in 2005. The White Sox, though, possessed one of the league's best offenses, leading the A.L. with 236 home runs, placing third with 868 runs scored, and finishing tied for fourth with a team batting average of .280. Paul Konerko, Jim Thome, and Jermaine Dye wielded the most potent bats in the Chicago lineup. Konerko hit 35 homers, knocked in 113 runs, and batted .313. Thome homered 42 times, drove in 109 runs, scored 108 others, and batted .288. Dye finished among the league leaders with 44 home runs and

120 runs batted in, batted .315, and scored 103 runs. He placed fifth in the MVP balloting. Although the Tigers placed only two players in the top 20 of the voting, they were the division's most well-balanced team. With a league-leading team earned run average of 3.84, Detroit had the A.L.'s best pitching staff. The Tigers also had a solid offense that finished third in the league in home runs (203), and that placed sixth in runs scored (822).

Justin Verlander and Kenny Rogers were the team's most effective starting pitchers. Verlander finished 17-9 with a 3.63 earned run average, while Rogers posted a record of 17-8 with a 3.84 earned run average. Hard-throwing Jeremy Bonderman won 14 games and led the staff with 202 strikeouts. Closer Todd Jones saved 37 games, while set-up man Joel Zumaya finished 6-3, with a 1.94 earned run average and 97 strikeouts in 83 innings of work.

On offense, outfielder Marcus Thames hit 26 home runs in only 348 at-bats. Leftfielder Craig Monroe led the team with 28 home runs, knocked in 92 runs, and scored another 89. Third baseman Brandon Inge went deep 27 times, drove in 83 runs, and scored 83 others. Catcher Ivan Rodriguez batted .300 and helped stabilize Detroit's young pitching staff. Rightfielder Magglio Ordonez hit 24 homers, knocked in 104 runs, and batted .298. Shortstop Carlos Guillen hit 19 home runs, drove in 85 runs, and led the team with 100 runs scored, 20 stolen bases, and a .320 batting average. Guillen finished tenth in the MVP voting.

Placing three players in the top ten of the balloting were the division champion Minnesota Twins. The Twins, who led the American League with a .287 team batting average, had a solid offense. They also posted the second lowest team earned run average in the league (3.95). Their staff featured the American League's best pitcher, one of its bright young stars, and one of its premier closers. Joe Nathan converted 36 of his 38 save opportunities, finished a perfect 7-0, compiled a brilliant 1.58 earned run average, and struck out 95 batters in 68 innings of work, while allowing only 38 base hits. Although he missed virtually all of the second half of the season with an injury, 22-year-old lefthander Francisco Liriano established himself as a future star, going 12-3 with a 2.16 earned run average, and striking out 144 batters in 121 innings pitched. Johan Santana won his second Cy Young Award in three seasons, leading all A.L. starters in wins (19), earned run average (2.77), strikeouts (245), and innings pitched (234). His exceptional performance also earned him a seventh-place finish in the MVP balloting.

On offense, Minnesota was led by the quartet of Michael Cuddyer, Torii Hunter, Joe Mauer, and Justin Morneau. Rightfielder Cuddyer hit 24 homers, drove in 109 runs, scored 102 others, and batted .284. In addition to playing an outstanding centerfield, Hunter hit 31 home runs, knocked in 98 runs, scored another 86, and batted .278. Mauer, who finished sixth in the MVP voting, and Morneau, who won the award, posted even better numbers.

Let's take a look at their statistics, alongside those of the other leading MVP candidates:

PLAYER	AB	HITS	RUNS	2B	3B	HR	RBI	AVG	OBP	SLG PCT
Frank Thomas	466	126	77	11	0	39	114	.270	.381	.545
David Ortiz	558	160	115	29	2	**54**	**137**	.287	.413	.636
Jermaine Dye	539	170	103	27	3	44	120	.315	.385	.622
Derek Jeter	623	214	118	39	3	14	97	.343	.417	.483
Justin Morneau	592	190	97	37	1	34	130	.321	.375	.559
Joe Mauer	521	181	86	36	4	13	84	**.347**	.429	.507

A valid argument could be waged on behalf of any of the six men, and a strong case could also be made for Johan Santana. Thomas, Jeter, Morneau, Mauer, and Santana all played for division winners. Ortiz posted the most impressive power numbers, and he was the league's most feared hitter. Dye also compiled some extremely impressive numbers, and he had a tremendous all-around year.

Thomas was the first to be eliminated from consideration. While his powerful bat was clearly the most potent weapon in the Oakland lineup, he batted only .270, he scored just 77 runs, and he never played the field.

Dye was the next to go. His numbers were very good, but they were no better than either Morneau's or Jeter's—both of whom played for first-place teams. Dye hit 10 more home runs than Morneau, and he compiled a significantly higher slugging percentage. But the Minnesota first baseman knocked in 10 more runs, and he finished with comparable numbers in every other statistical category. Dye's power numbers were much better than Jeter's. He hit 30 more home runs, drove in 23 more runs, and finished with a much higher slugging percentage. But the New York shortstop scored 15 more runs, accumulated many more hits and doubles, stole many more bases (34 to 7), and compiled a significantly higher batting average and on-base percentage. Jeter also played the more demanding defensive position of the two.

Ortiz was the next one to be eliminated from consideration. His overall statistics were better than anyone else's. But Ortiz had two things working against him. Firstly, after remaining in first place much of the year, his team fell out of the divisional race with several weeks still remaining on the schedule. Ortiz's chances were also damaged for the second consecutive season by the fact that he was predominantly a designated hitter. As good as his numbers were, it would be difficult to rank him above Jeter and Mauer, who played the two most demanding defensive positions on the diamond.

Santana was the next player to go. The Minnesota lefthander was the league's most dominant player during the regular season, winning the pitcher's triple crown and leading all A.L. hurlers in four different statistical categories. But Santana's numbers did not stand out enough to enable him to wrest the award away from three players who fielded their positions for their teams every day. Santana finished 19-6, with a 2.77 earned run average and 245 strikeouts. Those were certainly fine numbers. But they did not compare to Pedro Martinez's 1999 figures that made him the choice here for that year's MVP (23-4, 2.07 earned run average, 313 strikeouts).

As a result, we are left with Jeter, Morneau, and Mauer. In comparing Jeter's numbers to Mauer's, the two players were extremely close in most categories. Mauer had a slight edge in batting average, on-base percentage, and slugging percentage. Jeter, though, drove in 13 more runs, scored 32 more times, and accumulated 33 more hits. As a catcher, Mauer played an even more demanding defensive position than Jeter. Furthermore, he became the first American League receiver in history to lead the league in hitting.

But the Yankee shortstop had an edge in that he won a Gold Glove Award and appeared in 14 more games for his team (154 to 140). Jeter had an additional advantage in that he was clearly his team's most valuable player. While it is true that Johnny Damon, Robinson Cano, and Jorge Posada all had fine seasons, and that Alex Rodriguez posted impressive offensive numbers, it was Jeter who held the Yankees together after they lost Hideki Matsui and Gary Sheffield for virtually the entire year. He was New York's most consistent hitter, their emotional leader, and their best all-around player. Meanwhile, it is extremely debatable as to whether or not Mauer was even the best player on his own team.

A far more compelling argument could be made on behalf of Mauer's Minnesota teammate, Justin Morneau. Although the first baseman played a less-demanding position in the field than Mauer, his overall offensive numbers were better than the catcher's. They were also extremely comparable to Jeter's. Jeter finished well ahead in batting average, runs scored, hits, and on-base percentage, but Morneau hit 20 more home runs, compiled a much higher slugging percentage, and knocked in 33 more runs.

Jeter's importance to the Yankees, especially after the losses of Gary Sheffield and Hideki Matsu, has already been documented. However, Morneau's contributions to the Twins were equally significant. The Minnesota first baseman struggled during the first two months of the season, batting only .235, with just five home runs and 23 runs batted in. But Morneau posted the highest batting average in the major leagues after June 8 (.362). He also had the most hits in baseball (145), and the most runs batted in in the American League. Minnesota's record stood at 25-33 on June 7. But, after Morneau caught fire, the team posted the best record in the major leagues, going 71-33 after June 8.

It could be argued that Morneau received a tremendous amount of support from Mauer and Santana, who finished sixth and seventh, respectively, in the MVP voting. Yet, despite the losses of Sheffield and Matsui, Jeter had an excellent supporting cast in New York. Alex Rodriguez, Johnny Damon, Jason Giambi, Jorge Posada, and Robinson Cano all put up outstanding offensive numbers, with the first three members of that group all placing in the top 15 of the MVP balloting. Furthermore, even with the losses of two of their top sluggers, the Yankees still had a far more potent offense than the Twins. New York finished well ahead of Minnesota in both runs scored (930 to 801) and home runs (210 to 143). Therefore, it would seem that Morneau's offensive contributions to the Twins were every bit as important as Jeter's were to the Yankees.

Perhaps most important, though, is the fact that Minnesota finished first in the league's most competitive division. The Twins came from behind to edge out the Tigers for the Central Division title in the season's final days. Meanwhile, the Yankees all but wrapped up the A.L. East by early September. That last fact emphasizes the significance of Morneau's achievements.

Derek Jeter entered the league MVP voting as a slight favorite to win the award, and he certainly would not have been a bad choice. But the writers made the correct decision when they gave Justin Morneau 320 total points, to Jeter's total of 306 points.

NATIONAL LEAGUE

The San Diego Padres won 22 of their final 31 games to capture their second consecutive N.L. West title in 2006. San Diego and Los Angeles both finished the regular season with identical 88-74 records, but the Padres claimed first-place on the strength of their better divisional record. The Dodgers, who also played well down the stretch, winning nine of their last ten contests, had to settle for the wild-card.

The Dodgers' team earned run average of 4.23 was the fourth best in the league, and their staff featured two of the circuit's better starting pitchers. Brad Penny finished 16-9, while Derek Lowe went 16-8, with a solid 3.63 earned run average.

Los Angeles also finished fourth in the league in runs scored (820), while posting the N.L.'s highest team batting average (.276). The Dodgers' offense was led by Rafael Furcal, J.D. Drew, and Nomar Garciaparra. Furcal batted .300 and led the team with 37 stolen bases, 196 hits, and 113 runs scored. Drew batted .283, hit 20 homers, and drove in 100 runs. Garciaparra hit 20 homers, knocked in 93 runs, and batted .303.

The division-winning Padres had a less potent offense than the Dodgers, placing 13th in the N.L. in runs scored (731), and finishing 10th in team batting average (.263). Their top two offensive performers were first baseman Adrian Gonzalez and outfielder Mike Cameron. Gonzalez hit 24 home runs, drove in 82 runs, scored 83 others, and batted .304. Cameron went deep 22 times, knocked in 83 runs, scored another 88, and stole 25 bases.

The Padres' strength lay in their pitching staff, which posted the league's lowest team earned run average (3.87). Woody Williams finished 12-5, with a 3.65 earned run average, while Chris Young went 11-5, with an earned run average of 3.46. Although he finished just 11-14, Jake Peavy led the team with 202 innings pitched and 215 strikeouts. Closer Trevor Hoffman saved 46 games, while compiling an outstanding 2.14 earned run average. Hoffman finished tenth in the league MVP voting.

Despite posting a decidedly mediocre 83-78 record, the St. Louis Cardinals claimed the Central Division title, edging out the Houston Astros by 1½ games, and finishing 3½ games ahead of the Cincinnati Reds. The runner-up Astros featured one of the league's best pitchers in Roy Oswalt. The righthander finished 15-8, with a league-leading 2.98 earned run average. Houston's top player on offense was Lance Berkman, who batted .315 and placed among the league leaders with 45 home runs, 136 runs batted in, and a .621 slugging percentage. Berkman finished third in the MVP balloting.

The first-place Cardinals also had one of the league's best pitchers in Chris Carpenter. Coming off his 2005 Cy Young campaign, Carpenter compiled a record of 15-8, along with a 3.09 earned run average. But, with the St. Louis staff finishing ninth in the N.L. with a team earned run average of 4.54, it was not the Cardinals' pitching that enabled them to finish just ahead of the Astros in the divisional race. Instead, it was their offense, which was considerably stronger than Houston's. While the Astros finished last in the league with a team batting average of .255, the Cardinals placed fourth in the rankings with a mark of .269. They also outscored Houston by almost 50 runs (781 to 735), to finish sixth in the league in runs scored, as opposed to Houston's 12th-place ranking.

Still, the loss of Jim Edmonds for some 50 games due to injury greatly curtailed the Cardinals' run-production. In just 350 at-bats, Edmonds hit only 19 home runs and drove in just 70 runs. Veteran outfielder Juan Encarnacion picked up some of the slack, hitting 19 home runs and driving in 79 runs. Third baseman Scott Rolen also had a solid season, batting .296 and finishing second on the team with

22 home runs, 95 runs batted in, and 94 runs scored. The team leader in virtually every offensive category was Albert Pujols. Although he missed almost three weeks of the season with an injury of his own, Pujols placed among the league leaders with 49 home runs, 137 runs batted in, 119 runs scored, and a .331 batting average. He also led the circuit with a .671 slugging percentage. Those figures earned him a second-place finish in the league MVP voting.

The man who won the award came out of the N.L. East, where the New York Mets ended Atlanta's 11-year reign as division champions. Posting a league-best 97-65 record, the Mets were the National's League's dominant team during the regular season. They finished 12 games ahead of the runner-up Phillies, and 18 in front of the Braves, who slipped to third in the division. Yet, two of the league's finest performances were turned in by members of teams that finished even further back in the standings.

Washington Nationals outfielder Alfonso Soriano joined the select 40-40 club by finishing among the league leaders with 46 home runs and 41 stolen bases. He also finished near the top of the league rankings in runs scored (119) and total bases (362), while driving in 95 runs and batting .277. Florida Marlins third baseman Miguel Cabrera also had an outstanding season, hitting 26 home runs, knocking in 114 runs, scoring another 112, and placing among the league leaders with 50 doubles, 195 hits, a .339 batting average, a .430 on-base percentage, and a .568 slugging percentage. But Florida finished fourth in the division, 19 games out of first, while Washington came in last, 26 games off the pace. Therefore, Cabrera could do no better than fifth in the MVP voting, while Soriano was fortunate to finish sixth in the balloting.

The third-place Braves had one of the league's most potent offenses, leading the circuit with 222 home runs and placing second in runs scored (849) and batting average (.270). But, with longtime pitching coach Leo Mazzone accepting a lucrative offer to join the Baltimore Orioles during the off-season, the Atlanta pitching staff faltered badly. Their team earned run average of 4.60 placed them in the bottom half of the league rankings, causing Atlanta to finish below .500 for the first time in 16 seasons. As a result, the extremely productive year turned in by 2005 MVP runner-up Andruw Jones (41 home runs, 129 runs batted in, 107 runs scored) earned him just an 11th-place finish in the MVP voting.

Meanwhile, the first-place Mets not only possessed one of the league's best lineups, but they also had one of the circuit's more solid pitching staffs. Their team earned run average of 4.15 was the third best in the N.L., and their bullpen was as deep as any in the league. Closer Billy Wagner saved 40 games, while striking out 94 batters in 72 innings of work. Chad Bradford won four games in relief, Duaner Sanchez another five, and Pedro Feliciano went 7-2 with an outstanding 2.09 earned run average. Among the starters, Tom Glavine and Steve Trachsel each won 15 games, while Pedro Martinez and Orlando Hernandez chipped in with nine victories apiece.

On offense, the Mets finished third in the league in runs scored (834), and they placed fourth in home runs (200). Catcher Paul LoDuca batted .318 and scored 80 runs. First baseman Carlos Delgado hit 38 home runs, drove in 114 runs, and scored 89 others. Third baseman David Wright hit 26 homers, knocked in 116 runs, scored another 96, and batted .311. He finished ninth in the MVP balloting.

New York's top two candidates for the award were centerfielder Carlos Beltran and shortstop Jose Reyes. Beltran batted .275 and led the team with 41 home runs, 116 runs batted in, and 127 runs scored. Reyes was the Mets' offensive catalyst, providing them with a dynamic presence at the top of their batting order. Reyes hit 19 home runs, knocked in 81 runs, batted .300, finished among the league leaders with 122 runs scored and 194 hits, and led the N.L. with 17 triples and 64 stolen bases. It could be argued that, in spite of Beltran's superior run-production, Reyes was actually the team's most valuable player. Yet, Beltran finished fourth in the league MVP voting, while Reyes came in seventh.

Two of the leading contenders for the MVP trophy played for the second-place Phillies, who had a lineup that rivaled that of New York. In fact, Philadelphia led the National League with 865 runs scored, and finished third with 216 home runs. Outfielder Pat Burrell hit 29 homers and drove in 95 runs. Shortstop Jimmy Rollins homered 25 times, knocked in 83 runs, stole 36 bases, and finished among the league leaders with 127 runs scored. Second baseman Chase Utley was even better. He hit 32 home runs, drove in 102 runs, batted .309, collected 203 hits, and led the league with 131 runs scored. Utley finished eighth in the MVP balloting.

The man who won the award was Philadelphia first baseman Ryan Howard. A look at his numbers, alongside those of MVP runner-up Albert Pujols, clearly indicates that the two men were the National League's dominant players in 2006:

PLAYER	AB	HITS	RUNS	2B	3B	HR	RBI	AVG	OBP	SLG PCT
Albert Pujols	535	177	119	33	1	49	137	.331	.431	.671
Ryan Howard	581	182	104	25	1	58	149	.313	.425	.659

Howard and Pujols finished first and second in the N.L. in all the power-related statistical categories, and they also placed among the leaders in batting average, on-base percentage, and total bases.

In comparing the numbers compiled by the two men, Howard hit nine more home runs and knocked in 12 more runs than Pujols. But the St. Louis first baseman fiinished slightly ahead of Howard in most other statistical categories. It could be argued that Howard had a better offensive supporting cast in Philadelphia than Pujols had in St. Louis. After all, the Phillies hit 32 more home runs and scored 84 more runs than the Cardinals, and Howard had Jimmy Rollins and Chase Utley hitting immediately ahead of him in the Philadelphia lineup. But Pat Burrell, who usually followed Howard in the batting order, didn't instill fear in most opposing pitchers. Burrell hit 29 homers and drove in 95 runs, but he also batted only .258 and struck out 131 times in just 462 official at-bats. Opposing managers very much preferred to take their chances with Burrell, often choosing to pitch around Howard with men on base. The end result was a total of 108 bases on balls for Howard over the course of the season, and fewer and fewer opportunities for him to drive in runs as the year progressed. Howard received a total of 77 walks after the All-Star break.

Meanwhile, Albert Pujols generally had Scott Rolen hitting behind him in St. Louis. Rolen was a far more complete hitter than Burrell. The Cardinals third baseman hit 22 homers, knocked in 95 runs, batted .296, and struck out only 69 times. Since the thought of facing Rolen with men on base was not an appealing one for most managers, they frequently chose to pitch to Pujols in such situations.

Pujols walked a total of 92 times, certainly a substantial number. But he had many more opportunities to drive in runs than Howard.

It could also be said that Pujols' Cardinals finished first in a very close divisional race, while Howard's Phillies failed to advance into the postseason. But Philadelphia's 85-77 record was actually better than the Cardinals' mark of 83-78. Furthermore, while it is true that Houston finished just 1½ games behind St. Louis in the Central Division, the race wasn't really as close as the final standings would seem to indicate. The Cardinals had a 6½ game lead over the Astros with 10 games remaining on the schedule. But the Cards won only three of their final 10 contests, allowing the Astros, who went 8-2 over the same stretch, to get back into the divisional race.

Meanwhile, Howard helped keep the Phillies in playoff contention until the season's final days. Philadelphia finished just three games behind the Dodgers in the race for the wild-card. Therefore, Howard's tremendous performance was absolutely essential to any playoff aspirations the Phillies had, while Pujols' contributions were less vital to the Cardinals' playoff chances. It would have been difficult to argue with the writers had they selected Pujols as the league's Most Valuable Player. But they made the correct choice when they named Howard instead, giving him a total of 388 points, to the total of 347 points they awarded Pujols.

2007

AMERICAN LEAGUE

After failing to advance to the postseason the previous year, the Los Angeles Angels of Anaheim reclaimed the top spot in the A.L. West in 2007, posting a regular-season record of 94-68 to finish eight games ahead of the second-place Seattle Mariners. Still, the Mariners featured the division's best hitter, as well as its most effective relief pitcher. Ichiro Suzuki moved from rightfield to centerfield at the start of the season, but clearly did not permit the defensive shift to affect his performance at the plate. Ichiro placed second in the league rankings with a .351 batting average, he led the circuit with 238 base hits, and he also finished among the leaders with 111 runs scored and 37 stolen bases. Closer J.J. Putz tied for second in the league with 40 saves, while finishing 6-1 with a 1.38 earned run average and allowing only 37 hits in 72 innings of work. He also struck out 82 batters while walking only 13. Suzuki finished eighth in the MVP balloting, while Putz came in 13th.

The division-winning Angels had an outstanding closer of their own in bullpen ace Francisco Rodriguez. The 25-year-old righthander saved 40 games, won another five, and compiled a 2.81 earned run average. Rodriguez struck out 90 batters in 67 innings of work, and he allowed the opposition just 50 hits. The Los Angeles pitching staff compiled the fifth best team earned run average in the league (4.23), and it featured two of the circuit's top starters. John Lackey finished 19-9 with a league-leading 3.01 earned run average. Kelvim Escobar was almost as effective, going 18-7 with an earned run average of 3.40.

On offense, the Angels did not have a great deal of power, finishing 12th in the league with just 123 home runs. But they finished fourth in both runs scored (822) and batting average (.284), and they placed second in stolen bases (139). Shortstop Orlando Cabrera batted .301, drove in 86 runs, led the team with 101 runs scored, and won a Gold Glove Award for his outstanding defensive play. Despite missing almost two months of the season due to injury, Garret Anderson knocked in 80 runs and batted .297. After a terrible start, Chone Figgins compiled one of the highest batting averages in baseball over the final four months of the season. The versatile Figgins finished the year with a .330 batting average, 81 runs scored, and 41 stolen bases. Rightfielder Vladimir Guerrero was once again the focal point of the team's offense, leading the club with 27 home runs, and placing among the league leaders with 125 runs batted in, 45 doubles, and a .324 batting average. Those figures were good enough to earn him a third-place finish in the league MVP voting.

The Cleveland Indians rebounded from their disappointing 2006 performance to capture the Central Division title with a record of 96-66. The defending A.L. champion Detroit Tigers finished second, eight games behind Cleveland, while the third-place Twins finished a distant 17 games back.

Justin Morneau, who was named league MVP the previous year, had another solid season for Minnesota, leading the team with 31 home runs and 111 runs batted in. But the Twins' best player was centerfielder Torii Hunter, who homered 28 times, knocked in 107 runs, scored 94 others, and batted .287. However, with Minnesota finishing well out of contention in the divisional race, neither Morneau nor Hunter could be seriously considered for league MVP honors.

The first-place Indians compiled the third lowest team earned run average in the American League (4.05), and they featured two of the circuit's top pitchers. Twenty-three year-old righthander Fausto Carmona finished second in the league with a 3.06 earned run average, and he also placed among the leaders with 19 victories, against only 8 losses. Lefthander C.C. Sabathia was equally impressive, posting a record of 19-7 with a 3.21 earned run average, leading the league with 241 innings pitched, and finishing among the leaders with 209 strikeouts. For his efforts, Sabathia was presented with the A.L. Cy Young Award at the end of the season.

The Indians also possessed one of the league's better offenses, finishing sixth in runs scored (811) and fifth in home runs (178). Their attack was led by Grady Sizemore, Travis Hafner, Jhonny Peralta, Kenny Lofton, and Victor Martinez. Leadoff hitter Sizemore hit 24 home runs, stole 33 bases, and placed among the league leaders with 118 runs scored. Hafner had something of an off-season, but he still managed to hit 24 home runs and drive in 100 runs. Peralta hit 21 homers, scored 87 runs, and provided solid defense at shortstop. Lofton batted .296 and scored 86 runs. Martinez was Cleveland's most consistent performer all year, leading the team with 25 home runs, 114 runs batted in, and a .301 batting average. He finished seventh in the MVP balloting.

After advancing to the World Series the previous year, the Detroit Tigers failed to make the playoffs despite finishing second in the league in batting average (.287) and runs scored (887). The Tigers were kept out of the postseason by their pitching, which wasn't nearly as effective as it was in 2006. Detroit's staff, which led the A.L. with a team earned run average of 3.84 the previous season, faltered badly in 2007, finishing ninth in the circuit with a mark of 4.57. Only Justin Verlander remained an effective pitcher for the team, finishing 18-6 with a 3.66 earned run average.

If not for the Tigers' outstanding offensive production, they would have finished well out of contention. Fine seasons from Carlos Guillen,

Gary Sheffield, Placido Polanco, Curtis Granderson, and Magglio Ordonez kept Detroit in the divisional race for most of the year. Guillen hit 21 home runs, drove in 102 runs, and batted .296. Despite missing almost 30 games due to an injury, Sheffield hit 25 homers and scored 107 runs. Polanco scored 105 runs, finished among the league leaders with a .341 batting average, and played flawless defense in the field, committing no errors in his 141 games at second base. Granderson had a tremendous all-around year for Detroit, batting .302, scoring 122 runs, and compiling 23 home runs, 23 triples, 38 doubles, and 26 stolen bases. He finished tenth in the balloting for league MVP. The man who finished second in the voting was Magglio Ordonez, who had the greatest season of his career. The rightfielder hit 28 home runs, led the league with 54 doubles and a .363 batting average, and placed among the leaders with 139 runs batted in, 117 runs scored, and 216 base hits.

In most years, Ordonez's outstanding performance would have earned him the league MVP Award. But, due to the incredible season turned in by another A.L. slugger, Ordonez was denied that honor.

The eventual winner of the award came out of the league's most competitive division, the A.L. East, where Boston ended New York's nine-year reign as division champions. Compiling a regular-season record of 96-66, the Red Sox edged out the Yankees by just two games, to capture their first division title since 1995. Yet, one of the league's top offensive performers was Carlos Pena, who played for the last-place Tampa Bay Devil Rays. Although the Rays finished 30 games behind Boston in the divisional standings, Pena was one of the league's most productive hitters. The first baseman scored 99 runs and placed among the league leaders with 46 home runs and 121 runs batted in. Pena's outstanding season earned him a ninth-place finish in the league MVP voting.

The Red Sox were the division's most well-balanced team. Their deep pitching staff posted a league-best 3.87 team earned run average, and it featured the circuit's top starter and most dominant reliever. Josh Beckett finished 20-7 to lead all A.L. hurlers in victories, and he also placed near the top of the league rankings with a 3.27 earned run average and 194 strikeouts. He finished runner-up to C.C. Sabathia in the Cy Young voting. Jonathan Papelbon challenged Seattle's J.J. Putz for the distinction of being the league's top closer. The hard-throwing righthander saved 37 games, compiled a 1.85 earned run average, and struck out 84 batters in 58 innings of work, while allowing just 30 base hits. Boston's starting rotation also included Japanese import Daisuke Matsuzaka and veteran knuckleballer Tim Wakefield. Matsuzaka won 15 games and finished among the league leaders with 201 strikeouts. Wakefield finished second to Beckett on the Boston staff with 17 victories.

The Red Sox also possessed one of the league's top offenses, placing third in the league rankings with 867 runs scored, and posting the fifth highest team batting average, with a mark of .279. A.L. Rookie of the Year Dustin Pedroia had an outstanding year for Boston at second base. After starting off the season slowly, Pedroia ended up batting .317 and scoring 86 runs. Kevin Youkilis struggled somewhat during the season's second half, but he finished the year with a .288 batting average, 83 runs batted in, and 85 runs scored. He also played errorless ball in his 135 games at first base. Manny Ramirez wasn't nearly as productive as he was in past seasons, but the enigmatic outfielder still batted .296 and drove in 88 runs. The club's top two offensive performers were designated hitter David Ortiz and third baseman Mike Lowell. Ortiz finished among the league leaders with 35 home runs, 117 runs batted in, 116 runs scored, 52 doubles, and a .332 batting average. Lowell was Boston's most consistent hitter all year, leading the team with 120 runs batted in, hitting 21 home runs, and batting .324. Ortiz finished fourth in the MVP balloting, while Lowell placed right behind him in fifth place.

The second-place Yankees featured the league's most potent offense, leading the circuit in runs scored (968), home runs (201), and batting average (.290). However, their mediocre pitching staff, which finished eighth in the league with a 4.49 earned run average, prevented them from capturing their tenth consecutive division title. Chien-Ming Wang and Andy Pettitte were the team's only reliable starters, winning 19 and 15 games, respectively.

It was the Yankees' offense that sparked the team to a second-half surge—one that enabled them to eventually close to within two games of the Red Sox in the final standings and advance into the postseason as the league's wild-card entry. Outfielders Hideki Matsui and Bobby

Abreu were both prone to long periods of ineffectiveness during the season. Yet, Matsui ended up batting .285, scoring 100 runs, and finishing second on the team with 25 home runs and 103 runs batted in. Meanwhile, Abreu batted .283, knocked in 101 runs, and finished second in the league with 123 runs scored. After a slow start, Robinson Cano was one of the league's most productive hitters over the season's final four months. The young second baseman ended the campaign with 19 home runs, 97 runs batted in, and a .306 batting average. Derek Jeter and Jorge Posada were the team's most consistent hitters all year. Jeter batted .322, scored 102 runs, and placed among the league leaders with 206 base hits. Posada hit 20 home runs, knocked in 90 runs, scored another 91, and finished fourth in the league with a .338 batting average.

Yet, the man who was unquestionably New York's most dynamic player, and the best player in baseball all year, was Alex Rodriguez. The third baseman led the major leagues in home runs (54), runs batted in (156), runs scored (143), and slugging percentage (.645).

Let's look at his overall numbers alongside those of Detroit's Magglio Ordonez, his primary competition for league MVP honors:

PLAYER	AB	HITS	RUNS	2B	3B	HR	RBI	AVG	OBP	SLG PCT
Magglio Ordonez	595	216	117	54	0	28	139	.363	.434	.595
Alex Rodriguez	583	183	143	31	0	54	156	.314	.422	.645

Ordonez finished with a much higher batting average than Rodriguez, and he also compiled more hits and doubles. In fact, he led the league in two of those categories and finished second in the other. Rodriguez, though, finished well ahead of him in virtually every other statistical category. He hit almost twice as many home runs as Ordonez, drove in 17 more runs, scored 26 more times, and finished with a slugging percentage that was 50 points higher. In addition, since Rodriguez walked much more frequently than Ordonez, his on-base percentage was only 12 points lower. Furthermore, Rodriguez carried his team on his back the first half of the season, when New York stumbled out of the gate to an 8-14 start. With Matsui, Abreu, and Cano struggling at the plate the first few months of the campaign, and with New York's pitching staff decimated by injuries, Rodriguez kept the Yankees afloat long enough for them to mount a second-half comeback. The team eventually made it into the playoffs, something Ordonez's Tigers failed to do.

Still, Ordonez helped keep his team in the division race much of the season with his fabulous performance. In most years, that would have been good enough to earn him MVP honors. But Rodriguez had a year for the ages, becoming the first player since Roger Maris in 1961 to lead the majors in home runs, runs batted in, and runs scored. He clearly earned the MVP Award voted him by the baseball writers at the end of the season, by a margin of 382 to 258 points over Ordonez.

NATIONAL LEAGUE

The choice for National League MVP in 2007 was a far more difficult one, with three men heading the list of viable candidates.

The Chicago Cubs captured the N.L. Central Division, finishing the regular season with a record of 85-77, two games ahead of the second-place Milwaukee Brewers, and seven games in front of the defending world champion St. Louis Cardinals. St. Louis was hit hard by injuries all year, with top starters Chris Carpenter and Mark Mulder both missing virtually the entire season, and with sluggers Jim Edmonds and Scott Rolen also missing significant playing time. As a result, the Cardinals finished just 11th in the league rankings in both earned run average (4.65) and runs scored (725), while placing 13th in home runs (141). Albert Pujols was the team's only bright spot, finishing the campaign with 32 home runs, 103 runs batted in, 99 runs scored, and a .327 batting average. But, with St. Louis finishing the year with a record of only 78-84, Pujols could do no better than ninth in the MVP balloting.

The Cubs relied heavily on their improved pitching to edge out the Brewers for the top spot in the division. Compiling the second lowest team earned run average in the league (4.04), the Chicago staff featured two of the circuit's better starting pitchers. Righthander Carlos Zambrano finished among the league leaders with 18 victories, while lefthander Ted Lilly posted an outstanding 15-8 record. On offense, the Cubs were led by the trio of Derrek Lee, Aramis Ramirez, and Alfonso Soriano. Lee hit 22 home runs, drove in 82 runs, scored 91 others, and batted .317. Ramirez batted .310, homered 26 times, and led the team with 101 runs batted in. Soriano batted .299 and led

Chicago with 33 home runs and 97 runs scored. Soriano finished 12th in the MVP voting, and Ramirez came in 13th.

The division's leading contender for that honor played for the Brewers, who remained in the race until the season's final days. Milwaukee featured a well-balanced attack, leading the N.L. with 231 home runs and placing fifth in the circuit with 801 runs scored. Rookie third baseman Ryan Braun knocked in 97 runs, scored 91 others, and finished among the league leaders with 34 home runs and a .324 batting average. Outfielder Corey Hart hit 24 homers, drove in 81 runs, scored another 86, and batted .295. Shortstop J.J. Hardy hit 26 long balls and scored 89 runs. But the driving force behind Milwaukee's offense was first baseman Prince Fielder, who batted .288, knocked in 119 runs, scored 109 others, and led the league with 50 home runs and a .618 slugging percentage. Fielder placed third in the MVP voting.

The league's closest divisional race was waged out west, where just one game separated three teams at the conclusion of play on the season's final day. The Arizona Diamondbacks finished the regular season with a record of 90-72, to edge out the Colorado Rockies and the San Diego Padres for the division title. Both the Rockies and Padres concluded the regular season with identical 89-73 records, forcing the teams to face one another in a one-game playoff to determine the league's wild-card entry into the postseason tournament. The Rockies, baseball's hottest team over the final few weeks of the season, defeated the Padres in the head-to-head matchup, thereby advancing to the playoffs having won their last nine regular-season contests. They subsequently extended their winning streak to an amazing 16 games by sweeping both the Phillies and the Diamondbacks in the playoffs, before being swept themselves by Boston in the World Series.

Although they finished the regular season with identical won-lost records, Colorado and San Diego were extremely dissimilar in their respective approaches to the game. The Rockies scored the second-most runs in the league (860), led the circuit with a .280 team batting average, and finished eighth in earned run average, with a mark of 4.32. On the other hand, the Padres finished ninth in the league in runs scored (741), and they finished next-to-last in batting average (.251). However, they also posted the lowest team earned run average in the circuit (3.70). It should come as no surprise then that San Diego's leading candidate for league MVP was pitcher Jake Peavy. The righthander was the National League's top hurler, capturing the pitcher's version of the Triple Crown by leading the circuit with 19 victories (against only 6 defeats), a 2.54 earned run average, and 240 strikeouts. Peavy finished seventh in the MVP balloting.

Arizona somehow managed to win the division despite finishing behind San Diego and Colorado in practically every major statistical category on offense, and placing well behind the Padres in team earned run average. Although they hit the same number of home runs as both San Diego and Colorado (171), the Diamondbacks finished last in the league in batting average (.250), and they placed 14th in the circuit in runs scored (712). Their 4.13 team earned run average placed them fourth in the league rankings, but it still fell considerably short of San Diego's league-leading mark of 3.70. Arizona's starting staff was headed by Brandon Webb, who finished second in the league to Peavy in wins (18) and earned run average (3.01), led all N.L. hurlers with 236 innings pitched, four complete games, and three shutouts, and placed among the leaders with 194 strikeouts. Closer Jose Valverde led the league with 47 saves, while pitching to a 2.66 earned run average and striking out 78 batters in 64 innings of work. On offense, the Diamondbacks were led by outfielder Eric Byrnes, who hit 21 home runs, scored 103 runs, batted .286, and stole 50 bases. Byrnes finished 11th in the league MVP voting.

The Rockies were the division's most well-balanced team. Their best starting pitcher, Jeff Francis, compiled a won-lost record of 17-9, while bullpen aces Brian Fuentes and Manny Corpas saved 20 and 19 games, respectively. Colorado's lineup featured five players who had outstanding seasons. Veteran first baseman Todd Helton batted .320 and knocked in 91 runs. Outfielder Brad Hawpe hit 29 homers and drove in 116 runs. Third baseman Garrett Atkins hit 25 long balls, knocked in 111 runs, and batted .301. Rookie shortstop Troy Tulowitzki homered 24 times, drove in 99 runs, scored 104 others, and batted .291. The team's top offensive performer was leftfielder Matt Holliday, who hit 36 home runs, scored 120 runs, and led the league with 137 runs batted in, 216 hits, 50 doubles, and a .340 batting average. Holliday had to be considered a leading candidate for league MVP.

In the N.L. East, a collapse of historical proportions enabled the Philadelphia Phillies to capture the division title. The Mets appeared to have the division locked up, holding a seven-game lead over the Phillies with only 17 games remaining on the schedule. But New York faltered down the stretch, allowing Philadelphia to sneak into the playoffs as the Eastern Division representative with a record of 89-73. The Mets finished one game back, at 88-74.

Yet, two of the division's most outstanding performances were turned in by members of the last-place Florida Marlins, who finished 18 games behind the Phillies in the standings. Third baseman Miguel Cabrera and shortstop Hanley Ramirez both had sensational years for Florida. Cabrera hit 34 home runs, drove in 119 runs, and batted .320. Ramirez clubbed 29 homers and finished among the league leaders with 125 runs scored, 212 hits, 48 doubles, 51 stolen bases, and a .332 batting average. However, with the Marlins finishing well out of contention, Cabrera placed 15th in the MVP balloting, while Ramirez could manage only a 10th-place finish.

Veteran third baseman Chipper Jones also had an exceptional season for the third-place Atlanta Braves. After missing extended playing time with injuries in each of the previous two seasons, Jones bounced back with 29 home runs, 102 runs batted in, 108 runs scored, and a .337 batting average. Although the Braves finished third in the division, they ended up only five games out of the top spot, and Jones helped to keep them in the race most of the year. His efforts were recognized by the writers, who placed him sixth in the MVP voting.

Despite blowing what appeared to be an insurmountable lead in the closing weeks of the season, the Mets received solid efforts from a number of players. Starting pitchers John Maine and Oliver Perez finished with identical 15-10 records, and closer Billy Wagner saved 34 games. Outfielder Moises Alou appeared in only 87 games, but he hit 13 home runs, drove in 49 runs, and led the team with a .341 batting average. Although he faltered badly during the season's second half, Jose Reyes batted .280, scored 119 runs, and stole a league-leading 78 bases. Carlos Beltran led the team with 33 home runs and 112 runs batted in. New York's best player was third baseman David Wright, who remained consistently good the entire year. Wright hit 30 homers, knocked in 107 runs, scored 113 others, stole 34 bases, batted .325, and won his first Gold Glove Award for his solid defensive work at third. For his efforts, Wright was awarded a fourth-place finish in the league MVP balloting.

The winner of that coveted honor was a member of the Philadelphia Phillies, who featured three of the top ten vote-getters. Philadelphia's pitching staff, which finished 13th in the league in earned run average (4.73), was mediocre at best. Cole Hamels, who compiled a 15-5 record and a 3.39 earned run average, was the team's only consistently effective starter. But the Phillies' offense was the best in the National League. They finished first in runs scored (892), second in home runs (213), and fifth in batting average (.274). Leftfielder Pat Burrell hit 30 home runs and drove in 97 runs. Centerfielder Aaron Rowand had the finest season of his career. In addition to winning a Gold Glove Award for his superb outfield play, Rowand batted .309 and established new career-highs with 27 home runs, 89 runs batted in, 105 runs scored, 189 hits, and 45 doubles. Second baseman Chase Utley missed a month of the season, but still managed to hit 22 homers, drive in 103 runs, score another 104, and finish among the league leaders with a .332 batting average. Defending N.L. MVP Ryan Howard struck out 199 times and batted only .268, but he finished second in the league with 47 home runs and 136 runs batted in. He placed fifth in the MVP balloting, three notches ahead of Utley.

The man selected by the baseball writers as the National League's Most Valuable Player was Phillies shortstop Jimmy Rollins. Let's look at his offensive numbers next to those compiled by Matt Holliday and Prince Fielder, the two other leading candidates for the award:

PLAYER	AB	HITS	RUNS	2B	3B	HR	RBI	AVG	OBP	SLG PCT
Prince Fielder	573	165	109	35	2	**50**	119	.288	.395	**.618**
Jimmy Rollins	716	212	**139**	38	**20**	30	94	.296	.344	.531
Matt Holliday	636	**216**	120	**50**	6	36	**137**	**.340**	.405	.607

In evaluating the credentials of the three players, based strictly on statistics it would appear that Rollins was perhaps the least deserving. Holliday certainly posted the most impressive numbers of the three men, and Fielder's power numbers were far superior to those compiled by Rollins. The Milwaukee first baseman hit 20 more home runs than Rollins, knocked in 25 more runs, and finished with much higher on-base and slugging percentages. On the other hand, Rollins amassed a league-leading 20 triples, to the two three-baggers collected by Fielder, accumulated many more hits, and scored 30 more runs. Therefore, Rollins was actually the superior run-producer of the two men, especially when one considers that the Philadelphia shortstop's role as leadoff hitter precluded him from driving in as many runs as Fielder, who batted in the middle of his team's lineup. Furthermore, Rollins was a far more complete player than the ponderous Fielder, who, at 6'0" and 260 pounds, was a poor baserunner and a below-average fielder (he committed 14 errors at first base over the course of the season).

Meanwhile, Rollins finished among the league leaders with 41 stolen bases, committed only 11 errors at shortstop, and won the first Gold Glove of his career for his outstanding defense. Therefore, Fielder was the first to be eliminated from consideration.

In comparing Rollins to Holliday, a valid case could be made for selecting either man for league MVP. Holliday finished ahead of Rollins in every major offensive category except for runs scored, triples, and stolen bases. He placed among the league leaders in eight offensive departments, topping the circuit in four of those. Holliday was consistent all year, and he performed at an extremely high level during the season's final month, leading the Rockies on their inexorable march towards the playoffs down the stretch. Over the final four weeks of the regular season, Holliday hit 12 home runs, drove in 30 runs, scored 29 others, and batted .367. He was also a solid outfielder and a good baserunner, committing only three outfield errors and stealing 11 bases during the season. Therefore, it would have been difficult to find fault with the writers had they selected Holliday for league MVP.

However, a strong argument could also be waged on Rollins' behalf. He led the league in runs scored and triples, and he also finished among the leaders in base hits and stolen bases. He hit 30 home runs and knocked in 94 runs—exceptional numbers for a leadoff hitter. He played a more demanding defensive position than Holliday, and he was also his team's leader, both on and off the field. Perhaps most important, though, is the fact that Holliday's offensive numbers were inflated by playing in Coors Field. It is true that baseballs no longer fly out of that park as they once did, since they are now placed in a humidifier prior to the start of each game. However, Holliday's statistics clearly indicate that Coors Field remains a superb ballpark in which to hit.

The following "home and away" split for the Colorado outfielder illustrates that fact:

	AB	HITS	RUNS	2B	3B	HR	RBI	AVG	OBP	SLG PCT
HOME	327	123	67	28	5	25	82	.376	.435	.722
AWAY	309	93	53	22	1	11	55	.301	.374	.485

Rollins also had the advantage of playing in a hitter-friendly park in Philadelphia. But he posted "home and away" numbers that were far less incongruous:

	AB	HITS	RUNS	2B	3B	HR	RBI	AVG	OBP	SLG PCT
HOME	347	104	69	13	11	18	47	.300	.336	.556
AWAY	369	108	70	25	9	12	47	.293	.352	.507

The above numbers not only indicate that Holliday was a much better player at home than he was on the road, but they also illustrate that Rollins was superior to Holliday when the two men played away from their home ballparks. He compiled better numbers than Holliday in most offensive categories, and he was the more complete player of the two men. Furthermore, Rollins also excelled during the season's final month, as the Phillies overtook the Mets for first place in the Eastern Division. Over the final four weeks of the campaign, he hit six home runs, knocked in 18 runs, scored another 22, and batted .298.

Matt Holliday would not have been a bad choice by the writers, but, all things considered, they made the right decision when they awarded Jimmy Rollins a total of 353 points in the MVP balloting, to the total of 336 points they gave Holliday.

2008

AMERICAN LEAGUE

Baseball's most consistent team during the 2008 regular season was the Los Angeles Angels of Anaheim, who posted a major-league best 100-62 record in capturing the A.L. West title for the second straight year. The Texas Rangers finished a distant second in the division, 21 games back. Yet, it was the Rangers who boasted the league's most potent offense, leading the circuit with 901 runs scored and a .283 team batting average, and placing third with 194 home runs. Texas featured three of the American League's top offensive players in second baseman Ian Kinsler and outfielders Milton Bradley and Josh Hamilton. Kinsler hit 18 home runs, stole 26 bases, and placed near the top of the league rankings with 102 runs scored and a .319 batting average. Bradley finished among the league leaders with a .321 batting average and a .563 slugging percentage. Hamilton was the circuit's top offensive performer, leading the league with 130 runs batted in and finishing among the leaders with 32 home runs, 98 runs scored, 190 hits, a .304 batting average, and a .530 slugging percentage. But, with the Rangers finishing well out of contention, Hamilton could do no better than seventh in the MVP balloting.

The Angels' offense wasn't nearly as potent. They finished 10th in the A.L. with 765 runs scored, they placed ninth with 159 home runs, and they finished seventh with a .268 team batting average. Their top two offensive threats were Torii Hunter and Vladimir Guerrero. Hunter hit 21 homers, knocked in 78 runs, and scored 85 others. Guerrero led the team with 27 home runs, 91 runs batted in, and a .303 batting average.

The Angels' greatest strength was their pitching staff, which posted the third lowest team earned run average in the American League, with a mark of 3.99. The team's top two starters were righthander Ervin Santana and southpaw Joe Saunders. Santana finished 16-7, with a 3.49 earned run average and 214 strikeouts. Saunders compiled a record of 17-7, along with an earned run average of 3.41. John Garland chipped in with 14 victories, and John Lackey added another 12 wins. But the Angels' most outstanding performer all year was closer Francisco Rodriguez, who established a new major-league record by saving 62 games. The flamboyant reliever also pitched to an outstanding 2.24 earned run average, while allowing only 54 hits in 68 innings of work and striking out 77 opposing batters. For his exceptional performance, Rodriguez was awarded a sixth-place finish in the league MVP voting.

The topsy-turvy A.L. Central experienced another major shift in the balance of power in 2008, with the defending division champion

Cleveland Indians slipping to third place and the Chicago White Sox claiming the top spot by defeating the runner-up Minnesota Twins in a one-game playoff. Chicago finished the season with a record of 89-74, barely edging out the Twins, who failed to make the playoffs. The Indians finished a disappointing 81-81, 7½ games off the pace. Still, the division's most disappointing team was the Detroit Tigers, who were selected by many baseball experts to finish first prior to the start of the season. Detroit compiled the division's worst record, finishing one game behind fourth-place Kansas City, with a record of only 74-88. Nevertheless, Miguel Cabrera, who the Tigers acquired from Florida during the off-season, proved to be one of the league's most dynamic hitters. Cabrera led the A.L. with 37 home runs, and he also placed among the leaders with 127 runs batted in and a .537 slugging percentage.

Third-place Cleveland featured the league's best pitcher in Cliff Lee. The lefthander led all A.L. starters with a record of 22-3 and an earned run average of 2.54 en route to winning the Cy Young Award. Lee also placed 12th in the MVP voting.

Division-winning Chicago had neither outstanding hitting nor exceptional pitching. The White Sox finished fifth in the circuit with 811 runs scored, they placed 11th with a team batting average of .263, and they finished sixth with a team earned run average of 4.06. Their two most effective starters were lefthander Mark Buehrle and righthander Gavin Floyd. Buehrle finished 15-12 with a 3.79 earned run average, and Floyd compiled a record of 17-8 with a 3.94 earned run average. On offense, Chicago was paced by the trio of Jim Thome, Jermaine Dye, and Carlos Quentin. Thome batted only .245, but he hit 34 homers, drove in 90 runs, and scored another 93. Dye batted .292, also went deep 34 times, knocked in 96 runs, and scored 96 others. Quentin batted .288, also scored 96 runs, and finished among the league leaders with 36 home runs, 100 runs batted in, and a .571 slugging percentage. For his efforts, Quentin was awarded a fifth-place finish in the league MVP balloting.

The division's two leading candidates for that honor actually came from the second-place Twins, even though they failed to make the playoffs, albeit by the slimmest of margins. With 829 runs scored and a .279 team batting average, Minnesota featured one of the league's best offenses. That offense was paced by two of the circuit's top hitters—catcher Joe Mauer and first baseman Justin Morneau. Mauer drove in 85 runs, scored 98 others, and won his second batting title with a mark of .328. Morneau hit 23 homers, scored 97 runs, batted .300, and finished among the league leaders with 129 runs batted in and 47 doubles. Mauer placed fourth in the MVP voting, two places behind Morneau, who came in second.

The eventual winner of the award came from the A.L. East, which featured baseball's most surprising team. After compiling the worst record in the major leagues the previous year and finishing 30 games behind the division-winning Boston Red Sox, the Tampa Bay Rays won 97 games to capture the A.L. East title. Boston finished two games back, thereby advancing into the postseason as the league's wild-card entry. The Yankees, who finished eight games behind the Rays in the standings, failed to make the playoffs for the first time in 14 years.

The key to Tampa Bay's success was the team's improved pitching. The Rays' team earned run average of 3.82 was the second lowest in the American League, and their staff included five starters who finished in double-digits in victories. James Shields and Edwin Jackson both won 14 games, Andy Sonnanstine won another 13, and Scott Kazmir and Matt Garza chipped in with 12 and 11 wins, respectively.

On the other hand, Tampa Bay hardly had one of the league's most imposing offenses. Despite compiling the fourth-highest home-run total in the A.L., they finished ninth in runs scored and next-to-last in team batting average. Their top two offensive players were first baseman Carlos Pena and A.L. Rookie of the Year third baseman Evan Longoria. Pena batted just .247, but he led the team with 31 home runs and 102 runs batted in. Longoria finished second to Pena on the team with 27 home runs and 85 runs batted in. Second baseman Akinori Iwamura led the Rays with 91 runs scored and 172 hits, while centerfielder B.J. Upton placed second in the league with 44 stolen bases. None of those men, though, merited serious consideration for league MVP honors.

Two of the most serious contenders for that coveted prize came from the runner-up Red Sox, who were the American League's most well-balanced team. Boston's team earned run average of 4.01 was the fourth-best in the league, and Boston's offense placed second in the circuit in runs scored (845), second in batting average (.280), and sixth in home runs (173).

Boston's pitching staff was headed by lefthander Jon Lester and righthander Daisuke Matsuzaka. Lester finished 16-6 with a 3.21 earned run average, and Matsuzaka led the team with a record of 18-3 and a 2.90 earned run average. Closer Jonathan Papelbon saved 41 games, won another five out of the bullpen, and compiled an outstanding 2.34 earned run average.

The Red Sox lineup was also extremely solid. J.D. Drew batted .280, hit 19 home runs, and scored 79 runs. Despite appearing in only 109 games due to a left wrist injury, David Ortiz hit 23 homers and knocked in 89 runs. Mike Lowell also missed a significant amount of playing time with injuries, but he managed to hit 17 home runs and drive in 73 runs. Before forcing his way out of Boston with his lackadaisical attitude, Manny Ramirez hit 20 homers and knocked in 68 runs in only 100 games. His outfield replacement, Jason Bay, hit nine home runs, drove in 37 runs, and scored another 39 runs in his 49 games with the team. But Boston's two most important players all year were second baseman Dustin Pedroia and first baseman Kevin Youkilis.

Let's look at their numbers alongside those of Joe Mauer and Justin Morneau, the other two leading candidates for league MVP:

PLAYER	AB	HITS	RUNS	2B	3B	HR	RBI	AVG	OBP	SLG PCT
Justin Morneau	623	187	97	47	4	23	129	.300	.374	.499
Joe Mauer	536	176	98	31	4	9	85	**.328**	.413	.451
Dustin Pedroia	653	**213**	**118**	**54**	2	17	83	.326	.376	.493
Kevin Youkilis	538	168	91	43	4	29	115	.312	.390	.569

Although he finished with the highest batting average and on-base percentage, Mauer's overall numbers were the least impressive of the four men. His home-run total and slugging percentage were both significantly lower than those of the other three players, and he was much less effective as a run-producer. Mauer knocked in far fewer runs than Morneau and Youkilis, and he didn't score nearly as many runs as Pedroia. Therefore, Mauer was the first to be eliminated from consideration.

The statistics of Morneau and Youkilis were extremely comparable. The Minnesota first baseman had an edge in run-production, but Youkilis finished slightly ahead of him in batting average and on-base percentage. Youkilis also compiled a significantly higher slugging percentage. Neither man appears to have much of a statistical advantage over the other. It could be argued that Youkilis had an edge in that his team advanced to the playoffs, albeit as a wild card. But it took a one-game playoff at the end of the regular season to eliminate Morneau's Twins from playoff contention. Therefore, a valid case could be made for selecting either Youkilis or Morneau.

But, what of Youkilis' Boston teammate, Dustin Pedroia? The diminutive second baseman's power numbers were not as impressive as those posted by either Morneau or Youkilis. However, as a middle infielder, one would not expect them to be. And, considering that Pedroia usually batted second in the Red Sox lineup, he didn't have as many opportunities to drive in runs. Therefore, he was actually quite comparable to the two sluggers as a run-producer. Furthermore, Pedroia led the league in runs scored, hits, and doubles, and he finished a close second to Mauer in the batting race.

Looking beyond the sheer numbers, both Youkilis and Pedroia helped pick up much of the slack in Boston when injuries forced David Ortiz and Mike Lowell out of the team's lineup for extended periods. But, unlike Youkilis, whose obsessively intense nature occasionally irritated some of his teammates, Pedroia remained extremely popular in the Boston clubhouse, and he was generally considered to be one of the team's leaders. In addition, he appeared in 157 games for the Red Sox (12 more than Youkilis), committed only six errors all year, and earned the first Gold Glove of his young career for his exceptional work at second base.

All things considered, it would be difficult to find fault with the writers' selection of Pedroia as league MVP over both Morneau and Youkilis, who finished second and third, respectively, in the voting.

NATIONAL LEAGUE

The Los Angeles Dodgers came out on top in the decidedly mediocre National League West in 2008, finishing the regular season with a record of 84-78, two games ahead of the runner-up Arizona Diamondbacks. Yet, the third-place Colorado Rockies, the fourth-place San Francisco Giants, and the last-place San Diego Padres, all of whom finished well out of contention, featured most of the division's top individual performers. First baseman Adrian Gonzalez batted .279 for the Padres and placed among the league leaders with 36 homers and 119 runs batted in. Colorado outfielder Matt Holliday homered 25 times, knocked in 88 runs, scored 107 others, and finished third in the league with a .321 batting average. San Francisco righthander Tim Lincecum claimed the N.L. Cy Young Award after compiling an 18-5 record, a 2.62 earned run average and a league-leading 265 strikeouts during the campaign. But the poor showings of their respective teams prevented the three men from being serious contenders for the league MVP Award.

Brandon Webb, who finished second to Lincecum in the Cy Young balloting, was Arizona's leading candidate for league MVP. The righthander topped all N.L. pitchers with 22 victories (against only 7 losses), and he compiled a very respectable 3.30 earned run average. Still, Webb could do no better than 17th in the voting.

The first-place Dodgers had the circuit's best pitching staff, finishing the year with a league-leading team earned run average of 3.68. Their staff was headed by righthanders Derek Lowe and Chad Billingsley. Lowe finished 14-11 with a 3.24 earned run average, and Billingsley led the team with 16 victories, while compiling a 3.14 earned run average. The Los Angeles offense wasn't nearly as formidable, placing 13th in the league rankings in both home runs and runs scored, despite compiling the fifth highest team batting average. Centerfielder Matt Kemp hit 18 homers, drove in 76 runs, scored 93 others, and batted .290. First baseman James Loney batted .289 and led the team with 90 runs batted in. Catcher Russell Martin batted .280 and scored 87 runs. Outfielder Andre Ethier scored 90 runs and led the team with 20 home runs and a .305 batting average.

But the Dodgers' leading MVP candidate was Manny Ramirez, who spent only two months with the team after being acquired from the Red Sox on July 31. Ramirez drove in 53 runs in his 53 games with Los Angeles, while also hitting 17 home runs, batting .396, and compiling a .489 on-base percentage and a .743 slugging percentage. Ramirez also created a spark within the Dodger clubhouse, and he greatly changed the entire culture of the team. For his efforts, Manny was awarded a fourth-place finish in the league MVP voting.

The eventual World Champion Philadelphia Phillies captured their second straight N.L. East title by finishing the regular season with a record of 92-70, three games ahead of the runner-up New York Mets, who narrowly missed making the playoffs for the second consecutive year. Placing third in the division, just 7½ games off the pace, were the young and improving Florida Marlins, who compiled a regular-season record of 84-77. The Marlins featured a quartet of sluggers who picked up much of the slack for the departed Miguel Cabrera. First baseman Mike Jacobs batted just .247, but he hit 32 homers and drove in 93 runs. Second baseman Dan Uggla also homered 32 times, knocked in 92 runs, and scored another 97 runs. Third baseman Jorge Cantu hit 29 long balls, drove in 95 runs, and scored 92 others. Florida's best all-around player was shortstop Hanley Ramirez, who led the team with 33 home runs, 35 stolen bases, and a .301 batting average, while also leading the league with 125 runs scored. Still, Ramirez could do no better than 11th in the MVP balloting.

The second-place Mets possessed one of the league's top offenses, and they also had one of the circuit's best pitchers in Johan Santana. The lefthander finished 16-7, with a league-leading 2.53 earned run average and 234 innings pitched. Santana finished 14th in the MVP voting. The New York lineup, which tied for second in the league in runs scored, placed two members in the top ten of the balloting. After slumping terribly during the season's first half, first baseman Carlos Delgado had a torrid final three months to finish the campaign with 38 home runs, 115 runs batted in, and 96 runs scored. Third baseman David Wright was the team's most consistent performer, collecting 33 homers, batting .302, and placing among the league leaders with 124 runs batted in, 115 runs scored, and 189 hits. Delgado finished ninth in the MVP voting, while Wright came in seventh.

Improved pitching helped the Phillies capture their second straight division title. The Philadelphia staff compiled the fourth-lowest team earned run average in the National League, with a mark of 3.88. The starters were led by lefthanders Cole Hamels and Jamie Moyer. Hamels finished 14-10 with an outstanding 3.09 earned run average, while the ageless Moyer led the staff with 16 victories. In the bullpen, Brad Lidge pitched to an earned run average of 1.95, and he was a perfect 41-for-41 in save opportunities. He finished eighth in the MVP balloting.

The Phillies' greatest strength was their offense, which tied for second in the N.L. with 799 runs scored and topped the circuit with 214 home runs. Reigning MVP Jimmy Rollins had a sub-par season, driving in only 59 runs and scoring just 76 others. But he still managed to steal 47 bases. Outfielders Shane Victorino and Jayson Werth provided an offensive spark. Victorino batted .293, stole 36 bases, and scored 102 runs. Werth hit 24 homers and drove in 67 runs in only 418 at-bats. Veteran outfielder Pat Burrell hit 33 home runs and knocked in 86 runs. Philadelphia's best all-around player was second baseman Chase Utley, who was the team's hottest hitter during the season's first half. Utley finished the year with 33 home runs, 104 runs batted in, 113 runs scored, and a .292 batting average. Yet, Utley's solid performance earned him just a 15th-place finish in the MVP voting.

The man the writers perceived to be the Phillies' most valuable player was Ryan Howard. Despite putting up decent power numbers, the slugging first baseman struggled during the season's first half, posting a batting average of only .215. After a strong month of July, Howard slumped again in August, before catching fire in September to help lead his team to the division title. Over the season's final month, Howard hit 11 home runs, knocked in 32 runs, scored 26 others, and batted .352. He finished the year with a batting average of .251, 105 runs scored, and a league-leading 48 home runs, 146 runs batted in, and 199 strikeouts. The members of the BBWAA placed Howard second in the league MVP balloting.

The man who won the award came out of the N.L. Central, which featured the league's strongest team for much of the regular season. The Chicago Cubs compiled the circuit's best record, finishing 97-64, 7½ games ahead of the second-place Milwaukee Brewers, who were the league's wild-card representative. The Houston Astros came in third, 11 games back, just ahead of the fourth-place Cardinals, who finished 11½ games off the pace.

The division-winning Cubs were the league's most well-balanced team during the regular season. In addition to finishing third in the circuit with a team earned run average of 3.87, they led the N.L. with 855 runs scored, while also placing second in team batting average (.278) and fifth in home runs (184). Chicago's starting staff was as deep as any in baseball. Ryan Dempster compiled a record of 17-6 and finished among the league leaders with a 2.96 earned run average. Ted Lilly posted a record of 17-9, while Carlos Zambrano won 14 games and Jason Marquis chipped in with another 11 victories. After being converted to closer prior to the start of the season, Kerry Wood saved 34 games and won another five working out of the bullpen.

On offense, outfielder Kosuke Fukudome scored 79 runs, while shortstop Ryan Theriot scored another 85 and batted .307. Second baseman Mark DeRosa hit 21 homers, batted .285, knocked in 87 runs, and led the team with 103 runs scored. Outfielder Alfonso Soriano batted .280 and homered 29 times. First baseman Derrek Lee hit 20 long balls, drove in 90 runs, scored 93 others, and batted .291. Catcher Geovany Soto hit 23 homers, knocked in 86 runs, and batted .285. Third baseman Aramis Ramirez hit 27 home runs, scored 97 times, batted .289, and led the team with 111 runs batted in. He finished 10th in the league MVP voting.

Finishing fifth in the balloting was Lance Berkman, who had an outstanding year for the third-place Astros. The Houston first baseman hit 29 home runs, knocked in 106 runs, led the league with 46 doubles, and placed among the leaders with 114 runs scored, a .312 batting average, and a .567 slugging percentage.

Placing two players in the top ten of the balloting were the runner-up Milwaukee Brewers. Lefthander C.C. Sabathia played a huge role in the team's advancement into the postseason after being acquired from Cleveland on July 6. Sabathia went 11-2, with a 1.65 earned run average and a league-leading seven complete games and three shutouts with Milwaukee over the season's final three months. He finished sixth in the voting. Finishing three spots ahead of Sabathia, in third place, was outfielder Ryan Braun, who paced Milwaukee's offense most of the year.

Let's look at his statistics, alongside those of the other two leading candidates for league MVP—Ryan Howard and Cardinals first baseman Albert Pujols:

PLAYER	AB	HITS	RUNS	2B	3B	HR	RBI	AVG	OBP	SLG PCT
Ryan Braun	611	174	92	39	7	37	106	.285	.335	.553
Albert Pujols	524	187	100	44	0	37	116	.357	**.462**	**.653**
Ryan Howard	610	153	105	26	4	**48**	**146**	.251	.339	.543

Pujols, who was the choice of the writers, was clearly the best player. Braun compiled comparable numbers in most offensive categories, but Pujols finished with a significantly higher batting average and with much higher on-base and slugging percentages. In fact, Pujols' .357 batting average was higher than Braun's .335 on-base percentage. Although Howard hit 11 more home runs and knocked in 30 more runs than Pujols, the Cardinals first baseman posted much better overall numbers. Pujols outhit Howard by more than 100 points, and he also compiled on-base and slugging percentages that were more than 100 points higher.

It must also be remembered that Howard had a much better supporting cast in Philadelphia than Pujols had in St. Louis. Philadelphia's lineup also included the likes of Chase Utley, Pat Burrell, Jimmy Rollins, and Shane Victorino. Meanwhile, with Jim Edmonds and Scott Rolen both traded away during the off-season, the Cardinals' only other real threats on offense were Troy Glaus and Ryan Ludwick. Glaus hit 27 home runs and drove in 99 runs, while Ludwick hit 37 homers, knocked in 113 runs, scored 104 others, and batted .299. It is true that the Cardinals led the league with a .281 team batting average. But they hit 40 fewer home runs than the Phillies and scored 20 fewer runs. Furthermore, the effectiveness of the St. Louis pitching staff was greatly compromised for the second consecutive year by injuries to its two top starters. Both Chris Carpenter and Mark Mulder missed virtually the entire season once again, resulting in St. Louis finishing just seventh in the league in team earned run average, with a mark of 4.19.

Meanwhile, Philadelphia's staff finished fourth in the league with a 3.88 team earned run average. Milwaukee's staff was even better, placing second in the circuit with a mark of 3.85. As a result, Pujols' contributions to his team were absolutely essential. He held the Cardinals together for most of the season, keeping them relatively close in their division and enabling them to finish in fourth place, only four games out of a playoff spot. There is no telling where St. Louis would have finished without him.

And, finally, Pujols was far more consistent than Howard, whose erratic performance over the course of the campaign greatly diminished his legitimacy as a viable MVP candidate. The writers made the correct choice when they awarded Pujols 369 total points in the balloting, to the 308 points they gave Howard.

2009

AMERICAN LEAGUE

The Los Angeles Angels of Anaheim coasted to their third consecutive A.L. West title in 2009, finishing the campaign with a record of 97-65. Meanwhile, both the runner-up Texas Rangers and the third-place Seattle Mariners showed marked improvement over their performances from the previous season. Texas posted a record of 87-75, to finish 10 games behind Los Angeles, while Seattle compiled a record 85-77, to finish 12 games back. The Mariner pitching staff led the A.L. with a team earned run average of 3.87, and it featured one of the league's very best pitchers in Felix Hernandez. The 23-year-old righthander compiled a record of 19-5, to tie for the league lead in victories. He also finished second in earned run average (2.49), third in innings pitched (239), and fourth in strikeouts (217).

Seattle's lineup also included one of the circuit's top position players in perennial All-Star Ichiro Suzuki, who finished second in the league with a .352 batting average while amassing a league-leading 225 hits. Ichiro's outstanding performance earned him a ninth-place finish in the league MVP voting.

The second-place Rangers were once again one of the American League's better hitting teams, placing second in the circuit with 224 home runs and finishing seventh with 784 runs scored. But the Angels were the division's strongest team for the third straight year, even though their team earned run average rose to an unseemly 4.45 (it was 3.99 in 2008). Injuries and ineffectiveness plagued Ervin Santana for much of the year, limiting the righthander to 23 starts and causing him to finish the season with a record of only 8-8 and an earned run average of 5.03.

Lefthander Scott Kazmir was also extremely erratic, going just 10-9 with a 4.89 earned run average during the campaign. John Lackey missed the season's first month with an injury, and he finished the year with only 11 victories. Nevertheless, he posted a very respectable 3.83 earned run average. Jeff Weaver and Joe Saunders were the team's big winners, both compiling 16 victories over the course of the season. Closer Francisco Rodriguez left the Angels via free agency during the off-season, but the team signed Brian Fuentes to be his replacement. Although the 35-year-old southpaw struggled at times, blowing seven save opportunities, losing five games coming out of the bullpen, and pitching to a rather mediocre 3.93 earned run average, he ended up leading the league with 48 saves.

It was actually the Angels' improved offense that enabled them to capture the A.L. West crown. After finishing near the middle of the pack in runs scored and team batting average the previous season, the Angels placed near the top of the league rankings in both categories in 2009. In fact, their .285 team batting average led the American League, and they also finished second with 883 runs scored. Injuries limited Vladimir Guerrero to fewer than 400 official at-bats and prevented him from playing the outfield at all during the season. Guerrero batted .295, but he hit just 15 home runs and knocked in only 50 runs. However, several other players stepped up to give the team's offense a boost. Centerfielder Torii Hunter hit 22 home runs, drove in 90 runs, and batted .299. Second baseman Erick Aybar batted .312 and scored 70 runs. Leftfielder Juan Rivera batted .287 and established new career highs with 25 homers and 88 runs batted in. Rightfielder Bobby Abreu proved to be a free-agent bargain after signing with the team during the off-season. Abreu batted .293, hit 15 home runs, knocked in 103 runs, scored 96 others, and stole 30 bases. Chone Figgins batted .298 and placed among the league leaders with 114 runs scored and 42 stolen bases.

The team's top offensive performer was first baseman Kendry Morales, who scored 86 runs, batted .306, and finished among the league leaders with 34 home runs, 108 runs batted in, and a .569 slugging percentage. The writers placed Morales fifth in the league MVP balloting.

After failing to make the playoffs for the first time in 14 years the previous season, the New York Yankees compiled baseball's best record in 2009, finishing the year at 103-59, before eventually going on to win the World Series for the first time since 2000. The Boston Red Sox finished second in the A.L. East with a record of 95-67, advancing to the postseason as the league's wild-card entry. The defending A.L. Champion Tampa Bay Devil Rays slipped to third in the division, coming in 19 games behind first-place New York, while fourth-place Toronto finished 28 games behind the division winners. Yet, the Devil Rays and Blue Jays both featured some of the league's top offensive performers.

Toronto DH Adam Lind batted .305 and placed among the league leaders with 35 home runs and 114 runs batted in. Second baseman Aaron Hill batted .286, knocked in 108 runs, scored 103 others, and finished tied for third in the league with 36 homers. Tampa Bay third baseman Evan Longoria batted .281, hit 33 home runs, scored 100 runs, and finished among the league leaders with 113 runs batted in. Second baseman Ben Zobrist homered 27 times, drove in 91 runs, scored 91 others, and batted .297, to earn an eighth-place finish in the league MVP voting.

Injuries to two of Boston's top starters, Daisuke Matsuzaka and Tim Wakefield, adversely affected the team's pitching and prevented the Red Sox from mounting a serious challenge to the Yankees for the division title. Matsuzaka and Wakefield combined for a total of only 15 victories, and both men finished the year with an earned run average well in excess of four-and-a-half runs per-game. Boston's only dependable starters were Josh Beckett and Jon Lester. Beckett compiled a 3.86 earned run average and led the staff with a record of 17-6. Lester finished 15-8 with a 3.41 earned run average.

Boston's mediocre pitching forced the team to rely more heavily on its offense, which finished third in the league in runs scored (872) and home runs (212), while placing fourth in the circuit with a .270 team batting average. The Boston attack was led by the quartet of Dustin Pedroia, Victor Martinez, Jason Bay, and Kevin Youkilis. Reigning A.L. MVP Pedroia batted .296 and scored 115 runs. After coming over to Boston from Cleveland at the trade deadline, Martinez ended the campaign with 23 home runs, 108 runs batted in, and a .303 batting average. Bay scored 103 runs and placed among the league leaders with 36 home runs and 119 runs batted in. Youkilis hit 27 homers, knocked in 94 runs, scored 99 others, and led the team with a .305 batting average and a .413 on-base percentage. Youkilis and Bay finished sixth and seventh, respectively, in the league MVP voting.

Improved starting pitching and a powerful offense were the keys to New York's success throughout the season. The team's free-agent signings of C.C. Sabathia and A.J. Burnett during the off-season paid huge dividends. Although Burnett pitched inconsistently at times, he finished the year with a record of 13-9 and an earned run average of 4.04. Sabathia was the team's most reliable starter, compiling a record of 19-8 and an earned run average of 3.37, and throwing 230 innings. Andy Pettitte chipped in with 14 victories, while the incomparable Mariano Rivera showed no signs of aging, pitching to a 1.76 earned run average and compiling 44 saves in 46 save opportunities.

It was New York's offense, though, that truly separated them from the rest of the American League. The Yankees finished second in the league with a .283 team batting average, and they topped the circuit with 915 runs scored and 244 home runs. Catcher Jorge Posada batted .285, hit 22 homers, and drove in 81 runs. Designated hitter Hideki Matsui homered 28 times and knocked in 90 runs. Rightfielder Nick Swisher batted only .249, but he compiled a .371 on-base percentage, hit 29 home runs, and drove in 82 runs.

Second baseman Robinson Cano batted .320, knocked in 85 runs, and established new career highs with 25 home runs and 103 runs scored. Johnny Damon batted .282, hit 24 homers, drove in 82 runs, and scored 107 others. Alex Rodriguez missed the first month of the season recovering from hip surgery, but he still managed to hit 30 home runs and knock in 100 runs. New York's two most consistent performers during the season were Derek Jeter and Mark Teixeira. Jeter hit 18 homers, drove in 66 runs, scored 107 others, stole 30 bases, and finished among the league leaders with a .334 batting average and 212 hits. He also had an outstanding year in the field, committing only eight errors at shortstop and winning the fourth Gold Glove of his career.

Teixeira, who signed with the team as a free agent during the off-season, batted .292, scored 103 runs, and led the league with 39 home runs and 122 runs batted in. He also won a Gold Glove for his outstanding work at first base, stabilizing the right side of the Yankee infield and saving his infield mates numerous throwing errors over the course of the season. Equally important was the effect Teixeira had on New York's batting order. He gave the Yankees a consistently productive bat in the middle of their lineup, a powerful bat from both sides of the plate, and someone who could take some of the pressure off Alex Rodriguez to drive in runs. Along with Sabathia, he shifted the balance of power in the A.L. East to the Yankees.

The writers recognized Teixeira's contributions to his new team by placing him second in the MVP voting. Jeter finished right behind his teammate, in third place.

Finishing ahead of Teixeira and Jeter in the balloting was a member of the American League Central Division champion Minnesota Twins, who captured the division title by defeating the second-place Detroit Tigers in a one-game playoff. The Twins finished the year with a record of 87-76, while the Tigers failed to make the playoffs with a record of 86-77. Still, it was the last-place Kansas City Royals who boasted the American League's Cy Young Award winner. Pitching for a team that won only 65 games, Zack Greinke finished the year 16-8, with 242 strikeouts and a league-leading 2.16 earned run average.

The runner-up Tigers also had an exceptional pitcher in Justin Verlander. The righthander finished 19-9, to tie for the league lead in victories. Verlander also placed among the leaders with a 3.45 earned run average, and he topped the circuit with 269 strikeouts and 240 innings pitched. Equally impressive was the year turned in by Tiger first baseman Miguel Cabrera, who hit 34 home runs, knocked in 103 runs, scored 96 others, and finished near the top of the league rankings with a .324 batting average. Cabrera's outstanding season and Detroit's close second-place finish enabled the slugger to finish fourth in the league MVP balloting.

It was mentioned earlier that the winner of the award played for the division-winning Twins, who captured the division title despite lacking a true ace to their pitching staff and finishing 11th in the league with a 4.50 team earned run average. Righthander Scott Baker compiled an earned run average of 4.37 and finished 15-9, to lead the team in victories. Carl Pavano returned from several seasons of inactivity to finish 14-12, while posting a rather high earned run average of 5.10. Nick Blackburn and Kevin Slowey contributed 11 and 10 victories, respectively, but both men finished with an earned run average in excess of four runs per-game. The team's most reliable pitcher was unquestionably closer Joe Nathan, who finished the campaign with a 2.10 earned run average and 47 saves in 52 save opportunities.

On offense, the Twins finished ninth in the league with 172 home runs, but they nevertheless had one of the circuit's more productive lineups. The Twins scored the fourth most runs in the American League (817), and they posted the third-highest team batting average (.274). Designated hitter Jason Kubel hit 28 home runs, drove in 103 runs, and batted .300. Leftfielder Denard Span batted .311, scored 97 runs, and stole 23 bases. Before being sidelined for the final three weeks of the season with an injured back, Justin Morneau hit 30 homers, knocked in 100 runs, and scored 85 others. Rightfielder Michael Cuddyer hit 32 home runs, drove in 94 runs, scored another 93 times, and did a creditable job at first base after taking over for the injured Morneau.

But Minnesota's most valuable player was unquestionably Joe Mauer, whose league-leading .365 batting average was the highest figure posted by any catcher in major league history. In a season of historical proportions, Mauer became the first receiver in either league to win three batting titles and, also, the first catcher to lead his league in batting average, on-base percentage (.444), and slugging percentage (.587) in the same season. Despite missing the season's first month with a back injury, Mauer established new career highs with 28 home runs and 96 runs batted in. He also scored 94 runs and won a Gold Glove for his outstanding work behind the plate. Mauer punctuated his great season by batting .378, hitting two home runs, and driving in 14 runs in Minnesota's final 21 games, as he carried the team into the playoffs following the loss of Morneau to injury.

Both Mark Teixeira and Derek Jeter had outstanding years for the pennant-winning Yankees. But Joe Mauer was clearly the American League's Most Valuable Player. The members of the BBWAA recognized that fact by awarding the Minnesota catcher a total of 387 points in their balloting, to the 225 and 193 points they gave Teixeira and Jeter, respectively.

NATIONAL LEAGUE

The Los Angeles Dodgers captured their second straight National League West title in 2009, posting a league-best 95-67 record during the regular season to edge out the second-place Colorado Rockies by three games. Colorado advanced to the postseason as the league's wild-card entry. Yet, the third-place Giants and the fourth-place Padres each featured one of the league's best players. San Diego first baseman Adrian Gonzalez batted .277, drove in 99 runs, scored 90 others, and placed among the N.L. leaders with 40 home runs. Unfortunately for Gonzalez, the Padres finished 20 games behind the first-place Dodgers, preventing the slugger from placing any higher than 12th in the league MVP voting. The Giants finished only seven games behind Los Angeles, and they had the league's top pitcher in Tim Lincecum. The 25-year-old righthander compiled a 15-7 record, a 2.48 earned run average, and a league-leading 261 strikeouts en route to winning his second consecutive Cy Young Award. Still, Lincecum failed to place in the top 10 in the MVP balloting.

Receiving far more support than his teammate was San Francisco third baseman Pablo Sandoval, who hit 25 home runs, drove in 90 runs, and finished second in the league with a .330 batting average. Sandoval placed seventh in the voting.

The second-place Rockies finished just eighth in the league with a team earned run average of 4.22, but they nevertheless improved their pitching from the previous season. Lefthander Jorge De La Rosa led the staff with 16 victories, and righthanders Jason Marquis and Ubaldo Jimenez each contributed 15 wins. Huston Street won four games coming out of the bullpen and converted 35 of his 37 save opportunities.

But it was Colorado's offense that enabled them to advance to the playoffs. The Rockies finished second in the league with 804 runs scored and 190 home runs. Outfielder Brad Hawpe batted .285, hit 23 homers, knocked in 86 runs, and scored 82 others. First baseman Todd Helton drove in 86 runs and placed among the league leaders with a .325 batting average. Shortstop Troy Tulowitzki was the team's most potent offensive weapon. He batted .297 and led the Rockies with 32 home runs, 92 runs batted in, and 101 runs scored. Tulowitzki finished fifth in the MVP balloting.

First-place Los Angeles was the division's most well-balanced team for the second straight year. Although the Dodgers finished 11th in the N.L. with only 145 home runs, they compiled the highest team batting average (.270) and scored the fourth most runs (780). The Dodgers' team earned run average of 3.41 was also the best in the National League. Chad Billingsley led the staff with 12 victories, while Jon Garland and Randy Wolf chipped in with 11 wins apiece. Promising 21-year-old lefthander Clayton Kershaw finished the year just 8-8, but he led the team with a 2.79 earned run average and 185 strikeouts. Closer Jonathan Broxton won seven games in relief and converted 36 of his 42 save opportunities.

The Dodgers were led on offense by the trio of James Loney, Matt Kemp, and Andre Ethier. First baseman Loney batted .281 and knocked in 90 runs. Centerfielder Kemp hit 26 homers, knocked in 101 runs, scored 97 others, and batted .297. Rightfielder Ethier batted .272, scored 92 runs, and led the team with 31 home runs and 106 runs batted in. He finished sixth in the league MVP voting, four places ahead of Kemp, who came in 10th.

The Philadelphia Phillies won their third straight N.L. East title, finishing the year 93-69, six games ahead of the second-place Florida Marlins, and seven games in front of the third-place Atlanta Braves. Atlanta had one of the N.L.'s best pitching staffs, placing third in the league with a 3.57 earned run average. Javier Vazquez and Derek Lowe each won 15 games, and Jair Jurrjens added another 14 victories.

Florida's 4.29 team earned run average was considerably higher than Atlanta's, but the Marlins finished fifth in the league in runs scored (772), and they posted the third-highest team batting average (.268). Florida had the division's finest all-around player in shortstop Hanley Ramirez, who hit 24 home runs, knocked in 106 runs, scored 101 others, stole 27 bases, and led the league with a .342 batting average. Ramirez's exceptional play earned him a second-place finish in the league MVP voting.

However, Ramirez was not able to lead the Marlins to the N.L. East title since the Phillies were once again the class of the division. Philadelphia had decent pitching and the league's most explosive offense. The Philadelphia staff, which finished sixth in the N.L. with a 4.16 team earned run average, was headed by the trio of Joe Blanton,

Jamie Moyer, and J.A. Happ, each of whom won 12 games over the course of the season. In winning only 10 games and posting an earned run average of 4.32, Cole Hamels wasn't nearly as effective as he was in 2008. But the Phillies acquired Cliff Lee from the Cleveland Indians during the season's second half, and the lefthander pitched exceptionally well for Philadelphia down the stretch, going 7-4 with a 3.39 earned run average and excelling during the postseason. Unfortunately, the Phillies never found someone to replace the slumping Brad Lidge in their bullpen. After converting all 41 of his save opportunities the previous year, Lidge blew 11 of 42 such chances in 2009, while compiling a record of 0-8 and an inordinately high 7.21 earned run average.

The Phillies' powerful offense enabled them to overcome any difficulties their pitching staff may have encountered over the course of the season. Philadelphia led the league with 820 runs scored and 224 home runs. Leftfielder Raul Ibanez hit 34 home runs, knocked in 93 runs, and scored 93 others. Rightfielder Jayson Werth blossomed into a star, hitting 36 homers, driving in 99 runs, and scoring 98 times. Centerfielder Shane Victorino batted .292, scored 102 runs, and stole 25 bases. Shortstop Jimmy Rollins had something of an off year, batting only .250 and compiling just a .296 on-base percentage. But he still managed to hit 21 homers, drive in 77 runs, steal 31 bases, and score 100 runs. Second baseman Chase Utley was perhaps the team's most consistent performer, batting .282, compiling a .397 on-base percentage, homering 31 times, knocking in 93 runs, and scoring 112 times. He finished eighth in the MVP balloting.

Placing third in the voting was Ryan Howard, who was Philadelphia's most productive and powerful hitter. The slugging first baseman batted .279, scored 105 runs, tied for the league lead with 141 runs batted in, and finished among the leaders with 45 home runs and a .571 slugging percentage.

The man who was named the league's Most Valuable Player came out of the N.L. Central, where the St. Louis Cardinals replaced the Chicago Cubs as division champions by finishing the year 91-71, 7½ games ahead of the second-place Cubs. Yet, the Milwaukee Brewers, who finished in third-place, 11 games behind St. Louis, had one of the league's leading MVP candidates in Prince Fielder. The Milwaukee first baseman batted .299, scored 103 runs, tied Ryan Howard for the league lead with 141 runs batted in, and placed second in the league with 46 home runs, 356 total bases, and a .602 slugging percentage. Ryan Braun also had an outstanding year for Milwaukee, hitting 32 home runs and finishing among the league leaders with 114 runs batted in, 113 runs scored, and a .320 batting average. But the writers considered Fielder to be the team's most important player, placing him fourth in the league MVP balloting. Braun finished 11th in the voting.

Derrek Lee was the only member of the second-place Cubs who received any support in the balloting. The Chicago first baseman hammered 35 home runs, knocked in 111 runs, scored 91 others, and batted .306, to earn a ninth-place finish in the voting.

After failing to make the playoffs each of the previous two seasons, the St. Louis Cardinals overcame numerous injuries to capture the Central Division title. Third baseman Troy Glaus was lost to the team for all but 14 games. Arm problems plagued Mark Mulder for the fourth consecutive year, sidelining the veteran lefthander for the entire season. Ace righthander Chris Carpenter missed the season's first month. Nevertheless, the Cardinals managed to win the division rather handily, with several players making key contributions. Righthander Joel Pineiro finished 15-12 with a 3.49 earned run average. Veteran reliever Ryan Franklin excelled in the role of closer, compiling a 1.92 earned run average and converting 38 of his 43 save opportunities. Adam Wainwright had the finest season of his relatively young career, compiling a record of 19-8, to lead all N.L. pitchers in victories. The 28-year-old righthander also led the league with 233 innings pitched, and he finished among the leaders as well with a 2.63 earned run average and 212 strikeouts. Chris Carpenter pitched exceptionally well after he returned to the team, compiling a record of 17-4 and leading all N.L. hurlers with a 2.24 earned run average.

In fact, Wainwright and Carpenter comprised the most formidable pitching tandem in baseball, enabling the Cardinals to post the league's fourth lowest team earned run average (3.66).

The St. Louis offense was hardly overwhelming, but it was quite efficient. The Cardinals finished fourth in the league with a .263 team batting average, and they finished sixth in home runs (160) and seventh in runs scored (730). Catcher Yadier Molina drove in 54 runs and batted .293. Second baseman Skip Schumaker batted .303 and scored 85 runs. Outfielder Ryan Ludwick hit 22 homers and knocked in 97 runs. Matt Holliday made a huge impact after he was acquired from the Oakland Athletics during the season's second half. The leftfielder batted .353, hit 13 home runs, and drove in 55 runs in his 63 games with the Cardinals. Equally important, he provided protection in the St. Louis lineup for Albert Pujols, who carried the team on his shoulders most of the year. The first baseman led the National League with 47 home runs, 124 runs scored, 374 total bases, a .443 on-base percentage, and a .658 slugging percentage. He also placed among the leaders with 135 runs batted in, 45 doubles, and a .327 batting average.

Pujols was such an important part of the St. Louis offense that he had a hand in almost 36 percent of the 730 runs the team scored over the course of the season (135 runs batted in + 124 runs scored). He also hit almost 30 percent of the team's home runs (47 of 160). Although the addition of Matt Holliday to the St. Louis lineup for the final two months of the season forced opposing pitchers to think twice before pitching around Pujols, the Cardinals first baseman still compiled a career-high 115 bases on balls.

Pujols was the league's most feared hitter, and he was easily its best player. He unquestionably deserved the MVP Award that was unanimously voted to him at season's end.

SUMMARY

The evaluations have been completed, and the MVP selections for every year since 1900 have been made. Based on the selections made in this book, several players distinguished themselves as being particularly big winners. Following is a list of those players who, according to the selection criteria used here, should have been named league MVP on at least three separate occasions:

PLAYER	NUMBER OF MVP AWARDS
Babe Ruth	7
Barry Bonds	7
Mickey Mantle	6
Honus Wagner	5
Rogers Hornsby	5
Ty Cobb	4
Lou Gehrig	4
Ted Williams	4
Stan Musial	4
Christy Mathewson	3
Grover Cleveland Alexander	3
Al Simmons	3
Jimmie Foxx	3
Joe DiMaggio	3
Yogi Berra	3
Willie Mays	3
Hank Aaron	3
Mike Schmidt	3
Frank Thomas	3
Alex Rodriguez	3
Albert Pujols	3

This list includes the names of 21 players. However, for one reason or another, only seven of the 21 men (Bonds, Foxx, DiMaggio, Berra, Schmidt, Rodriguez, and Pujols) actually received the correct number of awards. And, according to my estimation, only Bonds, Foxx, Schmidt, and Pujols were named the winner in the correct year every time. It should also be noted that Bonds won his last four MVP Awards under a huge cloud of suspicion. His performance in each of those seasons was likely aided by the use of steroids, thereby lessening the validity of his accomplishments and diminishing the value of his awards—at least in this writer's opinion. Alex Rodriguez also won at least one of his MVP trophies (the 2003 Award he won as a member of the Rangers) under the same set of circumstances.

In addition, whether it was the *Chalmers Award* that was presented annually from 1911 to 1914, or the more familiar *Most Valuable Player Award* that has been presented almost every year since 1922, a total of 179 presentations have been made to players over the past 100 years. Based on the evaluations conducted in this book, 133 of the selections made were correct. However, 46 of the elections held resulted in an undeserving candidate being named the recipient of the honor. In other words, more than 25 percent of the players chosen league MVP should never have received the award.

There will undoubtedly be those who feel that I am no more qualified than any of the people who participated in the elections to decide which candidate was most worthy. In fact, many will feel that I am *less* qualified, since I was not able to follow most of the players on a day-to-day basis to the same degree as the writers. However, as I pointed out earlier, it has not always been clear through the years what the writers were looking for when evaluating viable MVP candidates. On the other hand, certain criteria were used throughout this book to judge the candidates—criteria that were spelled out earlier. A clear explanation has also been given as to why each player was chosen. It should also be emphasized that, to the very best of my ability, I remained completely objective when evaluating the credentials of possible candidates. In certain instances, it could be said that the writers may not have been able to do the same.

GLOSSARY

ABBREVIATIONS AND STATISTICAL TERMS

AB. At-bats. The number of times a player comes to the plate to try to get on base. It does not include those times when a walk was issued, the player was hit by a pitch, the player hit a sacrifice fly to score a runner, or the player advanced a baserunner via a sacrifice bunt.

AVG. Batting average. The number of hits divided by the number of at-bats.

BB. Bases on balls, which are better known as walks. A free trip to first base as a penalty to the pitcher when he fails to get the ball over the plate four times during an at-bat.

CG. Complete games pitched.

ERA. Earned run average. The number of earned runs a pitcher gives up, per nine innings. This does not include runs that scored as a result of errors made in the field and is calculated by dividing the number of runs given up, by the number of innings pitched, and multiplying the result by 9.

G. Games. The total numbers of games in which a player appears.

GS. Games started by a pitcher.

HITS. Base hits. Awarded when a runner safely reaches at least first base upon a batted ball, if no error is recorded.

HR. Home runs. Fair ball hit over the fence, or one hit to a spot that allows the batter to circle the bases before the ball is returned to home plate, if no error is recorded.

GLOSSARY

IP. Innings pitched.

L. Losses.

OBP. On-base percentage. Hits plus walks plus hit-by-pitches, divided by plate appearances.

PCT. Winning percentage. A pitcher's number of wins divided by his number of total decisions (that is, wins plus losses).

RBI. Runs batted in. Awarded to the batter when a runner scores upon a safely batted ball, a sacrifice or a walk.

RUNS. Runs scored by a player.

SAVES. While the rules used to determine "saves" have been altered through the years, a relief pitcher essentially compiles a "save" when he enters a game in the sixth inning or later, with his team in the lead by three runs or less, and pitches the remainder of the contest without permitting the opposing team to ever tie the score or take the lead.

SB. Stolen bases.

SHO: Shutouts. A game in which a pitcher works all the innings and allows no runs to score.

SLG PCT. Slugging percentage. The number of total bases earned by all singles, doubles, triples and home runs, divided by the total number of at-bats.

SO. Strikeouts.

3B. Three-base hits. Triples.

2B. Two-base hits. Doubles.

W. Wins.

BIBLIOGRAPHY

BOOKS

Dewey, Donald, and Acocella, Nicholas, *The Biographical History of Baseball.* Carroll & Graf, Inc., New York, 1995.

Halberstam, David, *October 1964.* Villard Books, New York, 1994.

Nemec, David, et al., *Players of Cooperstown—Baseball's Hall of Fame.* Publications International, Ltd., Lincolnwood, Il., 1994.

Okrent, Daniel, and Lewine, Harris, eds., with David Nemec, *The Ultimate Baseball Book.* Houghton Mifflin Co. / A Hiltown Book, Boston, Mass., 1988.

Ritter, Lawrence, *The Glory of Their Times.* Random House, New York, 1985.

Shalin, Mike, and Neil Shalin, *Out by a Step: The 100 Best Players Not in the Baseball Hall of Fame.* Diamond Communications, Inc., Indiana, 2002.

Thorn, John, and Palmer, Pete, eds., with Michael Gershman, *Total Baseball.* HarperCollins Pub., Inc., New York, 1993.

VIDEOS

New York Yankees: The Movie. Magic Video Publishing Company, 1987.

Pinstripe Power: The Story of the 1961 New York Yankees. Major League Baseball Productions, New York, 1987.

The Sporting News' 100 Greatest Baseball Players. National Broadcasting Co., 1999.

BIBLIOGRAPHY

Sports Century—Roberto Clemente. ESPN, 2003.

Sports Century—Stan Musial. ESPN, 2000.

When It Was A Game 3. HBO, 2000.

INTERNET WEBSITES

The Ballplayers, online at BaseballLibrary.com
(http://www.baseballlibrary.com/baseballlibrary/ballplayers).

Historical Stats, online at MLB.com
(http://www.mlb.com/stats.historical/individual stats player).

Team Histories, online at MLB.com
(http://www.mlb.com/history/mlb_history_teams)

MLB Awards, online at MLB.com
(http://www.mlb.com/awards/mlb_awards/mvp_history).

The Players, online at Baseball-Almanac.com
(http://www.baseball-almanac.com/players).

The Players, online at Baseballink.com
(http://www.baseballink.com/baseballink/players).

The Players, online at Baseball-Reference.com
(http://www.baseball-reference.com/players).

The Teams, online at BaseballLibrary.com
(http://www.baseballlibrary.com/baseballlibrary/teams).

Historical Stats, online at MLB.com
(http://www.mlb.com/mlb/xxx/stats_historical/xxx_historical_
team_stats).

INDEX

INDEX

INDEX

INDEX

INDEX

INDEX

INDEX